Sacred Rites in Moonlight

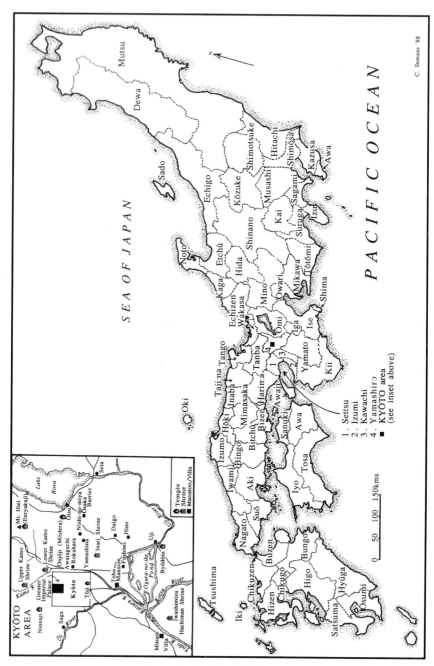

Japan in the Classical Age

Sacred Rites in Moonlight
Ben no Naishi Nikki

Introduced, translated, and annotated by
S. Yumiko Hulvey

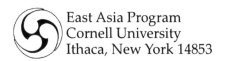

East Asia Program
Cornell University
Ithaca, New York 14853

The Cornell East Asia Series is published by the Cornell University East Asia Program (distinct from Cornell University Press). We publish affordably priced books on a variety of scholarly topics relating to East Asia as a service to the academic community and the general public. Standing orders, which provide for automatic notification and invoicing of each title in the series upon publication, are accepted.

If after review by internal and external readers a manuscript is accepted for publication, it is published on the basis of camera-ready copy provided by the volume author. Each author is thus responsible for any necessary copyediting and for manuscript formatting. Address submission inquiries to CEAS Editorial Board, East Asia Program, Cornell University, Ithaca, New York 14853-7601.

Cover illustration from *Takafusa-kyō Tsuyakotoba Emaki,* courtesy of the National Museum of Japanese History. Frontispiece from Helen Craig McCullough, *Classical Japanese Prose: An Anthology,* copyright © 1990; map of Kan'in Palace Seiryōden adapted from William H. and Helen Craig McCullough, *A Tale of Flowering Fortunes: Annals of Japanese Aristocratic Life in the Heian Period,* copyright © 1980; copyrights held by the Board of Trustees of the Leland Stanford Jr. University; reproduced with the permission of Stanford University Press, www.sup.org. Map of Kan'in Palace Reconstruction from Ōta Seiroku, *Shindenzukuri no Kenkyū,* p. 838, courtesy of Yoshikawa Kōbunkan. Cover design by Karen K. Smith.

Number 122 in the Cornell East Asia Series
Copyright © 2005 by S. Yumiko Hulvey. All rights reserved
ISSN 1050-2955
ISBN-13: 978-1-885445-40-7 hc / ISBN-10: 1-885445-40-7 hc
ISBN-13: 978-1-885445-22-3 pb / ISBN-10: 1-885445-22-9 pb
Library of Congress Control Number: 2004113790
Printed in the United States of America
23 22 21 20 19 18 17 16 15 14 13 12 11 10 09 08 05   9 8 7 6 5 4 3 2 1

⊖ The paper in this book meets the requirements for permanence of ISO 9706:1994.

To
JOHN AND JOHN JAMES

Contents

CONTENTS / ix

Translator's Acknowledgments

There are many people I would like to thank for generously giving their time and expertise to this project. I feel privileged to have worked with Helen Craig McCullough and William McCullough, two of the leading scholars of classical Japanese literature, as a graduate student at the University of California, Berkeley. Helen suggested *Ben no Naishi Nikki* as the topic of my dissertation and guided me through the translation and Bill provided encouragement and mentorship over the years. I mourn their recent passing and keenly feel the loss of wonderful teachers and esteemed friends. I would also like to thank Professor Joan Piggott who championed this little-known text and generously helped to revise the manuscript into publishable form. I also thank Kyoko Selden for helping me impart a more literary tone to my translations of Ben no Naishi's poetry. I express my gratitude to Professors Iwasa Miyoko and Imazeki Toshiko for their pioneering research that determined the direction of my study of *Ben no Naishi Nikki*. I would also like to thank Professor Ann Wehmeyer and Andrew Lewis for reading the manuscript and for offering guidance on technical aspects of the manuscript. I am also indebted to Margaret Joyner for carefully reading, editing, and formatting the manuscript to completion.

I am grateful for the support of the Northeast Asia Research Council, the Stanford East Asian Research Council, and the Asia Library Grant from the University of Michigan Center for Japanese Studies, for providing opportunities to visit research libraries while I was translating and studying the text.

I would also like to express my love and appreciation to my family: my husband John and my son John James, whose support and encouragement enabled me to complete this project; my mother, Miyoko, whose beautiful calligraphy inspired me to begin studying Japanese long ago; and my step-father, Jim, whose kindness and patience provided a wonderful role model.

Notes on the Format

This translation is based on Tamai Kōsuke's annotated text, *Ben no Naishi Nikki Shinchū* (1958), emended with reference to Iwasa Miyoko's annotated text, *Chūsei Nikki, Kikō Shū*, in Volume 48 of *Shinpen Nihon Koten Bungaku Zenshū* (1994).

Throughout my study and translation, I follow Joan R. Piggott's *The Emergence of Japanese Kingship* (1997) in refraining from the use of "empire, emperor, and imperial" because they are inappropriate for the Japanese context. Miner, Odagiri, and Morrell (1985) also refer to *tennō* as monarchs or sovereigns, rather than emperors, which assumes kingship based on martial-political conquest. Exceptions occur only in direct citations by other scholars.

Unless otherwise indicated, all translations of prose and poetry are mine. All endnotes, which are given at the end of each chapter, are also my own.

The following abbreviations have been used in the notes:

NKBT   *Nihon Koten Bungaku Taikei*. Takagi Ichinosuke, et. al., eds. Iwanami shoten, 1957–68, 102 Vols.

NKBZ   *Nihon Koten Bungaku Zenshū*. Akiyama Ken, et. al., eds. Shogakukan, 1970–76.

Part I
THE CONTEXT

1
Introduction

Ben no Naishi Nikki (The Memoir of Ben no Naishi, 1246–52) is a unique poetic account attributed to Ben no Naishi, a female courtier (*naishi*) who served at the court of Go-Fukakusa (1243–1304; r. 1246–59), the eighty-ninth sovereign of Japan. It belongs to the tradition of vernacular prose (*kana nikki*) written by women dating back to the Heian period (794–1185) and continuing through the Kamakura period (1185–1333). Most of the Heian literary canon has been translated into English, but of the Kamakura canon only a few works are available in translation. The primary purpose of this study is to add *Ben no Naishi Nikki* to that list. I also argue for a reassessment of the work. It is time to challenge the frequent negative criticism published by scholars in the early part of the twentieth century.

Ben no Naishi's devotion to duty, both sacred and secular, controlled her text. As one of the highest-ranking female officials of the Office of Female Courtiers (Naishi no Tsukasa), she was responsible for conveying and safeguarding the three sacred regalia (*sanshu no jingi*)—the mirror, the sword, and the jewels—during enthronement and abdication ceremonies. Her sense of duty dictated that topics in the memoir be limited to events in which she and her sister participated as *naishi*. Devotion to duty also compelled her to create the unusual device of a shared point of view with her sister in order to include events from which she was absent, but at which her sister was present. This shared point of view thus enabled her to present the most comprehensive view of court activities while allowing her to abide by the limitations she set for topics permitted in the account.

Perhaps a royal commission to maintain a poetic record of Go-Fukakusa's reign inspired Ben no Naishi to choose the moon as a vehicle to convey the thematic and literary goals of the *nikki*. The structure of the memoir is circular like the shape of the auspicious full moon. The memoir opens with the abdication of Go-Saga (1222–72; r. 1242–46). The second

3

entry joyously announces the enthronement of Go-Saga's three-year-old son, Go-Fukakusa. The final entry, no longer extant in the memoir but preserved in a near contemporary work, ends with Go-Fukakusa's forced abdication in 1259. The abdication and enthronement ceremonies echo the waning and waxing phases of the moon. The circular frame of the *nikki* is supported by the round of duties she performed as a female courtier. Her use of the secondary images of snow, frost, and wind have in common the characteristics of the cold and of a reflected brightness, clarity, and spiritual cleansing. The moon cast its light over the sacred winter rites, inducing the author to assess the cold as a positive attribute as a harbinger of new developing medieval aesthetics. The nocturnal nature of the author's court service and the moon as a timekeeper of that time contributed to the unique and notable presence of the celestial orb in the *nikki*.

Many poems in *Ben no Naishi Nikki* extol the royal court as sacred space and the royal family as sacred time through laudatory lexical items that resemble the vocabulary found in *norito* and *yogoto* of the Shintō liturgical canon. Auspicious words to augur long and prosperous reigns are found in both the Shintō liturgies and the poems in the memoir to perpetuate the myth of the divine origins of the royal and client families. There is also a sense of reverence for the performance of the enthronement ceremonies that legitimized the reign of the *tennō* (sovereign) and theoretically transformed human monarchs into divine rulers descended from *kami*. The moon also symbolized the Nakatomi/Fujiwara family role as ritualists in the enthronement rites.

Ben no Naishi was not only devoted to duty and scrupulous in comprehensiveness, she was also witty and innovative. When she challenges male courtiers to a battle of wits or describes the delight with which female and male courtiers engage in the custom of hitting each other on the buttocks with gruel sticks on the night of the full moon festivities on the fifteenth day of the first month (*mochigayu*), she resembles Sei Shōnagon.[1] Like *The Pillow Book of Sei Shōnagon (Makura no Sōshi*, ca. early 11th century) and unlike most texts by women of the Heian and Kamakura periods, *Ben no Naishi Nikki* presents more pleasant aspects of court life; however, unlike Sei Shōnagon, Ben no Naishi consciously structured pleasant events to be interpreted as auspicious signs for a tranquil, long-enduring reign. Again, there is a literary purpose behind emphasizing the positive aspects of court life, even to the point of altering facts to justify thematic intent, because her poetic record was probably commissioned by the retired sovereign Go-Saga to commemorate the reign of his son, Go-Fukakusa.

Ben no Naishi Nikki also offers glimpses of several familiar historical characters depicted in the *Memoirs of Nakatsukasa no Naishi (Nakatsukasa no Naishi Nikki*, ca. 1280–92) and *The Confessions of Lady Nijō*

(*Towazugatari*, 1271–1307). It is possible to trace Go-Fukakusa's development: as a child in *Ben no Naishi Nikki*, as a young man in the *Memoirs of Nakatsukasa no Naishi*, and finally as a man past middle-age in *The Confessions of Lady Nijō*. In contrast to the fictionalized, unflattering portrayal of Go-Fukakusa in *The Confessions of Lady Nijō*, Ben no Naishi refrains from describing Go-Fukakusa in concrete terms, perhaps because of her reverence for the reign of the royal family as a symbol of sacred time and for the site of the court as sacred space. Thus the monarch's presence in the memoir is minimal, intentionally left in the shadows in deference to his sacred position.

Of further historical interest are figures such as Fujiwara Tameie (1198–1275) and his son Fujiwara Tameuji (1222–86), and Fujiwara (Takatsukasa) Kanehira (b. 1227), who are also mentioned in the *Memoirs of Nakatsukasa no Naishi* and *The Confessions of Lady Nijō*. As son and grandson of Fujiwara Teika (1162–1241) and distant relatives of Ben no Naishi, Tameie and Tameuji occasionally appear in entries that feature poetic composition. Kanehira, who appears in *The Confessions of Lady Nijō* as an old lecher, is still a young man pursuing higher office and rank in *Ben no Naishi Nikki*.

Such women as Ben no Naishi, Nakatsukasa no Naishi, and Lady Nijō who served the Jimyōin line (later known as the Senior line or Northern Court, descended from Go-Fukakusa) wrote memoirs in the vernacular that fortunately survived the vicissitudes of time. On the other hand, there are no extant works by women who served the Daikakuji line (later to be known as the Junior line or Southern Court), descended from Kameyama (1249–1305; r. 1259–74), the younger brother of Go-Fukakusa. Perhaps there were none written by clients of the Daikakuji line. The subsequent split in the royal succession into the Northern and Southern courts caused a split in aesthetic tastes as well, with the Jimyōin line patronizing traditional Japanese culture and literary arts and the Daikakuji line supporting the newly imported Sung Chinese culture and ideologies.[2] Jimyōin line patronage accounts for the continuity of historical figures in texts written by women who served the descendants of Go-Fukakusa. Thus, as a client of the Jimyōin line, Ben no Naishi was perpetuating the tradition of women writing in the vernacular that began in the Heian period.

Although Ben no Naishi was known to her contemporaries primarily as a poet of *waka* (a 31-syllable poem) and *renga* (linked verse), today her renown rests on her memoir. *Ben no Naishi Nikki* originally recorded events from Go-Fukakusa's entire thirteen-year reign, but what is left of the final portion of the extant manuscript is badly damaged. Of the 175 sections, damage begins in Section 122 and intensifies as the text continues; my translation includes only entries that are not damaged.

Like other women of her time, Ben no Naishi is known only by a so-briquet. Even though we do not know her real name, we know she was a daughter of the court poet and portrait painter, Fujiwara Nobuzane (ca. 1177–1270). We know very few personal names of the women in works of the Heian and Kamakura periods, for it was the custom for female courti-ers at that time to be referred to by a combination of the name of the post they held at court and a post occupied by a male member of their family. The origin of *ben* (controller) in Ben no Naishi's pseudonym has not been connected to a particular male relative, but *naishi* refers to her official po-sition.[3]

Women who could compose poetry, write a good hand, or play musical instruments or who had mastered other aesthetic accomplishments desired by patrons were offered employment at the courts of sovereigns, retired sovereigns, or the households of the aristocracy. Ben no Naishi and her sister Shōshō no Naishi, who traced their lineage to a literary branch of the Fujiwara family, won their place at Go-Fukakusa's court for their skill in poetic composition. Their father, Nobuzane, was instrumental in bringing his daughters' skill at poetic composition to the attention of potential pa-trons by taking them to poetry gatherings sponsored by influential aristo-crats and members of the royal family. Nobuzane's tactic succeeded when Ben no Naishi was placed into service as "Controller in the Crown Prince's Household" (Tōgū no Ben) to the two-month-old Crown Prince Go-Fukakusa. Later, when Go-Fukakusa became sovereign, Ben no Naishi remained in his service. Her younger sister, Shōshō no Naishi, joined her at court after the accession of Go-Fukakusa.

In my translation of her memoir, the introductory material is divided into two sections: the historical context and the literary context. In the first part, I situate Ben no Naishi and her family in court society and trace the cultivation of patronage relationships which led to Ben no Naishi's post at court. I also examine the place *naishi* occupied within the court bureauc-racy. Next I look at the royal regalia and their relationship to *naishi* and the Office of Female Courtiers as a way of delineating the sacred and secu-lar duties of *naishi*. In the second part, I start with a description of Western and Japanese scholarship of the *kana nikki* tradition and set up a frame-work of the survey of Heian and Kamakura period *nikki* based on Konishi Jin'ichi's subdivision of public versus private and factual versus fictional *nikki*. In the final portion of this section, I focus attention on the unique literary aspects of the memoir, such as the moon and its relationship to kingship, initiation rites, New Year's celebrations, and sacred time. I also discuss the vital role the Nakatomi/Fujiwara played at the enthronement ceremonies of sovereigns and the family's relationship to the moon pre-served in a myth found in the Shintō liturgical canon (*norito, yogoto*). I argue that the sacred tone of poetry in the memoir was influenced by the *norito* and *yogoto* intoned at the enthronement ceremonies and other sacred rites held in the moonlight. I assess her reputation as a *waka* and *renga* (linked verse) poet and conclude that, far from being "imitative" of Heian models, *Ben no Naishi Nikki* is full of innovative techniques and devices that help achieve its literary goal.

Ben no Naishi Nikki perpetuates the Heian tradition of writing by women while at the same time subverting the family line of male literary creativity to the female side. Her memoir is a testament to the fact that the family genius for literary matters could indeed be capably sustained by a woman. Her innovative techniques enhanced the scope of *nikki* and successfully captured the flavor of the time in a unique manner, a further testament to her skill as a writer.

Notes

1. *Makura no Sōshi*, in *Nihon Koten Bungaku Zenshū* (hereafter NKBT), 11: 65–66, and Ivan Morris's translation of *The Pillow Book of Sei Shōnagon* (Morris 1967, 1:2–3; 2:4). Lady Nijō also includes an episode in *The Confessions of Lady Nijō* during which she beats Retired Sovereign Go-Fukakusa with a gruel stick (Brazell 1973, 68–69).

2. "The deepening hostility between the two lines, which had first begun as a succession dispute, later affected the entire court structure. Even in the cultural and religious spheres, the split was apparent. Whereas the Daikakuji line patronized the new Chinese culture—Sung-style Confucianism, Zen Buddhism, and the Chinese style of calligraphy—the Jimyōin line preferred the traditional (Heian) culture in literature, calligraphy, and Buddhism" (Ishii, 167).

3. Ben no Naishi is identified in headnotes to compositions in royal poetry collections as the "New Retired Sovereign's Ben no Naishi" (Shin'in Go-Fukakusa Ben no Naishi) in *Shokukokinshū* and "Retired Sovereign Go-Fukakusa's Ben no Naishi" (Go-Fukakusa'in Ben no Naishi) in *Shokushūishū, Gyokuyōshū, Shokugoshūishū, Shinshūishū,* and *Shinzokukokinshū.* Variant titles of *Ben no Naishi Nikki* occasionally include "Retired Sovereign Go-Fukakusa" (Go-Fukakusa'in) before her name.

2
The Historical Context

Ben no Naishi at Court

Who was Ben no Naishi? We do not know her real name, the circumstances of her early childhood, or the dates of her birth and death, but we can glean some information about her life by a close reading of *Ben no Naishi Nikki*, and by referring to contemporary historical sources. Many of her ancestors were employed by the court bureaucracy from around the eleventh century, so it is quite likely that Ben no Naishi was born and raised in the capital of Heian-kyō, and that her father, Fujiwara Nobuzane, trained her in the literary and social skills required for court service.

Most members of Ben no Naishi's family were involved in some form of court service. She had five older brothers, two older sisters, and a younger sister. The *Genealogy of the Exalted and the Base* (*Sonpi Bunmyaku*) does not record the names of the mothers of all of Nobuzane's children, but Tamai Kōsuke, one of the leading scholars of *nikki bungaku*, proposes that three of them, Sōhekimon'in Shōshō no Naishi, Ben no Naishi, and Shōshō no Naishi, shared the same mother. In the 1927 pioneer study of *Ben no Naishi Nikki*, Ikeda Kikan suggests a different order for the three sisters, listing in descending order: Sōhekimon'in Shōshō no Naishi, Shōshō no Naishi, and Ben no Naishi. But Tamai's study of poetry contest records proves Ikeda's thesis to be in error. All records support Tamai's conclusion and I believe his assessment to be correct.

After consulting the record of *The Poetry Contest of the Iwashimizu Deity* (*Iwashimizu Wakamiya Uta'awase*), which lists only Nobuzane and Sōhekimon'in Shōshō no Naishi, Tamai concludes that the omission of the names of Ben no Naishi and Shōshō no Naishi from the list suggests that they were too young to have participated in the poetry gathering of 1232. Based on this, Tamai maintains that the eldest sister, Sōhekimon'in Shōshō no Naishi, must have been at least ten years older than Ben no Naishi and Shōshō no Naishi because the younger sisters' names do not appear as participants in poetry contests until 1243.[1] Tamai also believes that although ten years or more separated Sōhekimon'in Shōshō no Naishi from Ben no Naishi and Shōshō no Naishi, the younger sisters themselves were probably only a few years apart in age.

Several conclusions about Ben no Naishi and her family can be drawn by referring to Tamai Kōsuke's study of the record of *The Poetry Contest of Kawai Shrine* (*Kawaisha Uta'awase*, 1243). It lists Nobuzane, Sōhekimon'in Shōshō no Naishi, "Shōshō's younger sibling" (Shōshō no otōto),[2] and "Controller in the Crown Prince's Household" (Tōgū no Ben) as participants. The older sister, Sōhekimon'in Shōshō no Naishi, is listed without a new court-related sobriquet, indicating that she did not reenter court service after the death of Sōhekimon'in (1209–33), the daughter of Kujō Michiie and a consort of Go-Horikawa (1231–42; r. 1232–42). Even though Sōhekimon'in Shōshō no Naishi was no longer actively engaged in court service, she periodically accompanied her father and sisters to poetry outings. Second, Ben no Naishi was old enough to have entered court service by 1243. Her sobriquet, "Controller in the Crown Prince's Household," indicates that she was already in service to the infant who would later ascend the throne as Go-Fukakusa.[3] Third, the youngest sister, listed only as "Shōshō's younger sibling" (later to be known as Go-Fukakusa'in Shōshō no Naishi), was probably still too young for court service in 1243; however, sometime during the three years between 1243 and 1246, Shōshō no Naishi entered court service because she is described as one of the *naishi* in attendance upon Go-Fukakusa in Section 4 of *Ben no Naishi Nikki*. Based on the fact that Tamai argued his case persuasively, I have presented Ben no Naishi as the older sister of Shōshō no Naishi. Tamai's thesis is supported by similar ideas proposed by Ōuchi Mayako.

The exact date that Ben no Naishi entered court service is uncertain, but Ōuchi Mayako argues that Ben no Naishi may have been in service to Ōmiya'in (1225–92, Fujiwara [Saionji] Kitsushi), Go-Fukakusa's mother, on the day of the crown prince's birth, the tenth day of the sixth month of 1243.[4] To support her claim, she cites the "Palace Snow" chapter (Uchino no Yuki) of *The Clear Mirror* (*Masukagami*, ca. 1376): *"uchi no onmenoto Dainagon no Niidono otonaotonashiki suke nado sabeki kagiri mairitamaeri . . ."* [The royal wet nurse, Dainagon no Niidono, and some mature-acting young female attendants and the like, whose presence was considered necessary.] Ōuchi suggests that Ben no Naishi was one of the *otonaotonashiki suke* (mature-acting young females) in attendance.

We cannot be certain that Ben no Naishi was among the young women described in *The Clear Mirror* entry, but there are documents that clearly state that she served the crown prince. Go-Fukakusa was named crown prince in the eighth month of 1243, and Ben no Naishi bore the sobriquet the "Controller in the Crown Prince's Household" at the poetry gathering in the eleventh month of 1243, so she must have entered court service at some point between the eighth month and the eleventh month of 1243. Ōuchi's contention merits attention: even if Ben no Naishi was not in Ōmiya'in's service before she was recruited for the crown prince's entourage, there are records to prove that she entered service soon after he was announced heir apparent and that she remained in Go-Fukakusa's service throughout his entire thirteen-year reign.

Assuming that both Tamai and Ōuchi's ideas are valid, we can gather clues about how Ben no Naishi secured her official position at court as a *naishi*. Evidence of a common interest among both patrons and practitioners lies in poetry contests (*uta'awase*). These occasions became elaborate affairs later in the medieval period, but during the mid-thirteenth century they were lively gatherings during which a new medieval aesthetic was being formed. Obviously, Nobuzane had educated his daughters well and they brought honor to the family by continuing one of the family "trades" anchored in the bay of poetry. Nobuzane planted the seeds of patronage relationships in the fields of both the regental Kujō family and the royal family itself. It seems both families contributed equal shares in securing court positions for Nobuzane's daughters.

Ben no Naishi, along with Nobuzane, Sōhekimon'in Shōshō no Naishi, and her younger sister, are listed as participants at *The Thirty-Poem Autumn Sequence of the Former Regent, the Lay Priest Kōmyōbuji* (*Kōmyōbuji Nyūdō Saki no Sesshōke no Aki Sanjusshu Uta*), a poetry gathering sponsored by Kujō Michiie in the ninth month of 1245.[5] The relationship between the sponsor, Kujō Michiie, and Nobuzane was one of long-standing friendship and mutual admiration. It was Michiie who reintroduced Nobuzane to the poetic milieu by inviting him to a poetry contest in 1216 after Nobuzane's poetic "exile," following the exclusion of his poems from the *New Collection of Ancient and Modern Japanese Poetry* (*Shin-kokinshū*, 1205), the eighth royal anthology and one of the most influential collections of the twenty-one anthologies. Ties between Kujō Michiie's family and Nobuzane become increasingly evident when we recall that Go-Fukakusa's regent was none other than Michiie's son Fujiwara (Ichijō) Sanetsune (1223–84, hereafter Ichijō Sanetsune). Therefore, the importance of the powerful Kujō family as supporters of Nobuzane and his daughters must not be underestimated.

However, the fortunes of the Kujō family plummeted when Ichijō Sanetsune was relieved of his duties as regent, placed under house arrest, and replaced by Fujiwara (Konoe) Kanetsune (1210–59, hereafter Konoe Kanetsune) (see Section 34).[6] Sanetsune's fall from grace came about as retribution for the part played by his brother, the former fourth shogun,

Fujiwara (Kujō) Yoritsune (1218–56; shogun 1226–44, hereafter Kujō Yoritsune), in a failed assassination plot against the Hōjō regent Tokiyori (1227–63; regent 1246–56) in 1246 in Kamakura. Repercussions extended even to the father of the two, the highly influential Michiie, who lived out the rest of his life in semi-retirement. Although Sanetsune was eventually to return to court as a chancellor (1265–67), it took him almost twenty years to do so. The loss of a powerful literary ally to Ben no Naishi's family is recorded in Section 34 of *Ben no Naishi Nikki*, noting the change in regents from Sanetsune to Kanetsune with poems suggesting that evergreens *can* change color, a metaphor for the diminished power of the dominant branch of the Fujiwara regental family. Sanetsune was dismissed from office on the nineteenth day of the first month of 1247. He was replaced by Kanetsune sometime before the twenty-eighth day of the second month. In Section 37, *Ben no Naishi Nikki* records the accompanying change in reign name from Kangen to Hōji after a "new" regent was selected as one of the repercussions of the power shift from the Kujō to the Konoe branch of the Fujiwara family. *Ben no Naishi Nikki* contains no hint of the assassination plot of Kujō Yoritsune that caused the downfall of the Kujō branch, but Section 42 records Ben no Naishi and Lady Chūnagon no Suke composing linked verse expressing their regret about Sanetsune's absence from an annual ceremony because he was still under house arrest.

The loss of the Kujō family as literary patrons to Ben no Naishi and her family was offset by the continued support of Retired Sovereign Go-Saga, the young and vibrant *in* (Retired Sovereign) who was an avid fan of *waka* and *renga* composition. Go-Saga's name appears a number of times in the pages of *Ben no Naishi Nikki*, either inviting Ben no Naishi and her sister to poetry gatherings or requiring them to reply to poems he had sent them. Go-Saga issued orders that resulted in the compilation of two royal poetry anthologies: in 1248, the *Later Collection of Gleanings of Japanese Poetry Continued* (*Shokugosenshū*, 1251) and in 1259, the *Collection of Ancient and Modern Japanese Poetry Continued* (*Shokukokinshū*, 1265). For the first, he selected Fujiwara Teika's heir, Tameie, as the sole compiler. For the second, he chose Tameie as the chief of five compilers, including Fujiwara (Kujō) Motoie (1203–80), Fujiwara Ieyoshi (1192–1264), Fujiwara Yukiie (1223–75), and Fujiwara Mitsutoshi (1210–76). The poetry gathering at the Tokiwai Palace in 1247 may well have been one of Go-Saga's first attempts to procure desirable compositions for the proposed anthology. Those invited included such influential poets as Fujiwara Tameie and his son Tameuji and powerful political figures such as Saionji Saneuji's (1194–1269) sons, Kinmoto (1219–74) and Kinsuke (1222–67), brothers of Go-Saga's consort Ōmiya'in.

Go-Saga sponsored two other poetry gatherings in 1248 to increase the pool of compositions for possible inclusion in the new anthology. The first, known variously as *The Retired Sovereign's Royal Hundred-Poem Sequence* (*In no Onhyakushu*), *The Hundred-Poem Sequence of the Second Year of Hōji* (*Hōji Ninen no Hyakushu*), *The Hundred-Poem Sequence of Hōji* (*Hōji Hyakushu*), and *The Royal Hundred-Poem Sequence of Hōji* (*Hōji Onhyakushu*), lists Nobuzane, Ben no Naishi, and Shōshō no Naishi among the participants.[7] The second, *The Retired Sovereign's Royal Poetry Contest* (*In no On'uta'awase*), also records as participants Nobuzane, Sōhekimon'in Shōshō no Naishi, Ben no Naishi, and Shōshō no Naishi.[8]

Go-Saga's interest in Ben no Naishi and Shōshō no Naishi was based, in part, on their ability to produce quick, impromptu linked verse (*renga*) compositions. In the mid-thirteenth century, the rules for composing linked verse had not yet been codified and linked verse parties were merely social games in court circles where speed of composition was valued over formal adherence to rules. There are several occasions recorded in *Ben no Naishi Nikki* when Go-Saga invited Ben no Naishi and Shōshō no Naishi to compose linked verse with him (see Sections 58, 97, and 117). When Ben no Naishi and Shōshō no Naishi lost the patronage of the Kujō house, Go-Saga seems to have assumed responsibility as patron.

Go-Saga's patronage is evident through poetic correspondence with Ben no Naishi and her sister. When Go-Fukakusa's town palace (*satodairi*), the Kan'in Palace, was destroyed by fire in 1249 (Section 81), the royal court moved to the Tominokōji Palace, where Go-Saga and Ōmiya'in had been living (see Appendix F, Map of Kyōto and Environs, ca. 1250). Thereafter, Go-Saga and his court moved to the Tokiwai Palace (also called the Madenokōji or Reizei-Madenokōji Palace), which belonged to Saionji Saneuji, the father of Ōmiya'in. The Tokiwai Palace seems to have been utilized as a town palace from the reign of Go-Horikawa on, even though it was nominally under the control of the Saionji family. The Tominokōji Palace and Tokiwai Palace were in close proximity, sharing Tominokōji Street as a common border. After the move to the Tominokōji Palace, the poetic exchanges between Go-Saga and Ben no Naishi became more frequent. A comment by the former chancellor Saionji Saneuji in Section 83 reveals that the unidentified poet who sent Ben no Naishi the composition in Section 82 was actually Go-Saga himself.

Ben no Naishi was frequently invited to poetry gatherings outside the royal court. One such was the *Six Notebooks of Extant Waka* (*Gensonwaka Rokujō*), held on the twelfth day of the twelfth month of 1249,[9] and another was the *Autumn Wind Selections* (*Shūfūshō*), held on the eighteenth day of the fourth month of 1250.[10] Tamai notes that Ben no Naishi had six poems in the first (two of which are the same as poems in *The Retired Sovereign's Royal Hundred-Poem Sequence*) and five poems in the second (three of which are identical to poems in *The Retired Sovereign's Hundred-Poem Sequence of Hōji*).[11] A third poetic gathering occurred in 1251, when Ben no Naishi, her father, and Shōshō no Naishi participated in another contest, *A Poetry Contest Held at a Special Event Venerating a Portrait of the Famous Poet Hitomaro (Eigu Uta'awase)*.[12] Later in the fourteenth century, Ben no Naishi and her younger sister were evidently considered female *renga* masters.

In 1249, *Ben no Naishi Nikki* features an incident during which Ben no Naishi's father, Nobuzane, exchanges poetry with high-ranking courtiers. The regent, Kanetsune, orders her to go to her father's house to get a branch of an early-blossoming red plum to present to the monarch (Section 79). The composition Nobuzane attached to the branch elicited a number of responses at court, and the branch itself was put on display at the Bush-Clover Door (Hagi no To).

Nobuzane's relationship with Go-Saga was sealed by a mutual interest in poetry. During his lifetime Nobuzane was valued as a court poet and linked verse poet of some repute even though he was a man of modest rank and social standing. In *A Tsukuba Collection (Tsukubashū, ca. 1356)*, Nobuzane had eleven *ku* (links) included in the collection. The famous poet and Nobuzane's relative, Fujiwara Teika, had twenty-six *ku* included in *A Tsukuba Collection*, followed by twenty-two for Go-Saga, and nineteen for Go-Toba (1180-1239; r. 1183-98).[13] Thus the eleven *ku* by Nobuzane preserved in *A Tsukuba Collection* is a testament to the high regard in which he was held in linked verse salons. Nobuzane fought to maintain his influence at court by capitalizing on his talent for poetry and painting, and he was successful in procuring official posts for his two youngest daughters. Nobuzane is not featured in many entries in *Ben no Naishi Nikki*, but events that occurred during the first six years of Go-Fukakusa's reign fill the pages of the surviving *nikki*.

Extant manuscripts of *Ben no Naishi Nikki* all come to an abrupt halt with the entry for the thirteenth day of the tenth month of 1252, but there is ample evidence that Ben no Naishi continued to serve Go-Fukakusa until 1259 when he was forced to abdicate in favor of his younger brother Kameyama. The fourteenth royal anthology, *Collection of Jeweled Leaves (Gyokuyōshū, ca. 1313)*, contains the following two poems by Ben no Naishi dated 1259, indicating that she was still in Go-Fukakusa's service:[14]

Gyokuyōshū 1878 (Miscellaneous 1). Go-Fukakusa'in Ben no Naishi. In the spring of the first year of Shōgen [1259], Go-Fukakusa Ben no Naishi saw flowers near the South Hall and composed this poem.

harugoto no	O cherry blossoms
hana ni kokoro wa	in the abode of clouds,
someokitsu	do not forget me,
kumoi no sakura	for my heart has been dyed
ware o wasuruna	by the flowers of springtime.

Gyokuyōshū 2760 (Gods). Go-Fukakusa'in Ben no Naishi. When the abdication of the first year of Shōgen [1259] was approaching, Go-Fukakusa'in Ben no Naishi composed this poem when His Majesty visited the Naishidokoro:

ōkata no	Though the world may change
yo wa utsuru tomo	do not forget
masukagami	the reflection of one
tanomi o kakeshi	who placed her trust
kage na wasure so	in the clear mirror.

It is apparent from the pseudonym "Go-Fukakusa'in Ben no Naishi" that the *Collection of Jeweled Leaves* was compiled after Go-Fukakusa had stepped down from the throne, but the headnote suggests that she composed the poem in 1259 in anticipation of Go-Fukakusa's upcoming abdication ceremony. Ben no Naishi expresses disappointment that the "clear mirror," an epithet for the sovereign she depended on, was clouding, alluding to Go-Fukakusa's forced abdication.

Even more explicit evidence that Ben no Naishi was still in service to Go-Fukakusa in 1259 is found in a passage from the chapter "Descending Clouds" (Oriiru kumo) in the historical tale, *The Clear Mirror* (*Masukagami*):[15]

On the twenty-eighth day of the eighth month of this year [1259], the eleven-year-old crown prince [Kameyama] performed the Coming-of-Age Ceremony. His former name was Tsunehito. The rumors that were circulating made His Majesty, Go-Fukakusa, indignant and un-happy. Late one night, while people were quietly talking, His Majesty calculated that 5,074 days had passed while he had made obeisance at the Naishidokoro. Ben no Naishi composed this poem:

chiyo to ieba	Surely the gods will not forget:
itsutsu kasanete	a reign endures for a thousand years,
nanasoji ni	and the days that have elapsed
amaru hikazu o	number only five times
kami wa wasureji	a thousand and a little over seventy.

Then on the night of the twenty-sixth day of the eleventh month, His Majesty abdicated the throne. Even the sky was sad; it began to rain, and everything looked terribly depressing. Sadly, it was as though Lady Ise had been speaking of this occasion when she said, "With no thought of return to the Hundred-Stones Palace." Although His Majesty had prepared himself mentally for the transferal of the sacred sword and sacred jewels, he was deeply distressed when the time came to bid farewell to the regalia that had been constantly at his side for the last thirteen years. Seeing him unable to hide his sorrow, Ben no Naishi composed this poem:

ima wa tote	Darkness spreads like a shadow
oriiru kumo no	within this heart of mine,
shigurureba	when the rain pours down
kokoro no uchi zo	from the descending clouds
kakikurashikeru	because "now is the time."

The two entries cited above are especially interesting in terms of the relationship between *The Clear Mirror* and *Ben no Naishi Nikki*. As pointed out by Tamai, an earlier entry in *The Clear Mirror* proves to be almost identical with Section 121 of the extant *Ben no Naishi Nikki*. As is well known, authors of historical tales relied heavily on *nikki* and similar materials, which they often incorporated with little or no revision.[16] When we observe that the style of *The Clear Mirror* passage above is almost identical to that in *Ben no Naishi Nikki*, a brief introduction followed by a poem composed by Ben no Naishi, it seems safe to conclude that the *nikki* was a source for *The Clear Mirror* entries. That is to say, *The Clear Mirror* entries in which Ben no Naishi laments Go-Fukakusa's abdication are compelling evidence that the work originally extended to that point, and we have simply lost the text for the seven years from 1252 through 1259. The two *Clear Mirror* excerpts describing Go-Fukakusa's abdication are most likely based on the closing entries of the original *nikki*, perfectly echoing the description of Go-Saga's abdication in the opening section and bringing to an end the poetic account of Go-Fukakusa's reign.

Little is known about Ben no Naishi's whereabouts after Go-Fukakusa's abdication, but we have evidence that she participated in two poetry contests during the autumn of 1265. For the first of these, *The Harvest Moon Poetry Contest* (*Hachigatsu Izayoi Uta'awase*), she composed a poem that later appeared in the *Collection of Ancient and Modern Poetry Continued* (*Shokukokinshū*), the eleventh royal anthology, compiled in 1265 from orders issued by the then Retired Sovereign Go-Saga:[17]

Shokukokinshū 442 (Autumn 2). Shin'in ["the New Retired Sovereign's] Ben no Naishi. Expressing sentiments similar to five compositions recited at [Retired Sovereign Go-Saga's] Kameyama Palace:

awade koshi	The stag bellows
tsuma o kou to ya	as he makes his way
aki no no ni	through bamboo grasses in autumn fields
sasa wakete naku	and returns full of longing
saoshika no koe	for his unseen mate.

She composed the following poem for *The Five-Poem Poetry Contest on the Night of the Thirteenth of the Ninth Month at the Kameyama Palace* ([*Kugatsu Jūsan'Yo no*] *Kameyamadono Goshu On'utaawase*). Because the headnote indicates that she received the topic from a royal messenger, Tamai thinks that she was not physically present at either of these two contests.[18] The poem below is preserved in *New Collection of Gleanings* (*Shinshūishū*, 1364), the nineteenth royal anthology ordered by Go-Kōgon (1338–74; r. 1352–71):[19]

Shinshūishū 1587 (Miscellaneous 1). Go-Fukakusa'in Ben no Naishi. A Weaver Maid Robe poem composed and submitted on receipt of a topic from Kameyama:

aki kite mo	Even though autumn has come,
tsuyu oku sode no	I can loan nothing
sebakereba	to the Weaver Maid,
tanabatatsume ni	my sleeves soaked
nani o kasamashi	with dew are too narrow.

Further information on Ben no Naishi's life after she left court service is found in *Notes from a Frog at the Bottom of a Well* (*Suia Ganmoku*, also *Suiashō*), a fourteenth-century work by the monk Ton'a (ca. 1289–1372). It states that Ben no Naishi's younger sister, Shōshō no Naishi, died in 1265 and that Ben no Naishi took Buddhist vows soon afterward. It concludes with a note that Ben no Naishi lived as a nun-recluse at a place called Ōgi, north of Sakamoto near the foothills of Mt. Hiei.[20]

More information about Ben no Naishi can be gathered from a headnote to a poem by Minamoto Michinari in the thirteenth royal anthology, *New Later Collection of Japanese Poetry* (*Shingosenshū*, 1303), confirming the fact that she outlived her younger sister:[21]

Shingosenshū 1505 (Miscellaneous 1). Tsuchimikado Nyūdō no Naidaijin [Minamoto Michinari]. One of a group of poems composed by people for Ben no Naishi at her request on the occasion of the Buddhist services after Shōshō no Naishi's death:

ato o tou	Probably the plovers
hito dani nakuba	will lose their way
tomochidori	on unfamiliar paths by the shore
shiranu hamaji ni	without anyone
nao ya mayowan	to ask for directions.

Before Ben no Naishi recovered from Shōshō no Naishi's death, in the same year she also lost her older brother, Tametsugu.[22] Traditional sources state that Nobuzane and Sōhekimon'in Shōshō no Naishi died fairly close to one another in the year 1266, but Inoue Muneo suggests a revised death date for Nobuzane falling between the eighth day of the fourth month of 1266 and the eighth month of 1270.[23] Since Sōhekimon'in Shōshō no Naishi is known to have outlived her father long enough to compose a poem lamenting his death, this could put Sōhekimon'in Shōshō no Naishi's death date as late as 1270 or beyond. Ben no Naishi in turn outlived her younger sister, Shōshō no Naishi (d. 1265), her eldest brother, Tametsugu (d. 1265), her father, Nobuzane, and her older sister, Sōhekimon'in no Shōshō. That Ben no Naishi lived longer than Sōhekimon'in Shōshō no Naishi is evident from the following headnote in the *Collection of Jeweled Leaves:*[24]

Gyokuyōshū 2044 (Miscellaneous 1). The former regent and chancellor [Fujiwara Mototada]. This response to the preceding poem was composed and sent at Ben no Naishi's request after the death of Sōhekimon'in Shōshō no Naishi:

sono na nomi	With only her name
katami no ura no	as a keepsake,
tomochidori	the plovers
ato o shinobanu	of Keepsake Bay
toki no ma mo nashi	never cease to miss her.

Although the headnote to this poem is not dated, it establishes the sequence in which members of Ben no Naishi's family departed the world. After Ben no Naishi lost her younger sister in 1265, she renounced the world, only to lose her older brother, Tametsugu, in the same year. It seems she lived as a nun for perhaps as little as a year to as many as five years. Sometime during this period between 1266 and 1270, Ben no Naishi lost her father, Nobuzane. Shortly after her father's death, her older sister, Sōhekimon'in Shōshō no Naishi, also died. Although we do not know when Ben no Naishi died, it seems safe to state that it was around the late 1260s or the early 1270s, for her name disappears from court records around this time. Thus, we can tentatively date her birth to around 1228 and her death to around 1270.

One last bit of chronologically ambiguous information remains to be discussed. At some time in Ben no Naishi's life, she met Fujiwara (Hosshōji) Masahira (1229–78), by whom she had a daughter known as Shin'yōmeimon'in no Shōshō[25] or Shin'yōmeimon'in nyōbō Chūnagon.[26] Ben no Naishi's daughter served Shin'yōmeimon'in (1262–96), a daughter of the Regent, Fujiwara Motohira (1246–68), who became the consort of Kameyama. Ben no Naishi must have borne her daughter before she took religious vows (ca. 1265), but unfortunately we do not know whether Ben no Naishi and Masahira were ever married. Ambiguities about their marital status hinge on the continuation of Heian-period marriage customs among the middle-ranking nobility of the mid-Kamakura period: ceremonies were civil; cohabitation was not the rule; children were raised in matrilocal households; matrilocal or uxorilocal still held dominance over patrilocal or virilocal residences; and endogamous marital alliances still prevailed among the middle aristocracy. Further, there seems to have been a fairly strong connection between Nobuzane's family and Hosshōji, a temple established by Fujiwara Tadahira in the Higashiyama district in 925. Nobuzane himself chose to reside there after he took religious vows, as did Sōhekimon'in Shōshō no Naishi.[27] Having lost almost all her immediate family, Ben no Naishi must have joined them sometime between 1266 and 1270.

There are no extant records of further contact between Go-Fukakusa and Ben no Naishi after she left court service, but she did receive a request for poetic compositions from his brother, Kameyama, in 1265. Perhaps this says more about the different characters and interests of the two sovereigns than the relationship between sovereign and *naishi*. In her post as *naishi,* one could not find a more devoted subject than Ben no Naishi.

Naishi (Female Courtiers)

In most translations and studies of classical Japanese literature in English, the various terms in Japanese referring to women in court service have been conflated into the all-purpose translation of "ladies-in-waiting." However, "ladies-in-waiting" does not convey the variety of ranks and posts the women held or the range of duties they performed at court. On the other hand, translations for men in court service preserve a better sense of rank: "gentlemen-in-waiting" (*jige*) for men who held the sixth or seventh ranks, "courtiers" (*tenjōbito*) for holders of the fourth and fifth ranks, and "senior nobles" for those of the three highest ranks. I wish to challenge the traditional translation of "ladies-in-waiting" for an alternative that better indicates their rank within the court hierarchy. In this section I argue that the translation "female courtier" is a more accurate translation of *naishi* in royal service than those commonly seen in translation, including "ladies-in-waiting," "handmaids," or "inner attendants." "Female courtier" more adequately reflects the high rank *naishi* held at court, whose status was at least the equivalent of male courtiers (*tenjōbito*) of the fourth or fifth ranks, or in some cases, equal to the level of senior nobles holding the three highest ranks. To adopt "female courtiers" as a translation for *naishi* requires a revision of the translation of *Naishi no Tsukasa*, which had evolved into the most important of the Twelve Offices (Jūni no Tsukasa) in the Back Palace (Kōkyū) by the Heian period, from the "Handmaid's Office" to the "Office of Female Courtiers."[28]

In order to gauge the rank of *naishi*, I define the term *nyōbō* (women of the upper ranks) because it refers to women of the first through fifth ranks without designating a specific post or duty assigned. Attempts to define *naishi* and *nyōbō* are hampered by the evolving nature of the ranks and duties assigned to women of the Back Palace since the system was established in the Nara period (710–94). Most studies focus primarily on the Nara and Heian periods and state almost nothing substantive of the Kamakura period situation. The process is also complicated by dictionaries using the characters for female and government (*onna* and *kan, tsukasa*) to define *naishi* that are now read as *nyōkan, nyokan*, or *jokan*. This results in confusion because, while dictionaries today use *nyōkan* and *nyokan* as general terms to indicate women in court service, in the premodern period the two terms referred to two distinct ranks in the female bureaucracy. Therefore, a ranking of the related terms used to define or distinguish *naishi* from other posts or levels within the Back Palace will aid our understanding of the system and serve as a justification for the translation "female courtiers."[29]

Naishi is simply defined as a female official (*jokan*) who served the Naishi no Tsukasa, but secondary definitions usually state that the term referred specifically to women who occupied the post of *naishi no jō* (assistant female courtiers), third in order of rank after *naishi no kami* (principal female courtiers) and *naishi no suke* (associate female courtiers). But before investigating the terms for female officials, it will be useful to start with *nyōbō*, the term for women of the upper five ranks of the bureaucracy and discover where *naishi* stood within the hierarchy of *nyōbō*.

Nyōbō, written with the characters for "female" and "room," was a general term for female officials serving at the courts of reigning or retired sovereigns, who were granted the privilege of private rooms at court. Originally, *nyōbō* referred specifically to the individual rooms given to female officials of the upper ranks; later, by extension, the term came to refer to the women who occupied those rooms. At that time, the privilege of being granted private quarters was confined to the upper ranks of the court bureaucracy. Therefore, *nyōbō* had a status equivalent to that of courtiers of at least the fourth or fifth ranks, or in other cases, to that of senior nobles of the top three ranks. The primary difference between the terms *naishi* and *nyōbō* is that *naishi* refers to specific posts within the court bureaucracy and *nyōbō* to a range of court ranks (the first through the fifth) without reference to specific posts.

William H. and Helen Craig McCullough divide *nyōbō* (which they translate as the "Emperor's ladies-in-waiting") into three categories in "Some Notes on Rank and Office" in *A Tale of Flowering Fortunes*:

> The upper grade (*jōrō*) consisted of a small, select group of women who had received specific individual authorization to wear forbidden colors and fabrics—the Mistresses of the Wardrobe, the two Principal Handmaids, any Assistant Handmaid of Second or Third Rank, and certain daughters and granddaughters of Ministers of State.

> In the middle grade (*chūrō*), the largest groups were the Handmaids (Naishi no Jō) and a sizable contingent of Myōbu (translated as Palace Lady, or transliterated).

> The lower grade (*gerō*) was made up of daughters of Stewards in regental households, daughters of priests who served at the leading Shintō shrines, and relatively low-ranking women known rather misleadingly as Lady Chamberlains (Nyokurōdo), who helped sew costumes and the like.[30]

McCullough and McCullough place *naishi* in two separate categories, higher-ranked principal handmaids (*naishi no kami*) and assistant handmaids (*naishi no suke* of the second or third rank) in the upper grade (*jōrō*), and handmaids (*naishi no jō* or *naishi*) in the middle grade (*chūrō*). There are no specific ranks for provisional handmaids (*gon no naishi*).

The *Kōjien* definition of *nyōbō* differs significantly from that of McCullough and McCullough, especially in its subdivision of the *jōrō* grade and the exclusion of *naishi no jō* from the *chūrō* grade. Their ranks were as follows—in descending order:

1. The *jōrō* (upper grade), an abbreviation of *jōrō no nyōbō*, included female officials (*jokan*) of high rank, such as mistresses of the wardrobe (*mikushigedono*), principal female courtiers (*naishi no kami*), assistant female courtiers (*naishi no suke*) of the second and third rank, and daughters or granddaughters of ministers of state (*daijin*) who were allowed to wear forbidden colors at court.[31] There were two levels of *jōrō*:

a. *Ōjōrō* (greater upper grade), the highest-ranking female officials (*jokan*) at court.[32]

b. *Kojōrō* (lesser upper grade), the daughters of ministers of state, counselors (*nagon*), or consultants (*sangi*), who became female officials (*jokan*).[33]

2. The *chūrō* (middle grade), an abbreviation of *chūrō no nyōbō*, designated female officials (*jokan*) serving in the Back Palace.[34]

3. The *gerō* (lower grade), an abbreviation of *gerō no nyōbō*, refers to lower-ranking female officials (*jokan*) who served in royal or regental households and at the Kamo and Hie shrines.[35]

While McCullough and McCullough identify *naishi no jō* as the largest group of women belonging to the *chūrō* grade, the *Kōjien* excludes *naishi* from the *chūrō* grade, thus suggesting that *naishi no jō* belong to the *kojōrō* subgroup of the *jōrō no nyōbō* grade. But because *naishi no jō* are not addressed specifically in the *Kōjien* definition, some doubt remains concerning the ranking of *naishi* within the three grades of *nyōbō*.

Asai Torao provides a wealth of details on the three grades of *nyōbō* in his book, *A Newly Revised Commentary on Female Officials* (*Shintei Jokan Tsūkai*, 1985):

1. *Jōrō no nyōbō* (upper grade), usually abbreviated to *jōrō*. Within the court bureaucracy, it refers to women who occupied at least the post of *naishi no suke*. In court rank, it refers to those who held at least the third rank. In court society, it refers to daughters of chancellors (*daijin*), major and middle counselors (*dainagon* and *chūnagon*), and occasionally granddaughters of chancellors. All in this grade were allowed to wear colors (red and blue) forbidden to others of lesser rank. They were divided into two sub-grades:

a. *Ōjōrō* (greater upper grade), women of the highest rank who held office as one of the directors of the Twelve Offices of the Back Palace, such as *naishi no kami* and *kura no kami*. Daughters of regental families allowed to adopt sobriquets incorporating the names of gates at the Royal Palace and to wear colors forbidden to women of lower rank often belonged to this, the highest grade.[36]

b. *Kojōrō* (lesser upper grade), women in the post of *naishi no jō*, daughters of senior nobles (first through third rank) or daughters of *jishin* (*tenjōbito* holding the fourth or fifth rank).[37] *Kojōrō* most often refers specifically to *naishi no jō*, although daughters of various masters of royal household offices (*daibu*) and consultants (*sangi*) also belonged to this grade.[38]

2. *Chūrō* (middle grade), women designated as *gemyōbu* (women whose husbands held the fourth or fifth rank), daughters of *jishin*, various masters of royal household offices (*daibu*), and noted families, such as the Kamo and the Abe who worked in the Bureau of Divination. They were assigned the duty of safeguarding the sacred sword and jewels stored in the Royal Bedchamber (Yon no Otodo).[39] Women below the level of *chūrō no nyōbō* were not allowed to serve in the Royal Bedchamber or the Dining Room (Asagarei no Ma).[40]

3. *Gerō* (lower grade), women holding posts such as female chamberlains (*nyokurōdo*) chosen from daughters of those who served at leading shrines such as Kamo or Hie, or daughters of those who held the sixth rank.[41]

Asai's definitions offer a range of detail missing in others. Unlike the other sources, Asai places *naishi no jō* in the *kojōrō* grade, confirming my contention that women who occupied the post of *naishi* belonged to one of the highest levels of court bureaucracy, equivalent in rank to courtiers and senior nobles. Even if *naishi no jō* belonged to the *chūrō no nyōbō*, as McCullough and McCullough stated above, they would still have been qualified to safeguard the royal sword and jewels, enter the royal presence, and serve in the Royal Bed Chamber and Royal Dining Room. Thus *naishi* as a group were equivalent in status to male courtiers, supporting my proposal to adopt the translation "female courtiers" to refer to women of high rank as a better alternative to "ladies-in-waiting," a term devoid of rank.

There has been a tendency to raise the rank of occupants of posts within the female bureaucracy. For example, in 807 (Daidō 2), ranks for the three types of *naishi* were raised two steps, confirming the contention that *naishi no jō* held at least the fifth rank and that corresponding ranks for *naishi* continued to climb from their original levels:

1. *Naishi no kami* (principal female courtiers; two positions), originally junior fifth, but raised to junior third rank.

2. *Naishi no suke* (assistant female courtiers; four positions, the first called *ōsuke*, the second *shin tenji*, the other two called by names of their posts at court), originally junior sixth but raised to junior fourth rank, although some *naishi no suke* held the second or third rank.

3. *Naishi no jō* (female courtiers; six positions, four regular and two provisional positions [*gon no naishi*]). The highest ranking *naishi no jō* was called *kōtō no naishi*, *ichi no naishi*, or later *nagahashi no tsubone*, originally seventh, but raised to junior fifth upper rank.[42]

From the time the Twelve Offices of the Back Palace were established in the Nara period, ranks for the most prominent incumbents of the female bureaucracy began to rise. Although reference sources usually describe conditions for the Heian period, the tendency to upgrade ranks and levels probably continued into the Kamakura period. To fully explore the importance of *naishi* in the female bureaucracy, a brief look at the Twelve Offices in the Back Palace is in order.

The Naishi no Tsukasa (Office of Female Courtiers) was the largest and most important of the twelve offices that constituted the Back Palace. The highest ranking *naishi* functioned as directors for the most prestigious office of that palace. The following list provides a general overview of the offices and administrators of each component of the Back Palace:

1. Naishi no Tsukasa (Office of Female Courtiers): largest of the twelve offices in the Back Palace, responsible for safeguarding the royal regalia, attending to the needs of the monarch, and transmitting his commands.[43]

> 2 *naishi no kami* (principal female courtiers), junior third rank
> 4 *naishi no suke* (associate female courtiers), junior fourth to senior fifth rank
> 4 *naishi no jō* (assistant female courtiers), junior fifth rank
> 2 *gon no naishi no jō* (provisional female attendants), senior sixth rank
> 100 *nyōju* (female assistants), women below junior eighth rank

2. Kura no Tsukasa (Storehouse Office): stored articles used by the sovereign and clothing presented as stipends to female courtiers. At one time occupants of this office performed duties of close attendance on royalty, but later these duties were assumed by *kōi* (royal concubines) and *mikushigedono* (mistresses of the wardrobe).[44]

> 1 *kura no kami* (principal storehouse courtier), senior third rank
> 2 *kura no suke* (associate storehouse courtiers), senior fourth to junior fifth rank
> 4 *kura no jō* (assistant storehouse attendants), junior seventh rank
> 10 *nyōju* (female assistants)

3. Fumi no Tsukasa (Scribal Office): in charge of storing sutras, registers, paper, charcoal, brushes, chairs, musical instruments, and the like.[45]

> 1 *fumi no kami* (principal scribal courtier), junior fifth rank
> 2 *fumi no suke* (associate scribal attendants), junior eighth rank
> 6 *nyōju* (female assistants)

4. Kusuri no Tsukasa (Pharmacy Office): managed medical supplies.[46]

> 1 *kusuri no kami* (principal pharmaceutical courtier), junior fifth rank
> 2 *kusuri no suke* (associate pharmaceutical attendants), junior eighth rank
> 4 *nyōju* (female assistants)

5. Tsuwamono no Tsukasa (Armory Office): exact functions unclear; presumably in charge of armor and ordinance .[47] Their duty was to accompany monarchs as guards.[48]

> 1 *tsuwamono no kami* (principal armory courtier), junior fifth rank
> 2 *tsuwamono no suke* (associate armory attendants), junior eighth rank
> 6 *nyōju* (female assistants)

6. Mikado no Tsukasa (Gates Office): originally in charge of keys to small gates within the palace enclosures; also handled receipts and disbursements. Responsible too for the collection of petitions to the sovereign from various offices and for distributing replies from the

sovereign to petitioning offices. However, most *tenjō* business was handled by *naishi* and *kurōdo* during the Heian period.[49]

> 1 *mikado no kami* (principal gates courtier), junior fifth rank
> 4 *mikado no suke* (associate gates attendants), junior eighth rank
> 10 *nyōju* (female assistants)

7. Tonomozukasa (Facilities Office, also Tonomori no Tsukasa):[50] in charge of such items related to lighting as lamp oil, animal oils, and torches, plus firewood to prepare water for bathing.[51]

> 1 *tonomo no kami* (principal facilities courtier), junior fifth rank
> 2 *tonomo no suke* (associate facilities attendants), junior eighth rank
> 6 *nyōju* (female assistants)

8. Kanimori no Tsukasa (Housekeeping Office; also Kamo no Tsukasa):[52] in charge of sweeping and sprinkling water on the grounds at shrines, preparing seats for Shintō and state functions, and so on.[53]

> 1 *kamo no kami* (principal housekeeping courtier), junior fifth rank
> 2 *kamo no suke* (associate housekeeping attendants), junior eighth rank
> 10 *nyōju* (female assistants)

9. Moitori no Tsukasa (Water Office; also Mondo no Tsukasa):[54] in charge of providing drinking water, preparing various rice gruels, and so on.[55]

> 1 *mondo no kami* (principal water courtier), junior fifth rank
> 2 *mondo no suke* (associate water attendants), junior sixth rank
> 6 *uneme* (gift maidens, ranked one level below female assistants)

10. Kashiwade no Tsukasa (Table Office): in charge of preparing food and wine, placed as offerings on serving trays.[56]

> 1 *kashiwade no kami* (principal table courtier), junior fourth rank
> 4 *kashiwade no suke* (associate table courtiers), junior fifth
> 41 *uneme* (gift maidens)

11. Sake no Tsukasa (Wine Office, also Miki no Tsukasa):[57] exact duties unclear, but providing rice wine for Shintō festivals and banquets (*sechie*) was probably the most important function of this office.[58]

1 *sake no kami* (principal wine courtier), junior fifth rank
2 *sake no suke* (associate wine attendants), junior eighth rank
(no other members indicated)

12. Nui no Tsukasa (Sewing Office; also Nuibe no Tsukasa):[59] in charge of sewing garments; later the Naishi no Tsukasa assumed this function.[60]

1 *nui no kami* (principal sewing courtier), junior fourth rank
2 *nui no suke* (associate sewing courtiers), junior fifth rank
4 *nui no jō* (sewing attendants), senior eighth rank

With over one hundred employees, the Office of Female Courtiers, the largest of the twelve offices, was charged with the most important duty, storing and guarding the sacred mirror in the Female Courtiers' Building (Naishidokoro, also known as Kashikodokoro and Unmeiden). Historically, however, the office was not the most important of the twelve offices. There was keen competition from the Storehouse Office.

The Office of Female Courtiers gradually achieved its preeminent position by appropriating duties assigned to other offices in the Back Palace. Originally, the Storehouse Office was the most powerful, based on its duties of safeguarding the royal regalia and attending to the personal care of sovereigns.[61] But when the mirror and sword were no longer stored in the building where the monarch lived, the principal female courtier of the Office of Female Courtiers (*naishi no kami*) and the principal female courtier of the Storehouse Office (*kura no kami*) began to reside with the monarch, sharing the duty of transporting and safeguarding the regalia.[62] Eventually the shared duty led to one person, the *naishi no kami,* emerging as victor. Thus, after the director of the Office of Female Courtiers assumed the duty of safeguarding the mirror and jewels, she claimed responsibility for the most significant duties of the Back Palace.

Most of what is written about the Back Palace is based on circumstances that existed during the Heian period. Unfortunately, little has been published on the state of the Back Palace in the Kamakura period. However, there are several issues about the Kamakura period that I must address. First was the fact that after the Jōkyū (also Shōkyū) Rebellion of 1221, there was a sudden decline in royal authority.[63] Second, in conjunction with the erosion of royal authority, there was a reduction in revenues following Go-Toba's rebellion. The extravagance of simultaneously layering twelve to twenty silk robes, described in *A Tale of Flowering Fortunes* (*Eiga monogatari*), was curtailed by decree in the Kamakura period to a maximum of five, perhaps because funds were needed for the upkeep of the warrior government in Kamakura. Finally, another startling change occurred early in the Kamakura period. The royal family abandoned the prospect of life within the Greater Royal Palace (Daidairi) after attempts to rebuild the palace ceased in 1219. Thereafter, royal residence shifted to mansions belonging to the regental families, some of which in the beginning were makeshift town palaces (*satodairi*), but which later evolved into smaller scale replicas of the royal palace (*dairizukuri*), such as the Kan'in Palace, the setting for Ben no Naishi's memoir. Town palaces were only a fraction of the size of the original Royal Residential Palace (Dairi), so the layout, number, and placement of buildings in the Back Palace, to say nothing of their functions, changed a great deal. Most reference sources do not mention this fact, but in trying to recreate equivalent charts of the original palace and the Kan'in Palace for this book, I realized that there was not enough room to situate all the original buildings of the Back Palace on the site occupied by this town palace. Without the traditional palace, a number of town palaces were created to house the royal family. No longer able to maintain the integrity of the sacred space of the court within the Greater Royal Palace, the royal family roamed from town palace to town palace, a symbol of the transient, transitional character of the Kamakura period. Though the nobility tried to preserve traditional court culture by perpetuating the tradition of writing in the vernacular, the resultant literature exuded the flavor of a new emergent culture even as it sought to keep at bay the tides of change.

In this section, I presented a more focused picture of *naishi*, *nyōbo*, and the Back Palace than that which had been available before concerning the Kamakura period. Now we are able to dispense with the all-purpose "ladies-in-waiting" instead using ones that designate more accurate positions of the ranks *naishi* held in court society. Next, I look at the duties performed by female courtiers, both sacred and secular, with reference to Ben no Naishi's duties in particular.

Sacred Duties of *Naishi*

It is easy to reject the mindset of premodern Japanese who believed in the divine nature of the royal family. The sacred mirror, the sacred sword, and the sacred jewels (*sanshu no jingi*, also *sanshu no shinpō*; or the three royal regalia) symbolize the legitimacy of the rule of Japanese monarchs. As descendants of the sun goddess Amaterasu Ōmikami, monarchs are considered the earthly recipients of the Yata Mirror (*Yata no Kagami*), which was not only a symbol of the sun goddess herself but also the receptacle for the soul of the sun and, as such, a *kami* (god) in its own right.[64] The Grass-Mowing Sword (*Kusanagi no Tsurugi*; also *Ame no Murakumo no Tsurugi*, Gathering-Clouds-of-Heaven Sword), embodies the lightning flash, or the terrible, awesome aspect of the god of light, whereas Amaterasu Ōmikami represents the beneficent aspect of light.[65] Finally, the Yasakani Curved Jewels (*Yasakani no Magatama*), a necklace with comma-shaped ornaments, represents the crescent moon as the final element of light-related gods signified by the regalia.

The origin of the three regalia is chronicled in creation myths. The *Record of Ancient Matters* (*Kojiki*, 712) preserves a legend that the eight hundred myriad deities commissioned the female deity Ishikoridome no Mikoto to make a mirror from iron excavated from sacred Mt. Kagu.[66] Next, the eight hundred myriad deities commissioned Tama no Ya no Mikoto to make a long string of jewels.[67] Later, the jewels were said to have been given to the sun goddess, who handed them over to her heavenly grandchild, Ninigi no Mikoto, when he descended to earth. The legend continues with the story of Susanoo no Mikoto, who slew a dragon and found the sword in its eight-spiked tail. Susanoo no Mikoto then presented it to his sister, the sun goddess, as he deemed it proper that she should possess such an extraordinary sword.[68]

In *Japanese Enthronement Ceremonies with an Account of the Royal Regalia* (1972), D. C. Holtom relates the legendary story of the sovereign Sujin (r. 97–30 BC in the traditional chronology) having replicas made of the Yata Mirror and the Grass-Mowing Sword. Compiled by Inbe Hironari, the *Gleanings from the Ancient Language* (*Kogoshūi*, 807) preserves legends not found in the *Record of Ancient Matters* or the *Chronicles of Japan* (*Nihongi*, alt. *Nihon Shoki*, 720):

> [He] "began to feel uneasy at dwelling on the same couch and under the same roof, beside the mirror sacred to Amaterasu-ō-mikami and the Herb-quelling Divine Sword, and being greatly overwhelmed by their awe-inspiring divine influence," he ordered them removed to the village of Kasanui in the district of Yamato where a new holy site was prepared for them. The emperor took the precaution, however, of having replica of the originals made which were kept near his person just as were the old. . . . The new mirror and sword are the identical sacred emblems which the Imbe family offer to the emperor as the divine insignia at his Enthronement Ceremony which protect the legitimate sovereign against hostile evil powers.[69]

Today the original Yata Mirror is said to be housed at the Ise Grand Shrine complex (Ise Daijingū) and the original Grass-Mowing Sword is reportedly stored at the Atsuta Shrine (Atsuta Jingū) near Nagoya.[70] The replica mirror, severely damaged during fires in 960, 1005, and 1040, has been handed down from generation to generation in sadly altered form to this day.[71] The replica sword, lost in 1185 during the naval battle of Dan no Ura, was never recovered. It was replaced in 1210 by a sword that had been stored at the Ise Grand Shrines. It is that sword that is used today at *Daijōsai* (enthronement ceremonies).[72]

Unlike the sacred mirror and the sacred sword, no replica was made of the sacred jewels. The Yasakani Curved Jewels were also thought lost during the naval battle of Dan no Ura, but legend states that they were later recovered, thanks to the buoyancy of the wooden box in which they were stored.[73] The Yasakani Curved Jewels were housed in the Naishidokoro within the Royal Residential Palace (Dairi) in Kyōto. Since the capital was transferred to Tokyo in 1868, the sacred jewels have been enshrined in the Unmeiden of the Royal Palace of Tokyo.[74]

The Naishidokoro was the building within the Royal Residential Palace which housed the sacred mirror. The highest-ranking female courtiers of the Office of Female Courtiers were responsible for safeguarding it. The *naishi* not only safeguarded the sacred mirror, they also transported it from its place of storage to the abdication and enthronement ceremonies and then back again to storage. Female courtiers also played a major role in transmitting the regalia from one monarch to another during the transfer of the regalia (Kenji Togyō no Gi) at those ceremonies.

Female courtiers charged with safeguarding the sacred mirror seem to have been extremely conscious of the efficacy of the rituals and ceremonies that shaped their daily existence. A near contemporary of Ben no Naishi and also a female courtier, Nakatsukasa no Naishi, the daughter of Fujiwara Nagatsune, left an account of the official, religious functions of female courtiers at the abdication ceremony of Kameyama's son, Go-Uda (1267–1324; r. 1274–87), and the enthronement ceremony of Go-Fukakusa's son, Fushimi, in the *Memoirs of Nakatsukasa no Naishi* (*Nakatsukasa no Naishi Nikki*, 1280-92).

Section 24 of the *Memoirs of Nakatsukasa no Naishi* is her account of the abdication ceremony of Go-Uda. In the memoir, a female courtier is described carrying the sacred jewels while a male courtier bears the sacred sword.[75] It also relates that Kōtō no Naishi (the highest-ranking member of the four *naishi no jō*) received the sacred sword from the male courtier, then conveyed it to the royal dais, while Shōshō no Naishi accepted the sacred jewels from the female courtier who had carried the regalia during the procession to the dais.[76] Nakatsukasa no Naishi records that it was almost dawn before the sacred mirror was finally brought in, but she does not record by whose hands it was borne to the ceremony. It seems likely that another female courtier was assigned that duty, since the sacred mirror was housed in the Naishidokoro.[77]

Section 46 of the *Memoirs of Nakatsukasa no Naishi* states that it was Nakatsukasa no Naishi herself who was entrusted with carrying the sacred jewels during the *Daijōsai* of Fushimi, son of Go-Fukakusa. The *nikki* records that another female courtier, Kōtō no Naishi, carried the sacred sword, while Nakatsukasa no Naishi was responsible for the sacred jewels in the procession toward the royal dais.[78] The *Memoirs of Nakatsukasa no Naishi* offers further glimpses of women performing important duties during the *Daijōsai*: *kojōrō* (lesser upper grade of *nyōbō*) acted as royal food bearers for the royal repast while other female attendants conveyed food trays to the *kojōrō*; another female attendant raised the curtain as the sovereign ascended the steps toward the throne; four female attendants and six female courtiers stood near the monarch's throne in close attendance; the same four female attendants led the procession, followed by the monarch and six female courtiers, divided into two groups, at the end of the procession; and finally another group of female courtiers was seated in places of honor as spectators of the ceremony.[79] Although *Ben no Naishi Nikki* is not as detailed as the *Memoirs of Nakatsukasa no Naishi*, a few examples will illustrate the variety of religious duties performed by female courtiers in *Ben no Naishi Nikki*.

Of all the duties delegated to female courtiers, perhaps the most important was safeguarding members of the royal family and the regalia during ordinary and extraordinary situations. Ben no Naishi is depicted guarding the sacred sword and jewels as part of her regular night duty in Section 31 of *Ben no Naishi Nikki*. In Section 81, Ben no Naishi and other female courtiers rush to the royal bedchamber to rescue the monarch and recover the regalia when fire was reported at the Kan'in Palace which served at the time as the royal residence. Throughout the uproar, the motivating factor among all female courtiers was the desire to safeguard members of the royal family and the regalia. Kōtō no Naishi collected the sacred sword, Niidono carried the seven-year-old Go-Fukakusa, Senji retrieved the guardian sword, and Chūnagon no Suke and Kunaikyō no Suke escorted Go-Fukakusa's aunt, Senkamon'in, to her carriage. Iwasa Miyoko states that Kōtō no Naishi was the female courtier responsible for the sacred sword and that Ben no Naishi was the female courtier delegated to take the sacred jewels to safety. (According to Tamai's annotated text, on which my translation is based, Noritoki rescued the *biwa*, the musical instrument known as Genjō, from the burning palace, but in a variant text, it is recorded that the *biwa* was recovered by "the daughter of Noritoki," perhaps another female courtier protecting an item precious to the royal family.) It was the duty of female courtiers to see that nothing was left behind during the evacuation of the palace.

Female courtiers kept watch over the monarch as he slept as part of their night duty. They were expected to keep vigil throughout the night near the sovereign's bedchamber, amusing themselves by composing clever poetic replies to questions posed by visitors (Section 30). But their primary function was to be on the alert for any sign of danger, such as the fire recorded in Section 81. In this section, we learn that *naishi* on official duty have their hair formally dressed (*kamiage no naishi*) and wear formal court attire, another indication of the ritual nature of their duty.

They also assisted the monarch in the performance of daily royal prayers. In Section 27, Ben no Naishi and other female courtiers wait in the Lime Altar Room (Ishibai no Dan, also Ishibai no Ma), the sacred space located in the southeastern corner of the Seiryōden, the sovereign's residential hall, that had a floor of dirt and lime. In this episode, female courtiers were waiting in the Lime Altar Room to receive word of the Kamo Return, a ceremony during which the Kamo Virgin paid homage to the sovereign while royal messengers entertained the gods with dances and horse races. It was there that the sovereign conducted daily prayers at dawn to the sun goddess Amaterasu Ōmikami and other *kami*. Evidently, the monarch sat on a bench surrounded by screens depicting the four seasons as he prayed to the sun goddess at dawn. Similarly, Section 36 notes that several female courtiers came to assist the sovereign with his petitions. A further detail about the duty of female courtiers is provided in Section 59 of the *Memoirs of Nakatsukasa no Naishi,* where a female courtier is depicted carrying water to the monarch so that he could be ritually cleansed before dawn prayers.[80]

Female courtiers also attended closely upon the monarch at meals. This included meals for ordinary times and those for more sacred occasions, such as the ritual of the Repast in the Presence of a *Kami* (*Jingonjiki*) and the First Fruits Service (*Niinamesai*). Both male and female courtiers assisted the sovereign during routine meals. In Section 53, Ben no Naishi is called upon by the regent, Konoe Kanetsune, to compose a poem about the moon while the monarch is dining.

Female courtiers were present at all sacred meals. At the Repast in the Presence of a *Kami*, First Fruits Service, and when the sovereign ate food previously offered to the gods (*himorogi*), the rituals emphasize the concept that the monarch becomes the repository of the sacred rice spirit when he eats ritually cleansed rice.[81] During the *Daijōsai,*[82] food offerings are placed on mats oriented toward the Ise Grand Shrines to indicate a special thanksgiving to the sun goddess.[83] In *Ben no Naishi Nikki*, although Ben no Naishi was not in personal attendance, Section 52 mentions the ritual of the Repast in the Presence of a *Kami* (*Jingonjiki*). In Section 71, there is an allusion to the First Fruits Banquet, perhaps one of the most important Shintō festivals, at which the sovereign eats new rice, which had been ritually cleansed to avoid any contamination during its growth, harvest, and preparation. In Section 57, *Ben no Naishi Nikki* records that, after a ceremony honoring Confucius and his ten disciples, the monarch engaged in a ritual of eating food that had been offered to the gods on the previous day.

Another sacred duty of female courtiers was to serve as royal messengers to a variety of Shintō shrines during such festivals as Hirano (Section 3), Matsunoo (Sections 4 and 89), Yoshida (Section 15), and Kasuga (Section 107). Section 15 is particularly interesting, for it offers a glimpse of Ben no Naishi's personality as she tries to persuade her attendants to take her carriage to the Suki Nyokudokoro where her sister, Shōshō no Naishi, was on duty during the *Daijōsai* while Ben no Naishi was serving as the royal messenger to Yoshida Shrine.[84] Several things about Ben no Naishi are revealed in this episode: she is resourceful, inventing a historical precedent that convinces her attendants to do her bidding; she is quick to reprimand the gate guard when he is slow to reopen the gate for the late-night visitors; and she displays a sense of humor when she recalls the encounter with the gate guard. The fact that Ben no Naishi's attendants indulged her whim, and the fact that the gate guard bent to her will speaks to the relative authority she possessed at court.

Ben no Naishi Nikki also records miscellaneous religious duties of *naishi*. For example, occasionally *naishi* were summoned to relay messages to other offices within the Royal Residential Palace, such as the Naishidokoro, during Shintō-related state occasions (Section 5). Other Shintō functions, such as the Obeisance to the Four Directions (Shihōhai) performed at the Seiryōden in the spring, required female courtiers to be in attendance.[85] Female courtiers also served as royal messengers during festivals, such as the Spirit-Pacifying Festival (Chiko no Sai, also Chinkonsai).[86]

The Spirit-Pacifying Festival exemplifies the importance in the relationship between monarchs and female attendants dating back to antiquity. According to the *Record of Ancient Matters*, the Spirit-Pacifying Festival originated with an incident that occurred during a First Fruits Service. The sovereign Yūryaku (r. 456–79) was seated beneath a *tsuki* tree (mulberry, but homophonous with "moon") during a First Fruits Service. An *uneme*, a female servant selected for court service from Mie province, unknowingly served a cup of rice wine with a leaf floating in the wine-cup. He became so angry that he held a knife to her neck before she was able to soothe him with a poem explaining that the leaf that fell into his wine-cup from the *tsuki* tree was an auspicious sign.[87] Thereafter, the "pacifying" poem she composed was set to music and called a *shizu-uta* ("pacifying song").[88]

Secular Duties of Naishi

Few secular duties performed by female courtiers are recorded in *Ben no Naishi Nikki*. Scribal duties were perhaps the most common official function of female courtiers. For example, female courtiers kept an attendance register (*chakutō*) with the names of women on official duty and those who visited the monarch (Section 34). The Upper Hot Water Room, located in the northwestern corner of the Seiryōden, served as an office for female courtiers who used the space to keep the attendance register, write records about annual events, draft royal documents, and perform other scribal duties. Speculation about the name, the Upper Hot Water Room, abound, but apparently the adjective "upper" derives from the room's elevation compared to the rest of the Seiryōden. The Upper Hot Water Room was also the place where water for the monarch's baths was heated and also where tea was prepared.

Occasionally, scribal duties of female courtiers included writing poems on behalf of others who were not as skilled at poetic composition. Because Ben no Naishi had won a place at court based on her skill as a poet, she was sometimes asked to write surrogate poems for high-ranking female courtiers such as Hyōe no Kami (Section 49) and Kōtō no Naishi (Section 56). Kōtō no Naishi was a noted virtuoso of the *koto* and the *biwa*, but occasionally she used Ben no Naishi's skill at impromptu compositions to her advantage. Ben no Naishi even wrote a surrogate poem for a female assistant known as Takatsunji when the latter received a love poem (Section 67).

Another secular duty of female courtiers was to convey messages at state functions. In Section 54, a male courtier has female courtiers wait in the Table Room for the announcement of the names of those who had been appointed to court posts. It was the responsibility of the female courtiers to announce the names of those appointed to the various court offices to the monarch. The Table Room, located in the southwestern portion of the Seiryōden overlooking the Table Room Court (Daibandokoro no Tsubo), received its name from the many dining tables (*daiban*) stored there. The spacious room served as the headquarters for the sovereign's female courtiers and as such was the equivalent of the Courtiers' Hall (Tenjō no Ma) for male courtiers. Unless given special permission, men were not allowed to enter it. Because the Table Room functioned as an office for female courtiers, the room contained a duty-board for female officials, a royal chair, and some furnishings, such as braziers and chests, similar to those found in the Courtiers' Hall. However, not all messages *naishi* conveyed were official; sometimes they simply carried messages to a consort's apartments (Section 62).

Another official duty of female courtiers was to educate a child monarch. In Section 47, Retired Sovereign Go-Saga commands senior nobles and courtiers, both male and female, to stage a mock festival ostensibly to entertain the monarch, but also to teach him proper conduct at banquets. Similarly, in Section 81, Ben no Naishi provides the monarch with a Chinese poem to copy during writing practice. In this way, entertainment and education were combined in an informal atmosphere to encourage learning. But occasionally entertainment is the only item on the agenda: when Ben no Naishi is commanded to put on a demon mask and try to scare people, it is simply because the child monarch is bored (Section 120).

Another duty *naishi* performed was to perfume robes to be given as royal gifts. Incense was burned beneath large baskets placed upside down (*fusego*) with silk robes draped over the baskets in a small confined space like a closet. In Section 24, female courtiers return to the monarch's quarters after failing to find a suitable place to view the sacred Shintō dance performance (*kagura*) at the Seisodō. There they occupy themselves by burning fragrance into robes to be handed out as rewards to worthy subjects. These are some of the most notable secular duties recorded in Ben no Naishi's memoir.

To conclude, Ben no Naishi secured a place as a poet at Go-Fukakusa's court due to her father's adroit handling of patronage relationships and her own recognized talent for impromptu compositions at poetry contests. Her official post as a *naishi* bound her closely to the sovereign as she assisted him in the performance of sacred duties that occupied much of Go-Fukakusa's time during his thirteen years of titular rule. Perhaps the most important legacy of her court duty is the memoir she left for posterity that reflects her prose and poetic impressions of her life as a *naishi* during the mid-Kamakura period. She played a significant role in the Back Palace as a high-ranking female courtier, taking her post seriously, performing her duties reverently, and recording her experiences of court service faithfully in a memoir she bequeathed to subsequent generations.

Notes

1. Tamai Kōsuke, *Ben no Naishi Nikki Shinchū* (Tokyo: 1958), 319–49.

2. In modern Japanese *otōto* refers only to younger male siblings, here the usage indicates a younger female sibling.

3. *Shinkō Gunsho Ruijū* (hereafter SGR) (Tokyo: 1938–39), 9:323.

4. Ōuchi Mayako, "*Ben no Naishi Nikki Kō*," *Ōsaka Furitsu Daigaku Kiyō* 12, Series C (1964):239.

5. SGR 9:281.

6. Henceforth, all references to "sections" followed by a number indicate numbered sections in my translation of *Ben no Naishi Nikki*.

7. *Kokka Taikan* (hereafter KT) (Tokyo: 1968), 4:371–447.

8. SGR 9:329–54.

9. SGR 7:153.

10. SGR 7:190.

11. Tamai, *Ben no Naishi Nikki*, 347.

12. SGR 9:355.

13. Kidō Saizō, "Ben no Naishi, Nakatsukasa no Naishi," *Nihon Joryū Bungakushi*, ed. Hisamatsu Sen'ichi (Tokyo: 1969), 1:418.

14. KT 1.1:459 and 1.1:480.

15. *Nihon Koten Bungaku Taikei* (hereafter NKBT), ed. Takagi Ichinosuke et al. (Tokyo: 1956–68), 87:318.

16. The case of Akazome Emon, the author of the first thirty chapters of *A Tale of Flowering Fortunes (Eiga Monogatari)* who incorporated sections almost verbatim from *Murasaki Shikibu: Her Diary and Memoirs (Murasaki Shikibu Nikki)*, is probably the best-known example of "borrowing" from texts by women.

17. KT 1.1:327.

18. Tamai, *Ben no Naishi Nikki*, 341.

19. KT 1.1:683.

20. SGR 13:377.

21. KT 1.1:418.

22. *Genealogy of the Exalted and the Base (Sonpi Bunmyaku)*, vols. 58–60 in *Kokushi Taikei* (Tokyo: 1929–64), 2:157–58.

23. Inoue Muneo, "Fujiwara Nobuzane Nenpu Kōshō: Jōkyū made," *Waka Bungaku Shinron*, ed. Morimoto Motoko (Tokyo: 1982), 378.

24. KT 1.1:463.

25. *Genealogy* 58:406–7.

26. Kidō, "Ben no Naishi," 413.

27. SGR 13:377.

28. The appendices, "Some Notes on Rank and Office" and "The Greater Imperial Palace," in *A Tale of Flowering Fortunes: Annals of Aristocratic Life in the Heian Period* (Stanford, Calif.: 1980) by William H. and Helen Craig McCullough set the standard for translations of terminology dealing with the court bureaucracy. In fact, the best account in English of duties performed by women who served at court appears in Appendix A, "Some Notes on Rank and Office," in which inhabitants of the Back Palace (in the McCulloughs' translation, Women's Quarters) are identified and described. For the most part, this study follows the translation for titles and ranks set forth in the appendices of McCullough and McCullough (2:790). "The Code divided the nobility into eight ranks plus initial ranks. First, second, and third each had two divisions, senior and junior. The other five ranks had four: upper senior and lower senior, upper junior and lower junior" (Miner, Odagiri, and Morrell, p. 445-46). Here holders of the first through third ranks

(*kugyo*) are translated as senior nobles (high nobility); those of the fourth and fifth ranks are translated as courtiers (attendant nobility), and to those of the sixth through eighth ranks are translated as gentleman (lesser nobility).

29. In this section, I am concerned only with women of relatively high rank within the Naishi no Tsukasa who held the posts of *naishi no kami, naishi no suke,* and *naishi no jo.* There were other women called *naishi* who belonged to a lower order of women serving in the Office of Female Courtiers, but these are not the object of my study. Furthermore, there were other women with pseudonyms of *naishi* who were not engaged by the royal court. Some women called *naishi* were female officials who served the Ise Virgin and Kamo Virgin and young women also known as *miko* (mediums or shrine maidens) who served the Itsukushima Shrine. Dictionary definitions concentrate on *naishi* of the highest rank and do not refer to *naishi* of a lower order who also belonged to the Office of Female Courtiers. I learned of the latter when I consulted Tsunoda Bun'e and Asai Torao's studies of the Back Palace. My study, therefore, cannot be definitive unless the various definitions can be correlated to specific points of reference at a particular period of history.

30. McCullough and McCullough, 2:822.

31. *Kōjien,* 1114.

32. Ibid., 275.

33. Ibid., 799.

34. Ibid., 1447.

35. Ibid., 701.

36. Asai Torao, *Shintei Jokan Tsūkai* (Tokyo: 1985), 38.

37. Ibid.

38. Ibid., 38–39.

39. Ibid., 38–40.

40. Ibid., 40–42.

41. Ibid., 43–45.

42. Ibid., 150–68.

43. Sugita Haruko, *Heian Jidai Kōkyū oyobi Joshi no Kenkyū* (*A Study of Women in the Back Palace during the Heian Period*) (Tokyo: 1982), 138–42, 153, 160–61.

44. Ibid., 167–71.

45. Ibid., 171–75.

46. Ibid., 175–77.

47. Ibid., 177–78.

48. Asai, 188.

49. Sugita, 178–79.

50. Asai, 191–93 and Tsunoda, "Kōkyū no Rekishi," 55.

51. Sugita, 190–92.

52. Asai, 193–94 and Tsunoda, "Rekishi," 55.

53. Sugita, 192–93.

54. Asai, 194–95.

55. Sugita, 194.

56. Sugita, 195–98.

57. Tsunoda, "Rekishi," 55.

58. Sugita, 198 and Asai, 199.

59. Asai, 200 and Tsunoda, "Rekishi," 55.

60. Sugita, 199.

61. Tsunoda, *Nihon no Kokyu*, 40.

62. Tsunoda, "Rekishi," 173.

63. Ibid., 57.

64. D. C. Holtom, *The Japanese Enthronement Ceremonies with an Account of the Imperial Regalia* (Tokyo: 1972), 12–13.

65. Ibid., 24.

66. Donald L. Philippi, trans., *Kojiki* (Tokyo: 1969), 82.

67. Ibid.

68. Ibid., 90.

69. Holtom, 16.

70. Ibid., 44.

71. Ibid., 41.

72. Ibid., 42.

73. Ibid., 40–41.

74. It is not clear where the sacred mirror was stored in the various town palaces (*satodairi*) of the Heian and Kamakura periods. There must have been a building that served as the Naishidokoro (Kashidokoro, Unmeiden) at the Kan'in Palace, the setting for most of *Ben no Naishi Nikki*, but it must have been called by a different name in a *satodairi*. There is no doubt that it was stored nearby, for its use is documented in the *nikki*. The *Nakatsukasa no Naishi Nikki* states that the sacred sword and sacred jewel were kept near the royal bedchamber at the Reizei-Tominokoji Palace. See Tamai, *Nakatsukasa no Naishi Nikki* (Tokyo: 1958), 190–92; Tamako Niwa, "*Nakatsukasa Naishi Nikki*" (Ph.D. diss., Radcliffe, 1955), 152. Today the replica sword and the reportedly original jewels are stored in a room in the royal palace known as the Room of the Sword and Seal (Kenji no Ma). The replica mirror is enshrined in the Kashikodokoro, one of the three palace shrines.

75. Tamai Kosuke, *Nakatsukasa no Naishi Nikki*, 85.

76. Ibid.

77. Ibid.

78. Ibid., 126.

79. In theory, there should have been only ten female courtiers: two *naishi no kami* (prinicpal female courtiers), four *naishi no suke* (assistant female courtiers), and four *naishi no jō* (female courtiers). (Occasionally there could be two additional *gon no naishi* [provisional female courtiers].) The list of female courtiers who participated in the enthronement ceremonies recorded by Nakatsukasa no Naishi exceeds ten because abdication ceremonies required the attendance of both the abdicating sovereign's entourage and the new titular monarch's female courtiers to complete the transferal of power and the royal regalia. The attendance of female courtiers in service to the soon-to-be retired sovereign swelled the number of *naishi* above the norm. The duplication of female pseudonyms in the accounts encountered in *Ben no Naishi Nikki* and *Nakatsukasa no Naishi Nikki* support the

fact that other members of the royal family also were fully attended by the required number of female courtiers for their personal entourage (see Section 56). Tamai, *Nakatsukasa no Naishi Nikki*, 124–26.

80. The importance of ritual purification by water is noted again in Section 69 of *Nakatsukasa no Naishi Nikki*, during which the monarch twice bathes and puts on ceremonial robes before going to the temporary shrine buildings for the enthronement ceremony. Tamai, *Nakatsukasa no Naishi Nikki*, 154.

81. Holtom, 113–14.

82. *Daijōsai* is difficult to translate. Literally, the characters for *Daijōsai* refer to a festival during which the harvest and food are worshipped, but actually the *Daijōsai* refers to the enthronement ceremonies of sovereigns. Another related ceremony is the *Niinamesai* (First Fruits Festival) that is strictly a harvest festival without enacting the enthronement ceremonies for new sovereigns.

McCullough and McCullough (1980) translate *Daijōsai* as the "Great Thanksgiving Service," D.C. Holtom as the "Great New Food Festival," and Robert S. Ellwood as the "Great Food Tasting." None of these translations, however, explicitly refers to the enthronement ceremonies. Further, Ellwood states that "it is only since the Meiji rituals that the terms *Daijōsai* and *Niinamesai* have been used strictly and exclusively to refer to the enthronement and annual festivals[,] respectively" (92). Therefore, I will use the original term *Daijōsai* to refer to the enthronement ceremonies that culminate offstage in the memoir in Section 24.

83. Suki (western) and Yuki (eastern) Nyokudokoro were responsible for the presentation and preparation of the new rice and the white and black wines for the *Daijōsai*. Suki and Yuki districts were chosen by divination. Those designated Suki were selected from either Tanba or Bitchu provinces and those elected Yuki were chosen from within Omi province. Temporary quarters for each side of the Nyokudokoro were built within the palace grounds for the participants.

84. See Section 77 of my translation.

85. See Section 22 of my translation.

86. Philippi, *Kojiki*, 362–66.

87. Robert S. Ellwood, *The Feast of Kingship: Accession Ceremonies in Ancient Japan* (Tokyo: 1972), 74–75.

3

The Literary Context

Ben no Naishi Nikki and the *Kana Nikki* Tradition

Ben no Naishi Nikki is a *kana nikki* detailing the public life of a woman serving at the court of Go-Fukakusa. *Kana nikki* are memoirs written, for the most part, in vernacular Japanese prose (*wabun*) in the cursive script (*hiragana*), closely associated with women and the literature written by women.[1] The *kana nikki* of the Heian period constitute the core of the premodern Japanese literary canon and many translations of its greatest works exist in English. Despite this, the Kamakura canon has received little critical attention thus far, perhaps because there are only a few translations available in English, the best known being Helen Craig McCullough's *The Journal of the Sixteenth-Night Moon* (1990) and Karen Brazell's *The Confessions of Lady Nijō* (1973).[2]

A glance at the studies of *nikki* by Helen Craig McCullough and Edwin A. Cranston offer some background on how Western scholarship has handled this genre. The term *nikki* has often been translated into English as "diary," "journal," or "memoir." In *Classical Japanese Prose: An Anthology*, McCullough divides Japanese prose into tales (*monogatari*) and memoirs (*nikki*), allowing for some overlapping of general categories.[3] She states that a memoir "corresponds roughly to the Japanese term *nikki bungaku*, which is usually translated literally as 'diary literature' or more freely as 'literary diaries.'"[4] McCullough excludes from consideration *nikki bungaku* writing that is clearly without literary intent.[5] She notes four major criteria distinguishing *nikki* from the "layman's notion (and the dictionary definition) of a diary":

1. The *nikki* is not always narrated in the first person or written by the main character. For example, *Izumi Shikibu nikki* (11th c.) is a third-person narration that may or may not have been written by the

protagonist, and *Kagerō nikki* (10th c.) fluctuates between third- and first-person narration.

2. Some examples of *nikki* contain daily or near-daily entries, but time is altered in such a way as to stop the action or to expand it greatly in a manner resembling that of fiction, history, autobiography, or biography.

3. *Nikki* contents are both more diverse and more selective than ordinary nonliterary diaries. For example, *Murasaki Shikibu nikki* (11th c.) contains not only autobiographical passages but also a critique of the author's fellow ladies-in-waiting in a section resembling a letter; *Kagerō nikki* excludes every aspect of the author's life not related to her marriage.

4. Most *nikki* contain such great numbers of poems that they resemble poetry collections with prose headnotes describing the circumstances which led to composition or the depth of feeling expressed by the act of composition. These works are not so much diaries as "life and times" autobiographical and biographical writings which transmit information of interest to the author and others. They can be of either confessional or conservatorial character.[6]

The characteristics McCullough identifies are primarily those associated with memoir-style *kana nikki*. Edwin Cranston, on the other hand, views the various kinds of *nikki* as historical records. In *The Izumi Shikibu Diary: A Romance of the Heian Court*, Cranston identifies the earliest usage of *nikki* as official records of court events maintained by the central bureaucracy. In these works "nikki" is written using the Chinese characters for "day" and "record." These official court records, which date back to 821, contain nothing that can be considered literary. He states that another type of early *nikki*, although not labeled as such, are private journals kept by court nobles, which record useful information, such as procedures followed on ceremonial occasions, which are written in a peculiar type of Chinese now often known as "memoranda Chinese" (*kiroku kanbun*). He notes that although such works are important sources for historians, they are seldom of literary interest. A third type of early *nikki* are the records of the poetry contests (*uta'awase*) that flourished in the Heian and Kamakura periods. If the records were written in Chinese, they were simply referred to as *nikki*; if they were written in the vernacular, they were called *kana nikki*. The animated descriptions found in some of the *uta'awase nikki* make them the first written with conscious literary intent.[7] They were among the direct precursors of the vernacular literary masterpieces of the tenth and eleventh centuries.

From Cranston's historical description, we gather that early *nikki* were records of actual events: official government records of state events, private journals of court nobles noting proper procedure and precedent, and accounts of poetry contests of some literary and social interest. He notes that there were variables among early *nikki*: they could be written in Chinese or in Japanese; they could adopt either a private or public stance; and they could be aesthetically presented or tersely factual.[8] Perhaps the most important legacy of the early *nikki* was their factual nature, which fostered in later readers a tendency to regard anything labeled as *nikki* to be a record of actual events.

From the tenth century on, *nikki* evolved into a type of personal account containing a blend of prose and poetry in which there was an interest in representing not only a public past but occasionally a personal one as well. These accounts, written in the vernacular and primarily in *kana* script, became the preferred mode of expression for aristocratic women. Ironically, the earliest surviving example of a *kana nikki* is *A Tosa Journal* (*Tosa Nikki*), written by a man, Ki no Tsurayuki. Because Tsurayuki adopted a female persona for *A Tosa Journal*, he unwittingly opened the sluice gate to a flood of writings by women who seemed to find in the *kana nikki* the perfect vehicle for personal and professional literary expression.

According to Konishi Jin'ichi's *History of Japanese Literature, Volume Two: The Early Middle Ages*, the current trend in Japanese scholarship is to divide vernacular prose into three major categories: *uta, rekishi,* and *tsukuri monogatari*; *nikki*; and *zuihitsu*.[9] Konishi claims that this classification system "does not always facilitate a proper understanding of vernacular prose works."[10] He suggests that medieval prose works were not given titles by their authors, but that titles were assigned later by others. This explains the existence of variant titles, for if works had been given titles at the inception, the problem of variant titles would not have arisen. Another reason for the existence of variant titles is that the reading audience and transmitters did not have a clear idea of what constituted a medieval prose genre; what one person might have perceived as a *monogatari* another might have viewed as a *nikki*.[11] He claims that for modern scholars to study texts based on labels assigned to works in the medieval period only creates obstacles preventing us from observing their original character.[12] Konishi's assertion is worth keeping in mind, although he seems to ignore his own advice when he turns his attention to the Kamakura literary canon.

From the three categories or types, *monogatari, nikki,* and *shū*, into which medieval readers divided untitled works, Konishi states that the following might have resulted "if the medieval audience's known and generally accepted criteria for differentiating categories [had been] put in the form of definitions":

1. *Monogatari*. A prose composition, written in the past tense, concerned with events involving either fictional or historical characters.

2. *Nikki*. A prose composition, written in the present tense, concerned with the life of a historical person.

3. *Shū*. A complex made up of prose in the *monogatari* or *nikki* style and a *waka* sequence.[13]

Tales of Ise (*Ise Monogatari*) and *Tales of Heichū* (*Heichū Monogatari*) are well-known examples of texts narrated in the mode of recollection; however, variant titles, such as *nikki*, indicate that tense was not the determining factor for medieval reading audiences.

Konishi finds in *An Untitled Work* (*Mumyō Sōshi*) further insights into the medieval criteria for categorizing works. In *An Untitled Work*, he distinguishes between "fabrications" (fiction) and "real events" (nonfiction) in *monogatari*. He categorizes both *A Tale of Flowering Fortunes* (*Eiga Monogatari*) and *The Great Mirror* (*Ōkagami*) as nonfiction.[14] He states that "'truth' and 'fiction' are matters of narrative stance that do not correspond to the historical reality of the content" and proposes that the current trend in Japanese scholarship, which continues to analyze works based on traditional classification of prose genres into *monogatari*, *nikki*, and *zuihitsu* (miscellany), is counterproductive. He suggests that the correct approach for looking at unclassifiable compositions is to understand the elements that make these works unclassifiable.[15]

I use Konishi's framework of classifying *nikki*, but the goal of my survey is limited to a discussion of the extant canon in terms of their similarities and differences to *Ben no Naishi Nikki*. The distinctions I adopt from Konishi are fictional versus factual *nikki* and private versus public stance. Subdividing *nikki* into fictional and factual is a major advance in the study of *nikki*. The difference between fictional *monogatari* and factual *monogatari* has been recognized historically, but Konishi's notable contribution lies in establishing the notion of a fictional *nikki* and challenging the traditional concept of *nikki* as "the record of actual events."[16]

A Tosa Journal, for example, has been traditionally regarded as factual, and Konishi concedes that the contents of *A Tosa Journal* are probably true, but he insists that because narrative persona is a technique used in fiction, *A Tosa Journal* is fictional.[17] This is the framework with which I begin my survey of the extant *nikki* from the Heian and Kamakura periods.

Nikki of the Heian Period (794–1185)

The earliest extant fictional *nikki* of the Heian period is Ki no Tsurayuki's (ca. 872–945) *A Tosa Journal* (ca. 935). Tsurayuki was known primarily as one of the compilers of the first royal poetry anthology, *Collection of Ancient and Modern Japanese Poetry* (*Kokinshū*, ca. 905), and as the author of the influential *kana* preface to the collection. He also compiled *New Selection of Japanese Poetry* (*Shinsen Wakashū*, ca. 935), which missed being designated a royal anthology because the monarch who commissioned it died before it was completed.[18] *A Tosa Journal* is Tsurayuki's only significant prose work.

In *A Tosa Journal*, Tsurayuki adopts a female persona to set down a short daily account of a provincial governor's return from Shikoku to the capital of Heian-kyō by boat.[19] *A Tosa Journal* is primarily devoted to recording about sixty poems, reported by the narrator to have been composed by members of the party, which roughly correspond in style to the poems in the Travel section of the *Kokinshū*.[20]

A Tosa Journal and *Ben no Naishi Nikki* are both arranged chronologically by dated entries and include a large number of poems, but that is the extent of their similarity. Tsurayuki's work is essentially a travel account of a journey by boat from Tosa province in Shikoku to the capital of Heian-kyō, while *Ben no Naishi Nikki* remains stationary at the royal court and is focused on duties performed by *naishi*. Tsurayuki gives a private, fictional account of a parents' grief over the death of a child, contrasting vividly with Ben no Naishi's adoption of a public persona from which she narrated her factual memoir.

The Gossamer Years (*Kagerō Nikki*, 10th c.), written by a woman known only as the mother of Fujiwara Michitsuna (Michitsuna no Haha [955–1020]), limits its subject matter largely to the narrow theme of the author's unhappy twenty-year marriage to the powerful court noble, Fujiwara Kaneie (929–90). Like other women writers of *nikki*, the mother of Michitsuna was born into the provincial governor class (*zuryō*). She ranks as the first in a group of women who left records of their lives in this genre. Written as a memoir, *The Gossamer Years* includes many poems exchanged by the couple throughout their marriage. Although it is extremely personal within the boundaries of its theme, it contains few details of other aspects of the author's life. The narration begins in the third person, but soon thereafter slips into the first person, where it remains until the close of the narrative.

There are a number of intriguing elements about *The Gossamer Years*, the first *nikki* written by a woman. Konishi categorizes this as a fictional *nikki*, although he does so on the basis of content, not narrative stance. An undoubtedly fictional element in *The Gossamer Years* was the author's decision to deny her own striking looks (she is listed as one of the three most beautiful women in Japan in *Genealogy of the Exalted and the Base*). Perhaps this was part of a ploy to challenge fantastic events in *monogatari* that were in vogue during her time. What she offered instead was a realistic narrative based on the life of an "ordinary person," although she was far from ordinary in her marital alliance to one of the most powerful political figures of her time.

The Gossamer Years differs from *Ben no Naishi Nikki* in that the author of *The Gossamer Years* adopts a private stance, whereas *Ben no Naishi Nikki* relates the public life of a *naishi* serving at court. As a result, the thematic contents of *The Gossamer Years* are restricted to those involving the author's unhappy marriage, while the public stance of *Ben no Naishi Nikki* excludes aspects of her private life. Thus, whereas the exchange of love poetry is a major part of *The Gossamer Years*, there is not one love poem in *Ben no Naishi Nikki*.

The Izumi Shikibu Diary (*Izumi Shikibu Nikki*, date uncertain) is considered an anonymous fictional story, based largely on poems written by the historical poet, Izumi Shikibu (fl. ca. 1000), and describing a love affair between a woman of the provincial governor class and a prince. Izumi Shikibu, whose father Ōe no Masamune was a provincial governor of Echizen and whose mother Suke no Naishi served as wet nurse to consort Shōshi, followed her mother into service at the court of Shōshi, where she worked with fellow female writers Murasaki Shikibu and Akazome Emon. *The Izumi Shikibu Diary* displays some characteristics of a fictional *nikki*, such as third-person narration and multiple points of view, which was probably responsible for the medieval audience's perception of the work as both *monogatari* and *nikki*. And while authorship was traditionally attributed to the historical poet Izumi Shikibu, Edwin Cranston favors the theory that the work was compiled by a later hand sometime in the Kamakura period.

The two most likely candidates as compilers are Fujiwara Shunzei (1114–1204) and his daughter, Fujiwara Shunzei-kyō no Musume (1175?–1250?). The daughter of "Lord" Fujiwara Shunzei was in fact his granddaughter, adopted as a daughter by Shunzei because of her poetic talent; she should not be confused with his biological daughter, Kenzu Omae (b. 1157). That one of the two may have compiled *The Izumi Shikibu Diary* is based on two colophons by Fujiwara Teika found in the manuscripts of *The Izumi Shikibu Diary* and *The Memoirs of*

Kenshunmon'in Chūnagon (*Kenshunmon'in Chūnagon Nikki*), the latter written by Kenzu Omae, elder sister of Teika.[21]

Once again it is easier to find differences rather than similarities between *The Izumi Shikibu Diary* and *Ben no Naishi Nikki*. Although both works contain a great deal of poetry, the focus on love in the former has no counterpart in *Ben no Naishi Nikki*. Further, *The Izumi Shikibu Diary* focuses narrowly on the private relationship between the female poet and her princely lover, precluding attention to the concerns of public court life preserved in *Ben no Naishi Nikki*.

Like *Ben no Naishi Nikki*, *As I Crossed a Bridge of Dreams* (*Sarashina Nikki*, ca. 1060) was set at the royal court, but includes a wider variety of topics than *Ben no Naishi Nikki* does. *As I Crossed a Bridge of Dreams*, written by a woman known as the daughter of Sugawara Takasue (Sugawara Takasue no Musume), contains about one hundred poems describing the author's dreams, religious retreats, pilgrimages, and travels. Sugawara Takasue also belonged to the provincial governor class, and at the opening of his daughter's account, his party is en route to the capital of Heian-kyō from the eastern province of Kazusa where he had just completed a tour of duty as governor.

The daughter of Sugawara Takasue was descended from Sugawara Michizane (845–903), a poet-statesman of the early Heian period whose literary accomplishments and posthumous honors had earned him the title, "the god of literature." The author describes the protagonist as an introverted, quiet person who seems to have found life extremely uncomfortable when she was sent into court service at the comparatively advanced age of thirty-one. It is apparent that a literary intent controls the contents of her work because she dwells on her emotions and says almost nothing about her life outside the court. The work is rather unusual in that its first part is essentially a travel account, the earliest extant example written by a woman. The work also contains internal evidence supporting the theory that it was written in retrospect in the author's old age. It looks back at the follies of youth with occasional regret and is frequently tinged with nostalgia at missed opportunities for religious devotion in her youth.

Konishi does not state why he regards this text as fictional. The historical attribution of *The Riverside Counselor's Stories* (*Hamamatsu Chūnagon Monogatari*) and *The Tale of Nezame* (*Yoru no Nezame*, also *Yowa no Nezame*) to Takasue's daughter may have influenced his decision, but it is hard to understand his conclusion without knowing his criteria. I personally see little in its contents to substantiate his choice.

As I Crossed a Bridge of Dreams and *Ben no Naishi Nikki* have little in common besides the setting. The former is intensely private and emotional, the latter decidedly public and intellectual. The daughter of

Takasue entered the court rather late in life, whereas Ben no Naishi probably became a courtier relatively young. The evident discomfort described by the older author of *As I Crossed a Bridge of Dreams* contrasts sharply with the enthusiasm expressed by Ben no Naishi, who performed her duties at court with a reverence bordering on the religious. Furthermore, the tone of reminiscence found in *As I Crossed a Bridge of Dreams* is missing from *Ben no Naishi Nikki*, which preserves a tone of immediacy even though it was probably revised after its initial composition.

Now we will turn to factual *nikki*, the contents of some of which, such as the diary of Murasaki Shikibu, provide the model for thirteenth-century *nikki* Konishi labels as "imitative," again without providing any criteria. *Murasaki Shikibu: Her Diary and Poetic Memoirs* (*Murasaki Shikibu Nikki*, early 11th c.), by the author of *The Tale of Genji* (*Genji Monogatari*, 11th c.), presents the public persona of the author in service to Fujiwara Shōshi (988–1074), a daughter of Michinaga (966–1027), and a consort of Ichijō (980–1011; r. 986–1011). Murasaki Shikibu, daughter of Fujiwara Tametoki, also belonged to the provincial governor class; her father served as the governor of both Echizen and Echigo provinces. Her brother Nobunori (d. 1011) was a minor bureaucrat in the Ministry of the Ceremonial (Shikibukyō), from whom a part of Murasaki Shikibu's pseudonym is derived. (There is considerable debate concerning the derivation of "Murasaki," the other part of her pseudonym.) Murasaki Shikibu's marriage to Fujiwara Nobutaka (d. 1001) produced one child, a daughter called Kenshi (b. 999), who later became known as the poet Daini no Sanmi. After the death of Murasaki Shikibu's husband, her reputation as a writer of fiction launched her onto the path of court service.

The diary of Murasaki Shikibu includes less poetry than is usual for the genre. Like *Ben no Naishi Nikki*, *Murasaki Shikibu Nikki* does not provide many personal details about the author, aside from aspects of her personality revealed through the entries she includes. All in all, the public persona Murasaki puts forward, namely her policy of limiting herself to her life as a woman in court service, resembles the public stance in *Ben no Naishi Nikki*. Another area in which the work is similar to *Ben no Naishi Nikki* is an interest in preserving for posterity a historical record of time spent in court service.

The diary of Murasaki Shikibu deserves closer inspection, since Konishi considers this work the model on which thirteenth-century public *nikki* were based. Murasaki Shikibu's memoir is not organized thematically, is not structured by daily entries, and is not a complete record of the time she spent in service. On the other hand, *Ben no Naishi Nikki*, labeled by Konishi as an "imitative" thirteenth-century factual *nikki*, is thematically focused, organized by daily entries, and originally covered the entire thirteen years Ben no Naishi spent in court service. Murasaki Shikibu's work, which is composed of sections resembling a memoir and a letter, finds no counterpart in factual, public *nikki* of the thirteenth century. Kamakura *nikki* remain within the bounds of pure memoir. The only outstanding similarity between the prototype and its thirteenth-century counterparts is the public stance from which the events of the memoir are narrated.

Sei Shōnagon, a contemporary of Murasaki Shikibu, produced a factual *nikki*, *The Pillow Book of Sei Shōnagon* (*Makura no Sōshi*, ca. early 11th c.), while serving at the rival court of Fujiwara Teishi (976?–1000). Her patron Teishi was the eldest daughter of Fujiwara Michitaka (953–95) and a consort to Ichijō (980–1011; r. 986–1011). She was a daughter of Kiyowara Motosuke (908–90), a scholar-bureaucrat and one of the compilers of the second royal poetry anthology *Later Collection of Japanese Poetry* (*Gosenshū*, ca. 950). Her pseudonym consists of the Sino-Japanese reading of her surname, Kiyowara ("Sei" is the Sino-Japanese reading of the first two syllables of "Kiyowara"), and the name of an office likely held by a male relative ("shōnagon" means "lesser counselor").

The Pillow Book is best known for its vignettes of court life written by a woman known for her verbal skill, extroverted nature, and lyrical prose style. The work is a composite of memoirs, essays, and lists of various kinds.

Although Japanese scholarship traditionally labels *The Pillow Book* as a *zuihitsu* because the word *nikki* does not appear in its title and because it contains some unusual lists, the work clearly belongs to the *nikki* tradition.[22] I agree with Konishi who proposes that the *zuihitsu* label be discarded in favor of factual *nikki*. He bases his reasoning on the fact that the method of composition for *nikki* and Sei Shōnagon's text are so similar that the latter ought to be considered a variant of the amorphous category known as *nikki*.[23] The memoir sections recount her pleasant experiences at court. In other sections, she chooses to write essays on specific topics such as why priests ought to be handsome or how a man ought to take leave of a woman in the morning after a tryst. The final category in *The Pillow Book* unique to this work is lists. The lists in *The Pillow* Book cover a great range of topics such as adorable things, disgusting things, squalid things, famous geographic place names, and so on.

The Pillow Book and *Ben no Naishi Nikki* share some similar features. The narrative personas are extroverted and always ready to face verbal challenges with clever wit. Both Sei Shōnagon and Ben no Naishi provide amusing vignettes of court life. Both Sei Shōnagon and Ben no Naishi held official posts at court, although Sei Shōnagon served a consort and

Ben no Naishi served a child monarch. The most striking difference between the two is the reverent tone of Ben no Naishi's poetry, a point that sets it apart from all other *nikki*. Sei Shōnagon's *Pillow Book* is the last factual *nikki* from the early eleventh century. Thereafter, Konishi states, the last two Heian factual *nikki* of the late eleventh century display a tendency toward *zoku* aesthetics (nonstandard, lower art) and a move toward informality.[24]

The Poetry Collection of Master Jōjin's Mother (*Jōjin Ajari no Haha Shū*, late 11th c.) is a poetic account focusing on the grief of an eighty-five-year-old mother whose sixty-two-year-old son has embarked on a journey to Sung China in 1071. The account ends in 1073, after the mother receives a letter from her son announcing his safe arrival. The first book of two begins in a manner resembling a *waka* collection, but a second book contains dated entries and resembles a *nikki*. For Konishi, it exemplifies a "strikingly informal tone shared by works of the twelfth and later centuries since the author fails to distinguish herself from the narrator of her *nikki*."[25]

Although both *The Poetry Collection* and *Ben no Naishi Nikki* contain a significant number of poems, the two works are strikingly dissimilar. The private, informal tone and the obsessive focus of Master Jōjin's Mother's poetry intended for her son's eyes only also makes this work vastly different from Ben no Naishi's conscious attempt to create a work of literary merit for a wider readership. Master Jōjin's Mother was an octogenarian when she wrote most of the poems, but, interestingly, the poetry of the younger Ben no Naishi is much more reverent in tone.

The Emperor Horikawa Diary (*Sanuki no Suke Nikki*, early 12th c.) was authored by the daughter of Fujiwara Akitsune. She first served Horikawa (1079–1107; r. 1086–1107) until his death and thereafter served his son, Toba (1103–56; r. 1107–23). The work is divided into two books, the first of which contains no poems but centers on events leading to the death of Horikawa, and the second of which includes twenty-three elegiac poems written after her return to serve Toba. Although the author was apparently not renowned as a poet, it is fairly obvious that her work was a conscious literary effort.

Konishi states that this work preserves some sense of formality, such as being written in the present tense as is the norm for the *nikki* tradition, but because it gives us such a vivid picture of Horikawa as a human being who suffered a great deal before his death, this work exhibits *zoku* characteristics.[26] Such a clear portrayal of the human aspects of the sovereign contrasts sharply with a lack of concrete descriptions of Go-Fukakusa in *Ben no Naishi Nikki*. Although *The Emperor Horikawa Diary*, like *Ben no Naishi Nikki*, records the experiences of a woman in service to a child sovereign, *Ben no Naishi Nikki* is more formal in tone and, rather than being imitative of the Heian canon, rejects the late eleventh-century tendency toward *zoku* aesthetics.

Nikki of the Kamakura Period (1185–1333)

It is obvious that Konishi devoted considerable time to the study of the Heian-period *nikki*, but his treatment of the works written by women of the Kamakura period is too cursory to provide a proper foundation for a meaningful analysis of this neglected canon. His broad generalizations about the three centuries comprising the Kamakura period are not supported by close examination of the texts in question. Rather, he makes sweeping assertions: that the *nikki* of the Kamakura period displayed a tendency toward the *zoku* aesthetic and a move away from the *ga* aesthetic (refined, high, precedented); for the thirteenth century, he claims that factual *nikki* imitated certain eleventh-century Heian *nikki*; and for the fourteenth century, he notes that *nikki* evolved toward a "quasi-classical" style in its language.[27]

I challenge some of the conclusions Konishi draws concerning the purported flaws of particular Kamakura-period *nikki*. Because his analyses are based on aesthetic criteria gleaned from the Heian period, his conclusions about some texts from the Kamakura canon are predictably negative. Without developing aesthetic criteria suitable for evaluating works that reflected the changing social and political conditions of the Kamakura period, he denigrates these later texts for failing to live up to the standards of the Heian period. Occasionally, he only mentions the title of a text from the Kamakura canon in passing, which suggests that he did not deem some texts worthy of his critical attention.

Had Konishi focused his formidable analytical skill on this neglected field, we might have benefited from his literary acumen. His condemnation of *Ben no Naishi Nikki* and the *Memoirs of Nakatsukasa no Naishi* as derivatives of esteemed eleventh-century models is not supported by persuasive arguments. In fact, Konishi seems to have fallen into the very trap he warned against: rather than carefully reading the texts under consideration, he accepts the judgment of traditional scholarship without trying to identify elements that make these texts unique products of the Kamakura period rather than as unsuccessful imitations of Heian-period models. The following adheres to the factual, fictional divisions in discussing the Kamakura canon.

Konishi proposes that factual, private *nikki*, such as *The Poetic Memoirs of Lady Daibu* (*Kenreimon'in Ukyō no Daibu Shū*, 1219) and *A Journal of the Sixteenth-Night Moon* (*Izayoi Nikki*, ca. 1280) by the nun

Abutsu, owe their present popularity to familiar characters and events described in well known contemporary texts. The tragic fate of Lady Daibu's lover, Taira no Sukemori (d. 1185), is described in *The Tale of the Heike* (*Heike Monogatari*, ca. 1371). *A Journal of the Sixteenth-Night Moon* depicts the progeny of Fujiwara Teika involved in a lawsuit to claim the right to carry on as legitimate heirs to his poetic tradition. Konishi's contention, that these works would not be so highly regarded today were it not for the inherent appeal of their subject matter to modern readers, denies the intrinsic value of the Kamakura canon and ignores specific contributions made by texts of the Kamakura period to the *nikki* tradition.

The Poetic Memoirs of Lady Daibu, by the daughter (b. 1157?) of Fujiwara Koreyuki (1123?–75), is a poetic account of the author's life from 1174 to 1232. Lady Daibu was in service to Kenreimon'in (1155–1213), a daughter of Taira no Kiyomori (1118–81), who bore Antoku Tennō (1178–85; r. 1180–83) when she was a consort. Lady Daibu's love affair with the young Taira no Sukemori is the main theme of her memoir, and her work is haunted by memories of Sukemori after his death at Dan no Ura. (Although Sukemori was the passion of her life, she had earlier been involved with Ben no Naishi's grandfather, Takanobu [1142–1205], a fact brought to light in 1934, when some of her poems were found in Takanobu's personal poetry collection.) We are told a great deal about the author's personal feelings through the poems she composes, but we learn relatively little about the everyday details of her life. Although *The Poetic Memoirs of Lady Daibu* is now categorized as a factual *nikki*, it contains such a significant number of poems arranged into sequences uninterrupted by prose that it was occasionally perceived by medieval reading audiences as a personal poetry collection (*shū*) rather than as a *nikki*.

Lady Daibu's work is thematically focused on her grief and is chronologically arranged, revealing a carefully constructed literary design. This thematic and literary focus seem to indicate that the text was revised at some point after its original composition. In this sense *The Poetic Memoirs of Lady Daibu* resembles *Ben no Naishi Nikki*, which was also composed while she was still in court service and revised into its present form at a later date.[28] A variant title of *Ben no Naishi Nikki* as a *shū* indicates that some of the medieval reading audience considered her work a poetry collection similar to Lady Daibu's work. In terms of content, however, the private nature of this text bears little resemblance to *Ben no Naishi Nikki*, in which matters of a personal nature are suppressed to present the public life of a *naishi* performing her sacred and secular duties at court.

Of the two factual, private *nikki* by the nun Abutsu (ca. 1220–83), the earlier *Fitful Slumbers* (*Utatane*, ca. 1240), is a curious blend of love story and travelogue. The second, *A Journal of the Sixteenth-Night Moon*, centers on Abutsu's attempt to secure an inheritance for her son. Abutsu, the second wife of Teika's son, Tameie, was known as an ambitious woman who took an inheritance dispute to the Kamakura courts to procure for her son Tamesuke (1260–1328) property claimed by Tameie's eldest heir, Tameuji. In a larger context, she was vying for the right of her sons to carry on the poetic heritage inherited from Fujiwara Teika.

Fitful Slumbers is divided into two parts: the first is a memoir of an unhappy youthful love affair with a married man of high social standing in the capital; the second is an account of a journey to Tōtōmi, where her adoptive father was posted and where she stayed until news of her wet-nurse's failing health called her back to the capital. The work is notable for its almost obsessive focus on the emotional state of the protagonist after being abandoned by a high-ranking lover.[29] She cuts her hair (indicating that she is renouncing the world), leaves home in the middle of the night, and sets out on foot for a nunnery.[30] (At this point, the plot resembles that of *The Tale of Genji*, when Ukifune flees Uji in the middle of the night, takes Buddhist vows, and finds temporary refuge in a nunnery.) After recovering her strength at a convent, the protagonist resumes her journey only to be reminded of her misery when she spots the entourage of her former lover en route to the capital.[31] She returns home and decides to accompany her father to Tōtōmi.[32] *Fitful Slumbers* combines an odd sense of immediacy focusing on the protagonist's emotional state with that of retrospection, suggesting the possibility that an earlier draft was edited later.

A Journal of the Sixteenth-Night Moon begins with a poetic exchange between the nun Abutsu and each of her five children as she bids them farewell and embarks upon a trip to Kamakura to petition the Bakufu (warrior government) to rule in her son's favor. Its many poems represent an attempt to maintain her high reputation as a poet, to safeguard her late husband's literary legacy, and perhaps to influence the Kamakura authorities by her eloquence. It also belongs in the category of a travel account written by a woman as the protagonist travels from the capital to Kamakura, composing poems along the way.

Fitful Slumbers and *A Journal of the Sixteenth-Night Moon* have little in common with *Ben no Naishi Nikki*. Both works are intensely personal accounts, the former focusing on love and the latter centering on a litigation for poetic hegemony, while Ben no Naishi's account excludes the personal for the public role she chose to highlight in the memoir. Abutsu's works are also more spatially mobile than the stationary setting of the royal court, the site for Ben no Naishi's account. Though both Abutsu and Ben no Naishi were renowned as poets to their contemporaries, it is for their prose accounts that they are remembered today.

Among factual, public *nikki* the earliest *nikki* is the *Memoirs of Kenshunmon'in Chūnagon* (*Kenshunmon'in Chūnagon Nikki*, also *Tamakiharu*, 1219), a record of life at court by Kenzu Omae, a daughter of Fujiwara Shunzei and the full elder sister of Teika. She served three female members of the royal family in her long career at court: Kenshunmon'in (1142–76, Taira no Jishi), a consort of Go-Shirakawa (1127–92; r. 1155–58); Hachijōin (d. 1219), a daughter of Toba; and Shunkamon'in (1183–1211), a daughter of Go-Toba. Even after Kenzu Omae took Buddhist vows, she continued her life at court.

Kenzu Omae's extant work is divided into two parts: the first, compiled by the author herself, contains recollections of her life as an attendant of Kenshunmon'in, a daughter of Taira no Tokinobu, who rose to the exalted position of consort of Go-Shirakawa and mother of Takakura (1161–81; r. 1168–80), after entering court as one of many women. The second part, compiled by Teika after the death of Kenzu Omae, is fragmentary and episodic in character, notable primarily for its precise descriptions of costumes and other cultural information.

Kenzu Omae's text is not a popular topic of study today, although it is obvious that a conscious literary design molded her narrative into its present form and structure. Konishi denigrates Kenzu Omae's text, stating that for all the time she devoted to her work, the "result is highly unoriginal." Yet he notes that she "was apparently rather proud of her *nikki*," based on a postscript she wrote soliciting opinions of her work and having a clean copy drafted by her daughter.[33] Konishi does not provide adequate textual detail to support his criticism of her text, suggesting a rather cursory treatment of the text. For our purposes, Kenzu Omae's memoir is interesting for the family relationship to Ben no Naishi: Kenzu Omae's mother, known as Bifukumon'in no Kaga because she served a royal consort of that name, was also the mother of Ben no Naishi's grandfather, the painter and poet Takanobu.

The *Memoirs of Nakatsukasa no Naishi* is attributed to the daughter of Fujiwara Nagatsune. The text describes life at the court of Fushimi (1265–1317; r. 1288–98) as seen through the eyes of a female courtier of delicate health, who lived at court for about ten years until an illness forced her to retire. The *Memoirs of Nakatsukasa no Naishi* devotes great attention to matters of ceremony, describing in detail enthronement and abdication ceremonies.

Although the work includes about 150 poems, Nakatsukasa no Naishi was not a renowned poet in her time; only two compositions not found in the work are included in royal poetry anthologies.[34] Like Ben no Naishi, Nakatsukasa no Naishi was a client of the Jimyōin line of monarchs, so familiar faces we encountered in *Ben no Naishi Nikki* appear again in the

Memoirs of Nakatsukasa no Naishi. The portrayal of Retired Sovereign Go-Fukakusa, father of the titular monarch Fushimi in the *Memoirs of Nakatsukasa no Naishi*, is especially interesting, for the adult Go-Fukakusa is given a distinct personality in the *Memoirs of Nakatsukasa no Naishi* quite unlike the veiled view of him as a child in *Ben no Naishi Nikki*. A further parallel with *Ben no Naishi Nikki* is the care with which the *Memoirs of Nakatsukasa no Naishi* records pleasant aspects of court life, as if to preserve for posterity a way of life that seemed then to be on the verge of disappearing.[35]

Traditional scholarship has often labeled *Ben no Naishi Nikki* and the *Memoirs of Nakatsukasa no Naishi* as "sister" works, the first "cheerful" and the second "melancholy." In addition, traditional scholarship has denigrated *Ben no Naishi Nikki* as a short, episodic work without any discernible theme, but has praised the *Memoirs of Nakatsukasa no Naishi* as a thematically focused work tinged with nostalgia. Upon closer inspection, however, *Ben no Naishi Nikki* displays more organization in almost all areas: the uniformity of dated entries followed by poetic composition(s), the thematic focus on pleasant aspects of life to commemorate the reign of the royal family, the rigorous devotion to duty, and so on. My intention is not to disparage the *Memoirs of Nakatsukasa no Naishi*, but to highlight the tendency of traditional scholarship to disparage Kamakura texts without adequate justification.

The *Memoirs of Takemuki* (*Takemuki ga Ki*, 1329–49), by Hino Meishi (1310–58), is the last in a series of *nikki* written by women in the medieval period. Hino Meishi was married to Fujiwara (Saionji) Kinmune (1310–35, hereafter Saionji Kinmune), who was killed during the tumultuous warfare that erupted when Go-Daigo (1288–1339; r. 1318–30) of the Daikakuji line achieved the short-lived Kenmu Restoration. She bore a son, Sanetoshi, who ordinarily would have inherited leadership of the Saionji clan but for the shogunate's decision to grant that honor to Kinmune's younger brother, Kinshige.

The *Memoirs of Takemuki* consists of two scrolls: the first focuses on the life the author shared with her husband before he was executed by adherents of the Daikakuji line during the succession dispute; the second describes her efforts to have her son assume leadership of the Saionji clan. The gap of four years between the extant first and second scrolls leaves out significant events in her life: her husband's execution, her father Sukena taking Buddhist vows, the murder of her older brother Ujimitsu, and the birth of her son Sanetoshi (1335–89). Donald Keene states that Hino Meishi refrained from making direct mention of events of a violent nature in her work because the conventions of the *nikki* tradition did not offer the vocabulary or the aesthetics to deviate so greatly from the norm.[36]

Hino Meishi, descended from a branch of the Fujiwara clan whose immediate family were clients of the Jimyōin line (Go-Fukakusa's descendants), suffered greatly during the years 1333–36 when adherents of the Daikakuji line gained the upper hand. Chapters 12 and 13 of *Taiheiki* state that Meishi was an eyewitness to her husband's execution by Daikakuji forces.[37] Later, when the shogunate denied her request to name her son Sanetoshi as the head of the Saionji clan, she and her son left the Saionji family. Concentrating on Sanetoshi's education, she persevered and secured a successful career for her son at court by continuing to serve Retired Sovereign Kōgon and his consort Kogimon'in. When the shogunate restored Kōgon of the Jimyōin side to the line of succession, Meishi and her son were in attendance during the enthronement ceremony, and she was placed in charge of bearing the sword in the procession.

The *Memoirs of Takemuki* exhibits some similarity to *Ben no Naishi Nikki*. Both accounts were written by female clients of the Jimyōin line, although almost a century had passed since the succession dispute began in 1272 at Go-Saga's death. Hino Meishi belonged to a higher social stratum than did Ben no Naishi, but their works form part of the heritage of women who kept memoirs of their service to the Jimyōin line of sovereigns.

The last major work of the Kamakura canon, *The Confessions of Lady Nijō*, was considered as a work of fiction by medieval readers, hence the absence of *nikki* from the title. The author, known as Go-Fukakusa-in Nijō, was the daughter of a major counselor, Minamoto [Koga] Masatada, and a concubine of Retired Sovereign Go-Fukakusa. Unlike most women writers who belonged to the provincial governor class, Nijō hailed from one of the highest rungs of aristocratic society. Her privileged social status was not the only aberrant element of *The Confessions of Lady Nijō*. According to Konishi, *The Confessions of Lady Nijō* was created as a result of "scrupulous care" and "meticulous planning" on its author's part with fictional elements woven into a factual *nikki* to heighten its dramatic and literary effects.[38]

Konishi's theory that *The Confessions of Lady Nijō* is fictional rests on two points: first, he believes the absence of *nikki* in the title of *The Confessions of Lady Nijō* reveals the medieval readers' perception of the work as fiction because it "contains many elements that are suggestive of the style of a *monogatari* [narrative in the past tense]";[39] and second, he states that "more than anything else, the happenings described in *Towazugatari* are too unusual for a factual nikki.[40] He notes that

> people tend to treat *Towazugatari* as a factual nikki, because most of the characters appear under real designations, and most of the

incidents depicted accord with historical facts. But the fictitious names given to two of the work's most central characters, Snow Dawn and Dawn Moon, are an indication of the author's intention of eliminating the factual nature of the work. Previous scholars have argued, for example, that Snow Dawn is Saionji Sanekanu (1249-1322). But Sanekanu is cited by name and appears in various places as Major Counselor Saionji (1:29, for example) and Sanekanu (1:82). Why would the author use both real names and elegant sobriquets for this character? The answer to this question is that Snow Dawn is used only in love scenes between the heroine and this character; when a character appears with a name that could not have existed in reality, it indicates the fictional nature of the episodes. Even if Sanekanu actually saw this nikki, he would have enjoyed immensely the depiction of himself as an elegant playboy, fully aware that it was fiction.[41]

Konishi's thesis that distinguishes between real names and elegant sobriquets for factual and fictional scenes is one of the most important contributions that addresses the aberrant nature of *The Confessions of Lady Nijō*.

Because *The Confessions of Lady Nijō* is fiction, it has little in common with *Ben no Naishi Nikki*. Stylistically, however, both works are part of a development toward what Konishi describes as "quasi-classical" language, characterized by "the gradual influx of Chinese words and the Japanese method of reading classical Chinese."[42] This "quasi-classical" language seems to be the result of the training women received in reading *kanbun yomikudashi* (forcing a Japanese syntax to read texts written in Chinese), a quality I noticed when I first began reading Ben no Naishi's text after studying works written in the Heian period. The stylistic change in language toward brevity and economy of expression began in the Kamakura period and continued its evolution toward a style Cranston might have called "memoranda Japanese" or *kiroku wabun,* noted in works such as the *Journal of the Upper Hot Water Room* (*Oyudono no Ue no Nikki,* 1477–1826), an official record of court events of little literary merit, though preserving cultural information of great historical value. *The Confessions of Lady Nijō* is also one of the few from the Kamakura literary canon to receive adequate critical attention in Japanese and in English, perhaps because it is available in translation.

The Kamakura *nikki* canon is in need of further study. It is unfair to judge the contributions of the Kamakura canon by criteria used to analyze works written in the Heian period. The Heian period aesthetic, which admired all that was new, up-to-date, and indigenous, that is, non-Chinese, evolved into an urge to preserve elements of traditional Heian culture that seemed on the verge of disappearing after armed conflicts erupted during the Kamakura period. Holdings of the royal family were decreased after the military government was established in Kamakura (1192) and were further reduced after Go-Toba unsuccessfully tried to regain royal power during the Jōkyū (also Shōkyū) era (1221), changing the lifestyle of the aristocracy and evoking a sense of insecurity among the inhabitants of the court. Although Kamakura *nikki* do not describe drastic events or wars of succession, it is clear that *The Memoirs of Lady Daibu* and the *Memoirs of Takemuki* were written as a result of the conflicts that claimed the lives of their lovers.

Other works in the Kamakura canon exhibit similar signs of a changed aesthetic. The nun Abutsu's *A Journal of the Sixteenth-Night Moon* is an account of her efforts to secure court ranks and posts for her sons when the royal succession alternated precariously between the Jimyōin and the Daikakuji lines. Abutsu was a key figure in a similar break that later occurred within the poetic dynasty inherited from Fujiwara Teika. The leadership of the Nijō school was bequeathed to Tameie's eldest son Tameuji, but a splinter group consisting of Tameie's sons in alliance with Tameie's sons by Abutsu, known as the Kyōgoku-Reizei school, challenged the main school with documents surreptitiously procured by Abutsu. Thus the succession lines of the royal family and the poetic dynasty were shaken by an instability unknown in the Heian period.

Some memoirists maintained detailed records of court life to commemorate a way of life under assault. No specific threat can be detected in the memoirs, but the very existence of such records seem to bear witness to an urge to preserve elements of a way of life undergoing dramatic changes. Ben no Naishi, devoted to performing her sacred duties, wrote poems that read like prayers to ensure the continuity of the reign of the royal family. Nakatsukasa no Naishi captured every detail of enthronement and abdication ceremonies so that her memoir could provide a point of reference if such a need ever arose. Yoshida Kenkō's *Essays in Idleness* (*Tsurezuregusa*, ca. 1310) embodies a similar aesthetic to preserve aspects of traditional court culture for posterity, indicating that insecurity about the future of court life crossed gender borders. Contributions made in the Kamakura period continued the tradition of producing *nikki*, but the texts exhibit signs that they were motivated by an aesthetic that sought to preserve traditional court culture, sometimes in innovative ways.

Literary Aspects of *Ben no Naishi Nikki*

Everything that makes *Ben no Naishi Nikki* unique among *nikki* written by women was dictated by the sacred duty Ben no Naishi performed at court:

the public persona and stance, the shared point of view, the choice of the moon as the dominant image, the formation of a new medieval aesthetic, the connections between the moon, the enthronement ceremony, and sacred time, and the laudatory tone of the poetry within the *nikki*. Finally, I argue for a reassessment of the *nikki*, leaving behind traditional views to focus on the unique path it forged in creating innovative techniques to achieve literary goals that were specifically inspired by the Kamakura period during which it was conceived.

In the past, most studies of *Ben no Naishi Nikki* have focused on the characteristics of "cheerfulness" (*akarusa*) and "innocence" (*mujōkisa*) first noted by Ikeda Kikan in the pioneer analysis of this memoir in *Literary Diaries by Women at Court* (*Kyūtei Joryū Nikki Bungaku*, 1927). With a few exceptions, almost all subsequent studies followed Ikeda's treatment of Ben no Naishi's text as the product of a "carefree, young girl" (*eien no otomegokoro*, the eternal maiden) who focused her account on amusing aspects of court life. As a consequence, many scholars view *Ben no Naishi Nikki* as a work of negligible literary merit comprised of a series of short, disconnected entries without a unifying theme or purpose.

One of the first scholars to forge a new path in studies of *Ben no Naishi Nikki* was Ōuchi Mayako, who in her 1964 article "Treatise on *Ben no Naishi Nikki*" introduced several perceptive lines of investigation. Ōuchi was the first to state that Ben no Naishi had adopted a formal and public stance, excluding from the *nikki* all events of a private nature. She was also first to cite *Ben no Naishi Nikki* as a possible forerunner of the *Journal of the Upper Hot Water Room*, an official journal compiled by women at the royal court, noting events in an unadorned manner reminiscent of *kanbun nikki* by court nobles. Ōuchi provides internal evidence that it was common knowledge that Ben no Naishi was keeping a written record of her court service and she also discussed relationships between Ben no Naishi and her female colleagues, drawing parallels with Murasaki Shikibu's critique of her colleagues. Finally, Ōuchi analyzed Ben no Naishi's use of poetic imagery and identified the importance of Ben no Naishi's role in the composition of linked verse (*renga*).

Imazeki Toshiko, a noted scholar of medieval literature, wrote a number of articles devoted exclusively to *Ben no Naishi Nikki* and, on this topic, has proved to be one of the most influential scholars from the 1980s to the present. Imazeki's focus on the public stance adopted in the *nikki*, the duties performed by *naishi* at court, the shared perspective, the poetic imagery, and the emphasis on the distinction between sacred and secular time in the *nikki* have been a great influence on my research.

Iwasa Miyoko's new annotation of *Ben no Naishi Nikki* in *Shinpen Nihon Koten Bungaku Zenshū* is extremely useful for its interpretation of *waka* and for information concerning the various *honka* (original poems) to which the poetry alludes. Iwasa's articles on the literary connections between Jimyōin line monarchs and extant *nikki* of the thirteenth and four-teenth centuries support my contention that Go-Saga'in from the Jimyōin line was the patron responsible for Ben no Naishi's post at court. Perhaps the public stance adopted by Ben no Naishi was the result of a command from Go-Saga that the author keep a poetic account of her time in court service to his son, Go-Fukakusa. Iwasa's textual study of Ben no Naishi Nikki contributed to my understanding that an early draft of the text was later revised into a tightly organized form and that the textual damage Tamai attributed to insect damage was actually caused by fire. I now turn to aspects that make *Ben no Naishi Nikki* unique, even among the fluid parameters of *nikki*.

Public Persona and Stance

Adopting a public stance made Ben no Naishi exclude significant events of a private or personal nature concerning even her immediate family. Go-Saga's royal patronage may have been a contributing factor to the public stance adopted for the memoir. Perhaps the sovereign ordered her to com-memorate his child's reign in a traditional poetic *nikki*. For example, in Section 75 Ben no Naishi mentions that the death of her mother caused her to spend most of 1248 at home in mourning. Because her stance did not allow her to include an entry that focused strictly on a private loss, she mentions her mother's death within the context of a poetic reply thanking someone at court for having sent a summer robe even though she was not in attendance. Her mother's death, therefore, serves as the explanation for the circumstances leading to her absence at court rather than as a source of personal grief.

Some scholars seem puzzled by Ben no Naishi's lack of emotional response to her mother's death and attribute her reaction to a shallow per-sonality incapable of expressing sorrow. I believe, however, that her choice of stance dictated that she record the event from the perspective of a *naishi* serving at court, rather than as a daughter grieving over the loss of her mother. In the public persona adopted for her *nikki*, she could only re-spond as a court official who had taken a leave of absence from her duties because of a death in the family. In my opinion, it is a testament to her skill as a writer that she was able to include such a matter of private sig-nificance in a *nikki* restricted to presenting a public persona.

Ben no Naishi's stance obliged her to treat other members of her fam-ily in a similarly public manner. In two entries of the *nikki*, she mentions her father, Nobuzane, recorded in the memoir as Jakusai after he took

Buddhist vows. In Section 79, the Regent Kanetsune asks for a branch of the red plum from Jakusai's garden where it bloomed earlier than in the capital. Jakusai sent a poem attached to the branch of red plum, calling forth poetic replies from the ruling faction at court: these included Saneuji, the former chancellor and grandfather of Go-Fukakusa; his sons Kinmoto and Kinsuke; and his younger brother Saneo. In this exchange of poetry, Jakusai is represented primarily as a member of the poetic circle, not as Ben no Naishi's father. Their family relationship is taken for granted, since the red plum came from his house, but her stance is maintained because the regent officially asked that a branch of red plum be sent to the monarch from her home. So long as Jakusai was presented within the context of court-related activities, the integrity of her stance was not compromised.

Jakusai makes another appearance in the *nikki* in Section 120, sending an abstinence charm (*monoimi*) to Ben no Naishi expressing parental concern for her safety when her antics during purification rites cause her to fall into the courtyard stream. The entry notes that the child monarch was bored because only a few people were serving at court during the purification rites, so he commanded Ben no Naishi to entertain him. In response to the royal command, she put on a demon mask, tied her divided skirt up to her chest, and put her chemise over her head to create the image of a frightful demon. Apparently she succeeded all too well. She managed to alarm the provincials serving as palace guards (*ōban*), who came at her with bows and arrows. They, ironically, frightened her, and she fell into the stream while fleeing them. The author stayed within the bounds of her stance by stating that she was performing her secular duty of entertaining the sovereign by direct command when she violated the sanction against entertainment during purification rites. When Jakusai heard of her action, he sent her an abstinence charm and suggested that she come home to perform penance for possibly having angered some spirits during the moratorium on entertainment of any kind. Once again, Ben no Naishi subordinates connections with family members to primary events that occurred to her as a *naishi* at court.

The same stance is apparent when dealing with her closest companion at court, her younger sister Shōshō no Naishi. Ben no Naishi invariably refers to her sister by her court sobriquet, not as her sibling. They shared many experiences at court, inhabited the same apartment, and stood in for each other when one of them was ill. Yet nowhere in her *nikki* does Ben no Naishi mention her, except in connection with her official status as a *naishi*.

Although Shōshō no Naishi was the younger of the two sisters, her frail health caused Ben no Naishi to perform Shōshō no Naishi's duties in addition to her own. Nonetheless, she never expresses concern for her sister's ill health in the *nikki*. In my reading, this omission is not callousness, but the result of maintaining a public stance. For example, Section 10 is the first of several instances in which Shōshō no Naishi's illness forces Ben no Naishi to serve in her stead. Ben no Naishi only mentions that she went to Suzaku Gate and composed a poem praying for a long and prosperous reign. Shōshō no Naishi is still ill in Section 14, when Kinsuke, the Ōmiya major counselor, sends her a poem, but Ben no Naishi refrains from expressing any concern over her sister's health. In Section 81, during the fire at the Kan'in Palace, Ben no Naishi hurries to her apartment to change clothes and to rouse Shōshō no Naishi, who again was unwell and lying down. Here again, Ben no Naishi presents herself as a member of the court, not as a member of Shōshō no Naishi's immediate family.

The author's stance focusing on the public persona of a *naishi* devoted to duty dictated the exclusion of topics of a personal nature, such as love, marriage, or children. *Ben no Naishi Nikki* contains not a single example of love poetry exchanged by Ben no Naishi or Shōshō no Naishi, except when Ben no Naishi wrote a surrogate love poem for a female servant called Takatsunji in Section 67. Through other sources, however, we learn that at some point in her life Ben no Naishi met Fujiwara Masahira and bore a child by him known as Shin'yōmeimon'in no Shōshō, though none of this personal information is recorded in her public *nikki*.

Such a consistent focus on a public persona in *Ben no Naishi Nikki* was probably the result of a highly organized revision. Rigorous revision honed toward praying for the longevity of the royal reign as sacred time and for the prosperity of the royal court as sacred space must have occurred at some point after the *nikki* was originally written and compiled. Moreover, the extant text was probably not written in the order that we have it; it was probably fashioned into its present form after the overall intention of the literary work had been conceived.[43] An unedited record kept on a daily basis would certainly contain more entries extraneous to the overall literary design than is discernible in *Ben no Naishi Nikki*. Perhaps these items were edited out of the original draft or revised to fit the thematic guidelines after she compiled her *nikki*. A later revision would explain the many discrepancies in titles noted in the *nikki*. Ben no Naishi refers to people by their former titles, indicating that some time had passed from the time the contents were written to the time the text was revised. For example, Ben no Naishi refers to Saionji Saneuji as the chancellor in Sections 46 and 79, although he already had relinquished the post sometime beforehand. Further examples of discrepancies in titles are found between Sections 93 and 112:[44] in the former, Minamoto Tomomi is called the Horikawa palace minister when he had already advanced to middle counselor by that time; and in the latter, Fujiwara Sanefuji is called the Muromachi major counselor when he was still a middle counselor at that time.[45] The problem is compounded because *Ben no Naishi Nikki* refers to people by their titles rather than by their personal or given names.

Ben no Naishi's thematic demands sometimes caused her to manipulate historical information from linear time to fit the literary purpose of the *nikki*. For example, in Section 2, Ben no Naishi writes that Go-Fukakusa's enthronement ceremony took place on a bright spring day, however, there is evidence to the contrary in *kanbun* diaries: that day was in fact marred by rain storms and lightning. But in Ben no Naishi's hands, her primary literary intention of presenting an auspicious beginning for her monarch's reign takes precedence over fact.[46]

Shared Point of View

Like other *nikki*, *Ben no Naishi Nikki* is narrated from the third-person point of view. But sometimes the perspective switches from Ben no Naishi's point of view to that of her younger sister, Shōshō no Naishi, making it a distinctive feature of the *nikki*. On several occasions (Sections 4, 18, 21, 98, 99, 100, and 101), Shōshō no Naishi's perspective is utilized to include in the memoir events at which Ben no Naishi was not present. In some sections of the *nikki*, I argue that this device is used to broaden the coverage of different events the sisters attended simultaneously. Perhaps the shared perspective was also predicated by Go-Saga's royal command that a poetic account preserve the memory of his child's reign. To present the most complete coverage of Go-Fukakusa's reign, a shared perspective gave the *nikki* another pair of eyes to look at events from a different angle.

Since *Ben no Naishi Nikki* is narrated in the third person, the shift from Ben no Naishi to Shōshō no Naishi's perspective is scarcely discernible until one notices that the poem in a particular section was composed not by Ben no Naishi herself but by Shōshō no Naishi. In the first occurrence of a shift from Ben no Naishi's perspective to that of Shōshō no Naishi in Section 4, a broader coverage of events in the life of *naishi* in court service results even though Ben no Naishi was not physically present at this particular activity. The paired entries of Sections 1 and 2, describing the abdication and enthronement, are paralleled by the topically related entries of Sections 3 and 4, commemorating the first time Ben no Naishi and Shōshō no Naishi acted as royal messengers to the Shintō shrines of Hirano and Matsunoo, respectively. These topically related entries also set up the expectation that the *nikki* will be presented henceforth from their combined perspectives, rather than from the usual convention of a constant, individual point of view found in most *nikki*.

Another set of topically related entries on the preparation of the *Yuki* and *Suki* sides for the enthronement ceremony is found in Sections 17 and 18.[47] In presenting Section 17 from Ben no Naishi's point of view as a participant on the *Yuki* side and Section 18 from Shōshō no Naishi's perspective on the *Suki* side, the *nikki* provides a more complete view of each side as they made preparations for the enthronement ceremony. By using a shared or combined point of view, Ben no Naishi is able to paint a comprehensive picture of the duties performed by female courtiers.

Shōshō no Naishi's perspective is tapped again in Section 21 to provide readers with a chance to view the younger sister as she tries to find a hairpin to arrange her hair in the formal *kamiage* style required of *naishi* participating in ceremonies. Ben no Naishi, busy with her own duties at the Council of State, sends a sympathetic poem, but is unable to provide her with the necessary hairpin. Once again this shared perspective enlarges the scope of coverage and provides a climatic buildup to the flurry of activities leading to the enthronement ceremony.

However, the longest series of entries exhibiting the shared perspectives of Ben no Naishi and Shōshō no Naishi are in the four sections beginning with 98 and ending with 101. Ben no Naishi's location is not indicated, but it is clear from her writing that she heard about the events secondhand from Shōshō no Naishi, the eyewitness observer of the events recounted in these sections. The usual pattern of Shōshō no Naishi's name appearing first in the section, followed by a poetic reply to a poem by her older sister, indicates that Ben no Naishi heard about the story or the poetic exchange later and then composed a reply to include as an addendum to the *nikki*. Section 98 is a good example of contents that are related to Ben no Naishi after which she composed a poetic reply to the earlier exchange. By way of contrast, Section 97 is a fine example of the sisters being in the same spatial location and composing poems together; secondhand narration had no part in this entry.

Among the usually separate entries in *Ben no Naishi Nikki*, Sections 100 and 101 hold a unique place in that they are connected to occurrences in another episode. In Section 100, Go-Fukakusa's female courtiers are invited to the town palace of Ōmiya'in to view the full moon. In Section 101, we learn that at the same time Ōmiya'in's female courtiers go to Go-Fukakusa's palace to view the moon, but fail to find their hosts at home. These connected entries are even more unusual because they are presented from Shōshō no Naishi's perspective. The usual pattern, Ben no Naishi composing her poem as a reaction to a story she had heard from Shōshō no Naishi, indicates that Ben no Naishi was not present at these events.

My interpretation concerning the device of shared perspective differs somewhat from Imazeki Toshiko's. She regards the perspectives of Ben no

Naishi and Shōshō no Naishi as being so similar that they could be considered the same viewpoint, rather than that of two distinct individuals. She regards Sections 3 and 4 as examples of a similar observer reporting events from essentially the same viewpoint.[48] Further, she maintains that this similarity of observer and viewpoint extends to the composition of poetry: it matters little who wrote the poems in the *nikki* since she considers *Ben no Naishi Nikki* to resemble more closely a *chokusenshū* (royal poetry anthology including the works of many poets) than an *ie no shū* (poetry collection written by an individual). She concludes that the shared perspective weakens the sense of the individual in the *nikki*[49] because it emphasizes the point of view of *naishi* performing their duties rather than the perspective of an individual. My reading of the device of shared perspectives hinges on the existence of two observers who occupy distinct spatial locations in order to provide the most comprehensive view of the duties performed by *naishi* at court. In my reading, the shared perspective maintains the integrity of distinct individuals who when spatially separated provide another source of observations to be included in the memoir. The other perspective supplements the primary point of view, but does not supplant it.

The Moon Divorced from Love

Ben no Naishi's public stance focusing on the duties of *naishi* also influenced the use of traditional poetic imagery in the *nikki*. Mention of winter with the images of snow and frost and the physical sensations of the wind and cold present the conditions during which the most sacred court rituals were performed. In exploring these conditions, the core of a new medieval aesthetic of austerity emerges in the *nikki*, a century and a half earlier than Konishi acknowledges its formation. The moon appears as the dominant image in *Ben no Naishi Nikki*, but before delving into the memoir's unique appropriation of the moon, I begin with a brief look at the traditional uses of the moon in the literature which preceded *Ben no Naishi Nikki*.

The moon is enveloped in an aura of mystery. In Heian-period aesthetics it was believed that the moon reflected one's innermost feelings or evoked a sense of nostalgia for the past. The development of a myth concerning the moon begins with the *Tale of the Bamboo Cutter* (*Taketori Monogatari*, hereafter *Bamboo Cutter*), which warns people against staring at the moon, since people then believed that mysterious and miraculous things could occur if they looked at the celestial image.[50] Like the *Bamboo Cutter*, *As I Crossed a Bridge of Dreams* also depicts the moon as a mysterious, almost fearsome phenomenon, since moonbeams striking a person's face were thought to be fatal.

A few poems in the *Kokinshū* also regard the moon as mysterious because it inspires passion and love. When love is thwarted, it brings on sad, melancholy thoughts:

Kokinshū 756 by Ise:

ai ni aite	How fitting it seems,
mono omou koro no	that tears should dampen the face
wa ga sode ni	even of the moon,
yadoru tsuki sae	whose image visits my sleeve
nururu kao naru	as I sit lost in sad thought.[51]

The face of the moon streaked by tears reflects the persona of the forsaken woman waiting in vain for the appearance of her lover. As in the poem above, the image of a lonely lady sadly gazing at the moon conveys the idea of love as a kind of suffering in *The Poetic Memoirs of Lady Daibu*; even when lovers are in accord, the moon functions as a stimulus to focus the lover's thoughts on each other when they are apart, as in the *Izumi Shikibu Diary*.

In *The Pillow Book*, the moon does not inspire melancholy thoughts, but rather a nostalgia for the past with a strong dose of personal reminiscence:

Moonlight makes me think of people who are far away and also reminds me of things in the past—sad things, happy things that delighted me—as though they had just happened. [52]

Another noted Heian poet shared the sentiment. Ariwara no Narihira's famous "*tsuki ya aranu*" poem emphasizes a return to the past, but on this occasion it is a man who passionately recalls a time when he and his beloved were in accord both spatially and emotionally. This nostalgia for the past evoked by gazing at the moon is also noted in the *Memoirs of Naka-tsukasa no Naishi*, a late-thirteenth-century work with a pervasive strain of personal recollection.

Some *nikki* employ the celestial images of the sun and moon as metaphors for the royal couple, as in *The Poetic Memoirs of Lady Daibu*:

kumo no ue ni	Here above the clouds
kakaru tsukihi no	I gaze upon the brilliance
hikari miru	Of such a sun and such a moon,
mi no chigiri sae	And I can only feel
ureshi to zo omou	How blissful is this fate of mine.[53]

And again from *The Poetic Memoirs of Lady Daibu*:

I was saddened to think what the Empress must have been feeling in her heart:

kage naraba	The sun that used to shine
teru hi no hikari	Beside the moon
kakuretsutsu	Has veiled its radiance;
hitori ya tsuki no	Surely the moon in its solitude
kakikumoruramu	Is overcast with grief.[54]

In the first poem, there is no hint of sadness or melancholy, but in the second, the solitary moon, a metaphor for the consort, is longing for the sun, a metaphor for the deceased monarch. Thus the second example is related to the traditional treatment of the moon, inspiring a lone observer to melancholy thoughts tinged with nostalgia. In *Ben no Naishi Nikki*, the moon is not used as a metaphor for the consort, as in the example cited above, but in Section 1 the celestial imagery of the sun and moon hint at the cosmological implications of the abdication and enthronement. The cosmological aspects of the sun and moon in this *nikki* are rarely found in other examples from this genre. Thus traditional uses of the moon in earlier literature inspired reverence and awe, evoked a nostalgic recollection of the past tied to romantic longing, referred metaphorically to the royal couple, and most important, were viewed in private.

In contrast to the Heian aesthetic of a solitary observer, the moon in *Ben no Naishi Nikki* is appreciated by a group of people engaged in a court-related activity. In her Section 9 poem, Ben no Naishi laments the fact that clouds obscure her view of the moon when she is sitting near the eaves with female courtiers Chūnagon no Suke and Kunaikyō. Ben no Naishi recalls an incident from the past, but her query does not evoke melancholy thoughts or a nostalgia for a personal past. Rather she wonders whether people in the past also fretted about being unable to see the moon unobstructed by clouds.

In *Ben no Naishi Nikki*, the moon functions as an object of admiration in an aesthetic seasonal setting during a court activity to show to advantage an incident or personality. For example, in Section 70 the moon appears to enhance the beauty of the young Gosechi dancers, favorites of powerful senior nobles at court. In Section 28, the moon lights the way for Azechi no Suke and Shōnagon no Naishi as they leave to hear the sacred music at the Naishidokoro (Naishidokoro no Mikagura). In Section 50, several female courtiers embark to hear the prayers at the Five Altars with the moonlight to guide them. In Section 76, the clear moon is seen as an auspicious sign by male and female courtiers as the Buddha's Names (Butsumyōe) and Spirit-Pacifying ceremonies are performed under its light. In Section 93, courtiers gather to watch the dawn moon rise as they listen to a lecture about the Golden Light Sutra (Konkōmyō Saishōkyō) at the Tominokōji Palace. The moon casts its luminous light on these and other court ceremonies or activities.

Unlike Heian period *nikki* in which the moon is linked with love, the public attitude in *Ben no Naishi Nikki* precluded the inclusion of such intensely personal or private matters. However, when the moon is hidden by clouds, *Ben no Naishi Nikki* treats a clouded moon or a moon that is hidden as inauspicious signs. When the regent Sanetsune is dismissed from office in Section 34, Ben no Naishi, dismayed by the news, uses the image of the clouded moon to symbolize her dismay for Sanetsune's fate.[55] Again when the Retired Sovereign Go-Saga's concubine dies in Section 58, the moon obscured by clouds symbolizes the sorrow over parting with a loved one. Word of her death casts a pall over the entire poetry gathering, leading Ben no Naishi to employ the clouded moon as a metaphor for Go-Saga's grief. There are not many occasions of a cloudy moon in *Ben no Naishi Nikki*, for the goal of the memoir was to show the court in the most auspicious circumstances possible, lit by a clear, unblemished moon.

The Moon and the Formation of a New Medieval Aesthetic

The moon and images related to the cold are treated as a positive aesthetic attribute in *Ben no Naishi Nikki* hundreds of years before literary historians such as Konishi acknowledge its development. Images that suggest the cold, such as snow, frost, and the wind, share attributes of a white, bright, clear, and transparent light. Like the moon, snow and frost are capable of reflected light or subdued brightness. The translucent wind imparts feelings of spiritual cleansing. Whiteness suggests the sacred in the medieval period.[56] Because *Ben no Naishi Nikki* is a product of the thirteenth century, consistently positive assessments do not prevail in two sections that describe the cold. In Section 18, words related to the cold weather, such as the moon, snow, and wind, appear together with negative terminology. The entry begins with an aesthetic remark about the beauty of the moon floating above the frozen snow and concludes with a composition by Shōshō no Naishi, who responds to a male courtier who said he was shivering too hard to talk:

> koto no ha mo Thinking of the way
> omou ni sa koso the wind blew and blew

nakarurame	all night long,
uki to fuku yo no	it seems even the "leaves of words"
kaze no keshiki ni	have disappeared in the wind.

Her poem makes a verbal pun on the actions of the man suffering from the cold. In the prose section that introduces the poem above, the cold was described with negative connotations: the "cold wind was blowing frightfully" (*kaze fukisaete, osoroshiki hodo narishi ni*) with the situation cited as "unbearable" (*taegatashi*). In Section 27, again "most unbearable" (*ito taegatashi*) was used to describe the situation as *naishi* waited in the Lime Altar Room (Ishibai no Dan) for the Kamo Return on a night with a luminous moon and glittering snow in the twelfth month.[57]

Negative reactions to the cold weather are countered by neutral or positive associations with the cold in other parts of the *nikki*. In Section 19, for instance, Ben no Naishi emphasizes the beauty of the moonlight during the Flushed Faces Banquet and reports objectively that the weather will continue to get colder:

kanete omou	Tonight's clear moon
toyonoakari no	anticipates how much colder still
samukesa o	the night will be
mashite ika ni to	when the "Flushed Faces" moon
sumeru tsuki kana	finally appears.

The factual description of the cold in this example is in sharp contrast to Section 27 when the cold is noted as "unbearable." In Section 20, the adjective *okashi* (charming, pleasant, amusing) is used to describe flurries of snow blown into the makeshift buildings in the Council of State compound. Here images of the frozen snow and cold wind promote the use of the adjective *okashi* to describe what would normally be thought of as anything but pleasant. In Section 74, "frost, shining white and cold on the stairs" is described as "interesting" (*omoshiroshi*), another positive assessment. An aesthetic similar to that found in *Ben no Naishi Nikki* is also found in the late Kamakura-period *Memoirs of Takemuki*, when the wind and the wintry landscape at a drinking party are described as "very pleasant indeed" (*ito omoshiroku zo*). Therefore, the *Memoirs of Takemuki* is another example of a traditional *nikki* that exhibits a heightened sense of appreciation for cold imagery in the mid-fourteenth century, a later stage in the development of a new austere medieval aesthetic that began in the mid-thirteenth century with *Ben no Naishi Nikki*.

Without noticing the indigenous examples cited above, Konishi attributes the origins of the appreciation of chill (*hie*) and coldness (*samusa*) in the *renga* of the fifteenth and sixteenth centuries to the Zen-inspired austere aesthetics of Sung dynasty *shih*.[58] Furthermore, he cites clarity (*heitan*) linked to brightness as another property of Sung poetic criticism. As I stated above, the mid-thirteenth-century *Ben no Naishi Nikki* and the fourteenth-century *Memoirs of Takemuki* predates Konishi's proposal of the development of the aesthetics of chill and coldness by one to two hundred years. In my view, *Ben no Naishi Nikki* with its positive aesthetic appreciation of the cold is an indigenous harbinger of the medieval aesthetics Konishi ascribes to the fifteenth and sixteenth centuries under the influence of Chinese poetics. Had he looked more closely at the texts of the Kamakura period as had Imazeki Toshiko, he would have found native examples such as the *Memoirs of Takemuki* that contain the same aesthetic appreciation for the cold that *Ben no Naishi Nikki* exhibits.

Spiritual cleansing associated with the cold and clarity adds another element to the developing medieval aesthetic. Feelings of spiritual cleansing described either as *sayu* (to be cold) or *sumu* (to be clear) are activated by auditory stimuli, such as Buddhist bells tolling, the ringing of small hand bells, or voices raised in song. Usually these sounds are combined with the feeling of cold or with cold weather imagery. In Section 97, the sound of the Buddhist bells "cleared their spirits" as Ben no Naishi and Shōshō no Naishi were urged to be quick with their poetic compositions at a linked verse gathering. In Section 93, the sound of the Shintō hand bells again "cleared her spirit," heightening a feeling of reverence for the occasion. In Section 27, voices raised in song sound clear as the song speaks of the celestial image of the Bright Star, moonlight, and courtyard fires illuminating the night. Luminous images combined with the cold, the clear, and the bright emphasize the sacred and the auspicious.[59]

The luminous purity and whiteness of the moon, snow, and frost are associated with the medieval perception of the auspicious and the spiritual. The wind imparts an impression of transparency or clarity. All these images are connected with the reverence in which the sacred rites were conducted during cold weather. The medieval aesthetic equating the cold weather and poetic imagery with the essence of spiritual cleansing developed independently in the Kamakura period and runs against the Heian aesthetic norm. Although Konishi attributes the aesthetics of cold and clarity to Sung dynasty poetics, I disagree. I hold that the positive appreciation for the cold and clarity is an indigenous development that began at least in the mid-thirteenth century, as recorded in *Ben no Naishi Nikki*. Later continental influences from Sung dynasty poetics may have accentuated this earlier trend toward a mature style, but texts written by women in the vernacular attest to its development earlier than that acknowledged by Konishi.

The Moon, the Enthronement Ceremony, and Sacred Time

Ben no Naishi Nikki enshrines the image of the moon for a variety of inter-related purposes. In this section, I examine the moon and its relationship to the enthronement ceremony, the moon's phases, and their correlation to time, the significance of the moon in ancient myths, and the laudatory tone of the poetry in the *nikki*. Imazeki Toshiko credits the sacred tone of Ben no Naishi's poetry to a desire to counteract feelings of insecurity caused by the uncertainty of the times, but I propose that this spirituality springs from the sacred ceremonies in which she participated as a *naishi*. Histori-cally, the Nakatomi and their Fujiwara descendants played vital roles at the enthronement ceremonies of sovereigns by voicing ancient Shintō prayers (*norito*) and congratulatory words (*yogoto*). I propose *norito* and *yogoto* as probable sources for the laudatory tone of Ben no Naishi's po-etry. As a member of the Fujiwara family descended from the Nakatomi, who as hereditary liturgists performed vital roles at the *Daijōsai* of sover-eigns, her participation in sacred Shintō rites would have given her access to the auspicious vocabulary, tone of supplication, and intent of *norito* and *yogoto*. Her clan lineage gave her the right to engage in court ritual and her family's more recent secular occupation as poets favored by royal pa-tronage provided Ben no Naishi the opportunity to fashion a unique poetic memoir based on the duties she performed at court. In her capable literary hands, her sacred and secular occupations are cleverly braided together.

The image of the moon woven into the fabric of *Ben no Naishi Nikki* suggests two ways of conceptualizing time:

> The accession of the king, when celebrated as a great festival of re-newal of nature, bridged two ways in which man experienced time. It brought the cyclical eternal-return time of nature and its seasons to-gether with time as history, the time of society which could only ap-proximate repeating itself in the line of kings.[60]

Ben no Naishi's job as a *naishi,* who assisted sovereigns in the perform-ance of cosmological rites, was intricately related to ceremonies that ef-fected a return *in illo tempore*, to the sacred beginning of time, represented by the royal line. But Ben no Naishi also wrote the memoir to perpetuate the tradition of writing her family was known for, thereby making a liter-ary contribution to be preserved in historical time.

The enthronement ceremonies of kings, royal initiation rites, celebra-tions for the New Year, and the phases of the moon are linked theoretically by the concept of a cycle: appearance, disappearance, and reappearance. The death of a king followed by the installation of a new sovereign, however "insignificant" he may be, hails the beginning of a "new era" or a regeneration that erases the past.[61] Further, a ritual death followed by a subsequent resurrection forms the essential part of royal initiation rites. Thus, the constant renewal of time erases the past and destabilizes the idea that time flows along a linear trajectory.[62]

Enthronement ceremonies and initiation rites are closely related to celebrations of the New Year.[63] The cosmic renewal that takes place at the New Year is related to the accession of a king that incorporates rituals re-enacting the beginning of time:

> Cosmogonic scenarios of the New Year can be incorporated into the coronation ceremony of a king. The two rituals pursue the same end— cosmic renewal, [thus] it is easy to understand why the installation of a king repeated the cosmogony or took place at the New Year. The king was believed to renew the entire Cosmos. The greatest renewals take place at the New Year, when a new time cycle is inaugurated. But the *renovatio* effected by the New Year ritual is, basically, a reitera-tion of the cosmogony. Each New Year begins the Creation over again.[64]

Separation of the New Year's rituals and enthronement ceremonies takes place when the concept of universal renewal breaks free of the cosmic rhythm (i.e., the rigid frame of the calendar) and becomes instead con-nected with historical persons (i.e., kings) and events.[65] In Japan, to signify the beginning of a new reign for sovereigns and a cosmic renewal for court society, a new reign name is chosen, turning the clock back to the original year (*gannen* or, theoretically, to the beginning of time) to signify the be-ginning of a new sovereign's titular rule. While the relationship between enthronement ceremonies of kings and royal initiation rites is easy to com-prehend, their relationship to the moon may seem tenuous at first glance.

The connection between the moon and enthronement and initiation rites lies in the phases of the moon: the new moon represents the figurative death of a sovereign and the reappearance of the moon signifies the acces-sion of a new monarch. The moon represented a "measure" of time with the phases of the moon determining the length of the lunar month by which ancients kept track of time. But the moon also symbolizes the idea of the eternal return by the cyclical nature of its appearance. The phases of the moon—its appearance or waxing and its disappearance or waning, followed by its reappearance after darkness—play an important role as the concrete expression of the "eternal return" that embodies the circular no-tion of sacred time. The phases of the moon serve as the archetype for a cyclical concept of time, reinforced by the cycle of the seasons in nature.

Similar to cycles in nature, the "unbroken" royal line follows the ebb and flow of time through the performance of ancient rituals.[66]

There are three major movements in the Japanese enthronement ceremony, or *Daijōsai*: the "treading the throne" (*senso*), the accession (*sokui*), and the enthronement accompanied by the ceremonial banquet.[67] The "treading the throne" element, similar to the *sokui*, signifies that a successor has achieved the rank of sovereign. The accession or succession to the throne, occurring soon after the demise of a sovereign or the abdication of a previous ruler, announces that an heir apparent has assumed the role of a new sovereign. The actual *Daijōsai*, in which the monarch feasts upon consecrated food and wine charged with religious and mythological implications, completes the cycle of ceremonies that transforms a human ruler into a divine successor to the royal line.

In the Heian period, the *sokui* closely resembled the Congratulation of the Monarch (*chōhai* or *chōga*) for the New Year since both were originally Chinese ceremonies adopted by the court.[68] The *sokui* was "an elaborate T'ang-style ceremony in which the entire court assembled with banners, incense, and drums at the Daigokuden [Great Hall of State] to pay homage to the sovereign."[69] The *sokui* is a public, civil accession based on Chinese models that require little preparation and, as a consequence, is usually performed soon after a change in sovereigns; in fact, the *sokui* is a formal announcement that a new sovereign has ascended the throne. The Congratulation of the Monarch, also derived from a public Chinese civil ceremony, celebrates the New Year on a grand scale, but lacks the cosmological implications of the native ceremonies. The indigenous Shintō rites, the *Niinamesai* and the *Daijōsai*, remain private and secret.

The moon casts its light on two of the most important and ancient nocturnal ceremonies of Shintō, the *Niinamesai* held each year to celebrate the fall harvest and the *Daijōsai*. Both ceremonies share the idea of a marriage between the earth and heaven:

The *Niiname* is basically a marriage feast—a celebration of the union of two forces, conceived of as male and female, to produce the harvest and renew the cosmos and with it the state. Several divergent themes combine to create the fullness of the festival, of course, but in both the mythology and the most archaic ritual forms, the concept of the marriage of heaven and earth, dominates the rest. Heaven is male, the earth is female; at harvest time the male descends to the earth, and for their nuptials a new house and banquet are provided at night, and singing and dancing take place. Of the union a child may be born who is perhaps the harvest itself, or perhaps the king or future king.[70]

The *Daijōsai* is the *Niinamesai* with the significant addition of the enthronement ceremonies of a new sovereign (*Senso Daijōsai*, or *Daijōe*).[71] Both Shintō ceremonies are conducted at night in strict secrecy, as they have been from ancient times. Unlike the *sokui*, the *Daijōsai* requires a great deal of preparation, such as rice cultivation determined by divination and ritual purification, the preparation of white and black rice wine, the construction of *Yuki*, *Suki*, and *Kairyūden* buildings, among numerous other activities. Thus the *Daijōsai* was usually performed late in the first year of a new reign or, if the reign began after the seventh month, it was held in the second year or even later depending on the circumstances. At first, there seems to have been no distinction between the *Niinamesai* and the *Daijōsai* in the archaic period during the reign of Tenchi (r. 661-71), but around the reigns of Tenmu (r. 673-86) and Jitō (female *tennō*, r. 690-97) the two separated and became distinct.[72]

The *Daijōsai* and the *Niinamesai* began and remain agricultural rites with strong religious and mythological connotations:

> There can be no harvest without the social order achieved by the state and the sovereign, and no sovereignty without that continuity of legitimacy which, in the face of the decay and mortality wrought by time, must be brought about by renewal. Moreover, the same themes [the popular and the imperial] animate both, but with a different though parallel meaning. On the popular side, the descent of the sky *kami* could be interpreted naturalistically; it was the action of heaven in fertilizing the land to produce the crops. On the other, it must be interpreted humanly, or, rather, divinely; it was the mating of the *kami* with an earthly maiden to generate a visible line of rulers. Yet the action is the same action. The distinction is not made; the marriage is at once heaven with earth and the sovereign and his (womanly or spiritual) consort; the child is at once the harvest and the next heir to the throne.[73]

Thus the myth of the divine marriage between heaven and earth is firmly linked to perpetuating the myth of the "unbroken" line of royal descent.

At the *Daijōsai*, the Nakatomi were vital participants, reciting *yogoto* and *norito* and providing sacred water for the monarch's use. *Yogoto*, which like *norito* belong to the Shintō liturgical canon, are formulaic invocations spoken in the Yamato language to gain desired results, either auspicious or calamitous, suggesting a connection with the archaic belief in word spirit (*kotodama*).[74] In the "Congratulatory Words of the Nakatomi" (*Nakatomi no Yogoto*), a myth specifically links the Nakatomi family to the moon during the *Daijōsai* of sovereigns. This *yogoto*, recorded in the

Taiki (the diary of Fujiwara no Yorinaga, 1120-1156) when it was performed at the *Daijōsai* of Konoe Tennō in 1142, preserves a mythological account of divine instructions given to the Nakatomi to obtain sacred water from the moon for use at the *Daijōsai*.[75] The following is the *yogoto* in its entirety:

Congratulatory Words of the Nakatomi (*Nakatomi no Yogoto*)

Before the Emperor Oho-yamato-neko,
Who rules the Great Eight-Island Land as an incarnate deity,
I [speak] the congratulatory words of the heavenly deities
And fulfill his praises. Thus I humbly speak.

By the command of the Sovereign ancestral Gods and Goddesses
Who divinely remain in the High Heavenly Plain
The eight myriad deities were convoked, [and the command given]:
"From the beginning in the High Heavenly Plain,
The Sovereign Grandchild is commanded to rule
The Land of the Plentiful Reed Plains and of the Fresh Ears of Grain
Tranquilly as a peaceful land.
Abiding upon the heavenly high seat of the heavenly sun-lineage,
He is to partake tranquilly and peacefully in the sacred ceremonial
    place
Of the fresh ears of grain for a thousand autumns, for five hundred au-
    tumns
As his heavenly food, his eternal food, his everlasting food."
Receiving this trust,
He descended from the heavens.
After this, Ame-no-ko-yane-no mikoto,
The distant ancestor of the Nakatomi,
Served before the Sovereign Grandchild,
And sent [his son] Ame-no-osi-kumo-ne-no-kami up to the heavenly
    double-peaked [mountain]
And had him speak humbly before the Ancestral Gods and
Goddesses in order to receive [their words].
He instructed him to speak humbly:
"We wish to present to the Sovereign Grandchild at his meals
Water of the visible lands, to which heavenly water has been added."
In accordance with this, Ame-no-osi-kumo-ne-no-kami, riding on a
    heavenly floating cloud,
Went up to the heavenly double-peaked [mountain]
And spoke humbly before the Ancestral Gods and Goddesses.

Then they entrusted him with a heavenly comb [and commanded]:
"Stand this jeweled comb up,
And from the time the waning sun goes down until the morning sun
shines
Recite the heavenly ritual, the solemn ritual words.
If you thus recite,
As a sign, sacred manifold bamboo shoots will sprout forth like young
water plants,
And from underneath many heavenly springs will gush forth.
Take this water and have him partake of it as heavenly water."
Thus it was entrusted.

In accordance with this trust, he partakes of the fresh ears of grain in
the sacred ceremonial place:
The diviners of the four lands have divined by means of the grand
divination
And have ceremonially determined as the Yuki [the county of] Yasu in
the land of Afumi
And as the Suki [the county of] Higami in the land of Taniha.
Those in charge of the ceremonial paddy:
The saka-tu-ko,
The saka-nami,
The ko-basiri,
The hahi-yaki,
The kamagi-kori,
The ahi-dukuri,
And the ina-mo-mi-no-kimi
Have all [performed their duties] and brought [the rice] to the sacred
ceremonial place of the Banquet of the First Fruits.
Thus, on the second day of the Hare of the eleventh month of this year,
[The rice] has been solemnly and strictly,
Fearfully and reverently purified and presented,
And a day in the month chosen and determined
For the great wine, the black wine and the white wine of the Yuki and
the Suki,
To be consumed by the Emperor Yamato-neko
With a ruddy countenance
As his heavenly food, his eternal food, his everlasting food,
In liquor and in fruit,
And for him to feast with ruddy countenance at the abundant
banquet.

May the Sovereign Deities also,
Whose praises are fulfilled with these congratulatory words of the
Heavenly Deities,
Concur together in this common First Fruits Banquet of a thousand
autumns and five hundred autumns,
Bless him as unmoving and eternal,
And cause [his reign] to flourish as an abundant reign;
And from this first year of Kōdi [1142]
May he, together with heaven and earth, with the sun and the moon,
Continue to give out light and radiance.
[With this prayer] as an intermediary,
As if grasping—not the top or bottom—
But the middle of an awesome spear,
I, the Nakatomi head-priest, Nakatomi no asomi Kiyotika,
Greater fourth court rank, higher official rank, assistant minister of
the Office of Rites,
Fulfill your praises with congratulatory words.
Thus I humbly speak.

Again I humbly speak:
You princes of the blood, princes, court nobles, many officials,
Who serve at the Emperor's court,
As well as the common people of the lands of the four quarters of the
kingdom,
Assemble all together and see,
Feel reverence,
Rejoice,
And hear.
May these words,
Praying that the Emperor's court will flourish as an abundant reign,
like luxuriant trees,
Be heard. Thus do I fearfully and reverently pray.
Thus I humbly speak.[76]

The Nakatomi clan's historical relationship to the moon may have affected
the paramount position of the moon in the memoir. Although Tsukiyomi,
the moon god, plays only a limited role in the standard creation myth, most
sacred Shintō rites are conducted at night under the light of the moon. In
archaic times, the day ruled by the sun was considered one with the fields
and the labors of man, but "it was the moon and night which were on the
other side, strange and numinous, and hence the source of rain and the
alien fecundating power necessary to bring the works of man to harvest."[77]

As clients and supporters of the royal line, the Nakatomi had a vested interest in perpetuating those myths that defined their role and responsibilities at court. In the *yogoto*, a Nakatomi was sent to the "heavenly double-peaked mountain" with a heavenly jeweled comb to recite the Heavenly Ritual from sunset to sunrise, watching for signs of sprouting bamboo shoots beneath which would gush forth heavenly water to be brought back for use in the ceremony.[78] Ellwood argues that the "heavenly double-peaked mountain" refers to the shape of the crescent moon with the points tipped upward to create a bowl in which sacred water collects. It is important to remember that the *Daijōsai* takes place at night under the light of the moon.

Strong associations between the moon, water, bamboo, and the royal line converge in the myths. Connections between the moon and water are easily discernible in the ocean tides and, in ancient times, the reproductive cycle of women. Furthermore, the moon was believed to be the source of underground sacred springs and wells both hot and cold, and was thought to be the abode of the Other, such as *yomi* ("underworld") or *tokoyo* ("other world"). The custom of bathing sovereigns in hot water at the *Daijōsai* was probably derived from the practice of bathing *tennō* at birth in the sacred well at Ōtsu.[79] During the *Daijōsai*, a Fujiwara as a descendant of the Nakatomi, bears the heavenly hot water in which the monarch is to bathe. Later still the monarch receives ablutions of sacred water from maidens described as "daughters of the Nakatomi," later bequeathed to female descendants of the Nakatomi, such as Ben no Naishi.[80]

Historical relationships between the moon, water, and Nakatomi maidens are found in the *Bamboo Cutter* (*Taketori Monogatari*) and a Japanese folk tale on which the Nō play *Hagoromo* (Feathered Robe) is based. Kaguyahime, the heroine of the *Bamboo Cutter*, discovered in a stalk of luminous bamboo, dons a heavenly feathered robe before she returns to the moon with her celestial escort.[81] When Kaguyahime puts on the feathered robe, she looses all memory of her experiences on earth, but regains her divinity. In one version of the Japanese folk tale, a fisherman finds a feathered robe that belongs to a heavenly maiden who shed the garment to bathe in the waters off the shore of Miho and makes her dance before returning it to her.[82] When the maiden disrobed, she lost her divine status, but after she dons the robe, she too regained her divinity. In the case of Kaguyahime and the heavenly maiden, the feathered robe confers divinity upon the wearer. After bathing during the *Daijōsai*, the sovereign dons a garment known as a *hagoromo* that signifies a transformation from human to divine status, thus suggesting some kinship to the *hagoromo* worn by *tennyo* (heavenly maidens serving the moon *kami*). Perhaps the *hagoromo* represents the "heavenly, if not lunar, descent and function" of the monarch in this rite.[83] The maidens who assist *tennō* (monarchs) with bathing rites at the *Daijōsai* can be interpreted as the earthly equivalents of the *tennyo* (moon maidens). Unlike the *yogoto* quoted above in which a "Nakatomi son" was sent to the moon to fetch sacred water, it was the descendants of the young women of the Nakatomi clan who fetched water for the sovereign's purification bath.

There are further mythical links between the moon, bamboo, and water. In the standard creation myth, bamboo plays a part in aiding Izanagi's escape from the Shikomi, hideous hags sent by Izanami to kill him for violating an earlier prohibition against looking at the female *kami*. In "Nakatomi no Yogoto," water was poured on bamboo shoots at night under the light of the moon. A *tamagushi* was set up from sunset to sunrise, thus conjuring up at night the strange and the mysterious that could not be evoked during the day. As mentioned earlier, Kaguyahime, the moon maiden, was found inside a luminious stalk of bamboo, providing another literary link between bamboo and the moon. Water which was held by Tsukiyomi, the moon *kami*, was known to rejuvenate all things. "The final line of the *yogoto* concerning heavenly underground springs makes no sense except in connection with an implicit lunar symbolism. Water and the sun could only be polarities, but the moon is everywhere the custodian and giver of water."[84]

> Thus the power of the moon is not limited to the sky which must be shared by the sun. But the moon controls the tides on earth, women through their cycles, snakes through their seeming rebirth. As the celestial bow, it is believed to send arrows to impregnate women and animals. It could easily release the wells of the underground. The moon, in fact, travels to the underworld and rules there, as the myth of Susanoo hints. The virtual identity of "*Tsukiyomi*" and "*tokoyo*"—*tukuyo*—and also the root of *yo* in *yomi*, the underworld, suggest that what belongs to the moon is not really so much the sky, which must after all be shared with the sun, as everything wherever found which is mysterious, numinous, nocturnal, extraordinary, running to extremes, yet fecundating and necessary, and fresh and renewing and marvelous.[85]

The most important aspect of the *yogoto* is the ascent of the Nakatomi son to the heavenly double-peaked mountain. He obtains the heavenly water and meets the royal ancestral *kami*, suggesting that it is from the heavenly double-peaked mountain that the royal line descends. It is the shape of the crescent moon with the points tipped up that represents the bowl into which the heavenly water collects.[86]

I have argued to provide evidence of a relationship between the phases of the moon, *Daijōsai*, initiation rites, New Year ceremonies, sacred time, and the significance of myths related to the Nakatomi/Fujiwara clans. Further, I introduced a Shintō prayer, *The Congratulatory Words of the Nakatomi*, to posit links between the heavenly water gathered by members of the Nakatomi clan and the significance of the moon, bamboo, and the heavenly maidens who assist *tennō* during sacred rites such as the *Daijōsai*. Now I turn to the laudatory tone of the poetry in the memoir that read like prayers.

Reverential Poetic Tone

Imazeki Toshiko, who has written extensively on sacred time and the reverent tone of Ben no Naishi's poetry, attributes the sacred tone of the poetry to a fear of the instability of the times and to a desire to preserve a record of court life that was on the point of disappearing. While this may have been the case in part, I hold that the religious tone in her poetry may have been derived from the sacred ceremonies Ben no Naishi performed at court. Perhaps the experience she acquired from participating in nocturnal ceremonies at which sacred *norito* and *yogoto* were intoned influenced the tone of her poetry and produced a memoir that reads like prayers for the continuation of the royal line as sacred time and the royal court as sacred space.

Ben no Naishi Nikki uses the image of the moon as a vehicle to praise the court and to pray for the continuity of the royal line. Some *norito* and *yogoto* use diction, tone, and imagery that are similar to those found in *Ben no Naishi Nikki*. From the opening sections focusing on the abdication and accession ceremonies until Section 24, when the actual *Daijōsai* takes place, the poetry focuses on the cosmological significance of the rites by concentrating on auspicious words and sustaining a laudatory tone. Like formulaic portions of *norito* and *yogoto*, the opening entries of *Ben no Naishi Nikki* contain words that set a reverent tone for the ensuing entries of the memoir. Although the entire memoir contains many references to the moon, for this analysis I concentrate only on the sections culminating in the *Daijōsai*.

In Section 1, celestial images of the sky (*sora*), moon (*tsuki*), and sun (*hi*), and the act of gazing upward to the heavens (*aogu*) prepare us for the accession of the child monarch in the second entry.[87] Likewise many *norito* begin with formulaic words humbly praising specific *kami*, heavenly and earthly shrines, the sun, the moon, the stars, and so forth.[88] The following is an excerpt from a *norito* that uses diction and tone similar to that in the *nikki*:

[With the prayer] that you do grant that the Sovereign Grandchild may
abide tranquilly and peacefully
Together with the heaven and earth, with the sun and moon,
Eternal and unmoving.[89]

The poem in Section 2 focuses on the novelty of seeing people dressed in
fine brocades at the accession ceremony, calling to mind "garments of col-
ored cloth, radiant cloth, plain cloth and coarse cloth," that form a part of
many *norito*.[90] Also in the second poem, Ben no Naishi chooses auspicious
words such as "a thousand-year reign" (*chitose*) that suggest the magical
nature of other numbers such as five (*io*) and eight (*yao*).[91] The phrase
tamayura ni ("briefly") suggests the image of "jewels" without the particle
ni, perhaps referring to the jeweled strand worn around the waist by *naishi*
at the accession ceremony. The jewels (*magatama*) are also part of the
royal regalia, which, like the strand worn as a belt by *naishi*, is made into a
necklace for sovereigns. In Sections 3 and 4, more auspicious words such
as "the mighty gods" (*chihayaburu*), "myriad years" (*yorozuyo*, another
number word which frequently appears in *norito* and *yogoto*), "pray"
(*inoru*), "gods" (*kami*), and two shrine names (Hirano and Matsunoo) are
included to continue the reverent tone of the opening poems. In Section 4,
the poet implores the gods to make the sovereign's reign as long-lasting as
the pines at Hirano Shrine that symbolize longevity. Then in Section 5, the
image of the clear mirror echoes the shape of the full moon to form com-
bined metaphors to implore the *kami* for an unblemished reign for the new
monarch. That the mirror is one of the three royal regalia further elevates
the tone of these opening entries. Whether consciously or unconsciously,
Ben no Naishi's poetry captures the awe-inspired spirit of *norito* and
yogoto that were voiced by her ancestors during ancient rites and ceremo-
nies.

The image of the moon and the gaze toward the heavens continue in
the next series of entries. In Section 7, the moon shines brightly on a small
group of poets composing linked verse, prompting Ben no Naishi and her
sister to capture the lyrical moment. Although the tone is not as elevated as
the poems in the opening section, the gaze upward (*aogu*) continues with
eyes fixed on the moon. Further, Ben no Naishi's poem focuses on remem-
bering the past as she looks at the moon, while her sister's poem cleverly
turns the sentiment around by stating that she misses it at the present mo-
ment (*ima*), anticipating the future when the moon will have already set.
Thus the image of the moon in their poetry toys with time-related words—
the past (*kinō*), the present (*kyō*), and the future (*ashita*)—that hints at the
timekeeping aspect of the moon. Section 8 keeps the gaze on the heavens
with the stars Vega and Altair during their annual meeting on the seventh

night of the seventh month. But this time, as clouds obscure the view, the sisters' composition speculates on the possibility of crossing the Milky Way (the Heavenly Stream) and implores the clouds to lift to reveal the light of the stars. The celestial imagery continues in Section 9 during which the sisters again exchange compositions laden with worries about seeing the moon. Ben no Naishi frets that a spiritual flaw might be preventing her from seeing the full moon of the sixteenth. A play on time-related words combined with the word "unclouded" for the full moon suggests the shape of the mirror mentioned in Section 5. Shōshō no Naishi's reply brushes aside Ben no Naishi's concern by stating that, since the palace is located "above the clouds" (*kumoi no ue ni*), it should be a perfect place to view the moon.

The tone of reverence heightens as Ben no Naishi and her colleagues begin in earnest to prepare for the *Daijōsai* ceremony. In Section 10, a progress through the Suzaku Gate to conduct monthly purification rites at the end of the month inspires Ben no Naishi to announce the upcoming enthronement of a new sovereign at the ruins of the old Greater Royal Palace (*Daidairi*) enclosure. The old and the new are joined in this poem by the phrase "new honorable reign today" (*miyo aratamaru kyō ni mo aru kana*) that anticipates the sacred *Daijōsai* that will be conducted three months hence. In Section 11, the shift in imagery to chrysanthemum blossoms may seem a digression, but when we recall that the dew collected from chrysanthemums was thought to ward off the effects of old age, the longevity-invoking tone of the poem is in keeping with others in this series. In Section 12, the image of hailstones raining down from the heavens is interpreted as an answer to countless prayers (*kazu mo miekeri*), emphasizing the reverent tone of associating celestial imagery with sacred portents. In Section 13, another purification rite is featured utilizing concepts of time and countless grains of sand (another number-related word) as metaphors for starting a long-enduring reign. Section 14, focused on "viewing the moon and the snow," inspires a series of poems laden with images of the snow, the nine-fold palace (*kokonoe*), thousand-year paths (*chitose no michi*), accumulations (*kasaneru*), and the passage of time on righteous paths (*chiyo no miyuki*). These are close in intent and tone to *norito* and *yogoto* that use auspicious words to pray for long reigns for sovereigns. In Section 15, preparations for the enthronement ceremonies continue with bustling activities in the *Suki*, *Yuki*, and *Nyokudokoro*, temporary buildings to shelter the sovereign during the rites. Although this entry contains no celestial imagery, linear time is evoked by citing a precedent from the past, creating a new precedent in the present for Yoshida Shrine messengers to use in the future. Thus with the images of the nine-fold palace, countless numbers of hailstones (*arare tama chiru*), and myriad prayers (*yaoyorozu*), auspicious words are used once again to implore the gods for a long reign for the sovereign.

The next series also contain some poetry in a sacred tone. The *Yuki, Suki,* and *Nyokudokoro*, mentioned in Sections 15, 17, and 18, indicate the approach of the *Daijōsai* that will be performed in each of these temporary halls. In Section 17, *chiyo* (one-thousand-year reign) signifies a desire that the new sovereign enjoys a long-enduring reign. The poem in Section 18, on the other hand, evokes images of the clear moon, white snow, and the cold to achieve the proper level of reverence during the winter season when the most sacred rites are conducted. Section 19 again incorporates the image of the clear moon and the cold to suggest the Flushed Faces Banquet (Toyonoakari no Sechie) that will be conducted under these harsh conditions. Section 20 extends the imagery of the bright moonlight and the cleansing wind toward the same Flushed Faces Banquet mentioned in the earlier section. However, the focus switches to sacred music in Section 22 as the poet wonders which *kami* is responsible for the auspicious musical performance. Finally Section 24 focuses on the Day of the Hare on which the *Daijōsai* is performed. Although the poem refers only obliquely to the *Daijōsai* by mentioning the sacred Shintō music that was performed for the occasion, the tone of the poetry is clearly auspicious as the sound of the *biwa* was described as unclouded, just as the moon is so described to denote a good portent. The poem in Section 25 also reads like a prayer that this new reign will follow precedents from the past at the royal court. Even the prose headnote in Section 25 emphasizes the sacred nature of the post-*Daijōsai* banquets. In Section 26, the dawn moon shines on the Flushed Faces Banquet finally performed on the Day of the Horse, as the events surrounding the *Daijōsai* come to an end. The poems are imbued with auspicious lexical items and a reverential tone that is combined with the image of the moon, linked not only to its ancient timekeeping function, but also to its connections with the Nakatomi/Fujiwara's clan's role at the *Daijōsai*.

In this section, I have argued for the possibility of Shintō *norito* and *yogoto* influencing the reverential tone of Ben no Naishi's poetry. The use of celestial images, auspicious lexicon, and laudatory tone is found in both Shintō prayers and some of Ben no Naishi's poetry. The moon as the central image of the *nikki* is related to all the important innovations found in the memoir. The laudatory tone in the poems leading up to the *Daijōsai* certainly appears to be focused on the moon, as discussed above. While the analysis focused only on the opening sections of the memoir, there are other poems with similar reverential tone in *Ben no Naishi Nikki*. Yet not all poems in the memoir are laudatory in nature. Ben no Naishi produced many conventional poems on various topics and engaged in witty exchanges with *Kokinshū*-style puns, for she was after all a poet who was patronized by the court for her skill in a variety of styles. She was even known as a linked verse poet, years before the art of *renga* had been elevated to the exalted level *waka* had enjoyed for centuries.

Waka and *Renga* Poet

Ben no Naishi gained her position at court due to her reputed skill in *waka* and *renga* composition. Her *waka* are embedded within the prose head-notes stating the occasion for which the poetry was composed and are noted for their reverent tone. In fact most of the poetry included in the memoir is *waka*, not *renga*, even when the occasion for a poetic gathering was for linked verse. Linked verse was rapidly gaining popularity in the mid-Kamakura literary salons, but the refined *ga* aesthetic had not yet been extended to linked verse and applied only to *waka* at that time. Therefore, the linked verse in the memoir is usually more secular and lighter in tone, perhaps reflecting the mid-thirteenth-century poetic mi-lieu's attitude toward linked verse.

In the poetic salons of the mid-Kamakura period, the speed with which poetry was composed was one of the decisive factors determining the success or failure of linked verse poets. Unlike in later times, im-promptu gatherings to compose linked verse functioned without the strict, codified rules that dictated every minute aspect of composition; thus, indi-viduals who could handily turn a verse were very much in demand at these gatherings. Ben no Naishi and her sister Shōshō no Naishi, whose father Nobuzane had labored to build their reputations as poets, were summoned by Retired Sovereign Go-Saga on several occasions to compose linked verse. In the following episode, Ben no Naishi and her sister were invited to the Madenokōji Palace to compose linked verse with the Retired Sover-eign Go-Saga, a noted aficionado of the art:

[Section 97] Royal Linked Verse

On the night of the fifteenth of the eighth month, there was a royal linked verse gathering at the palace of the retired sovereign. Al-though the night was growing late, particularly poignant and interest-ing linked verses continued to be composed. Just at that time, the sound of the temple bell drifted over, and someone asked, "Have the royal prayers begun?" The provisional major counselor Saneo came close to the bamboo blinds and ordered them to "hurry up and make linked verses because the late night prayers have begun." It was quite amusing. Hearing the sound of the bell cleared their spirits, so Shōshō no Naishi composed this poem, putting aside the linked verse:

aki no yo no	At the sound of the temple bell
tsuki ni saetaru	that tolls serenely
kane no oto ni	under a moon of an autumn night,
yagate mo toki no	I become aware
utsurinuru kana	that time has passed quickly.

Ben no Naishi:

toki utsuru	Is it because I hear the sound
kane no oto zo to	of the bell tolling the time
kiku kara ni	that it makes me feel
tsuki mo nakaba no	the mid-autumn moon
kage ya fukenuru	has begun to wane?

Although this section features an invitation to the retired sovereign's palace to compose linked verse, the poetic exchange recorded here involves two *waka* thematically linked to the sound of the temple bell introduced in the prose headnote. The linked verse the sisters were invited to compose is not recorded in this episode, although the *waka* they wrote later preserves the memory of the event. Below is still another episode during which Ben no Naishi and her sister are summoned by Retired Sovereign Go-Saga to compose linked verse, this time with the purpose of spelling out "*namu amidatsu*" (now pronounced *namu amidabutsu*) with the initial *kana* syllable of each link:

[Section 117] "Amida Buddha" Linked Verse

On the night of the fifteenth of the eighth month, there was the usual poetry gathering. It was indeed a pity that it rained. After the poetry gathering was over, the retired sovereign had the double doors opened so he could look outside, but he was disappointed because the moon was clouded over. He commanded saying, "As a farewell, let's just the three of us compose an 'Amida Buddha' linked verse sequence. It would be a pity if the compositions were forgotten. Shōshō no Naishi shall record them," he ordered.

Retired Sovereign:

nagori oba	What are you telling me
ika ni seyo tote	to do with my feelings,
kaeruran	that you go home and leave me alone?

Shōshō no Naishi:

| moshiya to matan | I will wait, for it may appear, |
| aki no yo no tsuki | the moon of an autumn night. |

Retired Sovereign:

akanaku ni	While not content,
meguri au yo mo	a night may come round
ari ya tote	when we meet again.

Ben no Naishi:

| michiuki hodo ni | The path is hard to travel along, |
| kaeru oguruma | little carriage wheels turn home. |

Retired Sovereign:

tagui naki	One of a kind,
waga koigusa o	I pick
tsumiirete	love grasses.

Shōshō no Naishi:

| tsutsumi amaru wa | To overflowing, |
| sode no shiratsuyu | the white dew on my sleeves. |

Since dawn had broken, he said, "We will save the rest for another linked verse gathering." They left full of memories.

Lady Dainagon no Sanmi heard of these links on this or that occasion and said, "These linked verse love grasses will be found memorable. You should compose a poem on this and include it in your poetry collection." Ben no Naishi:

omoide no	If these words
kotonoha to naru	are to be remembered,
kusa naraba	I will pick enough
nanakuruma ni mo	leaves to fill
ware zo tsumu beki	seven carriages.

One of the notable features of mid-Kamakura linked verse gatherings is the concept of spontaneous composition as a game of wits. Later in the medieval period, rules of linked verse composition dictated the order in which one contributed links and the images required or prohibited from appearing in links of close proximity. Clearly such complicated rules are not applicable here, as Go-Saga provides double the number of links allowed by later rules. Moreover, Go-Saga takes turns matching his compositions with each sister, rather than the three taking equal turns to provide links in the order prescribed later. Of further interest is the fact that Ben no Naishi closes the entry with a *waka* composition highlighting her emotional response to the honor of having been invited to compose linked verse with Go-Saga while indicating as well that it was common knowledge at court that she was keeping a poetic record of her service.

Sections 167 and 173 in *Ben no Naishi Nikki* also feature linked verse gatherings. Unfortunately because these episodes are located toward the end of the extant text, portions of the text are missing.[92]

[Section 167] Linked Verse

On the twenty-sixth, the Regent Kanetsune came [. . .] to the royal poetry gathering, which was interesting that the retired sovereign would command [. . .] The regent, saying that he would have the poems recorded once through, composed the opening verse. Lady Hyōe no Kami recorded the verses. With just three people, Ben no Naishi, Shōshō no Naishi and the regent, it was not very interesting. While the regent waited upon the retired sovereign all day long, the light of the evening sun shone brightly on the *kōshi* doors of the Jijūden [. . .]. The bamboo treetops bent [. . .] so she felt. Ben no Naishi:

kuretake no	Does the black bamboo
yo no ma no tsuki ya	[forget]
wasu[raren]	the moon of the night?
[eda ni utsuro]fu	The evening sunlight
yūhikage kana	reflecting on the branches.

[Section 173] Royal Linked Verse on a Rainy Night

At a royal linked verse gathering on the [. . .] day of the nineth month, it was raining and very [. . .]. The moon was especially unclouded [. . .] lower ranks, Hyōe no Kamidono [. . .] recite

ima sara ni	Though it is too late to regret
sono yo no sora no	I cannot refrain from regretting
tsura[ki kana]	the [unkind] sky of that night,
[koyoi no] tsuki no	all the more so because I see
kage o miru ni mo	the clear moon [tonight].

Reply:

tare mo geni	Everyone, not just you, but I also,
sono yo no sora wa	thought the night sky unkind,
tsu[rakariki]	since we knew the moon
[itsu] mo harekeru	[of enlightenment]
tsuki zo to omoeba	is [always] clear.

Ben no Naishi:

haruru yo mo	A clear night,
kumoru mo onaji	or a cloudy night,
sora [nareba]	[since] it is the same sky,
[tsura]shi tomo mizu	I do not see it as [unkind],
aki no yo no tsuki	the moon of an autumn night.

The irony in most of the sections dealing with linked verse gatherings is that only the *waka* compositions are recorded in the *nikki*, although the reason for the social occasion was to create linked verse. It is clear that Ben no Naishi considered *waka* as the proper vehicle for the expression of feelings related to reverential, serious times and linked verse as appropriate solely for secular occasions.

There are also sections from lost portions of *Ben no Naishi Nikki* preserved in a near contemporary text such as *Notes from a Frog at the Bottom of a Well* by Ton'a, which contribute much toward our understanding of Ben no Naishi's reputation as a linked verse poet.

During the honorable reign of the same *in* (Go-Saga), there was a royal linked verse gathering at Yoshida Springs. The female courtiers Ben no Naishi and Shōshō no Naishi were summoned to attend and were ensconced behind bamboo blinds. The Lay Priest of the Popular Affairs Ministry, sitting beside the bamboo blinds, acted as the oral transmitter of the poems composed by the women. But the Lay Priest was hard of hearing and the echoing sounds of the waterfall made it impossible for him to hear the linked verses they composed. Therefore, Lesser Captain Tamenori brought some kindling wood from the mountains, placed it beneath the waterfall, which reduced the sound considerably. This royal linked verse gathering was recorded in *Ben no Naishi Nikki* [but does not appear in extant texts].[93]

This entry preserved in Ton'a's fourteenth-century text provides another glimpse of a linked verse gathering to which Ben no Naishi and her sister were invited by Retired Sovereign Go-Saga. The entry probably dates somewhere between 1252, the year when the extant text breaks off, and 1259, when Go-Fukakusa was forced to abdicate the throne by Go-Saga, concluding the original memoir with the abdication. The fact that Ton'a chose to record almost verbatim from *Ben no Naishi Nikki* during his discussion of linked verse exhibits the high regard in which he must have held both Ben no Naishi and Shōshō no Naishi as linked verse poets. Apparently Ton'a was not alone in his high esteem for their literary prowess.

The medieval account *Tsukuba Disputation* (*Tsukuba Mondō*, ca. 1357–72) by Nijō Yoshimoto (1320–88) offers the following observation concerning "female linked verse masters" (*onna rengashi*):

> Female linked verse masters called Ben no Naishi, Shōshō no Naishi, and the like, let the richly fragrant sleeves of their plum robes protrude from the edge of the bamboo blinds and effortlessly pushed linked verses out from beneath the blinds to people who tirelessly chanted them in resounding voices. Likewise, there was a nun called Fukushu who was also a linked verse master, about seventy or eighty years old. This person was a contemporary of the Lay Priest Kyōgoku Middle Counselor [Fujiwara Teika]. It is a pity that nowadays there are no female linked verse masters.[94]

This entry emphasizes the rapidity with which Ben no Naishi and Shōshō no Naishi produced linked verse compositions. Although this entry is not dated, it provides another view into a lost portion of *Ben no Naishi Nikki*. A final testament to their reputation as "female linked verse masters" can be gleaned from the number of poems included in *A Tsukuba Collection*: thirteen by Ben no Naishi and fifteen by Shōshō no Naishi.[95] Retired Sovereign Go-Saga had only twenty-two compositions in the collection despite the unassailably high position he occupied. However renowned Ben no Naishi and Shōshō no Naishi were as female *renga* masters, it is clear that during the mid-thirteenth century it was *waka*, not *renga*, that was the medium of choice to memorialize one's name in court society.

Reassessment and Conclusion

Ikeda Kikan's chapter, "Ben no Naishi Nikki," in *A Study of Literary Diaries by Women* (1927) greatly influenced most critics' perception of the work for several decades. Ikeda's assessment of *Ben no Naishi Nikki* as the product of a cheerful "eternal maiden" who innocently focused her account on amusing aspects of court life condemned the work and kept it from serious consideration for decades. No research diverging from Ikeda's view appeared in print during the 1930s and 1940s. In 1958, when Tamai Kōsuke published an annotated version of *Ben no Naishi Nikki*, his study prompted new interest in the topic.

Nevertheless, the first significant departure from Ikeda's analysis occurred in 1964 when Ōuchi Mayako's article "Treatise on *Ben no Naishi Nikki*," introduced several new lines of investigation. She advanced the idea of Ben no Naishi's public stance and compared the work to the *Journal of the Upper Hot Water Room*, unadorned daily records compiled by women in court service during the fifteenth through the early nineteenth centuries. Ōuchi also drew attention to Ben no Naishi's skill in linked verse composition, emphasizing the role that speed played in mid-thirteenth-century linked verse composition.

Despite advances made by Ōuchi, decades later *Ben no Naishi Nikki* remains neglected by most male scholars. In *A History of Japanese Literature, Volume Three: The High Middle Ages*, Konishi Jin'ichi only mentions *Ben no Naishi Nikki* in passing, denigrating the work as "imitative" of eleventh-century Heian models without providing any concrete criteria for his judgment. Konishi's negative evaluation is the inevitable result of analyzing a Kamakura-period work using Heian-period aesthetic criteria. Although Konishi's discussion of factual and fictional *nikki* of the tenth through fourteenth centuries provides the framework for my survey situating *Ben no Naishi Nikki* within the tradition, his lack of attention to thirteenth-century *nikki* is regrettable.

Until the 1980s, when Imazeki Toshiko identified "praise for the court" (*kyūtei sanbi*) as the unifying theme for the distinct entries in *Ben no Naishi Nikki*, most scholars never attached any significance to Ben no Naishi's decision to adopt a public stance, that of a *naishi* performing her sacred duties. As I have argued, that decision determined the development of literary elements not found in other *nikki*, including the policy of limiting topics to court-related events, the shared perspective to expand coverage of court events, the aesthetics of cold weather imagery to symbolize the sacred ceremonies of winter, and the image of the moon as a vehicle to praise the court.

In my view, with all these innovative elements, it is hard to find anything "imitative" about *Ben no Naishi Nikki*. Konishi's model of an eleventh-century *nikki* was probably the diary of Murasaki Shikibu, a two-year account of court life which is not as thematically focused as *Ben no Naishi Nikki*. The main similarity between the two lie in their factual rather than fictional nature, and a stance that is public rather than private. Beyond these similarities, however, stand a host of differences.

The structure of *Ben no Naishi Nikki* distinguishes it from others in the genre. Its pattern of a prose headnote, followed by a poetic composition, suggests a conscious literary purpose that was achieved by revision at a later date. The brevity of most entries also points to later editing; a daily account would have produced a less regular pattern with a higher incidence of inflated and irrelevant details. The deliberate structure beginning and ending with entries centering on abdication ceremonies also carries a sense of completion rarely found in others of this genre. The sense of coming to a full circle hints at the cyclical nature of courtly sacred time and is the result of religious ceremonies efficaciously conducted.

Another innovative development in *Ben no Naishi Nikki* is the shared perspective, which enlarges the coverage of court events by including the viewpoint of Ben no Naishi's younger sister, Shōshō no Naishi. This unique technique of a shared perspective gives us another pair of eyes from which to view *naishi* performing their duties, providing access to events of another time and space than that experienced solely by Ben no Naishi. Controlled by a sense of duty, the shared perspective is the result of the public stance to narrate events from the view of *naishi* at work in their official capacity filtered through the eyes of a dominant individual. It gives us a more comprehensive picture of what happened at court ceremonies.

A distinct appreciation of cold weather represented by such images as those of the moon, snow, frost, and wind as symbols of the sacred rites conducted in winter reflects the development of a new medieval aesthetic in the Kamakura period. *Ben no Naishi Nikki* was one of the first to link cold weather images characterized by whiteness and brightness to the sacred. The nocturnal nature of the sacred duties performed by *naishi* becomes apparent when we note the predominance of moon imagery in her poetry, but the aesthetic of *Ben no Naishi Nikki* dictated that moon-viewing be conducted in a group, not by an individual reminiscing about a personal past as in typical love poems. There is a decided proclivity in this new medieval aesthetic toward a symbolic relationship between the cold and a purity of spirit. This indigenous development acted as a harbinger for the maturation of this aesthetic in the later medieval period combined with the influence of continental Sung poetics.

Perhaps one of the most unusual elements in *Ben no Naishi Nikki* is the emphasis on the moon and its relationship to *Daijōsai*, sacred time, myths of the Nakatomi/Fujiwara family, and the laudatory tone of some of the poetry that reads like Shintō prayers. The moon appears frequently in the memoir because so much of a *naishi's* duty was performed at night. However, there is more than meets the eye in the choice of the moon as the dominant image for the memoir. In the past, the moon was the timekeeper, the main celestial image in the night sky. The various phases of the moon—waxing and waning, appearing, and disappearing—acted as metaphors for the reign of kings, initiation rites, and New Year's celebrations with implications of cosmological renewal. Furthermore, myths of the Nakatomi/Fujiwara family role in the *Daijōsai* with the ancient relationship of that role with the moon as the source for the heavenly waters added to earthly waters indicates the marriage between heaven and earth at the *Daijōsai* of sovereigns. Like the *norito* and *yogoto* chanted at sacred ceremonies, poems that read like prayers dominate the opening entries of Ben no Naishi's memoir, suggesting that perhaps Shintō prayers influenced the tone of her poetry.

Ben no Naishi's reputation as a poet was more secure in the medieval period than it is now. Poetry aficionados valued her quick, impromptu compositions and included her poems in *waka* and *renga* anthologies. Her greatest fan was perhaps her patron Go-Saga who invited Ben no Naishi and her sister, Shōshō no Naishi, to several private sessions to compose linked verse with him. Go-Saga's request that she keep a poetic record of his son's reign probably gave her a venue to preserve her poetry, but it is ironic that because of this command she is known more today as a memoirist than a poet. Surely in her day she would have preferred being known as a *waka* poet than a memoirist, because the *ga* aesthetic in the mid-thirteenth century did not include *nikki* or *renga*. Her claim to fame was *waka*; the family's primary "business" was indeed literary.

Imazeki Toshiko suggested that the longing for an idealized past could be interpreted as a sign of the author's feelings of insecurity about the present. The mid-Kamakura period was shaken by disturbances that could have been interpreted in literary form as a nostalgia for an auspicious, stable monarchical reign of the past, when the court was in its heyday. However, constant allusions to the past may also be the result of the author's focus on time as a cycle. The fabric of *Ben no Naishi Nikki* is threaded through with two notions of time: as a part of historical time, the past, present, and future flow along a linear continuum, and as a part of sacred time, the cosmological beginning of time is renewed each time at the *Daijōsai* ceremonies of sovereigns performed under the light of the moon. The moon holds the key to almost all that is important in this memoir: as a timekeeper, the source for the sacred water used at the *Daijōsai*, the idea of renewal and rejuvenation, and so on. This may explain the many examples of poems and prose sections in which time-related and number words are used in the *nikki*.

Ben no Naishi's own devotion to the sacred duty of *naishi* controlled every aspect of the *nikki* she left to posterity, and her innovative methods for achieving a focused account of court life should be commended, rather than condemned. I see *Ben no Naishi Nikki* as having forged new paths into uncharted territory. This memoir is unique even in the amorphous genre of *nikki*, but, more importantly, it is a text with a conscious literary theme and purpose. Ikeda Kikan's assessment of *Ben no Naishi Nikki* as a frivolous account of a young girl interested only in describing pleasant occurrences at court needs revision. Recent research published in the 1980s and 1990s by Imazeki Toshiko and Iwasa Miyoko challenge previously accepted ideas about the memoir. While Ben no Naishi's work has long been disparaged as a flawed replica imitating Heian masterpieces, I see the author as having succeeded in producing a work that reflects a new medieval aesthetic quite different from the Heian norm. She also managed to invent unique literary devices that enabled her to achieve her purpose in a most creative manner.

Another interesting element must not be overlooked. Ben no Naishi's family made their mark as literary members of court society. Although her grandfather and father were known as painters in the new realistic style of Kamakura-period portraiture, they probably considered themselves poets rather than artists. Until Ben no Naishi wrote her memoir, all literary contributions were made by male members of the family. Though she followed in the footsteps of fellow female memoirists, she forged a new path for her family by being the first female to create a literary text. When Ben no Naishi laid down her brush, she must have felt satisfied that she had created a structurally integrated account focused on the sanctity of the royal reign, and that she had added new luster to the literary reputation of her distinguished ancestors.

Notes

1. The term *onnade* (woman's hand) refers to writing by women in which the majority is rendered in *kana*. On the other hand, the term *otokode* (man's hand) indicates writing in Chinese (*kanbun*) or a mixture of native and sinified styles from which modern Japanese is derived (*wakan konkōbun*). When women and men wrote Japanese poetry (*waka*), both genders used the *kana* syllabary to conduct courtship and social correspondence in the vernacular.

2. John Wallace's translation, "Fitful Slumbers: Nun Abutsu's *Utatane*," was published in *Monumenta Nipponica* 43.4 (1988): 391–416. But Wallace's translation is not as accessible as McCullough's and Brazell's translations which are published in book form.

3. Helen Craig McCullough, *Classical Japanese Prose: An Anthology* (Stanford, Calif.: 1990), 7.

4. Ibid., 15.

5. Ibid. The term *nikki bungaku* developed in the twentieth-century to refer to the tradition of accounts written in the vernacular. I do not endorse its use in my study; it is included in my text as direct citations from other sources.

6. Ibid., 15–16.

7. Edwin A. Cranston, trans., *The Izumi Shikibu Diary: A Romance of the Heian Court* (Cambridge, Eng.: 1969), 90–91.

8. Ibid., 91.

9. Konishi Jin'ichi, *A History of Japanese Literature, Volume Two: The Early Middle Ages*, trans. Aileen Gatten and Mark Harbison, ed. Earl Miner (Princeton, N.J.: 1986), 257.

10. Ibid.

11. Ibid., 252.

12. Ibid., 257.

13. Ibid., 256.

14. Ibid.

15. Ibid., 256–57.

16. In "Gender and Genre: Modern Literary Histories and Women's Diary Literature" in *Inventing the Classics: Modernity, National Identity, and Japanese Literature*, Tomi Suzuki credits Akiyama Ken (1965) with the idea of treating some *nikki* as fictional, rather than as records of actual events (92).

17. Ibid., 258.

18. McCullough, *Prose Anthology*, 70.

19. For the gender significance of adopting a female persona, see Lynne Miyake, "The Tosa Diary: In the Interstices of Gender and Criticism" in *The Woman's Hand: Gender and Theory in Japanese Women's Writing* (Stanford, Calif.: 1996), 41–73.

20. Helen Craig McCullough, *Kokin Wakashū: The First Imperial Anthology of Japanese Poetry* (Stanford, Calif.: 1985), 97–101.

21. Cranston, *Izumi Shikibu Diary*, 45–47, 63–70.

22. Edith Sarra states the contrary, "It [The Pillow Book] is clearly not a *nikki*, although scholars classify certain of its passages as being *nikki*-like," in *Fictions of Femininity: Literary Inventions of Gender in Japanese Court Women's Memoirs* (Stanford University, 1999), 10–11.

23. Konishi Jin'ichi, *A History of Japanese Literature, Volume Two: The Early Middle Ages*, trans. Aileen Gatten, ed. Earl Miner (Princeton, N.J.: 1986), 387–89.

24. Konishi Jin'ichi, *A History of Japanese Literature, Volume Three: The High Middle Ages*, trans. Aileen Gatten, ed. Earl Miner (Princeton, N.J.: 1991), 109–16.

25. Ibid., 109–10.

26. Ibid., 113.

27. Ibid., 109–16; 289–96; 471–85.

28. Iwasa Miyoko, interview with author, Tsurumi University, Yokohama, Japan, 26 October 1996.

29. S. Yumiko Hulvey, "Abutsu-ni" in *Japanese Women Writers: A Bio-Critical Sourcebook*, ed. Chieko Irie Mulhern (Westport, Conn.: 1994), 5.

30. John Wallace, trans., "Fitful Slumbers: Nun Abutsu's Utatane," *Monumenta Nipponica* 43, no. 4 (1988):391–416.

31. Ibid., 408.

32. Ibid., 410.

33. Konishi Jin'ichi, *A History of Japanese Literature, Volume Three: The High Middle Ages*, 291–92.

34. Tamako Niwa, "*Nakatsukasa Naishi Nikki*" (Ph.D. diss., Radcliffe, 1955), 49.

35. Donald Keene, *Seeds in the Heart: Japanese Literature from Earliest Times to the Late Sixteenth Century* (New York: 1993), 843.

36. Donald Keene, *Travelers of a Hundred Ages: The Japanese as Revealed Through 1,000 Years of Diaries* (New York: 1989), 171.

37. *Taiheiki* in *Shinpen Nihon Koten Bungazu Zenshū*, vol. 55, ed. by Hasegawa Tadashi (Tokyo: 1996): 108-110.

38. Konishi, *The High Middle Ages*, 473–75.

39. Ibid., 472.

40. Ibid.

41. Ibid., 480.

42. Ibid., 470.

43. Iwasa Miyoko, interview with author, Tsurumi University, Yokohama, Japan, 26 October 1996.

44. Imazeki Toshiko, "*Ben no Naishi Nikki* no Shipittsu Ito," *Nihon Bungaku* 519 (1996):25.

45. In the notes to the translation, I include Tamai and Iwasa's commentaries of significant discrepancies in titles and dates.

46. Imazeki, "Shipittsu Ito," 26–27.

47. *Yuki* is defined as "consecrated-purified" and *Suki* as the "next consecrated-purified" food or hall in D. C. Holtom's, *The Japanese Enthronement Ceremonies with an Account of the Imperial Regalia* (Tokyo: Sophia University Press, 1972), 90-93. Holtom provides a discussion of the highly contested meaning of these terms.

48. Ibid., 22.

49. Ibid.

50. *Taketori Monogatari* in *Nihon Koten Bungaku Taikei* (hereafter NKBT) (Tokyo: 1956–68), 9:58. Even in western lore the moon conjured up mysterious notions. The etymology of lunacy comes from the belief that gazing at the moon or sleeping in the moonlight caused insanity. Agricultural beliefs prescribe planting potatoes and other crops in the dark of the moon.

51. McCullough, *Kokin Wakashū*, 167.

52. *Makura no Sōshi* in NKBT, 19:305; Ivan Morris, *The Pillow Book of Sei Shōnagon* (New York: 1967), 1:239.

53. Phillip Tudor Harries, trans., *The Poetic Memoirs of Lady Daibu* (Stanford, Calif.: 1980), 79.

54. Ibid., 187.

55. Imazeki Toshiko, "Tsuki Akari no Kyūtei: *Ben no Naishi Nikki* Shōkō," *Teikoku Gakuen Kiyō* 10 (1983), 6. Imazeki states that the group longing for the past when court life was at its zenith was based on a longing for a stability they did not feel at the Kamakura court. While this may have been the case in some instances, I interpret the nostalgia for the past to a desire to perpetuate the myth of the legitimacy of the royal line that is inherent in the *norito* and *yogoto* intoned by

the Nakatomi/Fujiwara at the *Daijōsai* and First Fruits Banquet and much of the poetry composed by Ben no Naishi in her memoir.

56. Imazeki Toshiko, "*Ben no Naishi Nikki* Shōron: Kōryōsa e no Shiten o Megutte," *Teikoku Gakuen Kiyō* 11 (1985). The original idea of images related to the cold are derived from Imazeki's article, but the application of these ideas toward the development of a new medieval aesthetic is my own.

57. Ibid., 12.

58. Konishi, *The High Middle Ages*, 434-38.

59. Imazeki, "Kōryōsa," 18.

60. Robert S. Ellwood, *The Feast of Kingship: Accession Ceremonies in Ancient Japan* (Tokyo, 1972), 3.

61. Mircea Eliade, *Cosmos and History* (New York, 1959), 80-81.

62. Ibid., 85.

63. Ibid., 75.

64. Mircea Eliade, *Myth and Reality* (New York, 1963), 40-41.

65. Ibid., 41.

66. Eliade, *Cosmos and History*, 86-87.

67. D. C. Holtom, *The Japanese Enthronement Ceremonies with an Account of the Imperial Regalia* (Tokyo: Sophia University Press, 1972), 47 and Felicia Bock, *Engi-Shiki: Procedure of the Engi Era Books I-V* (Tokyo: Sophia University Press, 1970), 26, present similar information on the three elements of the Japanese *Daijōsai*.

68. Although archaic Japan did not observe the New Year as an occasion separate from the Harvest or Spring festivals, these two merged as celebrations of harvest and renewal. For details, see Ellwood, 55

69. McCullough and McCullough, *A Tale of Flowering Fortunes* (Stanford, Calif., 1980), 1:381.

70. Ellwood, 48.

71. The *Daijōsai* has no parallel in Chinese sources even though much of the Shintō sections of the Japanese Code were copied almost verbatim from originals in Chinese.

72. For a full discussion of the Tenmu-Jitō period Shintō revival movement, see Ellwood, p. 88-95. He states that though the two ceremonies separated around the time of Tenmu and Jitō's reigns, it was not until the Meiji period (1868-1912) that the two terms correlating to the two rites came to be widely used (90). On the other hand, Holtom cites the reign of Seiwa Tennō (r. 858-76) as the time when a distinction was made between the terms *Ohonihe matsuri* (*Daijōsai*) and *Nihinahe matsuri* (*Niiname matsuri*). In the beginning, he states that the *Ohonihe matsuri* was the annual Harvest Festival observed not only by the sovereign and his court, but by commoners as well (74).

73. Ellwood, 75.

74. Konishi believes that the concept of *kotodama* preceded its appearance in written works of the late seventh and early eighth centuries, because its practice was so widespread as to need little explanation. If certain words in the Yamato language were spoken in specific ways, the human breath would either bring about an auspicious or calamitous result. The *Kojiki*, recorded in written form from the

oral recitation of Hieda no Are, is an example of the importance of the spoken word and the oral tradition in archaic and ancient Yamato. Konishi Jin'ichi. *A History of Japanese Literature, Volume Two: The Archaic and Ancient Ages.* Princeton, NJ: Princeton University Press, 1984:163-64.

75. For other *norito* and *yogoto* recited only by the Nakatomi, see Donald L. Philippi, trans. *Norito: A New Translation of the Ancient Japanese Ritual Prayers* (Tokyo: 1959): II, VII, X, XIV, XV, XVI, XXI, and XXIII. To defend the late date during which the *yogoto* was recorded in the *Taiki*, Ellwood maintains that the conservative nature of liturgical materials argues for the faithful continuation of the earlier tradition, rather than a reconstruction (54).

76. Philippi, *Norito*, 76-79; *Norito* in vol. 1 of *Nihon Koten Bungaku Taikei* (Tokyo: Iwanami Shoten, 1959-77), 459-63.

77. Ellwood, 66-67.

78. In the standard creation myth, bamboo sprouts, hair ties, and combs play a significant part during Izanagi's escape from the land of Yomi while he is being pursued by the Shikome, hags from the world of darkness and ritual impurity. First, when Izanagi throws down the cords which bind his hair, they turn into grapes that the Shikome stop to devour. When the hags close in on him again, the teeth from a wooden comb that he throws down transform into bamboo shoots, causing another delay in the hags' pursuit while they stop to devour them. A further instance of the mysterious character of bamboo is found in the *Tale of the Bamboo Cutter*: an old bamboo cutter finds a miniature moon maiden glowing inside a bamboo stalk. After growing to adulthood in an incredibly short time, she ascends to the moon wearing a feathered robe (*hagoromo*).

79. Ellwood., 54-55. Tenchi, Tenmu, and Jitō tennō were all bathed in the sacred well at Ōtsu.

80. Ibid., 56.

81. Helen Craig McCullough, *Classical Japanese Prose: An Anthology* (Stanford, Calif., 1990), 36.

82. Royall Tyler, *Japanese Nō Dramas* (London: 1992), 104; Arthur Waley, *The Nō Plays of Japan* (New York: 1957), 222.

83. Ellwood, 135.

84. Ibid., 62.

85. Ibid., 62-63.

86. Ibid., 62.

87. For translations of the poetry, see relevant sections in my translation.

88. There is celestial imagery in many extant *norito* and *yogoto*.

89. Philippi, 66; *Norito* in vol. 1 of *Nihon Koten Bungaku Taikei* (Tokyo: Iwanami Shoten, 1959-77), 444-47.

90. For formulaic parallelisms of cloth imagery, see Philippi, I (18), II (23), III (25), IV (29-30),V (32), VI (34), VII (36), XII (52), XIII (53), XIV (55), XV (56), XVIII (59), and XXV (69); *Norito* in vol. 1 of *Nihon Koten Bungaku Taikei* (Tokyo: Iwanami Shoten, 1959-77), 387-93, 394-97, 397-99, 401-05, 405-07, 407-09, 409-14, 431-33, 434-35, 436-37, 440-41, and 447-51.

91. The number eight (*ya, yao*) was thought to possess magical power: such phrases as *yakumo tatsu* (eight-fold clouds rise) and *yakumo sasu* (eight-fold

clouds pierce) were employed as *engo* for Izumo, a sacred site in Shintō mythology; *yakumo no michi* (eight-fold cloud path) and *waka no uro* (bay of poetry) refer metaphorically to *waka* and its adherents. Further, *yaoyorozu* (myriad years) and *yachiyo* (eight thousand years; myriad years) are other examples of auspicious language found both in poetry and the Shintō liturgy.

92. Iwasa Miyoko, interview with author, Tsurumi University, Yokohama, Japan, 26 October 1996. Iwasa stated that she and Imazeki Toshiko believe that fire damaged the text of *Ben no Naishi Nikki*. Using the Shokōkanbon text, Iwasa holds that the pattern of damage in this scroll exhibit signs of having been *burned* while rolled in reverse order with the outside of the scroll containing the latter portion of the text. Iwasa states that Imazeki anticipates publishing an article about the pattern of textual damage due to fire. Tamai Kōsuke does not mention fire damage; instead he describes only "insect damage" (*mushi kui*).

93. SGR, 13:382.

94. Kaneko Kinjirō, *Rengashi no Kikō* (Tokyo: 1990), 17.

95. Kidō Saizō, "Kamakura Chūki no Renga," in *Rengashi Ronkō*, (Tokyo: 1973), 1:164.

Part II
THE TRANSLATION

4
Ben no Naishi Nikki

[Section 1] The Abdication Ceremony
On the twenty-ninth day of the first month in the fourth year of Kangen [1246], the monarch Go-Saga abdicated at the Tominokōji Palace.[1] It was hard to record everything that happened at that time. It was all so splendid. Ben no Naishi:

kyō yori wa	From this day forth
waga kimi no yo to	can I not but think,
nazuketsutsu	"This is my lord's world,"
tsukihi shi sora ni	when I look up at the sun
augazarame ya	or the moon in the sky?[2]

[Section 2] The Enthronement Ceremony
On the eleventh day of the third month, the enthronement ceremony was conducted at the Council of State.[1] Needless to say, the various ceremonies on this bright spring day were splendid. People appeared so novel. Ben no Naishi:

tamayura ni	Figures clothed
nishiki o yorou	briefly in brocades
sugata koso	are more novel still,
chitose wa kyō to	as today begins my lord's
iya mezuranare	one thousand-year reign.

[Section 3] The Festival at Hirano Shrine
On the first day of the fourth month, the Hirano Festival was held.[1] The presiding official was the Tsuchimikado major counselor Akisada, the controller was Tsunetoshi, the carriage officer was Suketsugu, and the general assistant was Tokitsuna. Ben no Naishi used the young maple combination for her skirt display.[2]

101

It was pleasant when someone said, "Give the female courtier water to cleanse her hands," and someone else moistened a piece of paper, inserted it in a cleft stick, and thrust it ceremoniously into the carriage. She was enjoying the scenery in the shade of a pine tree with a cool breeze blowing. Ben no Naishi:

yorozuyo to	I pray to the mighty gods
kimi o zo inoru	that our lord's reign
chihayaburu	will last a myriad years,
hirano no matsu no	as long-prospering
furuki tameshi ni	as the pines at Hirano Shrine.

[Section 4] The Messenger to Matsunoo Shrine in the Fourth Year of Kangen

On the same day, Shōshō no Naishi went to Matsunoo Shrine as the official messenger.[1] The presiding official was the middle counselor of the second rank Yoshinori, the controller was Chikayori, the general assistant was Tamenawa, and the carriage officer was Kanetomo. Shōshō no Naishi used the sweet-flag combination for her skirt display.[2]

Hearing the cuckoo's first song as it perched atop a densely foliaged tree, Shōshō no Naishi composed this:

chihayaburu	A cuckoo at mighty
matsunoo yama no	Matsunoo Mountain!
hototogisu	Today the gods, too,
kami mo hatsune o	are surely listening
kyō ya kikuran	to its first song.

[Section 5] The Messenger to the Naishidokoro

On the thirteenth day of the fourth month, Ben no Naishi went to the Naishidokoro as a special messenger.[1] Since she went by way of the Eaves Corridor and the Giyōden Altar Corridor,[2] she could see the moon shining clearly as it traversed the sky deep in the night. Ben no Naishi:

masukagami	I serve a lord
kumoranu michi ni	whose reign is as unclouded
tsukaete zo	as a clear mirror,
sayakeki tsuki no	thus I can behold
kage mo mirubeki	the light of the pure moon.

[Section 6] The *Katsumi* Poem

On the fifth day of the fifth month, someone had brought some *katsumi*[1] to the Dining Room.[2] His Lordship had said, "Take it and show it to His Majesty with a poem attached."[3] Since Ben no Naishi had thought the *katsumi* stalks were sweet-flags, she had attached a sweet-flag poem—an amusing mistake. Ben no Naishi:

katsumi ouru	Not knowing
Asaka no numa mo	the *katsumi*
mada shirade	of Shallow Marsh,
fukaku ayame to	I was deeply sure
omoikeru kana	they were sweet-flags.

[Section 7] Linked Verse

After the twentieth day of the fifth month, when the cloudless dawn moon was particularly pleasant, Ben no Naishi thought it was very elegant that His Lordship held a linked verse gathering in his retiring room.[1] Only Taie and Tametsugu were present,[2] so the number of people attending was very small. His Lordship said, "It would be nice to hear Kōtō no Naishi play the *biwa* next,"[3] but the moon was close to setting, therefore everyone went home. She hated to see the occasion end, so she lingered for some time beside the fishing pavilion.[4] Ben no Naishi:

tsuki o mite	If I gaze at the moon,
omoi mo ideba	remembering the past,
onozukara	I will no doubt
shinobarenubeki	remember this
ariake no sora	pale dawn sky.

Shōshō no Naishi's reply:

omoiiden	I do not say,
nochi to wa iwaji	"I will surely
ima no ma no	recall it later!"
nagori nomi koso	I miss it right now,
ariake no tsuki	this dawn moon!

[Section 8] The Tanabata Festival

For Kikōden night,[1] on the seventh day of the seventh month, head chamberlain-middle captain Masaie was appointed manager of the festivities. In the Dining Room, Kōtō no Naishi set up the bridges on the *koto* and played a little to check the tuning. The sound of her testing the tuning was very pleasant. When people said such things as "Could it be because the head chamberlain-middle captain is managing things? Tonight's rain falls ever so quietly," Shōshō no Naishi composed this poem:

shimejime to	By the nature of the rain
koyoi no ame no	falling quietly tonight,
furumai ni	we can guess
bugyō no hito no	the mood
keshiki o zo shiru	of the manager.

When she composed her poem, it was delightful that Lady Dainagon found the poem amusing enough to smile.[2] Everything was prepared: looking out from the Consort's Apartment and the Two-Bay Room,[3] the faint shadows created by the torch light were so pleasant that Shōshō no Naishi composed this poem:

tomoshibi no	The Herdsman thought he would
kage mo hazukashi	steal across the Heavenly Stream
ama no gawa	this rainy night, but now,
amemoyo ni to ya	is he unable to cross
watarikanuran	embarrassed by the torch light?

Ben no Naishi's reply:

hoshiai no	Show me the light of the stars
hikari wa miseyo	meeting in the abode of clouds,
kumoi yori	close to His Majesty's
kumoi wa chikashi	Royal Palace,
kasasagi no hashi	O bridge of magpies wings.[4]

[Section 9] Moonlight Meditation

On the sixteenth day of the eighth month, His Majesty went to the Gosechidokoro.[1] The Madenokōji major counselor Kinmoto, the commander of the left gate guards Sanefuji, the head chamberlain-middle captain Masaie, the head chamberlain-controller Akitomo, and others presented themselves, and there was music. While His Majesty was away, Lady Chūnagon no Suke, Lady Kunaikyō, and Ben no Naishi were among those who went out under the outer eaves of the Dining Room (*hirobishashi*). It was unbearable seeing the moon only faintly beyond the edge of the Horse Screen near the railing.[2] "It makes me think of the Nijō consort of the distant past, whose residence in the Kōrōden corresponds to the First Wing

Chamber here.³ I wonder if people of her time also worried about seeing the bright moon," she said. Ben no Naishi:

mukashi yori	Must it be a flaw in my heart
kumorazu to iu	that I cannot clearly see the moon,
tsukikage o	though it is said
sayaka ni minu wa	to have been unclouded
kokoro nariken	from times past?⁴

Upon returning with the royal party, Shōshō no Naishi heard of her poem and composed this reply:

kumo no ue ni	Since you dwell,
nao suminagara	after all, above the clouds,
aki no yo no	should you not be able
tsuki o sayaka ni	to see the moon clearly
nado ka mizaran	even on this autumn night?⁵

[Section 10] The Fields Outside the Walled Enclosure

On the final day of the eighth month, Shōshō no Naishi, one of the female courtiers who was to be in charge of the Nyokudokoro¹ and who was to proceed to the Suzaku Gate,² became ill, and Ben no Naishi was sent as her substitute. The wind that was blowing was very cool, and the fields were pleasant.³ Ben no Naishi:

ōuchi ya	I have come to visit
furuki mikaki ni	the ancient wall
tazunekite	of the Royal Palace,
miyo aratamaru	when there is to be
kyō ni mo aru kana	a new honorable reign today.

[Section 11] Chrysanthemum Covers

On the eighth day of the ninth month, someone from the consort came bearing some silk covers for chrysanthemums.¹ Ben no Naishi put the particularly attractive ones on some of the chrysanthemums in the Dining Room Courtyard. She had been concerned about the dew that night, but on the morning of the ninth the whole bed looked as though it were in bloom.² It was very delightful. Ben no Naishi:

kokonoe ya	Since these are the chrysanthemums
kyō kokonuka no	for today, the ninth,
kiku nareba	at the Nine-fold Palace, I view them,

kokoro no mama ni	having let them bloom
sakasete zo miru	to my heart's content.[3]

[Section 12] Court Proceedings at the Guards' Headquarters

On the first day of the tenth month, there was a meeting to decide the day for the annual prayers commemorating the death of the former sovereign Tsuchimikado, so the appointment ceremony, scheduled for the first, was postponed until the eleventh.[1] The Ōmiya major counselor Kinsuke, the Madenokōji major counselor Kinmoto, and others went to the guards' headquarters to conduct court affairs.[2] The chamberlains Tsunetoshi, Munemasa, Mitsukuni, and others also went there to decide upon matters concerning the prayers.[3] It was announced that the Golden Wheel Ritual, Calamity-Averting Rite[4] and the like were to begin on the nineteenth with the chamberlain-gentleman-in-waiting Munemasa as manager.[5] There was a violent hailstorm that day, and the weather turned very cold. Much intrigued, Ben no Naishi composed this poem:

yao yorozu	An answer to those
inoru shirushi mo	myriad prayers has appeared,
arawarete	countless numbers
arare tama chiru	of hailstones
kazu mo miekeri	scattering down.

[Section 13] A Great Purification Ceremony at the Riverside

On the twenty-fourth day of the tenth month, a great purification ceremony took place at the riverside.[1] It would be commonplace to call the occasion splendid. As Ben no Naishi looked out from the temporary building for His Majesty,[2] the distant river sand looked white and the river breeze was refreshing. Ben no Naishi:

kyō shi koso	It is likely indeed
kiyoki kawara no	that today is the beginning
isagoji ni	of a reign as endless
chiyo hen kazu mo	as the number of grains of sand
torihajimurame	on this beautiful river beach.

[Section 14] Viewing the Moon and the Snow

On the night of the fourteenth day of the eleventh month, a delightful snowfall covered the road and collected in drifts. Since the men on night guard duty, the Kazan'in consultant-middle captain Morotsugu and others such as the head chamberlain-middle captain had gone to the retired sovereign's residence,[1] several female courtiers left for the Seiryōden. The icy bamboo leaves blowing in the wind outside sounded charming. Moreover, the moon and the sky, clouding over as if it were going to snow again, had much to recommend it. The Ōmiya major counselor Kinsuke, the Madeno-kōji major counselor Kinmoto, and others who were at the palace watched the scene from the South Hall throughout the night.[2] It became piercing cold before dawn, and they told some courtiers to bring firewood from the Courtiers' Hall.[3] The courtiers said that the firewood supply there was exhausted, so they used withered branches from a bush-clover plant north of the Spacious Hall,[4] a most elegant expedient. Ben no Naishi:

shimogare no	Indeed it is
furue no hagi no	for budding spring
orimatsu wa	that we burn as firewood
moeizuru haru no	the ancient frost-withered branches
tame to koso mire	of the bush-clover.[5]

Not a cloud obscured the late moon[6] the bright light on the snow was delightful. Ben no Naishi had gone out to the railing beyond the His Majesty's Apartment[7] to gaze at moon when middle captain Kintada came along with the Ōmiya major counselor's inkstone, which he said he had been asked to fetch. She wondered where the letter's destination might be. Ben no Naishi:

akeyarade	Still in the depth of night,
mada yo wa fukaki	dawn has not yet broken.
yuki no uchi ni	Surely the letter-bearer
fumi miru michi wa	will see no path
ato ya nakaran	as he treads through the snow.

On the same night, the fourteenth, Shōshō no Naishi had gone to the Nyokudokoro[8] where, still unwell, she was lying sound asleep. Along toward dawn, she awoke and heard the sound of shoes plodding through deep snow in the distance. Despite her illness, she got slowly out of bed. She heard a voice say, "A message from the Ōmiya major counselor." She pushed open the double doors.[9] Although it was still dark, the whiteness of the snow on the Palace Meadow[10] created such an unforgettable scene that words fail to describe it adequately. She opened the letter and read the following poem from him:

kokonoe ya	How must it appear
ōuchiyama no	at the nine-fold
ikanaran	Royal Palace Mountain,

kagiri mo shirazu   this white snow accumulating
tsumoru shirayuki   in limitless deep drifts![11]

Shōshō no Naishi's reply:

kokonoe no   Tracing tracks
uchino no yuki ni   in the snow
ato tsukete   of the Palace Meadow
haruka ni chiyo no   within the Nine-fold Palace,
michi o miru kana   we see a thousand-year path.[12]

This following poem was sent to Ben no Naishi from Shōshō no Naishi on the morning after the snow:

kokonoe ni   On Royal Palace Mountain
chiyo o kasanete   thousand-year reigns accumulate
miyuru kana   into nine-fold layers,
ōuchiyama no   like the white snow
kesa no shirayuki   seen this morning.

Ben no Naishi's reply:

michi shi aran   Considering the thousand-year
chiyo no miyuki o   righteous path of our lord,
omou ni wa   neither the passing of time
furu tomo nobe no   nor the falling of snow
ato wa mienan   will obscure the meadow path.[13]

[Section 15] The Messenger to Yoshida Shrine

On the seventeenth day, the snow was still very deep. On the way home from having served as the messenger to Yoshida Shrine, Ben no Naishi told the attendants to take her carriage to the Suki Nyokudokoro,[1] which she was curious to see. The general assistants, Tamemochi and Kanetomo, and the chamberlains of sixth rank accompanying the carriage said that it was too late at night to make such a long detour, but she was determined to go. "There are precedents indeed for messengers on the return from Yoshida Shrine to visit the Nyokudokoro," she said. "Well, if there really are precedents," they said, and they made the long journey.

The gate guard was very slow in opening the gate, so they said angrily, "Is this the first time this has happened? It has always been the custom for the female courtier to come here on the return from Yoshida Shrine. Why are the gates suddenly kept closed?" She found it amusing to think that even their scolding words to the gate guard were likely to become precedents:

towamashi ya	Would I ask why this visit
tsumoreru yuki no	in the depth of night
fukaki yo ni	through deep drifts of snow,
kore mo mukashi no	were it not to follow
ato to iwazu wa	precedents of the past?

[Section 16] The Royal Haircut

The eighteenth was the middle Day of the Cock. His Lordship the regent came to announce a royal haircut and added that female courtiers should attend wearing ceremonial dress.[1] Ben no Naishi said, "We have no skirt-display robes ready. Would it do to wear our limp robes?" Ben no Naishi:

shioretaru	Do not make us wear
koromo na kise so	robes limp and worn;
ōumi no	people will mistake us
ama no sode ka to	for fisherwomen with sleeves
hito mo koso mire	drenched by the Great Sea.[2]

[Section 17] The *Yuki* Nyokudokoro

Kōtō no Naishi was in charge of the Yuki Nyokudokoro. Ben no Naishi was most impressed hearing Kōtō no Naishi play the *koto* throughout the night during the freezing snowy weather. Ben no Naishi:

yomosugara	White snow fell ceaselessly
nobe no shirayuki	on the meadow all night long
furu koto mo	and the *koto* played constantly.
chiyo matsu kaze no	Are these omens of a thousand-year reign
tameshi ni ya hiku	awaiting our lord?[1]

[Section 18] The *Suki* Nyokudokoro

Shōshō no Naishi's Nyokudokoro was located inside the earth-walled enclosure of the bodyguards of the left, so she could look far into the distance. Struck by the boundless beauty of the moon floating above the freezing snow, she composed this poem:

itsu no yo mo	Could I ever forget
wasure ya wa sen	this clear moon in any age,
shirayuki no	floating above the ancient wall

furuki mikaki ni	covered by drifts
sumeru tsukikage	of white snow?

Gate guards, stable hands, and others had been assigned to the various offices to carry things and perform miscellaneous tasks. One of them, a man shouldering a basket loaded with goods, begged in tears to be excused. "I have someplace I must go," he said. Moved to pity, Shōshō no Naishi composed this:

mi ni oeba	Shouldering a bamboo basket,
sazo omouran	the man seems
take no ko no	to lament being separated
te o hanatsu yo no	from his children
kokoromayoi ni	in a world full of worries.[1]

Interesting-looking robes of various colors, newly sewn, had been hung here and there. So that they would not be wet by dripping snow, some gate guards climbed up to the roof and raked the snow away. Hearing the interesting sounds of their activities, Shōshō no Naishi was moved to compose this poem:

abara naru	I wonder how so much
itaya no noki no	white snow has piled up
shirayuki no	on the eaves of the leaky plank roof,
kaku bakari nado	so much that
furitsumoruran	it has to be raked away.[2]

A cold wind was blowing frightfully at the time. The overseer,[3] Controller Chikayori, shivered as he said, "I felt I was being pinned to one spot by the wind at the Palace Meadow: it was terrible. I could not talk at all; the wind at the overseer's office has had me in a stupor ever since this morning. I cannot think of a more unbearable situation."

Female supervisors,[4] who were sitting close together in rows, found his remarks both natural and amusing. "Ah, here is the lord controller now," they said. There was a chorus of voices: "We have run out of dye substances. We are not going to finish the work in time."

"I could explain everything, but I am shivering too hard to talk," Chikayori said. Amused, Shōshō no Naishi composed this poem:

koto no ha mo	Thinking of the way
omou ni sa koso	the wind blew and blew
nakarurame	all night long,

fuki to fuku yo no	it seems even the "leaves of words"
kaze no keshiki ni	have disappeared in the wind.[5]

[Section 19] The Consort's Visit

The consort came two days before the royal progress to the Council of State compound scheduled for the twenty-second.[1] She arrived late at night on the twentieth at about moonrise. Ben no Naishi heard that the chamberlain-assistant commander[2] Tsunetoshi was looking for a female courtier, so she was waiting for him near one of the cloth partitions in the Table Room, thinking that he probably had something to be transmitted to His Majesty. While there, she heard the sound of Her Majesty's entourage approaching: the provisional master of the consort's household Michinari, the Kazan'in consultant-middle captain Morotsugu, the head chamberlain-middle captain Masaie, the lesser captain Michiyo, and others. It was interesting that she could even hear the clear sounds of the bows they were using as staffs. From the vicinity of the half-blinds,[3] she heard the chamberlain-gentleman-in-waiting Munemasa say, "What a splendid light the moon casts! It brings to mind the 'White Tissue Paper' season."[4] True enough, she could see all the way to the horizon. Ben no Naishi:

kanete omou	Tonight's clear moon
toyonoakari no	anticipates how much colder still
samukesa o	the night will be
mashite ika ni to	when the "Flushed Faces" moon
sumeru tsuki kana	finally appears.[5]

[Section 20] The Royal Progress to the Council of State Compound

There was a royal progress to the Council of State compound around dawn on the twenty-second. Although it was so cold the snow seemed to be frozen, the accommodations were makeshift, and the wind brought in flurries of snow through the spaces between the Sung screens,[1] which was quite charming. The Ōmiya major counselor came and lowered all the broken lattice shutters.[2]

His Majesty's apartment faced the throne.[3] Some men from the Palace Repairs Office had climbed up to the roof to clear away the white drifts of snow on the tiles. The sound of their axes seemed very near. Two-bay rooms, separated by partitions from the royal apartment, were equipped as substitutes for the Seiryōden, where His Majesty was to worship. The palace pantry (*Omonoyadori*) and kitchen office were below the double doors. Rooms for the *nyōbō*, women of the upper ranks,[4] had been divided into four sections each, and with two or three to a cubicle, it was unbearably crowded.

His Majesty went to the Consort's Apartment. It was pleasant viewing the Seisodō[5] from a room with a double-leaf door en route. Since all the arrangements were makeshift, everything seemed novel, even to the sound of people's footsteps.

The Curtain-Dais Rehearsal was scheduled for that night.[6] It was splendid to see the trailing robes of the Tokudaiji major captain Sanemoto and the other senior nobles, who were in one of the two-bay rooms furnished to serve as the Seiryōden (the one with a replica of the comb-shaped window in the Courtiers' Hall).[7]

The Table Room was next to His Majesty's Apartment. There higher-ranking *nyōbō* sat in rows with their trailing sleeves close together. Short Sung screens were set up along one bay, and it was amusing when *nyōbō* crawled like women of the past to avoid being seen by senior nobles while going to His Majesty's Apartment.[8] Since something like rough straw matting covered the floor, the skirts of their bombycine robes all got dirty.

The storm raged violently, knocking down all the dividing screens until one could see all the way to the connecting corridors. There was so much light that Ben no Naishi composed this poem:

hedatetsuru	The dividing screens
kaze no tayori mo	have been blown down
oshinabete	by the tidings of the wind
sara ni zo toyo no	letting in still more
akari narikeru	the brightness of flushed faces.[9]

[Section 21] Cascading Locks

When Shōshō no Naishi went to the Black Log Building,[1] she found that she had forgotten an ornamental hairpin to put up her hair in the formal style.[2] She sent a messenger over to Ben no Naishi's apartment at the Council of State compound, but she was unable to lend her one. With His Majesty's departure time approaching, people kept urging her to hurry. Exasperated, Shōshō no Naishi composed this:

shibashi mate	Please wait a moment,
uchitaregami no	at least until I have replaced
sashigushi o	the forgotten hairpin
sashiwasuretaru	with which I must put up
toki no ma bakari	my cascading locks.

Later, when Ben no Naishi heard about her poem, she composed this reply:

sashigushi no	I, too, was upset,
sashiau hodo no	as disordered as locks
toki no ma wa	cascading freely,
uchitaregami mo	when I could not give you
ware zo midareshi	an ornamental hairpin.

[Section 22] The Drinking Party in the Consort's Apartment

On the day of the Tiger, there was a drinking party[1] in the Consort's Apartment. His Majesty had retired for the night, since it was quite late, but he emerged again, awakened by voices singing "White Tissue Paper." Everyone stood up and danced. The major captain of the right Sanemoto danced three times, the Ōmiya major counselor Kinsuke five times, and the Madenokōji major counselor Kinmoto four times. The commander of the right military guards Arisuke sang. Ben no Naishi had heard that the commander of the left gate guards Sanefuji was to sing, and was most disappointed to learn that suddenly he had had to go into mourning.

The Kazan'in consultant-middle captain Morotsugu, as well the Nakanoin third rank middle captain and others, were all present. That night Ben no Naishi served as the messenger to the Spirit-Pacifying Festival.[2] The controller Akitomo did not arrive until after the visit to the retired sovereign's[3] drinking party, so it was nearly dawn when the event began. The music was delightful in the clear atmosphere of the shrine. Ben no Naishi:

koyoi shi mo	What god's past pledge
ika naru kami no	might have been
chikai nite	responsible
mono no ne narasu	for the music
ato to nariken	we present tonight?

[Section 23] Should Royal Bodyguards Escort the Regent?

The chamberlain-gentleman-in-waiting Munemasa said, "A sudden private inspection meeting has been called. Should royal bodyguards escort His Lordship from the banquet to the site of the meeting?"[1] With so much going on, Ben no Naishi had no opportunity to convey his message. He kept urging her to inquire at once, and so Lady Chūnagon no Suke said, "Do not bother the regent about it; answer him yourself as you see fit, with a poem, perhaps." Ben no Naishi mentally composed these lines, amused by the thought of how irritated Munemasa would be to hear a poem chanted as a response at such a hectic time:

sa shi mo mi ni	Because this midnight moon
shitagau yonaka no	is always following us,
tsuki nareba	it will doubtless go
utsuru kata ni zo	to whatever place
kage wa meguran	someone moves.[2]

[Section 24] Sacred Music at the Seisodō

On the Day of the Hare, there was sacred music at the Seisodō.[1] The female courtiers said that they wanted to listen to the music near the Consort's Apartment, but they were disappointed when they found His Lordship the regent there.[2] They went out toward the Seiryōden, only to find rows of chamberlains. Likewise, the courtyard was already full of women with their faces covered by robes. There was no place left to go, so they returned to His Majesty's Apartment. Near the Curtain Dais, they heard the sacred music faintly as they burned incense to perfume robes to be given as gifts. It would be needless to say that the music was pleasant with the Ōmiya major counselor on the *biwa*, the Kazan'in major counselor on the flute, and the commander of the military guards beating time with a pair of wooden slats. Ben no Naishi:

kumoi yori	They are probably
nao haruka ni ya	heard even beyond
kikoyuran	the abode of clouds,
mukashi ni kaesu	the music of "Asakura,"
asakura no koe	returning us to the distant past.[3]

After the performance was over, the Ōmiya major counselor went to His Majesty's Apartment and asked Kōtō no Naishi, "How did the *biwa*, Mokuma, sound?"[4] "Mokuma's tone resembled that of the Great Hall of State's *biwa*. Its sound was so unclouded that it could be heard everywhere," she replied. Ben no Naishi quite agreed. Her poem:

inishie no	Even compared to the *biwa*
kumoi ni hibiku	of the distant past
biwa no ne ni	whose sound reverberated
hikikurabete mo	in the abode of clouds,
nao kagiri nashi	Mokuma is unrivaled still.

[Section 25] The Throne

The Banquet was held on the Day of the Dragon.[1] Unfortunately, His Majesty's trousers made him stumble on the high stone steps as he prepared to ascend the throne, and the fan slipped from in front of his face.

Enough cannot be said about the splendid things that occurred that night. Ben no Naishi:

kumo no ue to	The royal progress
omou mo takaki	today resembles
inishie no	the path preserved
michi o zo aogu	in high antiquity
kyō no miyuki wa	above the clouds.

[Section 26] The Dawn Moon
When the Flushed Faces Banquet, the pages' performances, the platform dancing, and the command performances had ended, everyone found the light of the dawn moon on the Seisodō deeply moving.[1] Ben no Naishi:

kokonoe ni	Could I ever forget
yo o kasanetsuru	the dawn moon floating
yuki no ue no	above the snow
ariake no tsuki no	during these manifold nights
itsuka wasuren	at the Nine-fold Palace?

Thus, His Majesty returned to the Kan'in Palace.[2] Ben no Naishi recalled things at the Greater Royal Palace[3] and composed this:

kumoi nite	That I long
arishi kumoi no	for the ancient abode of clouds
koishiki wa	in the abode of clouds
furuki o shinobu	is due to a heart
kokoro narikeri	that yearns for the past.

[Section 27] The Ceremony of the Kamo Return
Although Ben no Naishi had heard that the Kamo Special Festival was set for the first day of the twelfth month, it was postponed until the twelfth.[1] The moon shone bright on the fallen snow and the air was unbearably cold while the female courtiers were in the Lime Altar Room[2] eagerly awaiting the Kamo Return. Most amusingly, Shōnagon no Naishi and Shōshō had a disagreement over the placement of the straw matting to be used by attendants serving His Majesty's meal.[3] Only the regent and one other senior noble, the Kazan'in consultant-middle captain Morotsugu, were present for the occasion. Mitsukuni was in charge. The moonlight shone clear above the light of the courtyard fires. It looked pleasant, so Ben no Naishi composed this poem:

akaboshi no	Voices singing
koe mo sa koso wa	of the Bright Star
suminurame	must be clear indeed;
niwabi ni tsuki no	moonlight reflected
kage zo utsurou	in the courtyard fires.[4]

[Section 28] Sacred Music at the Naishidokoro

Sacred music at the Naishidokoro was performed on the fifteenth day of the twelfth month.[1] The assistant female courtier was Lady Azechi no Suke[2] and the female courtier was Shōnagon no Naishi. Because the moon was utterly enchanting, Lady Dainagon invited other women to go listen to the music. But when they saw the Nakanoin third rank middle captain and the middle captain Masatada in the Eaves Corridor, unfortunately they had to turn back. Lady Dainagon asked, "What do you think of these tactless barrier guards?" Ben no Naishi:

uchi mo nenu	Feeling they were barrier guards
sono sekimori no	keeping constant vigil
kokochi shite	without so much as a wink,
tōsanu michi ni	we returned sadly from paths
tachikaeru kana	where passage was denied.[3]

[Section 29] The Directional Taboo on the Seasonal Divide

On the twenty-first, there was a royal progress to the Council of State for the directional taboo on the seasonal divide.[1] Recalling the previous nights they had spent at the Greater Royal Palace,[2] Shōnagon no Naishi and Ben no Naishi spent the entire night gazing at the moon in the place that had been prepared as the Seiryōden. Ben no Naishi:

akazarishi	Insatiably longing
kumoi no tsuki no	for the moon
koishiki ni	in the abode of clouds,
mata megurikinu	the moonlight came back
ariake no kage	to gaze at the dawn.[3]

[Section 30] The Koga Chancellor's Banquet

On the twenty-fourth, there was a banquet held at the residence of the Koga chancellor.[1] Late at night the chancellor came to the Table Room where Shōnagon no Naishi and Ben no Naishi were the on-duty female courtiers with their hair put up in the formal style.[2] The chancellor said, "Is it very late? Is it around the time for the Ox Card?"[3] When no one replied, Shōnagon no Naishi whispered in Ben no Naishi's ear, "You've probably thought up a clever reply. Please answer him." Ben no Naishi:

utatane ni	Since you do not seem
ne ya suginamashi	quite aware that time
sayonaka no	has advanced to the Ox Card,
ushi no kui to mo	I wonder if you did not doze
sashite shirazu wa	through the Hour of the Rat.[4]

[Section 31] The Healing Buddha Recitation Rites

Although Ben no Naishi had heard that the Healing Buddha Recitation Rites[1] were to commence on the eighteenth day of the twelfth month and end on the twenty-fourth,[2] they were prolonged until the twenty-sixth, which was also the night of the Buddha's Names Ceremony.[3] Attentively carrying out her duty of guarding the sacred sword and sacred jewels, she heard voices reading the sutras. The sacred sounds moved her to compose this poem:

nanuka zo to	I can hear voices
omoeba akanu	performing rituals
hi o nobete	that have been prolonged,
okonau hō no	those rituals of which I thought,
koe zo kikoyuru	"Seven days will not be enough."

[Section 32] The Congratulation of the Monarch

The spectacle of the Congratulation of the Monarch[1] on the first day of the fifth year of Kangen [1247] was truly auspicious. Ben no Naishi:

kyō zo tote	Spring has arrived
sode o tsuranuru	in the crowded courtyard
morohito no	where people seated in rows
muretatsu niwa ni	with sleeves aligned, think,
haru wa kinikeri	"O auspicious day!"

[Section 33] The Green Horse Banquet

The Green Horse Banquet took place on the seventh.[1] Since the interior controller, the Kujō major captain of the right,[2] looked glorious in the mild spring sunlight, Ben no Naishi composed this poem:

toneri mesu	Probably it will endure a myriad years,
haru no nanuka no	the light of this sun
hi no hikari	on the seventh day of spring

iku yorozuyo no   when His Majesty
kage ka meguran   summons the attendants.[3]

That night, while watching the Green Horses making their rounds, Ben no Naishi composed this poem:

hikitsurete   Led by their attendants,
uchi mo tayumanu   the horses with unflagging feet
koma no ashi   have paraded by,
hayaku kono yo wa How quickly indeed
fuke ya shinuran   this night has passed![4]

[Section 34] The Change of Regents

On the nineteenth, there was a meeting of senior nobles in connection with the change of regents.[1] The presiding official was the middle counselor of the junior second rank Yoshinori, and the chamberlain-in-charge was the head chamberlain-controller Akitomo.

At the moment Akitomo came to inform His Majesty of the retired sovereign's decree, the moon clouded over and without any reason, Ben no Naishi was saddened. Her poem:

haruru yo no   Can anyone think of this
tsuki to wa tare ka as a moon on a clear night?
nagamuran   There seems to be haze
kata e kasumeru   clouding over part of the sky
haru no sora kana on this spring night.[2]

Shōshō no Naishi, witnessing the report to His Majesty from the Upper Hot Water Room,[3] tore off the edge of the bound attendance register,[4] made of recycled paper, and wrote this poem on it:

iro kawaru   What must I have been thinking
ori mo arikeri   when I said the pines
kasugayama   on Mt. Kasuga are evergreen?
matsu o tokiwa to There are times
nani omoiken   when the color changes.[5]

Ben no Naishi's reply, when she saw her poem:

kasugayama   Although the color
matsu wa tokiwa no of the pines on Mt. Kasuga
iro nagara   is still evergreen,

| kaze koso shita ni | the wind which blows |
| fukikawarurame | beneath them seems to change. |

[Section 35] The Memoir

Around the time of the Ōdairi,[1] a memoir[2] in three bound volumes was left in the charge of Lady Chūnagon no Suke. Mitsukuni came stating that it ought to be returned and was there not something Ben no Naishi could say to convince her. Ben no Naishi knew the loss would be painful, so she composed this poem:

hamachidori	Regret, though you must,
ato o katami no	parting with the keepsake tracks
urami dani	of the plover,
nami no ue ni wa	it is hard to remain
ikaga todomen	on the waves.[3]

[Section 36] Attendants for the Royal Prayers

On the twenty-third, Lady Dainagon, Lady Chūnagon no Suke, and others arrived as the attendants for the royal prayers.[1] As they stood on the veranda of the Two-Bay Room,[2] snow was falling though the sun was shining, and a cold wind was blowing on the frozen Black Bamboo. Lady Chūnagon no Suke said, "I feel like echoing Fun'ya no Yasuhide's complaint. But he was not so very old, was he?"[3] Ben no Naishi:

ta ga mi ni ka	Was he any different
wakite itowan	from others,
haru no hi no	in hating to see snow
hikari ni ataru	falling on the blossoms
hana no shirayuki	on a bright, sunny spring day?[4]

[Section 37] The Change of the Era Name to Hōji

On the twenty-eighth day of the second month, there was a change of era name to Hōji.[1] Among those who attended the announcement at the guards' headquarters were Lord Ōkura, the Hachijō major counselor Michitada, the Tsuchimikado major counselor Akisada, and others whose names Ben no Naishi had heard but now had forgotten completely. The regent, Lord Okanoya Kanetsune, came, saying, "The illustrious Four Counselors must have been truly impressive in the past when they participated in decisions at the guards' headquarters. The shining middle captain and the radiant lesser captain thought that for them to aspire to high office and rank would be shameless; together they decided to renounce the world."[2] His reminiscences stimulated Ben no Naishi's imagination and she composed this poem:

inishie ni	Leaves of words
sadameokikeru	considered worthy
koto no ha o	in the distant past,
ima mo kasanete	now return to us
omoiyaru kana	to be admired yet again.

[Section 38] The Light Offering

When the Light Offering[1] took place on the first day of the third month, Ben no Naishi was in light mourning,[2] staying in one of the apartments under the outer eaves of the Jijūden, across from the left gate guards' headquarters. It was novel to be able to see the treetops in the East Sanjō district[3] from such close quarters. It was interesting to see the arrival of the counselor Tsunemitsu, the head chamberlain-middle captain, and the head chamberlain-controller, accompanied by palace guards[4] for the official proceedings at the guards' headquarters today. Munemasa, Mitsukuni, and others also attended. Just when she was admiring the blossoming flowers, the Ōmiya major counselor came into view. He was so remarkably handsome in his informal robes that she composed this poem: (Accompanying him were attendants clad in deep green hunting robes.)

hana no iro ni	Side by side
kurabete ima zo	with the flower's radiance,
omoishiru	I now realize
sakura ni masaru	there can be beauty
nioi ari to wa	that surpasses the cherry.

[Section 39] The Mock Gosechi

On the ninth day of the third month, the commander of the left gate guards Sanefuji arrived as the night guard, and because he had to spend the entire night on duty, required the presence of the commander of the right gate guards Michinari in the event that he was bored by a lack of amusement. Sanefuji said that someone should go to the Courtiers' Hall to summon some of those present to join him. Lord Arisuke obeyed his order and came back accompanied by Kintada, Kinyasu, Michiyo, Takatsune, and others. There was a mock Gosechi with boisterous dancing. Needless to say, it was amusing to hear the commander of the left gate guards take the lead in singing "Goematsu Pine on Mt. Ryōzen"[1] with the commander of the right gate guards and commander of the military guards joining in as the chorus. Someone said that the events of this evening should be written down. Ben no Naishi:

itsuwari no	How could we forget
koto shi mo ikaga	even this mock performance?
wasurubeki	The Flushed Faces Banquet
toyonoakari wa	knows
toki zo to mo nashi	no seasonal limitation.

[Section 40] The Promised Flowers
Since the consort was to visit around the time of the full moon in the third month, the Madenokōji major counselor suggested that the consort's female courtiers be invited for flower-viewing. "The cherries would not dare refuse to bloom, if they knew the consort were visiting us," he said. But for some reason, it never happened. It was a tremendous disappointment. Ben no Naishi:

hana min to	What happened
tanomeshi koto ya	to the flower-viewing
ikanareba	we relied on?
tazunu bakari no	Not even the name of the event
na dani tomaranu	remains for mere inquiry.

Shōshō no Naishi's reply:

hana sakanu	Can flowers
hana ya adana ni	that do not bloom
tachinuran	be named flowers?
soradanome ni mo	We have relied
narinikeru kana	on an empty promise.

[Section 41] Voices Calling the Roll
Ben no Naishi heard that prayers were to be offered on the twenty-first day of the third month.[1] The chamberlain-gentleman-in-waiting was the manager.[2] She heard that the chancellor[3] was responsible for the Golden Wheel Ritual and the regent for the Buddha's Eye Ritual. While preparations for the arrival of the former Tendai abbot[4] were being made in the Jijūden, she heard the voices calling the roll[5] and realized that the hour had grown late. When she asked, "Why hasn't the roll been called until now?" Someone replied, "The delay was caused by a meeting at the guards' headquarters about a Council of State report."[6] Somehow she found the answer amusing. Ben no Naishi:

ware naranu	Not alone am I to feel
hito mo sa koso wa	that indeed
kikitsurame	it is unusual to hear,
akatsukigata no	near dawn,
takiguchi no koe	the voices of the palace guards.

[Section 42] The Seasonal Reading of the Sutra

On the twenty-third, there was the Seasonal Reading of the Sutra.[1] The Ōmiya major counselor, the Madenokōji major counselor, the commander of the left gate guards, and others[2] went before the sovereign. Seeing His Lordship the regent present His Majesty with little balls attached to a branch of maple,[3] Lady Chūnagon no Suke said, "This reminds me of last year when the former regent presented His Majesty with a boat with ten little balls inside it." She murmured two lines of a poem:

| fune no tomari wa | I long for the boat |
| nao zo koishiki | in the harbor.[4] |

Ben no Naishi added three lines to complete the poem:

minatogawa	At the mouth of the river,
nami no kakari no	waves approach
seto arete	from the raging sea.[5]

Somebody said, "I wish that someone would treat the two verses as one poem and compose a reply." Ben no Naishi:

ika ni shite	In what way
kaketaru nami no	could the rough waves
ato ya sono	have caused
ukitaru fune no	the floating boat
tomarinaruran	to remain in harbor?[6]

[Section 43] The Kazan'in Consultant-Middle Captain's Sorrow

Ben no Naishi was saddened when she heard of the Kazan'in consultant-middle captain's extreme sorrow over the death of his mother,[1] which had occurred while he was accompanying the royal progress to view the flowers at Saionji.[2] She sent this poem to Shōshō no Naishi, who was staying at home:

| kanashisa no | Unaware that the sad |
| saranu wakare o | final parting had taken place, |

shirazu shite	he probably counted
chiyo mo to hana no	on her longevity
kage ya tanomeshi	happily beneath the flowers.[3]

Shōshō no Naishi's reply:

harugoto no	One may count on another view
hana wa mata to mo	of blossoms in springtime
tanominan	yet when will he be able
saranu wakare yo	to see her again
itsu o matsuran	after this final parting?

[Section 44] Sen'ninmon'in Renounces the World

On the twenty-eighth day of the third month, word came that Sen'nin-mon'in,[1] aged nineteen, had cut her hair and renounced the world on the thirteenth anniversary of the death of the Tō'in regent Norizane.[2] It was raining at the time and Ben no Naishi felt sad. She sent this poem to Shō-shō no Naishi:

tachinarenu	Have the sleeves
koromo no ura ya	of the new fisherwoman
harusame ni	perhaps been drenched
hajimete ama no	by the spring rain as she sets out
sode nurasuran	in her robe toward the bay?[3]

Shōshō no Naishi's reply:

tsu no kuni no	Why must she drench
naniwa mo shiranu	her sleeves,
yo no naka ni	the young, innocent
ika de ka ama no	fisherwoman of Naniwa
sode nurasuran	in Tsu Province?[4]

[Section 45] The New Yoshino River

The provisional major counselor came for daytime duty and produced some impromptu entertainment near the railing of His Majesty's Apartment. Kintada, Kinyasu, Sukeyasu, and others were also present. When Lady Dainagon saw kerria blossoms floating on the palace stream (*mikawamizu*), she said, "It seems as if there is a new Yoshino River."[1] Other women in the Upper Hot Water Room said, "What a delightful scene. It would be nice to compose a poem." Keeping it to herself, Ben no Naishi:

yamabuki no	Because it is water
hana no kage miru	in which kerria blossoms
mizu nareba	are reflected,
utsusu yoshino no	perhaps we can say
kawa to iu nari	Yoshino River has moved here.[2]

[Section 46] The Cuckoo at Kitayama

While the chancellor[1] was in Kitayama around the tenth day of the fourth month, some women of the upper ranks were there to hear the cuckoo's first song. Just when women of the upper ranks were able to hear its song, the chancellor successfully composed this poem:

hototogisu	The cuckoo's first song,
tazune ni kitsuru	sought successfully by those
yamazato no	who visit the mountain village,
matsu ni kai aru	can be heard
hatsune o zo kiku	on the pine in the ravine.[2]

Shōshō no Naishi's reply:

hototogisu	The cuckoo
sa koso wa yama no	is in the mountain ravine
kai arite	as expected,
ōmiyabito no	those from the palace
hatsune kikurame	were able to hear its first song[3]

Ben no Naishi:[4]

kumoi yori	Would not
tazunezariseba	the cuckoo's first song
hototogisu	have been to no avail
hatsune mo yama no	if they had not journeyed forth
kai ya nakaran	from the abode of clouds to hear it?[5]

[Section 47] The Royal Progress to the Records Office

On the fourth day of the fifth month, there was a royal progress to the Records Office.[1] The Ōmiya major counselor, the Madenokōji major counselor, the commander of the left gate guards, the commander of the right military guards, the head chamberlain-middle captain Masaie, Kinyasu, Sukeyasu, and Michiyo were directed to stage mock banquet festivities for His Majesty to watch.[2] Commanded to say something interesting and perform a dance, the Ōmiya major counselor said, "I am the head of the palace storehouse Takayuki." (He probably thought that people considered it unusual for him to appear in informal court dress.)³ The Madenokōji major counselor sang "Ah, the Clear Moon," the commander of the left gate guards sang "Ten Thousand Years," and the commander of the right military guards sang, "Will They Come from the Left Gate Guards' Headquarters?"⁴ As usual, their voices sounded beautiful; the songs were all delightful, well worth hearing. Through the assistant commander of the left gate guards, who had accompanied him from his residence, the retired sovereign commanded Ben no Naishi to compose a poem describing his personal feelings. Ben no Naishi:

itowaji yo	No one will be refused,
izukata yori mo	come from everywhere!
tazune toe	If you come,
akanu nagori ni	I will be reluctant
kinaba kaesaji	to let you go.

[Section 48] The Annual Lectures on the Golden Light Sutra in the First Year of Hōji

The annual lectures on the Golden Light Sutra began on the eighteenth and ended on the twenty-second.¹ In the lamplight, Ben no Naishi could barely recognize the Takatsukasa minister of the left, the Kazan'in major counselor Sadamasa, the provisional major counselor Saneo, and others who were in charge of distributing the incense. She could not identify anybody else at all. His Lordship the regent was in the Demon Room.² As she listened to the unfamiliar voices discussing the sutra, it was somehow nostalgic to realize that the final day of the lectures had arrived. Ben no Naishi:

kurabemiru	Should we compare
minori no chie no	their knowledge to a flower,
hana naraba	it must seem that the bud
kyō ya hatsuka ni	is just about to open
tsubomi hiraken	on this day, the twentieth.³

[Section 49] Sending Condolences to the Kazan'in Consultant-Middle Captain

While the Kazan'in consultant-middle captain was in seclusion during his period of mourning, Ben no Naishi composed this poem on behalf of Lady Hyōe no Kami, who said that she wanted it sent attached to a branch from the blossoming orange tree at the Shishinden:

arazaramu	Do not forget the scent
sode no iro ni mo	of the familiar orange blossoms
wasuruna yo	though your sleeves
hanatachibana no	are colored
nareshi nioi o	by the sadness of parting.[1]

The consultant-middle captain's reply was written on thin, dark gray paper attached to a branch of star anise:

inishie ni	Remembering the familiar
nareshi nioi o	fragrance of the past,
omoiidete	if my sleeves touch them,
waga sode fureba	these blossoms, too,
hana ya yatsuren	may fade away.[2]

[Section 50] The Prayers at the Five Altars
The prayers at the Five Altars,[1] which had begun on the seventeenth, were to end on the twenty-third, the last of the seven consecutive days. On the final night, someone, regretting that the prayers would soon be over, said, "Let us make sure we hear the prayers around dawn." They leaned against the railing on the verandah of His Majesty's Apartment until the moon sank toward the west. As Lady Hyōe no Kami, Lady Kōtō no Naishi, Shō-shō no Naishi and Ben no Naishi were engaged in idle chatter, someone said, "What would we do if someone were to unexpectedly drop by while we were wearing these informal night-duty robes?" Then someone else replied, "Why would anyone come here at this time of night?" No sooner had that been said than Lady Azechi appeared and said that she thought she had just seen the tip of someone's hat over the top of the lattice room dividers[2] near the Upper Hot Water Room. She added that she thought she had also heard someone talking. "Let's find out if there really is someone over there," someone said and sent the nyōju, Takatsunji, to investigate. Takatsunji reported that the Sanjō middle counselor Kinchika was there. How unpleasant! Ben no Naishi was upset and regretted that she might have been seen over the top of the lattice room dividers. At that moment, the dawn bell rang, and the sound of the prayers made her feel absolved of the sin of worrying about such a trifling matter. Reverently, she composed this:

nani to naki	For no particular reason,
kokoro no tsumi mo	the sin that blemished
kienuran	my heart has melted away

tsuki mo ariake no	at the bell echoing at dawn
kane no hibiki ni	with the moon still in the sky.

[Section 51] Akichika Renounces the World

On the first day of the sixth month, the Tsuchimikado middle counselor Akichika was scheduled to be on night duty. Possibly because he was also on night duty at the retired sovereign's residence, he arrived around noon, which was especially early. When Lady Kōtō no Naishi was told of his arrival, she said that it was most unusual and greeted him. Ben no Naishi looked through the half-blinds[1] she was sitting behind and saw that he looked extremely handsome in his dazzling, carefully chosen informal robe. Some of the women said that it would be hard to find a person of his caliber in this world. She overheard him telling Lady Kōtō no Naishi in great detail that he had not neglected his duty here and that he must not neglect his duty elsewhere either. He took his leave but Ben no Naishi found herself thinking of him thereafter.

Someone said such things as, "Shall we go in the Spacious Hall to peep at Akichika since he is going out of the Palace Guards Office?" He stood for quite a long time in the Courtiers' Hall looking at the duty board,[2] the attendance register,[3] and the like. He also spoke to a female official from the Facilities Office[4] and even after he signed his name in the attendance register, still he did not leave. He stood near the sounding boards[5] looking as if each detail his eyes rested upon was a source of fond memories. Someone said, "Why should such a busy man, who diligently served the retired sovereign and who only rarely came to serve His Majesty, be acting this way. It is strange." The next day when Ben no Naishi asked about Akichika, someone said, "He renounced the world at Ryōzen[6] at dawn this morning." She felt as if she were hearing a story from the distant past. She felt her sadness was limitless and composed this:

somukiete	I can indeed imagine him
kokoro mo kaze mo	on the precipitous mountain path
suzushisa no	walking in the cool wind,
iwa no kakeji o	his mind refreshed,
omoi koso yare	after renouncing the world.

[Section 52] Thinking of Akichika

On the eighth, Ben no Naishi remembered that, had Akichika not renounced the world, he would have been here today for daytime duty.[1] It was sad to think he was probably somewhere on the road to Kumano.[2] She whispered this poem to Lady Dainagon:

tabigoromo	I wonder how many days
tachite iku hi ni	it has been since he left
narinuran	in his travel robes;
aramashikaba to	it is sad today to speculate
kyō zo kanashiki	on how things might have been.

When the controller Tokitsugu was talking to them about the Repast in the Presence of a *Kami*[3] ceremony in the Table Room, he said, "It is sad indeed about the Tsuchimikado middle counselor. No one possessing sensibility failed to praise him. Those who are not aware of life's evanescence are like beasts in the guise of human beings." Greatly saddened, Ben no Naishi composed this poem:

kaku kikeba	When I hear this
sasuga mi no ke mo	a chill runs through my body,
tatsu mono o	even though I am
tori ni otoranu	as lacking in sensitivity
kokoro naredomo	as a bird.[4]

[Section 53] The Seiryōden Moon

On the fifteenth day of the seventh month, the moon was especially pleasant. Sitting near the Curtain Dais while His Majesty's meal was being served, he[1] looked out through the open lattice shutters and called for a poem on the appearance of the moon at the Seiryōden. Ben no Naishi composed this because the moon was exceptionally clear: (Tameuji was in charge of serving His Majesty.)[2]

koyoi mada	Although this is still
hajime no aki no	only the midpoint
nakaba tote	of the first autumn month,
katsugatsu tsuki no	already we have
kage zo michinuru	a brilliant moon.

[Section 54] The Appointment Ceremony

On the sixteenth, there was an appointment ceremony.[1] His Lordship the regent arrived; Tsunetoshi, Mitsukuni, and some others also came. Tsunetoshi told the female courtiers to wait in the Table Room for the announcement to His Majesty.[2] The female courtiers gazed at the moon, saying such things as, "When one is waiting for something, it seems to take forever. In the past, we have often stayed up all night to see the moon without feeling impatient. But now I feel impatient because an official function is involved." Ben no Naishi:

kore mo mata	This, too,
matsu to shi nareba	is a kind of waiting:
aki no yo no	I gaze at the autumn moon
fukenu saki ni to	thinking, let it happen
tsuki o miru kana	"before the night deepens."[3]

She had a *nyōju* take the poem to Shōshō no Naishi, who was in the Upper Hot Water Room. Shōshō no Naishi's reply:

kokoro ni mo	Who are you waiting for,
arade koyoi no	I wonder,
tsuki o mite	as you gaze at the moon,
fukenu saki ni to	thinking,
tare o matsuran	"before the night deepens"?

[Section 55] Incense from the Consort
On the first of the eighth month, someone brought over some wonderfully fragrant incense from the Consort's Apartment. Ben no Naishi:

kyō wa mata	Today in particular
soradakimono no	"imperceptible incense"[1]
na o kaete	changes its name
tanomeba fukaki	into deep fragrance
nioi to zo naru	as we deepen our trust in her.[2]

[Section 56] The Bush-Clover at the Bush-Clover Door
The Ben no Naishi who served the retired sovereign wrote Kōtō no Naishi a letter which asked, "Has the bush-clover at the Bush-Clover Door bloomed?" Ben no Naishi broke a branch off and composed a reply for Kōtō no Naishi:

aki o hete	Would that you might see
narekoshi niwa no	what the heart desires,
hagi no e ni	branches of bush-clover
tomeshi kokoro no	blossoming in the familiar
iro o misebaya	autumn garden.[1]

The reply of the retired sovereign's Ben no Naishi:

omoiyaru	The dewdrops
hagi no furue ni	on the old bush-clover branch
oku tsuyu wa	are the tears of longing

| moto mishi hito no | from one who saw it |
| namida narikeri | long ago in the past. |

[Section 57] The Ceremony Honoring Confucius and His Ten Disciples

There was a ceremony honoring Confucius and his ten disciples on the eleventh.[1] Aritsugu announced the proceedings to His Majesty in the Dining Room.[2] Someone said, "I would have liked to watch eminent scholars amuse themselves by composing Chinese poetry. I wonder why they could not have performed the ceremony in the Courtiers' Hall or some other nearby place? If they had, then we could have gone to hear the lectures." Ben no Naishi:

michi shi araba	If there were a path
tazune zo kikan	would we have journeyed
shikishima ya	there to listen?
yamato ni wa aranu	Leaves of Chinese words
kara no koto no ha	that are not of Yamato.[3]

[Section 58] The Retired Sovereign's Linked Verse

On the night of the fifteenth day of the eighth month, the retired sovereign held a poetry gathering at the Tokiwai Palace.[1] The Ōmiya major counselor, the Madenokōji major counselor, the Fujiwara major counselor Tamcic, the provisional major counselor Sanco, the commander of the right gate guards Michinari, the Yoshida middle counselor Tametsune, Tameuji, Tamenori, and lesser courtiers were present.[2] The Kazan'in major counselor Sadamasa arrived a bit late, just as the poems were being read aloud.[3] It was a pity that the moon was obscured by clouds.

The gathering took place in an atmosphere of sadness because Mikushigedono had died that morning around dawn.[4] Linked verses were composed, and Ben no Naishi heard the retired sovereign murmur part of an old poem, "Why may I never see her again?"[5] Moved, Ben no Naishi composed this poem:

aki no yo no	If the floating clouds clear away,
ukigumo haruru	we could see the moon again
tsuki wa aredo	on this autumn night,
mata minu kage o	but who might it be who mourns
tare shinoburan	an image never to be seen again?[6]

[Section 59] The Horse-Leading Ceremony

There was a Horse-Leading Ceremony on the sixteenth.[1] (The presiding official was the Nijō middle counselor Sukesue.)[2] The moon was especially bright and pleasant tonight. The controller Akitomo said, "I am sorry it was cloudy on the fifteenth, but tonight's moon is brilliant. What do you female courtiers say to this?"[3] Amused that he should go around apologizing as though he had been to blame for last night's clouds, Ben no Naishi composed this:[4]

sumimasaru	I wonder why
koyoi no tsuki no	the moon tonight
ikanareba	is so exceedingly clear,
nakaba yori ke ni	more brilliant than even
sayakekaruran	the brightest autumn moon.

Middle captain Kinyasu was to have overseen the distribution of the remaining horses, but he sent word that he would be unable to serve because he had suddenly had to go into mourning for Mikushigedono.[5] Upon hearing a question about his replacement, Ben no Naishi composed this poem:[6]

kumoi yori	Who will act as the messenger
konata kanata e	to lead the horses to be presented
hikiwake no	here and there
tsukai wa tare zo	at the abode of clouds,
kirihara no koma	those horses of the misty field?[7]

[Section 60] Eternal Moonlight
On a bright moonlit evening, the master of the consort's household Takachika[1] sent a poem written on a slat of a cypress fan to a number of female courtiers who were amusing themselves in the Seiryōden eaves-extension chamber. Takachika:

yorozuyo mo	Tonight may we pledge
sumubeki tsuki no	that somehow
kage zo to wa	the light of the clear moon
ikani ka koyoi	will dwell with us indeed
chigiri okuran	for myriad years.[2]

Shōshō no Naishi's reply:

chigiri arite	There is a pledge.
sumubeki tsuki no	Even the light of the clear moon
kage made mo	in the sky is a sign indeed

sora ni zo shiruki	that it will endure
aki no yorozuyo	for myriad autumns.[3]

Ben no Naishi:

yorozuyo to	A pledge of myriad years
chigiri okite mo	is still not enough
amari ari	for one who lives
tsuki ni tomonau	above the clouds
kumo no uebito	with the moon.

[Section 61] Time to Stay Awake
The provisional major counselor had arrived for night duty and was amusing himself by the Bush-Clover Door when he was asked the time by His Lordship the regent. He replied, "The Hour of the Boar for staying awake."[1] But since the female courtiers were already asleep, Ben no Naishi said to herself that it was later than that:

tadaima wa	Even though someone
okite i zo to wa	seems to have said,
iumeredo	now is the time to stay awake,
koromo katashiki	each spread a robe
tare mo nenanan	to sleep on.[2]

[Section 62] Old Bush-Clover Plants
While Ben no Naishi was going toward the Consort's Apartment as a messenger, she was delighted to see the bush-clover in full bloom through the chinks of the slatted fence near the Bush-Clover Door.[1] There was mist rising in the sky and the plaintive cries of wild geese could be heard. Ben no Naishi:

yoyo ni saku	Blooming for generations,
furue no hagi no	branches of the bush-clover
moto nareba	flower.
kiri tachiwatari	Wild geese cry as they cross
kari mo nakunari	the rising mist.[2]

[Section 63] Kōtō no Naishi's *Biwa*
Kōtō no Naishi spent the entire night playing her *biwa* in the Edge Apartment.[1] Lady Azechi no Sanmi said, "It would be interesting to imagine what she has been thinking of during the night." Ben no Naishi:

amasosogi	The light of the half-moon
sode ni ya tsuyu no	seems to be losing its brightness.
kakaruran	Can it be that the player's sleeves
nakaba no tsuki no	have been drenched by rain
kage zo fukeyuku	dripping from the eaves?[2]

[Section 64] The Moon in the Abode of Clouds

The regent's Resignation Request Ceremony[1] took place on the fourteenth day of the ninth month. After it was over, His Lordship arrived very late at night and said, "Since the moon is so pleasant, I would like to invite some women of the upper ranks to go moon-viewing." They viewed the moon from the Shishinden, the fishing pavilion and other places. His Lordship said, "A moonlit night like tonight reminds me of the reigns of the sovereigns Murakami and Ichijō,[2] when young senior nobles and courtiers sang popular songs[3] and competed at putting sutras to music. It is a pity that there's no one around to sing for us. Who is on duty tonight?" It was a shame that they had let the Madenokōji major counselor leave a moment ago without asking him to stay. Amusingly, His Lordship summoned the sixth-rank chamberlain Sukeyoshi and instructed him in the etiquette of moon-viewing.

When His Lordship went to his retiring room as dawn was breaking, Lady Hyōe no Kami said, "It would be nice to express our sentiments on parting from him." Ben no Naishi:

iza to iite	Had you not invited us,
sasowazariseba	saying, "Come along,"
hisakata no	which of us
kumoi no tsuki o	would have seen
tare ka nagamen	the moon in the abode of clouds?[4]

[Section 65] Love Separated by the River

During the same month, the Madenokōji major counselor invited Lady Azechi no Suke, Lady Chūnagon no Suke, and others to spend the night strolling on the other side of the Kamo River. When Lady Azechi no Sanmi heard of the excursion after their return, she said to Ben no Naishi, "That was most amusing. Compose a poem on the topic 'Love Separated by the River.'" Ben no Naishi:

sode nurasu	Dwelling on the other side
kawa yori ochi ni	of the sleeve-drenching river,
sumu tsuki no	must I continue to yearn

| kage ni mo hito o | for the person in the light |
| koi ya wataran | of the clear moon?[1] |

[Section 66] Long Autumn Nights

Since nights in autumn are long with plenty of leisure time, after His Majesty had retired one night, Lady Dainagon, Lady Azechi no Suke, Lady Chūnagon no Suke, Shōshō no Naishi, and Ben no Naishi amused themselves by composing linked verse. Lady Kōtō no Naishi refused to join them, and they heard her playing the *koto* in her Edge Apartment. Lady Azechi no Suke said, "I would like to reproach her." Ben no Naishi:

waka no ura ni	The waves are distressed
uramuru nami mo	at Waka Bay:
aru mono o	please blow
matsu no arashi yo	with a sympathetic heart,
kokoro shite fuke	O storm wind in the pines.[1]

[Section 67] Hidden Love

The master of the consort's household gave this poem to the *nyōju*, Takatsunji,[1] saying, "I want to tell you this. What do you say?"

omoisomuru	I have not yet shown
kokoro no iro zo	the colors
mada misenu	steeped in my heart.
yosome bakari ni	The years pass as I look
toshi wa henuredo	only from afar.[2]

Ben no Naishi composed a reply on her behalf:

hito shirenu	Loving someone only
yosome bakari wa	from afar is to no avail:
kai mo nashi	I would like
mienu kokoro no	to see the colors
iro o shirabaya	hidden in your heart.

[Section 68] Unkempt Hair

Among the autumn plants growing in the courtyard of His Majesty's Apartment, there was an adorable little plant called *kashirakezurazu*[1] growing in the spaces between the rocks. When the provisional major counselor saw it, he said that the plant's name had an unkempt feel to it. People thought his remark amusing. Ben no Naishi:

midaretaru	The tangled locks
sono na bakari no	are black hair
kurokami ni	in name alone.
tsuge no ogushi mo	How am I to take
ikaga torubeki	boxwood comb in hand?[2]

[Section 69] Potted Chrysanthemums

On a moonlit night, the commander of the left gate guards Sanefuji picked one of the attractive chrysanthemums growing in the same courtyard[1] and brought it in for the monarch. His Lordship[2] said, "Go pick another and bring it here." Ben no Naishi:

tsukikage ni	Saying a regretful farewell
oriken hito no	to the one who plucked
nagori tote	the flower in the moonlight,
musubi na tome so	dew-laden white chrysanthemum
kiku no shiratsuyu	do not obstruct my promise.

At about the same time, the Ōmiya major counselor, the Madenokōji major counselor, and the commander of the left gate guards presented some extraordinarily beautiful chrysanthemums, which were then planted in the courtyard. His Lordship said, "Pick any branch you find the most beautiful and bring it here." Ben no Naishi:

izure to ka	How am I to choose
wakite mo oran	the one to pluck from among
iroiro no	the white chrysanthemums
hito no kokoro mo	to express the sincerity
shiragiku no hana	of the donor's heart?

[Section 70] The Gosechi Festival

The Gosechi Festival began on the sixteenth.[1] The moon was especially bright and delightful. Peeping out of the Two-Bay Room to get a glimpse of the Curtain-Dais Rehearsal, Ben no Naishi could recognize no one other than His Lordship Kanetsune wearing the thick-hemmed willow combination,[2] the palace minister Sanemoto in the red plum combination,[3] and the Ōmiya major counselor in the pine combination.[4]

On the Day of the Tiger, the moon was very bright. His Lordship the regent came for the royal progress to the Gosechidokoro.[5] While the Taka-tsukasa minister of the left was accompanying His Lordship to the Go-sechidokoro, someone gave him a comb, saying, "This is for you." Words cannot adequately describe the elegance with which he let the comb fall from his sleeve after making a show of putting it in his breast.[6] Ben no Naishi:

shimo kōru	Although it is not a dewdrop
tsuyu no tama ni mo	freezing into frost,
aranaku ni	it does not linger
sode ni tamaranu	on the sleeve,
yowa no sashigushi	the midnight comb.

His Lordship presented his protégés for the Royal Viewing of the Girl Attendants.[7] The girls looked extraordinary. One of them, who had served in His Lordship's household for quite some time, was an adorably plump child. Another was slender and pensive, quite patrician in appearance. Each was delightful in her own way. It was amusing that the courtiers were adjusting the sleeves and trailing robes of the girl attendants. Ben no Naishi:

akazu miru	Are not the hearts of those
otome no sode no	who dwell above the clouds
tsukikage ni	captivated by the moonlit sleeves
kokoro ya tomaru	of the maidens
kumo no uebito	as they gaze still unsatisfied?

[Section 71] The Banquet
The Banquet[1] was held on the eighteenth. The moon was very bright as Ben no Naishi proceeded toward the stairway to summon the courtiers.[2] She told Lady Chūnagon no Suke that it would be hard to forget the beauty of the moonlight on the royal stairway. Ben no Naishi (wearing the red plum under snow combination[3] with her hair formally dressed):

yuki no shita	Even the fragrance
ume no nioi mo	of the red plum under snow
sode saete	on my sleeves seems frozen,
susumu mihashi ni	as I gazed at the moon
tsuki o mishi kana	on the royal stairway.

Having heard that the provisional middle counselor was to present one of the Gosechi dancers,[4] she thought that she would like to ask him for some of the combs. She sent this poem to him.

omoiyare	Please be sympathetic:
tare ka wa misen	nobody will show me

kokonoe ya	the midnight combs
toyonoakari no	from the Flushed Faces Banquet
yowa no okigushi	at the Nine-fold Palace.

The major counselor's reply:[5]

tarekomete	Secluded at home,
toyonoakari mo	I did not go to
shirazariki	the Flushed Faces Banquet.
kimi koso miseme	It is you who should show me
yowa no sashigushi	the midnight combs.

She felt bad about having sent the poem asking for the combs, unaware that he had been ill. Ben no Naishi:

tarekomeshi	It has grown late for the moon
koro tomo shiranu	of the Flushed Faces,
okotari ni	as I let time slip by
toyonoakari no	unaware that you were
tsuki wa fukeniki	at home in seclusion.

[Section 72] The Ninety Clouds

On the night of the Royal Inspection of Horses for the Kamo Special Festival, the Ōmiya major counselor was in attendance. When he noticed the decorative "ninety clouds" [*kujū kumo*] shelf in His Majesty's Apartment, he laughed and said, "Somebody is supposed to have written a 'hidden topic' poem about that shelf. The topic was concealed in the line, 'The topic is too hard; I cannot think of anything witty [*Naniwa uku shūku moeji*]' or some such."[1] Then he said, "Why not use 'ninety clouds' as the topic for a 'broken stanza'?"[2] Ben no Naishi immediately wrote a poem and put it down near the Curtain-Dais. "That was fast! I've got myself into a pretty fix, just like a frog being swallowed by a snake," he said. His poem:

*ku*ruru yo wa	As the night deepens,
*shi*no no hagusa no	dew and rain drip down
*u*waba made	and threaten to break
*ku*dakuru tsuyu no	even the upper leaves
*mo*ru shigure kana	of the bamboo grass.

Shōshō no Naishi's poem:

*ku*mo no ue ya	Is it only here,
*shi*ruki mikaki no	above the clouds,
*u*chi ni nomi	only within this familiar fence,
*ku*ruru yosugara	that people stay on guard
*mo*ru ya tonomori	all through the night?

Ben no Naishi:

*ku*retake no	On a night when frost
*shi*mo oku yowa no	covers the black bamboo,
*u*wakaze ni	wind blows through the upper
*ku*moranu tsuki no	branches revealing glimpses
*mo*ru o miru kana	of the cloudless moon.

[Section 73] How Splendid the Waters!

When the promotions[1] took place, Ben no Naishi heard some royal guardsmen go by singing lines like "Nostalgic thoughts"[2] and otherwise showing their regret at leaving their old posts. Then she heard someone singing, "How splendid the waters!"[3]

As she was wondering about the sudden change, she learned that Nakayasu was rejoicing because he had become the Ichirō.[4] How time flies! Amused, Ben no Naishi composed this poem:

shiboritsuru	In place of sleeves
sode no nagori o	drenched by memories,
hikikaete	the waters
tsutsumu amari ni	of a roaring cascade,
naru taki no mizu	too abundant to be contained!

[Section 74] The Royal Progress to the Records Office

There was a Royal Progress to the Records Office on the twenty-fourth.[1] The Madenokōji major counselor, the commander of the left gate guards Sanefuji, the commander of the right gate guards Michinari, the commander of the right military guards Arisuke, the head chamberlain-middle captain Masaie, the head chamberlain-controller Akitomo, and others came. As usual, there were all sorts of musical entertainment, when someone asked, "What did you find especially pleasant?" Shōshō no Naishi answered, "The sound of the commander of the left gate guards' *koto* was especially superior." Her poem:

kashiwagi no	O god who is said
hamori to ieru	to guard oak leaves,[2]

kami mo kike	ask the name of one
sono koto no ne ni	who is not drawn
kokoro hikazuba	by the sound of the *koto*?

"The singing of the mock Gosechi was by far the best," said Ben no Naishi:

koto no ne ni	The sound of the wind
kokoro wa hikazu	blowing through the oak leaves
kashiwagi no	pierces my being;
ha ni fuku kaze no	I am not drawn
koe zo mi ni shimu	by the sound of the *koto*.[3]

The provisional major counselor came late. Arriving after His Majesty had gone to bed, he stood near the lattice-shutter door, singing again and again, "Of pines on a hill where [the moon] glimmers [at dusk]."[4] His singing lingered in Ben no Naishi's ears and she wondered if there were anyone there to acknowledge his feelings. Ben no Naishi:

yūzukuyo	I cannot know
sashite shirubeki	who it is
kata zo naki	whose indifference toward you
tsurenaki matsu ni	is as unchanging
somuru kokoro o	as the color of the pine trees.

Someone said that they heard the sound of the bell announcing the change to late night,[5] and so His Majesty returned to the palace. Although almost everyone had gone home, a few were in attendance since there was a rumor of a fire nearby. The provisional major counselor, accompanied by some female courtiers, amused himself on the side of the building that faced the Shishinden. The frost, shining white and cold on the stairs leading to the left gate guards' headquarters,[6] was most interesting. Ben no Naishi:

okimayou	It is a night cold enough
shimo mo sanagara	for abundant frost.
sayuru yo ni	I wonder who was unable
tare kechikanuru	to extinguish the fire
honoho naruran	that started the blaze nearby.

[Section 75] In Mourning for Mother

While secluded at home in mourning for her mother in the second year of Hōji [1248], Ben no Naishi thought of the events surrounding the Iwashimizu Special Festival[1] and composed this poem on the twentieth:

hikage sasu	Unaware of the season,
haru no kazashi no	I am indeed saddened
iroiro mo	not being able to see
ori shiranu mi no	the sundry decorations
hodo zo kanashiki	of sun-drenched spring.[2]

At about this time, she received an unlined summer robe.[3] Ben no Naishi:

kakaru mi wa	To one living thus
toki shimo wakanu	heedless of the season,
koromode ni	these sleeves announce
kyō koso natsu no	that indeed today
tatsu to shirinure	is the beginning of summer![4]

[Section 76] The Buddha's Names Ceremony

It was pleasant that there was a clear moon on the night of the twenty-ninth of the twelfth month when the Buddha's Names Ceremony was performed.[1] As usual, the chamberlains of the fifth and sixth ranks assembled in the Demon Room to determine the duty allotments.[2] Mototomo and Kinyasu, the head chamberlain-middle captains of the left and right, did not come. Tsunetoshi, Munemasa, Mitsukuni, and others . . . [3] Ben no Naishi heard that Munemasa and some others were in charge of the Spirit-Pacifying Festival.[4] Someone said, "In the past, there was a *kosode* contest on this night."[5] The presiding official was Morotsugu, the provisional master of the consort's household. Ben no Naishi thought that the voices chanting the unfamiliar names of the Buddhas and the speaker's own names truly had the power to expunge sins. Ben no Naishi:

makoto ni wa	Those who dwell
tare mo hotoke no	above the clouds
kazu nare ya	chanting their names in unison
nanori tsuzukuru	with the Buddhas' names
kumo no uebito	are indeed one with the Buddhas.

[Section 77] Obeisance to the Four Directions
On the first day of the first month of the third year of Hōji [1249], the Obeisance to the Four Directions took place during the Hour of the Tiger.[1] Lady Azechi no Sanmi, Lady Chūnagon no Suke, and Lady Kōtō no Naishi accompanied His Majesty to the Seiryōden. Munemasa was in charge. Ben no Naishi found the signs of budding spring truly auspicious. Ben no Naishi:

kyō ni naru   How awe-inspiring
toki o ba haru no   the customary prayers,
hajime tote   when this hour ushers in
inorinaretaru   the day that marks
kata mo kashikoshi   the beginning of a new year!

[Section 78] Full Moon Gruel Sticks
Since the moon was interesting on the fifteenth day of the first month, Lady Chūnagon no Suke invited some people to view the moon over the South Hall. When they walked out of the Gekka Gate,[1] they spotted a man wearing informal attire[2] coming toward them from the Aburanokōji Gate.[3] Someone asked, "It is very late, I wonder who it could be? Is it the master of the dowager's household?"[4] After dashing into a conveniently located woman's room, someone verified that it was the provisional major counselor Saneo. It was a rare opportunity. While Lady Hyōe no Kami was talking to him in the Table Room, someone said, "Today is the day for hitting people.[5] How can we ambush him?" Someone else said, "We must hit him on his way out. Since we will not know which way he will leave, we must post someone at each exit." Mashimizu and Sumutsuru[6] stood guard at the Kunming Lake Partition.[7] Lady Kōtō no Naishi and Lady Mino waited in a room below the Upper Hot Water Room.[8] Chūnagon no Suke and Lady Hyōe no Kami[9] stood at the foot of the half-blinds, and Shōshō, Ben, and some others peeped out from behind the Partition of the Annual Ceremonies.[10] But even when it was almost dawn, he still had not come out.

Feeling very misused, they had lesser captain Sukeyasu check discreetly to see where he was. Sukeyasu said that he was standing in the small courtyard south of the Courtiers' Hall gazing at the moon. Lady Hyōe no Kami put out the lights in the His Majesty's Daytime Chamber,[11] looked through the arched window, and saw him standing with his back carefully to the wall so that he could not be hit. It was most aggravating of him. Dawn arrived while they were discussing whether they should write a note of some kind attached to a stick and thrust it out through the arched window, or whether they should try some other such thing. Nothing seemed to go right. Finally, to their intense irritation, they learned that he was already leaving through the Aburanokōji Gate. They sent someone after him with a poem on thin white paper inserted in a cleft at the end of a stick. Shōshō no Naishi:

uchiwabinu	What wretchedness!
kokoro kurabe no	It is sad to see you go
tsue nareba	at the end of a night
tsuki mide akasu	spent waiting in vain to use
na koso oshikere	our sticks in a game of wits.[12]

The major counselor's reply:

uchiwaburu	Unaware of hearts
kokoro mo shirade	bent
ariake no	on wretchedness,
tsuki no tayori ni	I left relying
idenikeru kana	on the dawn moon.[13]

Then the next day around sundown, they received a note from him, bearing the address, "To those who got cold feet." When Lady Hyōe no Kami, Lady Kōtō no Naishi, and others opened it in the Hand-Washing Room,[14] they saw the following poems:

uchiwabite	Disappointed,
nenikeru yowa no	you fell fast asleep.
kane no ne ni	I wonder if you gazed at the moon
odorokasarete	awakened by the sound
tsuki ya nagameshi	of the midnight bell.

machikaneshi	Tired of waiting,
mi wa natsumushi no	like fireflies
tomoshi kechi	with the lights out,
itazuragoto ni	you must have been chagrined
mono omoiken	at your failed mischief![15]

onhagi no	I will not forget
futoki hosoki mo	the moonlit scene
tachisoite	last night when legs
tsuki ni wasurenu	both thick and thin
yowa no omokage	sought to strike me.

Ben no Naishi's replies:

uchihaete	What can you mean
nuru to wa nani zo	by fell asleep?
ariake no	You, who discarded the chance
tsuki o misuteshi	to see the dawn moon,
kokoro narai ka	are quite mistaken!

isa shirazu	I do not know
tare natsumushi no	who extinguished the firefly lights;
tomoshi kechi	do you not think it was perhaps
take no ha kaze ya	the wind blowing
fuki mo shitsuran	through the bamboo leaves?

wasurezu yo	Your legs, too, must have hurt,
tsuki no omokage	from standing so long.
tachisoite	I can never forget the sight
sono onhagi mo	of you standing
kurushikariken	in the moonlight that night.[16]

[Section 79] The Early Red Plum

When His Lordship[1] heard that there was a red plum tree at Ben no Naishi's home that blossomed exceptionally early in the spring, he said, "Break off a branch and present it to His Majesty." She obeyed the command and attached a poem by Jakusai[2] to a branch in full bloom:

kumoi made	It is awe-inspiring indeed
ito mo kashikoku	that the fence-bound plum
niou kana	at my home
kakinegakure no	sends its fragrance
yado no umegae	even to the abode of clouds.

She put the branch in a vase and placed it in front of the Bush-Clover Door with the various replies tied onto it.

[Former] chancellor Saneuji:

kumoi made	Since the plum blossoms'
nioi kinureba	fragrance permeates
ume no hana	even the abode of clouds,
kakinegakure mo	they are fence-bound
na nomi narikeri	in name alone.

Shijō major counselor Takachika:

kakine yori	The flowers
kumoi ni niou	show their pleasure
ureshisa o	in being summoned
iro ni idete mo	to the abode of clouds
hana zo misekeru	by blooming in splendid fashion.

Reizei major counselor Kinsuke:

sakisomuru	The early blossoming
kakinegakure no	fence-bound flowers
ume no hana	of the plum
kimi ga yachiyo no	were plucked to serve as decorations[3]
kazashi ni zo oru	celebrating His Majesty's eternal reign.

Madenokōji major counselor Kinmoto:

kimi ga yo ni	How splendid that even
kakinegakure mo	the fence-bound early plum blossoms
arawarete	should come into prominence
amaneku niou	and diffuse their fragrance abroad
ume no hatsuhana	in His Majesty's reign!

Provisional major counselor Saneo:

kumoi made	In the awe-inspiring
kakine no ume wa	spring sunlight,[4]
nioikeri	the plum beside the fence
ito mo kashikoki	sends its fragrance
haru no hikari ni	even to the abode of clouds.

Ben no Naishi was commanded to add her reply:

kumoi nite	The beauty of the plum blossoms
mireba iro koso	that grew beside the fence
masarikere	at my home
ueshi kakine no	seems to be heightened
yado no umegae	when viewed in the abode of clouds.

[Section 80] A Small Book of Thin White Paper
The provisional major counselor [Saneo] brought over a small book of thin
white paper that had been presented to His Majesty by Lady Dainagon no
Nii, daughter of the Koga chancellor.[1] It contained a group of interesting
love poems written in an exquisite hand. When Shōshō no Naishi saw it,
she composed this poem:

koi su chō	Is she inviting us
na o nagashitaru	to drench our sleeves
mizukuki no	as we look
ato o mitsutsu mo	at the poems
sode nurase to ya	in which they revealed their love?[2]

Ben no Naishi:

na o nagasu	Many people have left records
sono mizukuki no	commemorating their love,
ato ni shimo	but I, alas, sad to say,
koi chō koto o	have yet to experience
minu zo kanashiki	any such emotion.[3]

[Section 81] The Burning of the Kan'in Palace
Late at night on the first day of the second month [of 1249], Ben no Naishi
went from the Table Room to fasten the cloth partition at the entrance to
the Demon Room, but the lights looked dim, and she sensed something
unusual. When she went through the Dining Room to His Majesty's
Apartment, she found Lady Kunaikyō no Suke, Lady Hyōe no Kami, Lady
Kōtō no Naishi, and others in attendance.[1] His Majesty, who had not yet
retired for the night, was in the middle of writing practice. He commanded
Ben no Naishi to write an interesting Chinese poem for him, so she wrote
down the line, "Reeds of the sandbar, where a lone ship dreams of home,"
and added this poem nearby:

mi hitotsu no	Has the lone traveler
uree ya nami ni	succumbed
shizumuran	to waves of loneliness?
ashi no karine no	Dreams must be fleeting
yume mo hakanashi	when one sleeps among the reeds.

While someone said, "Chinese autumn poems are all most interest-
ing," middle captain Kintada came on duty looking very flustered. He said,
"It's terrible. A fire has been reported in the Royal Dowager's

Apartment."[2] She was astounded; dumb struck. She could not believe it was happening. Removing the willow combination robes and a lined Chinese jacket of golden yellow[3] she had been wearing, she went to her apartment wearing just her divided skirt and pounded on the door. Hurriedly she changed into the plum combination robes that had been hanging in her apartment and put on a Chinese jacket of a maroon-plum color.[4] When she left her room, Lady Kōtō no Naishi was already in the Royal Bedchamber taking out the Sacred Sword.[5] She went to the Aburanokōji Gate. Lady Nii cradled His Majesty in her arms and went out to the same gate with Lady Chūnagon no Suke.[6]

Shōshō no Naishi had been lying down to rest after having been dispatched to serve as the messenger to Ōharano, but she was aroused by the sound of Ben no Naishi pounding on the door. After Ben no Naishi informed Shōshō no Naishi of the fire, Ben no Naishi hurried to His Majesty, only to find his apartments deserted and full of smoke. As she wandered about wondering if everyone had gone off somewhere with him, she heard a voice calling from a bay in the Royal Bedchamber. She approached cautiously, wondering if it were a ghost, and saw someone wearing a light Chinese jacket over triple-layered robes of an indiscernible color. Despite the confusion, this person calmly covered her face and her long hair hung neatly to the hem of her robes. It was Lady Senji, holding the Guardian Sword,[7] saying, "Ask Lady Azechi no Sanmi where I should take the sword." Ben no Naishi answered, "I know neither where to take it nor what to do."

Ben no Naishi went out the double doors[8] toward Aburanokōji Street and saw crowds of people milling about. When she said, "Lady Senji has the Guardian Sword," Lady Hyōe no Kami offered to guide Lady Senji. His Majesty, the royal dowager,[9] Lady Chūnagon no Suke, and Lady Kunaikyō no Suke got into the provisional major counselor's carriage, which was the first to arrive. Outside the gate, His Majesty was transferred to a palanquin. Although the royal dowager said that she would use the Reizei major counselor's back to get into the palanquin, somehow she was extremely calm as she climbed aboard. The provisional major counselor, the Madenokōji major counselor, the Reizei major counselor, and others worked admirably and quickly in the midst of all the confusion.

After having taken care to see that the silk curtains of the palanquin were properly in place, Lady Chūnagon no Suke climbed aboard. Later she told them that the royal dowager did not let ordinary people see her even at night.

Kōtō no Naishi and Ben no Naishi had ascended into Lady Nii's carriage carrying the Sacred Sword. "The Sacred Sword is not inside the palanquin. Did anyone bring it out?" people clamored. Someone said it had

been brought, and someone else said, "Has anyone seen it?" "Kōtō no Nai-
shi and Ben must have brought it out," Lady Hyōe no Kami said. Then the
men galloped around on horseback, asking, "Which carriage are Kōtō and
Ben in? Which one is it?"

Ben no Naishi was wondering what on earth was going on, when she
heard someone say, "Do you have the Sacred Sword? Have you got it? We
have asked about it until we are hoarse. Somebody said you have it. Is that
right?" No wonder they were worried.

It was Noritoki who brought out Genjō.[10]

The mounted major counselors stood guard at the gate with bow and
arrows at the ready; it was unbelievable, quite like a dream. When some
people said that there were repeated fires even in the august reigns of Engi
and Tenryaku,[11] Ben no Naishi composed this poem.

yakenu tomo	Although the palace
mata koso tateme	has burned down,
miyabashira	let us rebuild it once again.
yoshi ya keburi no	Brace up, do not lament
ato mo nagekaji	in the lingering smoke.

[Section 82] The Tominokōji Palace

His Majesty took up residence at the Tominokōji Palace.[1] On a misty
moonlit night around the time when the red plum was blooming near the
edge of the Spacious Hall,[2] someone[3] sent the following poem, written on
white tissue paper attached to a blossoming sprig:

iro mo ka mo	O blossoms of the plum,
kasanete nioe	put forth your color
ume no hana	and fragrance in manifold layers
kokonoe ni naru	as symbols that your home
yado no shirushi ni	has become the Nine-fold Palace.[4]

Told that the reply was to go to the retired sovereign's residence, Ben no
Naishi composed this poem:

iro mo ka mo	The color and fragrance
sa koso kasanete	will indeed be of manifold layers,
niourame	as the abode of the plum
kokonoe ni naru	becomes the home
yado no umegae	of the Nine-fold Palace.

[Section 83] The Familiar Plum

Lady Kōtō no Naishi's apartment[1] had formerly been occupied by someone called Lady Saishō when it was the residence of the retired consort.[2] When that person sent a letter asking if the plums were in bloom, Ben no Naishi composed a reply for Kōtō no Naishi:

iro mo ka mo	The flowers of the plum
nareshi hito o ya	probably longs
shinoburan	to show their blossoms
misebaya ume no	to someone familiar
hana no sakari o	with both its color and fragrance.

The provisional major counselor composed a reply for Lady Saishō:[3]

nagamebaya	How I long to gaze at them!
narekoshi ume no	Probably the fragrance
hana no ka mo	of the familiar plum blossoms
ima kokonoe ni	has been enhanced now that its abode
iro wa souran	has become the Nine-fold Palace.

When the chancellor[4] heard about these poems, he said, "It was inauspicious to use the same phrase found in the splendid poem 'iro mo ka mo.'[5] Furthermore, the reply should not have used a variant, 'ima kokonoe' of the superior phrase 'kokonoe ni naru,' which was a most fitting line. Both of these poems are inappropriate."

When Ben no Naishi heard his criticism, rather than being embarrassed, she was amused. Ben no Naishi:

nioi naki	Colors of the plum blossoms
iro o kasanete	without any fragrance
ume no hana	clustered in manifold layers—
tsuraku mo hito ni	I was criticized
togamerarenuru	with undisguised might.

[Section 84] The Karahashi Major Counselor

The twenty-seventh day [of the second month of 1249] was the Seven Shrines Offering.[1] Because that day was also to be the Seven Rivers Purification,[2] the female courtiers were in the Dining Room making preparations to dress the dolls[3] and intently gazing at the pleasant profusion of flowering blossoms. Even His Majesty was present for the flower-viewing. The Ōmiya major counselor, who came bearing robes for His Majesty and who before long was serving as an attendant, said that His Majesty ought to start kickball this year.[4] The Karahashi major counselor Masachika[5] came before the senior nobles looking as if he were not one year shy of a hundred and as if his hair were completely covered by snow and frost, with not one strand of black visible. It was most painful to behold. Seeing him standing in the shade of a flowering tree, Ben no Naishi composed this poem:

kimi ga yo ni	The snow on your head
hana o shi mikeru	is not at all disagreeable
shirushi ni wa	for there are signs
kashira mo yuki mo	that you saw flowers indeed
itowazarikeri	during His Majesty's reign.[6]

[Section 85] The Cockfight

This year for the cockfight[1] on the third day [of the third month of the third year of Hōji, 1249], women of the upper ranks heard that they, too, would be allowed to enter gamecocks, so the younger ones exerted considerable energy searching for suitable ones. Lady Kunaikyō no Suke said that she would enter a rooster called Harima that belonged to the middle captain Tamenori. The Madenokōji major counselor presented Ben no Naishi with a red rooster with a strong coxcomb and beautifully-colored feathers from His Majesty. While she was keeping it in a vacant apartment, the sixth-rank chamberlain Moriari came and said, "I was suddenly ordered to come for this rooster." Before handing it over, Ben no Naishi said, "Please do not, under any circumstances, let this rooster fight."

A while later the red rooster returned in an almost unrecognizably altered form: one of his eyes had been put out, blood flowed from his coxcomb, and his tail feathers were missing, among other pitiful things. It was utterly horrible. Ben no Naishi said again and again lamenting, "Now that it has come to this, it means nothing even though this rooster had been splendid. Since this bird was a gift from His Majesty, I thought it would have been very popular." Ben no Naishi:

ware zo mazu	Indeed I feel
ne ni tatsu bakari	that I shall be the first
oboekeru	to break into sobs
yūzukedori no	when I see the rooster's
nareru sugata ni	altered appearance.

Finally the cockfight was held on the third. His Majesty also went to the Spacious Hall[2] in the Tominokōji Palace. The Reizei major counselor, the Madenokōji major counselor, the commander of the gate guards, the

Sanjō middle counselor Kinchika, the head of the middle captains Kinyasu, the Iyo middle captain Kintada, the middle captain Sukeyasu and all the chamberlains were in attendance. For some time, the royal roosters called Hatsuyuki, Naruaka,[3] Koguro, and others, had been placed under inverted baskets[4] and individually cared for by attendants who performed tasks such as rubbing floral perfumes and musk oil on their birds, burning incense nearby to make them fragrant, and competing with others about which of the birds had the best color or fragrance. When the bird was taken from behind the royal bamboo blinds, the Madenokōji major counselor received it, and we heard it was quite splendid as a cockfight was set up with this bird and another. Although it was an undeniable fact that the bird had been raised under His Majesty's indulgent care since it was a chick, the bird itself was a pathetic weakling and it was amusing that considerable labor was expended searching for an opponent weak enough for the royal bird to beat.

When Kintada and Kinyasu's roosters were to be matched against each other, we heard that the Iyo middle captain Kintada's bird began flailing about aimlessly so that everyone laughed, the Reizei major counselor Kinsuke composed the first verse of a linked poem, "It is amusing that the bird dances about aimlessly in the celestial skies."[5] But Kintada only said, "Indeed." Amused, Ben no Naishi composed this:

kumoi to wa   Even you know that this
nare sae shiru ya   is the abode of clouds.
hisakata no   The bird also dances
soraodori suru   aimlessly about
tori ni mo aru kana   in the celestial skies.[6]

[Section 86] The Iwashimizu Special Festival
On the twentieth there was the royal viewing of the horses at the Special Festival.[1] Formerly, there had been just a low-ranking stable hand[2] leading the horses around the courtyard, but this time, it was most exciting as the royal cavalryman Kanemine had the steeds vigorously prance and gallop. The senior noble in attendance was the Madenokōji major counselor. The official in charge of recording the color of the horses[3] was the middle captain Suezane. The moonlight in the courtyard was most pleasant. Ben no Naishi:

na ni shi ou   How suitable the name
tsukige no koma no   for steeds dusted by moonbeams
kage made mo   and shadows too,

kumoi wa sazo to   as I watch them parade
miewataru kana   across the abode of clouds.[4]

[Section 87] Kickball Is Admirable

Around the time that blossoming cherries were most delightful, middle captain Tameuji[1] was placed in charge of a kickball game.[2] The participants were the Kazan'in major counselor Sadamasa, the Reizei major counselor Kinsuke, the Madenokōji major counselor Kinmoto, the commander of the left gate guards Sanefuji, the commander of the right gate guards Michinari, Sukehira, Kintada, Tameuji, Tamenori, and Takayuki.[3] It was especially pleasant when the sun was about to set. Ben no Naishi:

hana no ue ni   The ball seemed to linger
shibashi tomaru to   above the flowers for a while,
miyure domo   then it fell
kozutau eda ni   among the branches
chiru sakura kana   scattering cherry blossoms.

Shōshō no Naishi:

omoi amari   The ball scattering
kokoro ni kakaru   the cherry blossoms
yūgure no   lingers in the heart as memories
hana no nagori mo   on such an evening,
ari to koso kike   or so I have heard.[4]

The number of consecutive kicks had increased and then the ball soared to the treetop. The commander of the left gate guards Sanefuji ran toward the ball so rapidly that Lady Hyōe no Kami said, "Kickball is admirable indeed to make the commander of the left gate guards run so quickly." When Lady Dainagon heard Lady Hyōe no Kami's remark she said, "How clever! I was thinking the same thing as I watched. Are you not showing partiality for the commander of the left gate guards? Ben no Naishi, I would like for you to reply." Ben no Naishi:

chiru hana o   It seems the wind
amari ya kaze no   blew so much
fukitsuran   it scattered the blossoms,
haru no kokoro wa   though hearts in spring
nodoka naredomo   are calm[5]

[Section 88] The Change of the Era Name to Kenchō

On the twenty-eight day of the third month, there was a change in era name. Ben no Naishi heard that among the eight senior nobles who attended were Kazan'in major counselor Sadamasa as the presiding official and counselor Tsunemitsu. While the female courtiers chatted to while away the time as they waited late into night for the decision to be announced in the Table Room, someone said, "In the Enryaku and Engi eras of the distant past, reign names continued for over twenty years. Indeed it is a pity that era names constantly change in our time." Ben no Naishi:

hodo mo naku	Constant change
kawaru mo tsurashi	is trying,
inishie wa	though in the distant past,
futatō amaru	era names often continued
toshi mo aru yo ni	for more than twenty years.

[Section 89] The Messenger to Matsunoo Shrine in the First Year of Kenchō

On the seventh day of the fourth month, Ben no Naishi set off as the official messenger to Matsunoo Shrine. The presiding official was the Yoshida middle counselor Tametsune and the controller was Tsunetoshi. Upstream from where the party crossed the Katsura River, there were fishing weirs called *yana* placed in the water that made the waves surge loudly. Ben no Naishi:

kawa no se ni	Fishing weirs placed
yana uchiwatasu	across river rapids
mizunami no	shatter sound,
amari mo oto no	making the water surge
kudakeyuku kana	as it flows by.[1]

[Section 90] The Royal Progress for a Directional Taboo

On the seventeenth day [of the fourth month], there was a royal progress to avoid a directional taboo.[1] His Majesty went to the Imadegawa Mansion.[2] The retired consort was about to move there very soon.[3] The commander of the left gate guards Sanefuji[4] waited in attendance at the temporary royal quarters. The assistant bodyguard in charge of presenting the Royal Sword[5] was consultant-middle captain Masaie. Two head chamberlains[6] were in attendance until His Majesty was to return to the palace. Everyone gazed at the especially lovely moon throughout the night without sleeping. The Reizei major counselor Kinsuke and the Madenokōji major counselor Kinmoto, together with the commander of the left gate guards Sanefuji, expressed their deep appreciation by saying, "It is not often we see a moon this lovely." The light of the dawn moon shining on the white *nusa* cloth[7] was exceptionally charming and just at that moment Ben no Naishi heard the cry of a cuckoo. Ben no Naishi:

kaerusa no	While waiting
kane matsu hodo no	for the bell to toll
ariake ni	announcing the Royal Return,
tsure nakaraji to	the cuckoo cries at dawn,
naku hototogisu	thinking, "I will accompany the moon."[8]

[Section 91] Summoning the Guards

Because the festival[1] was to be celebrated on the twentieth day [of the fourth month], the Summoning of the Guards took place on the eighteenth.[2] The presiding official was the provisional middle counselor Fuyutada. People in the Table Room said, "Let us press some of them in books," when some heartvines were presented by Kamo Shrine and they were selecting some small ones when head chamberlain of the left-middle captain Mototomo came in wearing informal robes[3] in unusually festive colors with each of his guards also beautifully attired.[4] Head chamberlain of the right-middle captain Kinyasu entered in similar style, wearing more festive colors than usual. It was pleasant that he seemed self-satisfied. Ben no Naishi heard that Kintada also was given the privilege of wearing a narrow sword.[5] The guards' attire was so pleasing, Ben no Naishi composed this:

chihayaburu	Since it has come to be
matsuri no koro ni	the time for the age-old festival
narinureba	for the mighty gods,
chikaki mabori mo	those who guard closely also
kokoro shite keri	pay special heed to their attire.

[Section 92] While Waiting for the Moon

The regent[1] came on the night of the twenty-first and was waiting in uncertain expectation for the moon to appear.[2] Each time he asked if the moon had appeared, people devised various responses. Someone said, "The moon has already appeared on this side of the mountain, but its light has not reached us yet." Everyone said that some thought was placed into that reply and that it was convincing. Ben no Naishi:

yama no ha ni	On a night when the moon is late,
semete mo tsuki no	even when it is at the rim
osoki yo wa	of the mountain,

konata to omou mo	we urge it appear on this side
nao zo mataruru	for we cannot stop waiting.[3]

[Section 93] The Annual Lectures on the Golden Light Sutra at the Tominokōji Palace

The annual lectures on the Golden Light Sutra began on the twenty-second and ended on the twenty-sixth.[1] It was the first time that these Buddhist rites were performed at the Tominokōji Palace, so it was novel; it was pleasant when the incense was distributed. Here the Demon Room was located north of the Hand-Washing Room and the Table Room.[2] Those in charge were the Horikawa palace minister Tomomi,[3] the Reizei major counselor Kinsuke, the provisional major counselor Saneo, the new major counselor,[4] the commander of the left gate guards Sanefuji, and the Sanjō middle counselor Kinchika. The attendants were Sadahira[5] and Kintada. The Buddhist rites began quite late and everyone came out around the time the dawn moon appeared. Around the time they emerged, the archbishop of Shōgo'in performed the Shōkan'on esoteric rites[6] in the Spacious Hall. The rites were to end on the twenty-seventh, but because there was to be a royal progress that night, the appointed time of dawn for the rites was moved up to an earlier time and they were performed in the evening. The sound of the handbells[7] cleared her spirit, so Ben no Naishi reverently composed this:

akatsuki no	The special time
kane yori mo keni	of ringing the handbells
yūgure no	in the evening
reiji ni rei no	sounds clearer than
koe mo sumikeri	the usual bell at dawn.[8]

[Section 94] A Royal Chair for the Table Room

On the last day of the year, the regent came to see the delivery of a royal chair for the Table Room.[1] The regent rejected the chair, saying, "It should not have been made from the same wood as chairs made for banquets. It should have been made of rosewood."[2] When the armrest of the royal chair in the Courtiers' Hall was broken while the Priestly Kanpyō Sovereign and Narihira no Ason[3] were *sumō* wrestling, a precedent has been handed down from the distant past that all subsequent chairs be made incorporating the broken armrest. Ben no Naishi said it was very interesting to hear the story:

furinikeru	Perhaps these vestiges
mukashi no ato o	we see still unchanged

sono mama ni	from the distant past
kawarazu miru ya	are to become keepsakes
nagori naruran	in our time.

[Section 95] Special Royal Prayers

For the Special Royal Prayers,[1] which began on the twenty-eighth day of the sixth month, the Royal Dowager's Daytime Chamber[2] was prepared so that Jikken,[3] the head priest of Daigo Temple,[4] could perform longevity rites before the image of Fugen.[5] The Reizei major counselor was in charge. The rites for the Seven-Buddhas Healing Buddha were conducted in the Spacious Hall with the chancellor in charge.[6] While the prayers were being intoned, autumn arrived with very cool winds blowing and with faint cries of pine crickets chirping in the royal dowager's courtyard garden. It was very pleasant. Ben no Naishi:

kimi ga hen	Voices intoning the rites
chitose o inoru	pray for a thousand-year reign
nori no koe	for His Majesty;
konata kanata ni	here and there
matsumushi zo naku	waiting pine crickets are chirping.

[Section 96] The Tone of the Plucked Bowstring

The thunder was quite frightening so His Majesty moved to the Dining Room. While they were waiting for the arrival of a Tsuruuchi ("One Who Plucks a Bowstring") of the sixth rank,[1] the Reizei major counselor Kinsuke took the palace guard's bow and plucked its string. He plucked the bowstring so in tune with the thunder that His Majesty said, "Now that was in the Ichikotsu key!"[2] When His Majesty had Sukeyasu play a tune on the flute in that mode, Lady Kōtō no Naishi also said, amused, "It was in that key!" It was most interesting. Ben no Naishi:

mono no ne o	Without even playing an instrument,
hiki mo narasade	how does the plucked bowstring
azusayumi	of the birchwood bow
oshite shirabe o	elicit a tune
ikade shiruran	so unwittingly?[3]

[Section 97] Royal Linked Verse

On the night of the fifteenth day of the eighth month, there was a royal linked-verse gathering at the retired sovereign's palace.[1] Although the night was growing late, particularly poignant and interesting linked verses continued to be composed. Just at that time, the sound of the temple bell drifted over, someone asked, "Have the Royal Prayers begun?" Provisional major counselor Saneo came close to the bamboo blinds and ordered them to "hurry up and make linked verses because the late night prayers have begun." It was quite amusing. Hearing the sound of the bell cleared their spirits, so Shōshō no Naishi composed this poem, putting aside the linked verse:

aki no yo no	At the sound of the temple bell
tsuki ni saetaru	that tolls serenely
kane no oto ni	under a moon of an autumn night,
yagate mo toki no	I become aware
utsurinuru kana	that time has passed quickly.

Ben no Naishi:

toki utsuru	Is it because I hear the sound
kane no oto zo to	of the bell tolling the time
kiku kara ni	that it makes me feel
tsuki mo nakaba no	that the mid-autumn moon
kage ya fukenuru	has begun to wane?[2]

[Section 98] Night Duty above the Clouds
On the eighth day of the ninth month, Shōshō no Naishi heard the Madenokōji major counselor Kinmoto leave for night duty in the Spacious Hall, so she sent him the following poem attached to a chrysanthemum:[1]

kiku no ue ni	How can anyone doze,
okiiru tsuyu mo	when there are those who,
aru mono o	like the dew that lies
tare itazura ni	on chrysanthemums,
nete akasuran	pass the night awake?[2]

The major counselor's reply:

kokonoe no	Though lying down
kumo no uebushi	in the Nine-fold Palace
sode saete	above the clouds,
madoromu hodo no	there is no leisure time
toki no ma mo nashi	for dozing on cold sleeves.[3]

Ben no Naishi thought that "kumo no uebushi" [lying down above the clouds] was very elegant:

madoromanu	I know there is
hodo o kiku ni zo	no time for those
omoishiru	above the clouds to doze,
tsuyu o katashiku	lying alone on dew-laden
kumo no uebito	chrysanthemums.[4]

[Section 99] Third Rank for Lady Dainagon
Shōshō no Naishi sent a congratulatory poem to Lady Dainagon when she was promoted to the third rank:

akikaze no	Your delight at that time
mi ni shimu bakari	must have pierced your body
ureshiki ya	like the autumn wind,
nao hito shirenu	a happiness still
kokoro naruran	unknown to others.[1]

Ben no Naishi's poem:

kai arite	Worthy of your effort,
ima koso mitsu no	now you have at last ascended
kuraiyama	Third Rank Mountain,
mayowanu michi wa	all the more joyous
nao zo ureshiki	that you were not lost on the way.[2]

Lady Dainagon no Sanmi's reply:

mi ni shimite	Only the first breeze
ureshiki mono to	of an ordinary autumn,
ima zo shiru	now indeed I realize
tada ōkata no	a happiness
aki no hatsukaze	that pierces my body.[3]

[Section 100] The Moon at the Tokiwai Palace
Since the palace[1] was very close to this palace,[2] every night around the time the moon rose, the Madenokōji major counselor Kinmoto invited some women of the upper ranks to spend the entire night in entertainment there. The moon reflected in the water[3] looked very pleasant. Shōshō no Naishi:

yagate waga	Instantly my heart
kokoro zo utsuru	reflects itself in the water,
tokiwai no	even though it is not the moon

mizu ni yadoreru	that dwells in the everlasting
tsuki narandomo	Tokiwai waters.

When Ben no Naishi heard the poem, she composed her reply:

orifushi o	Since the moon knows
sora ni shirikeru	the change of seasons in the sky,
tsuki nareba	perhaps its reflection
nao tokiwai no	in the Tokiwai waters
kage zo sayakeki	is all the clearer.

[Section 101] The Moon on an Autumn Night

While the female courtiers were away visiting like this,[1] they were told that a large number of the retired consort's women of the upper ranks had arrived, intending to view the moon at the palace. Although the retired consort's women had asked, "Where have His Majesty's women gone?" they were told, "Well, I'm not sure where they have gone off to." When His Majesty's women returned to the palace, they learned that the retired consort's women had gone back saying, "It was disappointing not to find them here when we had taken the trouble to visit." After hearing this, Shōshō no Naishi sent this poem to a person called Lady Hizen,[2] who served the retired consort:

akugaruru	Since we can compare
kokoro kurabe mo	the depths of hearts
aru mono o	enticed away by the moon
nao tazunemiyo	of an autumn night,
aki no yo no tsuki	please come again.[3]

Lady Hizen's reply:

mata mo min	I would like again to see
nodokeki miyo no	the moon of an autumn night
aki no tsuki	in this peaceful, honorable reign.
chikaki kumoi ni	Please do not be distant
kokoro hedatsuna	at the nearby abode of clouds.[4]

Ben no Naishi found this reply most interesting, so she composed this:

tazune min	If you were to visit,
kokoro no hedate	you would see our hearts
kuma mo araji	without distance or shadow,

chikaki kumoi no	the moon of an autumn night
aki no yo no tsuki	at the nearby abode of clouds.[5]

[Section 102] The Gosechi at the Reizei Palace

Since this palace[2] was too small for the Gosechi Festival, there was a royal progress on the sixteenth[2] to the Reizei Palace,[3] with events beginning on the eighteenth. The moon was unclouded and most pleasant. Because both *kanzu*,[4] Mototomo and Kinyasu, possessed various polite accomplishments, they were especially favored during the Kisaimachi Boisterous Dancing[5] and the like.

The Retired Consort's Drinking Party was held on the Day of the Tiger.[6] The Shijō major counselor Takachika invited some women of the upper ranks to attend and what they saw from behind the shadows of the curtain stand was most interesting indeed. The Kan'in major counselors,[7] all of whom were accomplished in the arts, were engaged in dance, but the palace minister Sanemoto[8] could not be induced to dance even though everyone urged him to participate. When the commander of the right military guards Arisuke raised the key to a higher pitch and sang, "White Crane, I am going to capture you,"[9] Sanemoto displayed his fan, stood up and danced. His actions somehow looked very splendid to Ben no Naishi:

shirasagi wa	I wonder
ikanaru iro no	if there is a precedent
tameshi nite	for the beauty of the white crane
tachimau sode no	as it sways
kage nabikuran	to take wing in flight.[10]

On the Day of the Rabbit, the Royal Viewing of the Girl Attendants[11] took place. This year was different from usual with all the girl attendants participating in the royal viewing, so it was very novel. Ben no Naishi:

inishie no	Without knowing the practices
narai wa kikazu	of the distant past,
kokonoe ya	indeed we see a great number
amata otome no	of young maidens
kazu o miru kana	in the Nine-fold Palace.

[Section 103] From Kinosaki

When the provisional major counselor Saneo went to the hot springs at Kinosaki,[1] around the time that snow was deeply piled, he sent word to Lady Hyōe no Kami that the following poem be "transmitted to female courtiers."

kokonoe ni	Like the Nine-fold Palace,
furitsumoruran	the white snow piles up
shirayuki o	layer upon layer
fukaki miyama ni	deep in the beautiful mountains.
omoi koso yare	Indeed I beg your sympathy!²

Shōshō no Naishi:

kokonoe no	Snow also piles up
yuki no uchi ni mo	within the Nine-fold Palace,
tabibito no	when I see the traveler's
fumi miru michi o	letter from the path,
omoi koso yare	I am indeed sympathetic.³

Ben no Naishi:

kokonoe ni	I cannot imagine
nao kasanete mo	that white snow in the mountains
omowazu yo	has piled up as much
fumi miru hodo no	as in the Nine-fold Palace,
yama no shirayuki	for I saw the letter-bearer.⁴

[Section 104] The Sound of Someone in the Demon Room
On the eighteenth day of the twelfth month, a night with a cloudless moon, the head chamberlain-middle captain Mototomo arrived for night duty. Someone in the Demon Room said to middle captain Sukeyasu, "I heard the rustling sound of robes. Go see who it is." The middle captain went to investigate and returned with this poem:

oni no ma ni	I wonder who made
hito oto no suru	the rustling sound
tare naran	in the Demon Room;
yumi toru kata no	taking the bow with his left hand,
tō no chūjō	the head chamberlain-middle captain.¹

"What a clever way of conveying the meaning of 'left,'" praised Lady Azechi no Sanmi. After Ben no Naishi heard that Mototomo had left, she composed this:

ya to iite	I should have called out "ya,"
hiki ya tomemashi	though not to draw the birchwood bow,
azusayumi	to detain

| iru kata shiranu | the head chamberlain-middle captain, |
| tō no chūjō | who knows not his destination.[2] |

[Section 105] A Cold Night with Frost

On the nineteenth day, as usual there was the Buddha's Names Ceremony.[1] Since they heard that Royal Dowager Senkamon'in's[2] Buddha's Names Ceremony was also being conducted that night, it was performed in haste. At a place where the moon was most pleasant, the courtiers of ceremony[3] seemed to tend the bonfire right before their very eyes, since at this palace[4] the Table Room was very close to the covered corridor.[5] Sadahira, Koreyori, Korenaga, Motomasa, and others were present.[6] It was amusing that Sadahira noticed the novel way in which the *nyōju* had hitched up their divided skirts as they assisted him by adding the kindling wood to the fire. Ben no Naishi:

ito semete	At best a consolation
sayuru shimoyo no	for a cold night with frost,
nagusame ni	courtiers who dwell
shiba orikuburu	above the clouds,
kumo no uebito	make sport with kindling wood.[7]

Late at night, Shijō major counselor Takachika, consultant of the right-middle captain Kinmasa, provisional master of the Dowager's Household Morotsugu, Tsuchimikado consultant-middle captain Masaie, and major controller of the left-consultant Akitomo distributed the incense. Sadahira and Koreyori assisted those distributing the incense.

[Section 106] A Drinking Party for Courtiers

On the third day of the first month in the second year of Kenchō [1250], there was a drinking party for courtiers. Since they heard that this time two *kanzu*[1] were to be promoted to the post of head chamberlain at the spring appointment ceremony, the Shijō major counselor Takachika, who was in charge of the event, told people to enjoy themselves heartily. His Majesty[2] also watched the event through the small window.[3] Since Sanetaka, Tsunetada, Koremoto[4] and others with good voices cheered them on, both *kanzu* danced about ten times. It looked very pleasant. Ben no Naishi:

midaretsutsu	In constant disorder they sing
utau chikuwa no	"leaves of the bamboo,"
matsu no iro ni	the color of the thousand-year pine
chiyo no kage sou	joins the light of the moon
kyō no sakazuki	in the wine cup today.[5]

Finally they went to the Royal Dowager's Apartment. From the Two-Bay Room, it looked very pleasant with everyone singing, "The boat approaches the harbor of our thoughts." Ben no Naishi:

shibashi mate	Please wait a moment,
tachiyoru nami ni	there is something I would ask
koto towan	the inbound waves,
omoi no tsu ni zo	a boat approaches
fune yobau naru	the harbor of our thoughts.[6]

[Section 107] The Messenger to Kasuga Shrine

On the fifth day of the second month, Ben no Naishi set out as the messenger to Kasuga Shrine.[1] The presiding official was the provisional master of the dowager's household Morotsugu. When they arrived at Nashihara[2] around sunset, Ben no Naishi composed this while the evening moon pleasantly began emitting its light:

nashihara no	That name, "Nashihara,"
sono na wa aki ni	does not make it autumn.
narinarazu	How should we see
nete ya wa yowa no	the midnight moon
tsuki o mirubeki	if we are asleep?[3]

General assistants Tamenawa and Sadamura made much of a maid called Sakuya,[4] who accompanied them as they served wine. Choosing the *shidai* key, they sang "Now winter yields its place to springtime, flowers blooming on the trees."[5] Ben no Naishi was amused that Sakuya seemed to relish being the center of attention. Ben no Naishi:

haru o miru	Because your name "Sakuya"
waga mi hitotsu no	blooms all by itself,
na ni oite	showing spring's arrival,
sakuya to hito ni	people ask you
iwarenuru kana	if flowers are blooming.[6]

[Section 108] The *Buppōsō* Bird

A bird that cries "*buppōsō*,"[1] presented by the chancellor,[2] was placed in the eaves chamber of His Majesty's Apartment and on rainy days it sang especially well. As expected, it could be heard chanting its name[3] quite clearly. It looked like a *hiedori*,[4] but it was a little larger. Ben no Naishi:

to ni kaku ni	Because it is indeed
kashikoki kimi ga	His Majesty's awe-inspiring reign,
miyo nareba	the Three Treasures' Bird
mitsu no takara no	cries its name
tori mo nakunari	in various quarters.

[Section 109] The Great Willow Facing Kyōgyoku Avenue

Shōshō no Naishi's apartment was located on the edge[1] of the Second Wing Chamber,[2] so whenever she went out late at night after going off duty, she felt as if the bright moon she saw between the branches of the large willow tree facing Kyōgyoku Avenue[3] was shining just for her. It was very pleasant. Shōshō no Naishi:

aoyagi no	Even at night,
ito wa yoru tomo	green strands of the willow
mienu kana	are visible;
kokage kumoranu	the light of the moon unclouded
tsuki no hikari ni	by the shade of the tree.[4]

Ben no Naishi, sharing the same apartment when she was off duty, found the moonlight truly pleasant. Ben no Naishi:

aoyagi no	Like green strands of the willow
ito ni wa kage mo	hanging without disorder,
midareneba	the light of the moon
onaji suji ni zo	piercing the shadows
tsuki wa sayakeki	is bright indeed.[5]

[Section 110] The Seven Rivers Purification

On the sixteenth day of the third month, the Seven Rivers Purification rites were performed.[1] While waiting for the return of the messengers, the women went out to the Eaves Corridor[2] outside the Table Room. They discussed such things as, "Compared to the Kan'in Palace, the only thing that is better at the palace is the flowers." Shōshō no Naishi:

sakurabana	Though cherry blossoms
yae ni sakedomo	always bloom with eight folds,
kokonoe to	just thinking that
omoi nasu ni zo	this is the Nine-fold Palace
iro masarikeru	increases its color![3]

Again, Ben no Naishi:

nanigoto mo	Everything evokes
shinobu mukashi no	memories of the hidden
kumoi ni wa	abode of clouds of the past;
hana koso oyobu	only the fragrance
nioi narikere	of these flowers rivals it.[4]

[Section 111] More than a Thousand Years

On the twenty-ninth day of the third month, there was a royal kickball game.[1] In attendance were the Reizei major counselor Kinsuke, the Madenokōji major counselor Kinmoto, the provisional major counselor Saneo, the commander of the left gate guards Sanefuji, the commander of the right gate guards Michinari, the Minamoto commander of the right military guards Arisuke, the head chamberlain-middle captain Tameuji, Tamenori, Sukehira, Kintada, and Tokitsune.[2]

Most of the blossoms[3] had scattered, so it was sparse, but those at the treetop were quite pleasant, as if in preparation for those who came to view them. Around sunset, the royal cavalryman Yorimine[4] was sent as a royal messenger from the retired sovereign's residence with a branch of *goematsu* pine[5] to which a kickball was attached. The head chamberlain-middle captain (Tameuji) received it, then presented it. There was a thin white paper attached to it.[6] His Majesty opened it and read the following:

fuku kaze mo	Even the blowing wind
osamari ni keru	has settled down.
kimi ga yo no	The number of His Majesty's
chitose no kazu wa	thousand-year reign
kyō zō kazouru	is counted today![7]

Ben no Naishi's reply:

kagiri naki	Without limit,
chiyo no amari no	the count is more
ari kazu wa	than a thousand years,
kyō kazufu tomo	though today we count,
tsukiji to zō omou	the numbers are hardly spent.[8]

After the kickball game was over, they talked about their recollection of how the players had stood in rows beneath the shade of the tree. Shōshō no Naishi:

| kazukazu ni | Almost too abundant, |
| amari naru made | memories of longing |

koishiki wa	for this and that,
ika ni nagameshi	as we watched this evening
yūbe to ka shiru	with considerable excitement.[9]

Ben no Naishi's reply:

kaze ni niou	Fragrance on the wind
amari wa hana no	enhances the flowers'
iro ni idete	emerging color;
kazu kagiri naki	count without limit
yū to zō mishi	what we saw this evening.[10]

After that someone said that they should play kickball again and first the Madenokōji major counselor was ordered to attend as the manager in charge of matters. But he refused saying that he was feeling unwell with a cold and could not serve. In fact, His Majesty had heard that there was a secret kickball game going on at the Tokiwai Palace. "How hateful! I do not care what you say, but send him our complaint," he ordered.

harukaze no	Pretending you are suffering
tsurasa o kakotsu	from a spring cold,
itsuwari no	your lies
mi ni amari nuru	are too much,
hodo zo shiraruru	known by all![11]

The major counselor's reply:

harukaze no	My heartfelt excuse
tsurasa o kakotsu	of suffering
kokoro yori	from a spring cold,
mi no itsuwari ni	makes me sad
naru ga kanashisa	you think it a lie.[12]

There was some discussion such as, "He still insists that he was not lying!" Ben no Naishi:

hana no tame	For the flower
amari zo nao mo	it must be very painful,
tsurakaran	for the wind must blow
itsuwari ni ya wa	though people ask,
kaze wa fukubeki	"Is it a lie?"[13]

[Section 112] The Buddha's Anointment Ceremony
On the eighth day of the fourth month [of 1250] when the Buddha's Anointment Ceremony[1] was performed, the Muromachi major counselor Sanefuji[2] brought as an offering a superb crimson glossed silk robe[3] embellished with designs of grapevine[4] and sweet maple[5] leaves most elegantly suggesting Mt. Utsu, attached to a branch crafted of beaten gold. Since he came late, the other people's offerings had already been taken to the Courtiers' Hall. Lady Azechi no Sanmi and Lady Hyōe no Kami received it in the Table Room and said, "It belongs to that person," and gave it to the chamberlain. They remembered that there should be special preparations such as appointing Mitsukuni as the manager.[6]

tsutae kiku	Like the grapevine and sweet maple
tsuta mo kaede mo	bequeathed to posterity,
wakaba nite	the young leaves
mada utsurowanu	have not yet changed color
utsu no yamamichi	on the path of Mt. Utsu.

[Section 113] The Female Messenger to the Festival
When Lady Chūnagon no Suke was to proceed to the Festival[1] as the female messenger,[2] Ben no Naishi said that she would like to give her a set of robes in the wild pinks combination.[3] Ben no Naishi:

kurabemiru	When I compare them,
koko ni wa iro no	I see this color is too light.
usukereba	How should I dye the robes
kara nadeshiko ni	to make the color as deep
ikaga somubeki	as the Chinese wild pinks?

[Section 114] Repast in the Presence of a *Kami*
On the eleventh day of the sixth month, the Repast in the Presence of a *Kami* was conducted.[1] The presiding official was the Tsuchimikado middle counselor Michiyuki,[2] the controller was Akimasa.[3] The female courtier[4] had already left, but the controller said, "The presiding official has already left. Hurry up, female courtier." Shōshō no Naishi:

ososhi to wa	Who do you say
tare o iuran	is late?
kimi o koso	Time passes
matsuran to omou	while she is waiting
toki mo suginure	for you.

When Ben no Naishi returned, Shōshō no Naishi told her about what had happened. "I left much earlier than the presiding official and it was I who waited," said Ben no Naishi. She wrote:

itsumo sate	Though you always say
ware o matsu to wa	you wait for me,
iishikado	it is I
matareshi mono o	who waited for you
sayo fukuru made	deep into the night.

[Section 115] Black Door Guard
As the provisional major counselor [Saneo] has a tendency to absent himself from Black Door Guard and not report for duty, Shōshō no Naishi said, "I believe he came in the seventh month last year around the Stars Meeting."[1] Shōshō no Naishi:

kumoi oba	Without any connection
yoso ni nomi shite	to the abode of clouds,
ama no gawa	the crossing
tōki watari ni	of the Heavenly Stream
haya narinikeri	has quickly grown distant.[2]

Ben no Naishi's reply:

kumoi nite	The Heavenly Stream
tōshi to wa mishi	looks quite distant
ama no gawa	from the abode of clouds.
hito no kokoro ya	Will you, I wonder,
watari naruran	cross over?

[Section 116] Rebuilding the Kan'in Palace
On the thirteenth day of the seventh month, the controller Tsunetoshi came to report to His Majesty that reconstruction on the Kan'in Palace had begun.[1] Somehow, Ben no Naishi felt excited, wondering when the construction work might be finished:

momoshiki no	Has construction on the hundred-layered
ōmiyazukuri	palace begun today?
kyō yori ya	I wonder when the date
kanete sono hi to	for completion will be,
sadame okuran	decided some time ago.

[Section 117] "Amida Buddha" Linked Verse

On the night of the fifteenth of the eighth month, there was the usual poetry gathering.[1] It was indeed a pity that it rained. After the poetry gathering was over, the retired sovereign had the double doors[2] opened so he could look outside, but he was disappointed because the moon was clouded over. He[3] commanded saying, "As a farewell, let's just the three of us compose an 'Amida Buddha' linked-verse sequence."[4] "It would be a pity if the compositions were forgotten. Shōshō no Naishi record them," he ordered.

Retired Sovereign:

> nagori oba
> ika ni seyo tote
> kaeruran

> What are you telling me
> to do with my feelings,
> that you go home and leave me alone?[5]

Shōshō no Naishi:

> moshiya to matan
> aki no yo no tsuki

> I will wait, for it may appear,
> the moon of an autumn night

Retired Sovereign:

> akanaku ni
> meguri au yo mo
> ari ya tote

> While not content,
> a night may come round
> when we meet again.[6]

Ben no Naishi:

> michiuki hodo ni
> kaeru oguruma

> The path is hard to travel along,
> as little carriage wheels turn home.[7]

Retired Sovereign:

> tagui naki
> waga koigusa o
> tsumiirete

> One of a kind,
> I pick
> love grasses.[8]

Shōshō no Naishi:

> tsutsumi amaru wa
> sode no shiratsuyu

> To overflowing,
> the white dew on my sleeves.[9]

Since dawn had broken, he said, "We will save the rest for another linked-verse gathering." They returned full of memories.

Lady Dainagon no Sanmi[10] heard these links on this or that occasion and said, "These linked-verse love grasses will be found memorable. You should compose a poem on this and include it in your poetry collection."[11] Ben no Naishi:

omoide no	If these words
kotonoha to naru	are to be remembered,
kusa naraba	I will pick enough
nanaguruma ni mo	leaves to fill
ware zo tsumu beki	seven carriages.[12]

[Section 118] The Horse-Leading Ceremony

On the sixteenth day, there was a Horse-Leading Ceremony.[1] The presiding official was the Madenokōji major counselor. The consultant was Masaie. The messenger leading the horses was Motomasa. After the ceremony was over, the major counselor wrote this poem on the edge of a fan with Kintada acting as messenger:

kimi ga yo ni	Because I serve
tsukaete koyoi	in His Majesty's reign,
mitsuru kana	tonight I see
yoso ni kikikoshi	the full-moon steeds
mochizuki no koma	of which I had only heard before.[2]

Shōshō no Naishi's reply:

kimi ga yo ni	Is it because it is you
tsukaete shi mi wa	who devotedly serves
mochizuki no	in His Majesty's reign,
koma mo chitose no	the full-moon steeds also
tameshi ni ya hiku	are led toward a "thousand years"?[3]

Ben no Naishi considered his action especially elegant:

ima mo sazo	Have vestiges of past generations
yoyo no omokage	changed from the way
kawarame ya	things are now?
aki no koyoi no	The full-moon steeds
mochizuki no koma	on this autumn night.

[Section 119] Shining, Shining Sun-Child

On the night before His Majesty was to make a royal progress to the Imadegawa Mansion,[1] it looked as if it were going to rain, so seven people[2] braided Torch Stakes.[3] The last person tying the cord has the job of dancing while singing, "Shining, shining Sun-Child," and that task always fell to Shōshō no Naishi, but since she had gone home, everyone said that Ben no Naishi should dance in her place. Ben no Naishi thought she could not possibly perform and hid in her apartment. When she heard that someone called Iyo danced, Ben no Naishi:

kaji o toru How could I have prayed successfully
sono funabito ni for fair weather tomorrow,
aranu mi no when I am not
asu no hiyori o that boatman who takes
ikaga inoran the oars of the boat?[4]

[Section 120] The Cowardly Demon

Around the time of the *Kami* Observances when there were only a few people at court,[1] His Majesty grew bored and said to Ben no Naishi, "Put on a demon mask and scare people." She stood at the entrance to the Large Room[2] with her long divided skirt tied up to her chest and her burgundy chemise draped over her head. She startled the *ōban* guards[3] who came armed with bows at the ready, so she became frightened and fell into the courtyard stream. This evoked laughter from the onlookers, who called out, "You cowardly demon!"

The next day, she received an abstinence charm from home stating that she had reason to guard herself.[4] Moved by her parent's concern, Ben no Naishi wrote:

azusayumi Birchwood bows
hikitagaetaru poised in readiness,
inochi koso yet guarding my life
soekeru oya no was the protective spirit
mamori narikere of my parent.[5]

[Section 121] Mock Festivals

When His Majesty had female courtiers perform mock banquets, special festivals, procedures,[1] and the like, so he could see them, the chancellor[2] said with interest, "This amusement is very pleasant" and had female courtiers make batons[3] to present to His Majesty. The head chamberlain-middle captain Tameuji wrote the procedures for the banquets and presented them to His Majesty. Others present were Lady Dainagon no Sanmi, daughter of the chancellor-lay priest;[4] Lady Azechi no Suke, daughter of Lord Takahira, Lady Dainagon no Suke, daughter of Lord Takachika; Lady Chūnagon no Suke, daughter of Lord Saneie; Lady Kunaikyō, daughter of Lord Akiuji; Lady Hyōe no Kami, granddaughter of Lord Iemichi; Lady Kōtō no Naishi, daughter of lay priest Takatoki;[5] and Shōshō, Ben, and Iyo no Naishi.[6] The names of everyone the women were to impersonate were written on the batons.

Lady Chūnagon no Suke played the provisional major counselor, but then at the banquet when she was asked to play the palace controller, she refused, saying, "I have an illness that will not allow me to wear socks,"[7] and withdrew to her apartment. Ben no Naishi wrote a poem on a leaf of a reed and stuck it in the bamboo blinds of Chūnagon no Suke's apartment:

tsu no kuni no	Why are your feet
ashi no shitane no	drenched and disordered
ikanareba	by waves,
nami ni shiorete	like the roots of reeds
midare kao naru	in Tsu Province?[8]

Each time Lady Dainagon no Sanmi made a mistake, she said, "This is the way we do it at home." Lady Chūnagon no Suke said, "When we always hear the same thing, it is rather detestable and we cannot believe it unless we are shown a legitimate diary from her home in which it is recorded." Naturally, everyone agreed with her. Shōshō no Naishi played the part of the Sanjō major counselor, but all she did was make mistakes, leaving her baton on the floor after the Lesser Obeisance and dancing without it. Later Lady Hyōe no Kami was told by the person himself,[9] "I do not think I make that many mistakes, so it is rather hard to bear." It was very amusing.

Iyo no Naishi, who was always the director[10] of the dancers at Special Festivals made a hoop[11] on her own and held it while she twirled about dancing. Someone said such things as, "She ought to shake her head more vigorously." Ben no Naishi recalled with amusement that Iyo had said, "I did not even want to perform this role." Everyone agreed with Iyo's complaint. Ben was given the role of whistling[12] while en route on the royal progress and was concerned about not being inferior to the director. She was delighted when the Reizei major counselor, who came for night duty, joined their activity and offered to take on the whistling duty in her stead. Lady Azechi no Suke said, "If it is just among us,[13] let us display our skill at round singing[14] and boisterous dancing.[15] It is unlikely that others will come." She explained everything beforehand using especially elegant gestures as she set to work.

Everyone who served His Majesty closely was included in these amusements. It was amusing that the Madenokōji major counselor and others showed them how to dance by inserting just their sleeves from the room below the lintel[16] and saying, "Do it this way." At the mock banquet, it was very amusing that just when Lady Kunaikyō ought to have led the singing, the commander of the left gate guards[17] came in, so she could not sing or raise her voice enough to be heard. It was amusing that Lady Azechi no Sanmi said, "There is no need to force yourself." So much time went by without her singing that it became uncomfortable and the commander of the left gate guards thought that something was strange and left. It was very amusing. Ben no Naishi composed this in her mind:

kikihayasu	How ought we continue
shirousuyō no	with the "stolen" brush,
ori kara wa	while listening
ikaga iu beki	and keeping time
makiage no fude	to "White Tissue Paper?"[18]

[Section 122] Royal Progress to a Morning Audience
On the thirteenth day of the tenth month, His Majesty went to the Toba Mansion[1] for a Morning Audience.[2] During the night, they thought that it might rain, but it was most auspicious that by morning it had cleared up. The scenery at the residence of the Toba Mansion was extremely pleasant. It felt as if the various colors of autumn foliage were at their best. Words cannot capture the beauty of the autumn colors at the edge of the lake where the Dragon- and Bird-Headed boats[3] floated. Female courtiers with their hair put up in the formal style were Kōtō no Naishi and Shōshō no Naishi.[4] They spent the entire day with their hair formally dressed watching various interesting and auspicious events from inside. Someone said such things as, "There will be plenty of tales to tell when we get old." Shōshō no Naishi:

katariiden	I want to transmit tales
yuki sue made no	to later generations
ureshisa wa	of the happiness
kyō no miyuki no	with which we made
keshiki narikeri	the royal progress today.[5]

Hearing this, Ben no Naishi:

yoyo o hete	Leaves of words
katari tsutahen	to be transmitted as tales

koto no ha ya	to later generations
kyō [niwa] no	are like the autumn-colored leaves
momiji naruran	in the [garden] today.[6]

After returning to the palace, they talked of all the splendid things that happened that day and Shōshō no Naishi wrote down the dyed color combinations[7] each person wore. Ben no Naishi thought that the white-on-white combination[8] of the chancellor was magnificent and especially memorable:

shirotae no	Like feathered wings
tsuru no kegoromo	of the white crane,
nan to shite	I wonder why is it called
somenu o somuru	a "dyed" color
iro to iuran	when it was not dyed at all?[9]

Notes

[Section 1]

1. Tominokōji Palace was one of the many town palaces (*satodairi*) that served as royal residences during the Kamakura period (1185–1333) after the practice of rebuilding the Royal Residential Palace (Dairi) within the Greater Royal Palace (Daidairi) was abandoned in 1219 (Ōta 1987, 789–90). The Tominokōji Palace, located to the east of the Greater Royal Palace, served as the town palace of Go-Saga (1222–72; r. 1242–46) and his consort, Ōmiya'in (1225–92, Fujiwara [Saionji] Kitsushi), during his rule as titular monarch. Even after Go-Saga's abdication, he and Ōmiya'in continued to live at the Tominokōji Palace, which was then called the retired sovereign's residence (*in no gosho*). After the *Daijōsai* (enthronement ceremony) of Go-Saga's eldest son, Go-Fukakusa (1243–1304; r. 1246–59), the Kan'in Palace, located to the southeast of the Greater Royal Palace, served as the main town palace. Ben no Naishi lived at the Kan'in Palace in Go-Fukakusa's service until it was destroyed by fire on the first day of the second month of 1249 (see Section 81). Go-Fukakusa moved to the Tominokōji Palace, where Go-Saga and Ōmiya'in had lived, after his parents moved to the nearby Madenokōji Palace, also owned by the Saionji family, Ōmiya'in's relatives. After living at the Tominokōji Palace for over two years, Go-Fukakusa's court returned to the Kan'in Palace when reconstruction was completed on the twenty-eighth day of the sixth month of 1251 (Section 138). For details on the Kan'in Palace, see Section 26, note 2.

2. "My lord" refers to Go-Fukakusa, the eighty-ninth sovereign of Japan, who was only three years old when he was enthroned. His parents, Go-Saga and Ōmiya'in, deposed him in 1259 in favor of his younger brother Kameyama (1249–1305; r. 1259–74), the ninetieth sovereign. This lateral move set up a dispute in

the line of succession that resulted in an uneasy alternation between the Jimyōin (Go-Fukakusa's descendants, also Senior or Northern Court) and the Daikakuji (Kameyama's descendants, also Junior or Southern Court) lines until the reign of Go-Daigo (1288–1339; r. 1318–39). Go-Daigo's failed attempt to maintain succession in the Daikakuji line and to restore power to the royal family during the short-lived Kenmu Restoration (1334–36) hastened the collapse of the Kamakura shogunate and gave impetus to the usurpation of power by Ashikaga Takauji (1305–58), founder of the Ashikaga shogunate. The succession dispute was concluded in 1392 when Go-Komatsu (1377–1433; r. 1392–1412) of the Jimyōin line (the Northern Court monarch, r. 1382–92) was declared the descendant of the main line of succession. In the translation, Go-Fukakusa is most often referred to as "His Majesty."

[Section 2]

1. Council of State (Daijōkan) refers to both the supreme organ of government and to the building located in the central portion of the southeastern corner of the Greater Royal Palace, which housed its members: ministers of state (*daijin*), major counselors (*dainagon*), middle counselors (*chūnagon*), and consultants (*sangi*). For details, see McCullough and McCullough 1980, 2:796–801.

[Section 3]

1. Hirano Shrine, relocated in 794 to the Kita ward of Kyōto, was founded by Kanmu (737–806; r. 781–806) when he moved to the new capital in Yamashiro province from the former capital in Yamato province. Considered one of the original Twenty-two Shrines (Nijūnisha) by the Heian court, Hirano Shrine received royal patronage and special privileges, such as visits by crown princes before investiture (McCullough and McCullough 1980, 1:119). Traditionally, the Hirano Festival took place during the fourth lunar month, as did other Shintō *kami* observances (*kamigoto*) celebrated at the Kamo, Inari, Yamashina, Matsunoo, Umenomiya, Hirose, Tatsuta, Hiyoshi, and Yoshida shrines (1:334).

2. Young maple (*wakakaede*), a summer color combination for robes, worn from the beginning of the fourth lunar month, traditionally noted as the advent of summer, with all five robes and linings [in] a light sprout-green, with a chemise of white or scarlet-pink (Dalby 1987, 27). The fabric, a translucent gauze-woven silk called *ra*, was lined, thus giving the impression of coolness without achieving that effect for the wearer of the garment (24).

[Section 4]

1. Matsunoo Shrine, located in the Nishikyō ward of Kyōto, was one of the original Twenty-six Shrines (Nijūrokusha). These were Shintō shrines supported by the government. Its festival was formerly celebrated during the fourth lunar month on Matsunoo Mountain.

2. Sweet flag (*shōbu*), another color combination for summer with robes arranged as follows: (1) deep blue-green; (2) pale blue-green; (3) white; (4) deep plum-pink; (5) pale plum-pink; with a white, raw silk chemise (*susushi*) (Dalby 1987, 25).

[Section 5]

1. Naishidokoro (also Kashikodokoro, or Unmeiden), a building located east of the Jijūden in the Royal Residential Palace, housed the replica of the sacred mirror, one of the three royal regalia said to legitimize the rule of the royal family. *Naishi* were responsible for safeguarding the royal regalia: the replica sacred mirror, the replica sacred sword, and the original sacred jewels (threaded into a necklace). The original sacred mirror is housed at the Ise Grand Shrine and the original sacred sword is preserved at the Atsuta Shrine near Nagoya. Replicas of the sacred jewels were never made (Holtom 1972, 44).

2. The Giyōden, southeast of the Shishinden, housed valued treasures such as heirloom musical instruments. The Eaves Corridor (Konrō) extended from stairs on the east side of the Shishinden to the Giyōden. The eaves of this corridor covered a raised, hard-packed dirt floor (*dobisashi*) called the Giyōden Altar Corridor (Giyōden no Dan no Ue). *Dobisashi* corridors connected most of the subsidiary buildings in the original Royal Residential Palace and probably were also used in town palaces such as the Kan'in Palace. The Shishinden, located to the northeast of the Seiryōden in the Royal Residential Palace, was the main ceremonial building where Buddhist services, coming-of-age ceremonies (*genpuku*) for monarchs and crown princes, and annual ceremonies (*nenjū gyōji*) were conducted. Like other buildings in the Royal Residential Palace, the Shishinden was built with cypress-bark roof, raised-floor construction, and unpainted wood surfaces. The South Court of the Shishinden contained the famous trees: the Cherry Tree of the bodyguards of the left and the Orange Tree of the bodyguards of the right. The Shishinden in the Royal Residential Palace was sometimes called the Naden (South Hall).

[Section 6]

1. The sweet-flag festival, celebrated on the fifth day of the fifth month, was intended to ward off the diseases that accompany hot weather. Sweet-flag (*Acorus calamus* var. *angustatus*) leaves and/or roots were stuffed under the eaves of private dwellings and palace buildings, made into "medicinal balls," and formally presented to the monarch by court physicians at the Sweet-flag Banquet. There was, however, no custom for substituting *katsumi* (a kind of wild rice) for sweet-flags in the capital. Because there was no such custom, Ben no Naishi is surprised and makes her "amusing mistake." When Fujiwara Sanekata (d. 908) was appointed governor of Mutsu province, he discovered that sweet-flags did not grow there. Therefore, he ordered that *katsumi* from the Asaka Marsh be substituted for sweet-flags. For details, see McCullough and McCullough 1980, 1:412. The Shallow Marsh (Asaka no Numa) was located in Asaka-gun in Fukushima prefecture (formerly Michinoku province). There is a play on *asaka* (shallow) and *fukaku* (deep) in her poem. *Asaka* is a pillow word (*utamakura*) dating back to the time of *Man'yōshū* (*Collection of Ten Thousand Leaves*, ca. 759).

2. The Dining Room (Asagarei no Ma) was located in the northwestern portion of the Seiryōden, the monarch's residence, south of the Hand-Washing Room (Michōzu no Ma), overlooking the Dining Room Court (Asagarei no Tsubo). Some of the monarch's meals were served in the Dining Room.

3. "His Lordship" probably refers to the regent, Fujiwara Sanetsune (1223–84).

[Section 7]

1. A retiring room (*onchokurō*) was a place where regents (*sesshō, kanpaku*), ministers of state (*daijin*), major counselors (*dainagon*), and other high-ranking officials rested between court duties. Tamai again thinks that "His Lordship" is a reference to Sanetsune (Tamai 1958a, 8).

2. Taie, listed as "Kataie" in *Gunsho Ruijū*, has not been positively identified. Tamai believes that it could have been an abbreviation for Tameie, son of Fujiwara Teika. Iwasa Miyoko thinks the custom of abbreviating names was usually applied to those of low rank and suggests Minamoto Masaie as a possible candidate. Both Tamai and Iwasa agree that Tametsugu may refer to Ben no Naishi's older brother, known later as a portrait painter.

3. A court title used as a sobriquet. *Kōtō no naishi* refers to the head post among four positions of female courtiers (*naishi no jō*). This particular *kōtō no naishi* bore three children by Go-Saga while in his service, so she enjoyed some privileges at Go-Fukakusa's court. Perhaps she transferred from Go-Saga's service to Go-Fukakusa's when the latter ascended the throne.

4. Fishing pavilion (*tsuridono*), a corridor-like building which projected out over a pond in a south garden in a "sleeping hall" style (*shindenzukuri*) architectural complex.

[Section 8]

1. The Tanabata Festival (Kikōden) occurred on the seventh day of the seventh month to celebrate the annual meeting of the stars Altair (Herdsman) and Vega (Weaver Maid). The couple met by crossing a bridge made of magpie wings (*kasasagi no hashi*) spanning the Heavenly Stream (Ama no Gawa, the Milky Way) for one night together after a year apart. Thereafter, the couple was separated for another year until the trajectory completed its cycle for another annual visit. This festival was adopted from the Chinese, whose virilocal marriage practices required the Weaver Maid to cross the Heavenly Stream to visit the Herdsman on his side of the river. In Japan during the Heian (794–1185) and Kamakura periods when uxorilocal marriage practices prevailed, the Weaver Maid remained in her residence and the Herdsman crossed the river to visit her. Iwasa states that here Kikōden refers to a court ceremony in which nine torch platforms were set up in the Seiryōden courtyard with offerings, cloth, thread, musical instruments, and other objects placed on a table. The person placed in charge of the festivities was known as the manager (*bugyō*).

2. Throughout this translation, "Lady" approximates the honorific suffix "dono" attached to the sobriquets of Dainagon, Chūnagon no Suke, Kunaikyō no Suke, Azechi no Sanmi, Hyōe no Kami, and Kōtō no Naishi, indicating female courtiers higher in rank than Ben no Naishi and Shōshō no Naishi. The use of "dono" in the *nikki* indicates the desire of the author to note distinctions in rank between female courtiers of higher rank and Ben no Naishi or Shōshō no Naishi. Invariably, Ben no Naishi, Shōshō no Naishi, and Shōnagon no Naishi are referred

to without the honorific suffix "dono." It would rob the *nikki* of its proper flavor to leave out this honorific suffix for women of higher distinction because the society it depicts was highly conscious of rank. "Dono" or "Kyō" attached to a male name is usually translated as "Lord."

3. In the Royal Residential Palace, the Kokiden Royal Apartment (Kokiden no Ue no Mitsubone), one of two Consort's Apartment (Ue no Tsubone), was located in the northeast corner of the Seiryōden just north of the Two-Bay Room (Futama). One of the functions of the Two-Bay Room was to serve as a chapel for Buddhist monks on night duty. Tamai thinks that the two rooms may have been combined into one room at the Kan'in Palace.

4. There is a play on *kumoi* (abode of clouds; Royal Palace); *kasasagi no hashi* (a bridge made by the wings of magpies) suggests a stairway (*mihashi*) at the royal palace.

[Section 9]

1. Gosechidokoro (synonymous with Gosechi no Tsubone and Gosechi no Tokoro), temporary residential quarters for dancers performing in the *Daijōsai* of the eleventh month. The quarters were usually in the various sections of the Jōnei-den in the Royal Residential Palace. For details, see McCullough and McCullough 1980, 1:376–77.

2. The Horse Screen, a single-paneled screen, stood near the railing at the northern end of the corridor connecting the west side of the Seiryōden to the east side of the Dining-Room Courtyard (Asagarei no Tsubone). Ben no Naishi makes the poetic gesture of worrying because she was not able to see the mid-autumn moon on a clear night, famous for being the brightest and most beautiful for moon-viewing. The mid-autumn moon disappointed Ben no Naishi because it was only faintly visible to her on the fifteenth, the time when the viewing most likely occurred. (In lunar reckoning, the full moon predictably fell on the fifteenth. Although the event probably took place on the fifteenth, the entry is dated the sixteenth.)

3. The Nijō consort, Fujiwara Kōshi (842–910), is said to have been the person who prompted Ariwara no Narihira (825–80) to write the famous *Tsuki ya aranu* poem (see McCullough 1968, 71). According to the *Tales of Ise* (*Ise Monogatari*), Kōshi was staying in the western wing of a house in the eastern part of the capital with her aunt, Former Consort Junshi (809–71), at the time of her putative affair with Narihira, not at the Royal Residential Palace as Ben no Naishi assumed. The Kōrōden (Royal Kitchen) was located directly west of the Dining Room Court and Table Room Court (Daibandokoro no Tsubo) in the Seiryōden of the Royal Residential Palace. Presumably, the corresponding structure at the Kan'in Palace was the First Wing Chamber (Ichi no Tai).

4. Since the Royal Palace was "above the clouds" (see Section 8), the moon should have been visible. Perhaps it also refers to the moon of Buddhist enlightenment rather than just to the clear moon of mid-autumn.

5. There is a pun on *sumi*, a form of *sumu* (live; be clear). The poem could also be read as: "Even as the moon shines brightly above the clouds, why do you not see the clear sight of the autumn moon?" Sei Shōnagon mentions being worried

and restless because she wondered whether the weather would be clear or overcast. If the weather were clear, the Weaver Maid and the Herdsman would be able to meet; if it were overcast, then they would be denied their annual assignation.

[Section 10]

1. The Nyokudokoro (or Nyokodokoro) was an office established on a temporary basis to help prepare items necessary for the *Daijōsai*, which took place in the first year of a new reign, or in the second year if the reign began after the seventh month. Preparations for the ceremonies began as early as the fourth month and as the eleventh month approached, the activities increased rapidly. Two female courtiers appointed to the *Yuki* (eastern district) and *Suki* (western district) sides were required to report to the Suzaku Gate for the ceremony. Because Shōshō no Naishi became ill, Ben no Naishi was sent as her replacement. Certain districts were chosen to supply new rice: from Ōmi province for the *Yuki* eastern side and from Tanba or Bitchū provinces for the *Suki* western side. For details, see McCullough and McCullough 1980, 1:375–78.

2. The Suzaku Gate was the site for great purification ceremonies (*onharae*) performed monthly on the last day of the month from the eighth until the eleventh month when the *Daijōsai* took place. It was the main palace gate leading out onto the main north-south thoroughfare known as Suzaku Ōji. The Suzaku Gate, located on the southern boundary of the palace, was probably in ruins by Ben no Naishi's time.

3. "Fields" is an approximate translation of *mikakigahara* (fields [outside] the walls) a term associated in early poetry with the environs of the Yoshino royal villa. Here it refers to the area outside Suzaku Gate. *Ōuchi* is another way of referring to the Greater Royal Palace.

[Section 11]

1. Held on the ninth day of the ninth month, the Double Yang Banquet (Chōyō no En, also Chōyō no Sechie) was one of the Gosechi banquets held at court. The banquet imitated the chrysanthemum banquets of China and was based on the belief that chrysanthemum blossoms and their scent possessed the power to avert diseases and promote longevity. The flowers were placed inside floss silk covers to protect the flowers from fading caused by the dew. On the ninth day of the ninth month, custom dictated that one rub the dew-soaked scented cloth on one's face to receive the legendary benefits of the chrysanthemum (McCullough and McCullough 1980, 1:272).

2. Apparently the attractive covers resembled actual chrysanthemums in bloom when placed over the entire bed growing in the Dining-Room Courtyard, thus prompting the poem.

3. The poem makes clever use of the "k" sounds in *kokonoe* (nine-fold; Royal Palace), *kokonuka* (the ninth), and *kokoro* (heart).

[Section 12]

1. Appointment ceremonies (*jimoku*) were court functions to determine appointments of various government officials other than those of minister of state.

Ceremonies for provincial offices were conducted in the first month (unless they were postponed until the second or third month) and were called spring appointment (*agatameshi no jimoku*). Ceremonies for central offices were held in the autumn and was known as fall appointments (*tsukasameshi no jimoku*). Special appointment ceremonies (*rinji no jimoku*) were held at various times. The postponement of the appointment ceremony from the first to the eleventh month added another function to be performed on that occasion. This was the fifteenth annual worship service performed on the death date of the former sovereign Tsuchimikado (1195–1231; r. 1198–1210), who died on the eleventh day of the third month of 1231. Tsuchimikado, son of Go-Toba (1180–1239; r. 1183–98), was the father of Go-Saga and the grandfather of Go-Fukakusa.

2. The guards' headquarters (Jin no Za) was the place where senior nobles sat during Shintō rituals, banquets, appointment ceremonies, and other court events.

3. *Shikiji* was a general term for head chamberlains and fifth- and sixth-rank chamberlains.

4. Little seems to be known about the Golden Wheel Ritual (Konrin no Hō) and the Calamity-Averting Rite (Tenchi Saihen Sai). Apparently they consisted of prayers for the souls of the dead to prevent calamities such as earthquakes, floods, and famine.

5. The nineteenth was presumably the day of the prayers.

[Section 13]

1. A great purification ceremony (*onharae*), part of the *Daijōsai*, was performed after the accession of a new monarch. The simple rites, such as ceremonial hand-washing, followed by cleansing rituals performed by Department of Shrines (Jingikan) officials in which the monarch went to the west side of the dry bed of the Kamo River, were preceded by a magnificent procession that began at the Royal Palace to the rolling of drums. For details, see McCullough and McCullough 1980, 1:376.

2. A structure provided for royal use by the riverside.

[Section 14]

1. Retired Sovereign Go-Saga, father of Go-Fukakusa.

2. For South Hall, see Section 5, note 2.

3. The Courtiers' Hall (Tenjō no Ma), located along the southernmost portion of the Seiryōden, served as the headquarters for senior nobles of first through third ranks (*kugyō*) and male courtiers of the fourth and fifth ranks (*tenjōbito*) while on court duty. The room contained a duty board for courtiers on assignment, a royal chair (*goishi*), some lacquered dining tables, and a free-standing screen known as the Partition of the Annual Ceremonies (Nenjū Gyōji no Shōji) (McCullough and McCullough 1980, 2:843).

4. Spacious Hall (Hirogosho), apparently a building located to the north of the Shishinden within town palaces such as the Kan'in and the Tominokōji Palaces, which substituted for the Jijūden, originally designed as a royal residence for monarchs. At town palaces, these buildings sometimes were called the North Wing Chambers (Kita no Tai) of the Shishinden. According to *The Clear Mirror* (ca.

1376) which contains an entry based on *Ben no Naishi Nikki*, the terms Hirogosho and Kita no Tai both seem to refer to buildings located north of the Shishinden (corresponding to the Jijūden at the original Royal Residential Palace). Both the Kan'in and the Tominokōji palaces had Spacious Halls.

5. There are some *engo* (word associations) and pivot words (*kakekotoba*) at work in the poem. *Furue* (ancient branch) and *furu* (fall) are linked to *shimo* (frost); *moeizu* (sprout; bud) and *moe*, a form of *moyu* (burn), are related to *orimatsu* (firewood).

6. Properly speaking, *ariake no tsuki* (late moon) means the moon in the second half of the lunar month, which is still in the sky at dawn. Here the date is the fourteenth.

7. His Majesty's Apartment (Tsune no Gosho) is identified by Iwasa as a room to the north of the Royal Bedchamber in the Seiryōden in the Royal Residential Palace; Tamai does not indicate a location.

8. For Nyokudokoro, see Section 10, note 1. Later it is recorded that Shōshō no Naishi was in charge of the *Suki* side and that Kōtō no Naishi was responsible for the *Yuki*.

9. Double doors (*tsumado*) opening out from the center connected interior rooms to exterior hallways surrounding "sleeping-hall" style structures. These hinged double doors were usually placed at the corners of buildings, rather than centered along a broader axis. Double doors were permanent fixtures, unlike paper-covered sliding doors (*fusuma*) in "sleeping-hall" style interiors which functioned as movable walls separating areas within the main room ("mother" room, *moya*) inside buildings.

10. The Palace Meadow refers to the site of an open area within the former Greater Royal Palace.

11. *Kokonoe* (nine-fold; Royal Palace) is a decorative preface (*joshi*) for *ōuchiyama* (Royal Palace [Mountain]). Here *ōuchiyama* means *uchino* (Palace Meadow) the site of the former palace, where the *Daijōsai* was to take place.

12. The poem wishes the new monarch a long reign.

13. This poem also hopes the monarch will have a long reign. There is also a pun on *furu* (fall as of snow; a form of *fu*, elapse). *Michi shi aran* can mean both "there will be righteousness" and "there will be a path."

[Section 15]

1. For *Suki* and *Yuki*, see Section 10, note 1. Ben no Naishi wants to visit her sister Shōshō no Naishi at the Suki Nyokudokoro. Yoshida Shrine is located in the northeastern section of Kyōto on the eastern bank of the Kamo River. The Yoshida festival was celebrated twice a year: on the middle Day of the Rat in the fourth month and on the middle Day of the Monkey in the eleventh month. The date in question here is the latter, which was celebrated on the seventeenth day (middle Day of the Monkey) of the eleventh month in 1246. The female courtier assisting the royal messenger to the Yoshida Festival had the responsibility of organizing the offerings placed before the altar.

[Section 16]

1. Ceremonial dress consisted of a train (*mo*) and short Chinese jacket (*karaginu*). Both were required garments for female courtiers on official duty.

2. This poem implores the regent to delay the haircutting ceremony until proper robes could be prepared for the event. *Ōumi* (Great Sea), which can mean "wave pattern" (in fabrics), is an *engo* for *koromo* (robe). Tamai thinks she is asking to be excused from attending the ceremony.

[Section 17]

1. There are two pivot words: *koto* (zither; matter, thing) and *matsu* (wait; [to] pine). *Matsukaze* (pine wind; pine (long for someone) untranslated) is an *engo* for *koto* (zither).

[Section 18]

1. The poem contains a number of pivot words lost in translation: *ko* (bamboo baskets; child), *yo no* (the world; society; bamboo joints), *ou* (grow old, age; carry on the back). *Yo* also functions as an *engo* for *take* (bamboo).

2. There is a pun on *kaku* (in this way; rake).

3. During the *Daijōsai*, blind court musicians, overseers, and other temporary workers were brought in to help with the preparations. The overseers, one for the *Yuki* side and another for the *Suki* side, were given makeshift offices near the Gyō-jidokoro (Ceremony Building).

4. Female supervisors (*nyōkan*), occupying posts such as *nyōju* (female assistants), formed the middle hierarchy of women who served in the Back Palace. *Nyōju* supervised the lowest level of women known as *nyokan* (female servants), the shorter syllable *nyo* indicating a status lower than those referred to by the longer syllable *nyō* used for their supervisors. Here the female supervisors were assigned the task of sewing and dyeing garments for the Nyokudokoro. Many *nyōju* of the *nyōkan* class appear in Ben no Naishi's account but only two *nyokan* are mentioned.

5. *Koto no ha* (leaves of words; fallen leaves [scattered by the wind]). The poem also makes an implicit comparison between the wind and the women's complaints. Their complaints made Chikayori speechless much as the wind made speech impossible for him.

[Section 19]

1. Since Go-Fukakusa was going on an outing to the Council of State on the twenty-second for the *Daijōsai*, his mother, Ōmiya'in, visited the Kan'in Palace on the twentieth to view all the various patterns and designs.

2. A chamberlain-assistant commander (*kurōdo no suke*) refers to someone who concurrently held the positions of chamberlain (*kurōdo*) and assistant master of the gate guards (*emon no suke*).

3. Half-blinds (*kirimisu*), half the usual length of bamboo blinds (*sudare*), hung along the western side of the Table Room (Daibandokoro).

4. "White Tissue Paper" (*Shirousuyō*), a song traditionally sung by courtiers during the Gosechi festivities. Although there were only five Gosechi dancers

among the many groups providing entertainment at the final *Daijōsai* banquet, they were the most prominently mentioned group in literary sources because each was a protégé of someone influential at court. Two of the dancers, along with their women and girl attendants, maids, and other servants, were sponsored by the provincial governor class. The remaining three dancers were sponsored by higher-ranking members of court, such as royal consorts, senior nobles, and courtiers. The dancers were provided quarters and a practice platform in the Jōneiden where they were coached by teachers. They first performed before the monarch, senior nobles, and courtiers in the Jōneiden in the Curtain-Dais Rehearsal (Chōdai no Kokoromi). This was followed by the Gosechi Royal Rehearsal (Gozen no Kokoromi) performed in the Seiryōden eaves-chamber. The formal presentation of the dance was performed after the Flushed Faces Banquet (Toyonoakari no Sechie). For details, see McCullough and McCullough 1980, 1:376–78.

5. "Flushed Faces" (Toyonoakari), part of the *Daijōsai*, centered around the presentation of "white" and "black" wine made from the new rice. The Gosechi dances were formally presented at this time. For details, see McCullough and McCullough 1980, 1:378.

[Section 20]

1. The Sung screens, used on important ceremonial occasions, depicted Chinese polo players.

2. Of the buildings in the Greater Royal Palace, only two buildings, the Council of State and the Department of Shrines (Jingikan), were still in usable condition by the mid-thirteenth century. The broken lattice shutters are a testament to the sad state of disrepair of the two buildings remaining on the palace grounds. This is the first of six days Ben no Naishi spends at the Council of State in attendance upon the sovereign.

3. The throne (*takamikura*), an octagon-shaped chair placed in the exact center of the room for the monarch's use. Here it refers to the room behind the throne.

4. Women of the upper ranks is a descriptive phrase for *nyōbō*. See Chapter 2 for details.

5. Seisodō (also Seishōdō, Burakuin Kōbō, and Furōmon Nainandō), one of the nine buildings in the Court of Abundant Pleasures (Burakuin), was the place where sacred music (*kagura*, see Section 24, note 1) was performed. The Seisodō, situated to the north of the Burakuden in the Burakuin and to the west of the Great Hall of State (Daigokuden) in the Greater Royal Palace, was a special structure designed primarily as a temporary residence for the Gosechi dancers and as a theater to stage the Gosechi dances and *Daijōsai* festivities. The Burakuin, equal in size to the Court of Government (Chōdōin) situated to the east of the complex, was the court's formal banquet facility (McCullough and McCullough 1980, 2:837). Because the Seisodō no longer existed in the mid-Kamakura period, the reference here is probably to a temporary building borrowing its name. This passage reflects very clearly attempts made by the court to replicate the original Royal Residential Palace. The use of town palaces instead of the Royal Residential Palace within the Greater Royal Palace is another example of the use of replicas prevalent during the Kamakura period.

6. The Curtain-Dais Rehearsal, one of the preliminaries to the formal appearance of the Gosechi dancers at the final *Daijōsai* banquet, was performed for the sovereign in the Jōneiden, located in the heart of the Back Palace in the north-central part of the Royal Residential Palace. The Jōneiden had served as a residential hall for sovereigns Ninmyō (810–50; r. 833–50), Yōzei (868–949; r. 876–84), and Suzaku (923–52; r. 930–52), but by the mid-Heian period it was utilized as the staging place for the Gosechi dances and as temporary residential quarters for the Gosechi dancers, their attendants, and their teachers (McCullough and McCullough 1980, 2:847). For details of other activities occurring during the eleventh month, see McCullough and McCullough 1980, 1:376.

7. The "comb-shaped window" (*tenjō no kushigata*) in the Courtiers' Hall was an arch-shaped window in the wall between the Demon Room (Oni no Ma) and His Majesty's Daytime Chamber through which the monarch could view the Courtiers' Hall.

8. Although it had been customary for women in the Heian period to crawl (*izariaruku*) when approaching the sovereign, by the Kamakura period this practice was considered old-fashioned and rather comical. This was but one of the many social changes that occurred in the Kamakura period, some of which are recorded in *Ben no Naishi Nikki*.

9. The poem plays on *toyonoakari* (flushed faces; brightness from outside) and *kaze no tayori* (tidings of the wind; the wind that blew down the screens).

[Section 21]

1. Black Log Building (Kuroki no Ya), round logs used to build various structures for the *Daijōsai*. Here it seems to refer to the Kōritsuden (Royal Bath Chamber).

2. The "formal style" (*kamiage*) was a hairstyle women of the upper ranks, especially *naishi*, were required to wear on ceremonial occasions. The hair from the crown of the head was put up in a tall bun and kept in place by an ornamental hairpin. *Kamiage no naishi* refers to female courtiers on official duty with their hair put up and wearing the required formal attire, a train and a short Chinese jacket.

[Section 22]

1. Drinking parties (*enzui*) were part of the *Daijōsai* celebration. Courtiers, offered *sake* to their heart's desire, composed poetry, sang, and danced in an advanced state of inebriation.

2. The Spirit-Pacifying Festival (Chiko no Sai, also Chinkonsai) was a series of rites based on the belief that both illness and death resulted from the loss or weakening of the soul. The purpose of the rites was to return the wandering soul to its proper place or to quiet and strengthen it. Here, the rites were to preserve the soul of the sovereign and thereby ensure a long reign. The rites were performed every year on the middle Day of the Tiger in the eleventh month, with a female courtier bearing the sovereign's garment box to the ritual site, either the Royal Household Ministry (Kunaishō) or the Department of Shrines (Jingikan). On this occasion, Ben no Naishi was the female courtier on duty.

3. Apparently an unofficial Gosechi event. The retired sovereign was Go-Saga, father of Go-Fukakusa.

[Section 23]

1. A private inspection (*nairan*) decree authorized the holder to review documents of state as the monarch's representative and, therefore, to act as de facto regent. Here the term seems to indicate a meeting at which *nairan* powers were to be exercised. Royal bodyguards (*mizuijin*), attendants (*toneri*) armed with swords and bows, were assigned to accompany people of high rank whenever they went out. Rank determined the number of bodyguards assigned an individual; the regent was assigned ten bodyguards.

2. Ben no Naishi thinks that bodyguards should escort the regent wherever he goes.

[Section 24]

1. Sacred music (*kagura*) can be any performance presented for the benefit of *kami*. It may also be used to refer to a specific kind of sacred music developed for use at court during the Heian period. Because it was thought to be related to the performance that had lured Amaterasu Ōmikami out of her cave, *kagura* was performed at night in areas lit by courtyard fires (*niwabi*), which functioned both as illumination and symbols of ritual purity. Here, the *kagura* was performed on the Day of the Hare rather than on the usual Day of the Snake. Called the Seisodō *kagura*, it was performed in a building designated as the Seisodō after the actual building was destroyed by fire (see Section 20, note 5).

2. Because Go-Fukakusa was still a child, both he and the regent went to the Consort's Apartment to hear the *kagura*. Had he been of age, they would have listened to the performance in the Seisodō replica. In the polygynous society of the Heian and Kamakura periods, aristocratic women were required to hide their faces behind fans or remain behind curtain stands (*kichō*) in the presence of men. When female courtiers found the regent in the Consort's Apartment, they had to leave to avoid being seen by him. When they tried the courtyard, they found that the best places were already taken by women who had come earlier armed with robes to cover their faces.

3. Asakura, referring to the name of an ancient *kagura* and to the temporary palaces of Yūryaku (r. 456-79) and female sovereign Saimei (r. 655-661), signifies a symbolic return to the fifth and seventh centuries.

4. The *Gunsho Ruijū* text gives the name of the esteemed *biwa* as Bokuba rather than as Mokuma. The lute-like instruments, Mokuma and Genjō (see Section 81), survived to the fourteenth century because they are mentioned in *Essays in Idleness* (*Tsurezuregusa*) Section 70 (NKBT 30, 147) and *The Great Peace* (*Taiheiki*) Book 14 (NKBT 35.II:81).

[Section 25]

1. The Day of the Dragon fell on the twenty-fifth in 1246. Traditionally during the *Daijōsai*, the *Yuki* Banquet takes place on the Day of the Dragon, but the

Flushed Faces Banquet took place on that day in this reign. Here, reference is presumably being made to the Flushed Faces Banquet.

[Section 26]

1. "Pages' performances" is an approximate translation of *warawa nobori*, a term of uncertain meaning. *Rodai no ranbu* (platform dancing) was boisterous informal singing and dancing by courtiers.

2. The Kan'in Palace was a town palace located south of Second Avenue and one block (*chō*) west of Nishinotō'in. Originally it was a residence of Fujiwara Fuyutsugu (775–826), but it later became Go-Sanjō's (1034–73; r. 1068–72) residence. It was also the royal residence of Takakura (1161–81; r. 1168–80). Go-Toba designed the layout of the Kan'in Palace to replicate the plan of the Royal Residential Palace as closely as possible, and then had the shogun Minamoto Yoritomo (1147–99) pay for the cost of renovation and construction (Ōta 1987, 818).

3. Although Ben no Naishi "recalls" the Greater Royal Palace, only the Council of State and Department of Shrines were still in usable condition in the mid-thirteenth century. The Council of State was where Ben no Naishi had spent the previous six days in attendance upon the monarch for the *Daijōsai* enthronement ceremonies.

[Section 27]

1. The Kamo Special Festival (Kamo no Rinji no Sai) was supposed to be held annually on the last Day of the Cock in the eleventh month. Because there was also a "regular" Kamo Festival in the fourth month (middle Day of the Cock), this one was called the Kamo Special Festival. (Despite its name, it was a regular court event which kept the elaborate Kamo Return ceremony.) The Return *kagura* was a relatively short performance. For details, see McCullough and McCullough 1980, 1:408–9.

2. The Lime Altar Room (Ishibai no Dan, Ishibai no Ma), located in the southeastern corner of the Seiryōden, was the site of the sovereign's daily prayers, assisted by female courtiers.

3. The matting was being appropriated to help ward off the bitter cold. Shōnagon no Naishi is unidentified. The name Shōshō probably refers to Ben no Naishi's sister.

4. The Bright Star (Venus) figures in one of the songs presented on occasions such as the Kamo Return.

[Section 28]

1. Sacred music at the Naishidokoro (Naishidokoro no Mikagura) was traditionally performed in the courtyard between the Naishidokoro (also Kashikodokoro or Unmeiden) and the Ryōkiden (McCullough and McCullough 1980, 2:848). Regardless of the season, *kagura* was almost always performed at night. Beginning at around the time courtyard fires were needed, the sacred dances continued until dawn. A *kagura* building was constructed in the courtyard with three of the four sides draped by curtains. The fourth side facing the courtyard fires was left open. A Naishidokoro performance consisted of two sides, the *moto* and the *sue*, totaling

sixteen men; a *gagaku* (ancient court music) instrumental group of seven musicians (two Japanese zithers [*wagon*], three Japanese flutes [*yokobue*], and two oboes [*hichiriki*]); and a director (*ninjō*), who gave cues, made announcements, performed dances, and generally set the course for the entire performance. Everyone gathered within the curtained structure, divided into *moto* or *sue* sides, seated themselves and waited for the flute signal followed by the oboe, cues that the performance had begun. At this time the director went before the courtyard fires and, after performing the Kicking of the Earth Ritual, proceeded to lead the *moto* and *sue* sides in the performance. The "things taken" (*torimono*) ended with a dance by the director, after which there was an intermission supplied with wine and light entertainment. This was followed by the lighter *saibara* and the more serious *kamuagari* sections. A second and final dance by the director signified the conclusion of the performance. The sacred music at the Naishidokoro was performed annually on an auspicious day in the twelfth month (McCullough and McCullough 1980, 1:410–11.

2. Azechi no Sukedono and Azechi no Sanmi are related: Azechi no Sanmi is the older sister of Azechi no Sukedono; both are daughters of Fujiwara Takahira (d. 1254). The elder sister, Azechi no Sanmi served Go-Saga and bore him a son, Prince Saijohō, and the younger sister served Go-Fukakusa.

3. An allusion to a poem in the *Tales of Ise* (*Ise Monogatari*):

Hito shirenu	Would that he might fall asleep
Waga kayoiji no	Every night,
Sekimori wa	This guard
Yoiyoigoto ni	At the secret place
Uchi mo nenanan	Where I come and go.
(McCullough 1968, 72)	

[Section 29)

1. Seasonal divide (*sechibun*) was the term for the night before the beginning of one of the four seasons of the year as determined by the twenty-four fortnights (*nijūshi sekki*) calendar:

Season	Months	Western Equivalents
spring	1-3	February 5-May 5
summer	4-6	May 6-August 7
fall	7-9	August 8-November 7
winter	10-12	November 8-February 4

Directional taboos (*katatagae*) originated in China when a detailed cosmology was developed according to which the universe was conceived as an organic structure that was controlled by Heaven, consisting of *yin* (negative) and *yang* (positive) forces, and the five elements (earth, fire, metal, tree, and water). The ruler played a pivotal role as mediator between Heaven and the natural order, and it was the ruler's job to instruct his subjects to follow Confucian moral precepts. The ruler's success or failure was gauged by Heaven's response through occurrences of auspicious events, portents, or visitations. This system gave rise to a school of divination and a body of literature that dealt with directional taboos and calendrical superstitions. Known as Onmyōdō (Chinese, *Yinyangjia*), this system was only marginally

Confucian and went against the rational ideology of Confucius' teaching, but exercised great influence on both the Chinese and Japanese of the time. Directional taboos required people to temporarily abandon their own homes and spend a night or two at another house in a safe direction (*katatagae dokoro*) to avoid one that was deemed dangerous by Yin-yang diviners. Usually people who were in an unlucky direction contacted a family in a safe direction and arranged to spend the night as a guest until conditions changed that made their own residences "safe" again. The host family was expected to offer hospitality and be of service to their guests (*Kōdansha Encyclopedia of Japan* 1983, 1:353). On this night, custom required sovereigns, former sovereigns, women of the royal family, ministers of state, and other people of high status to change their residences. Advised by divination masters to avoid certain inauspicious directions to avert bad luck, the monarch and his entourage celebrated the advent of spring in other quarters.

2. A reference to events recorded in Section 26.

3. *Kumoi* (abode of clouds) refers to the Royal Palace and also the sky; *meguru* (return; encircle) is an *engo* for *tsuki* (moon).

[Section 30]

1. A misappropriation of the term *sechie* (official court banquets) to refer to a party given by the newly-appointed chancellor Minamoto (Koga) Michimitsu (1187–1248) at his home.

2. The Table Room, located in the southwest corner of the Seiryōden north of the Demon Room (Oni no Ma) and west of His Majesty's Daytime Chamber (Hi no Omashi), served as the headquarters for female courtiers. For "the formal style," see Section 21, note 2.

3. In the Courtiers' Hall's small courtyard near the Seiryōden, there was a stake on which cards showing the time (*toki no kui*) were posted. Chancellor Michimitsu is asking whether it is time for the card designating the Hour of the Ox (1:00 A.M.-3:00 A.M.) to be attached.

4. There is a wordplay between *Ne no koku sugite* (past the Hour of the Rat [11:00 P.M.-1:00 A.M.]) and *nesugi* (oversleep). The meaning of the poem is: The Hour of the Rat has passed. It is now the Hour of the Ox. However, it could also read: If by sleeping overlong, you dozed through the Hour of the Rat, you would not have known that the Ox Card had already been posted on the stake.

[Section 31]

1. The Healing Buddha Recitation Rites (Yakushi no Mishiho) celebrated the wondrous powers of the Healing Buddha. The rites consisted of recitations, either habitual daily devotions or continuous ones, which were performed for a fixed period, usually seven or twenty-one days.

2. *Kechigan* can also mean to offer prayers to a deity, but here it refers to the final day of the rites.

3. Buddha's Names Ceremony (Butsumyōe), usually celebrated annually at court for three successive nights from the nineteenth to the twenty-first day of the twelfth month, was to purge the sins one had accumulated during the year. The services consisted of recitations of the names of the three thousand Buddhas of the

past, the present, and the future listed in the Butsumyō sutra. In this section, it was celebrated on the twenty-sixth.

[Section 32]

1. *Hairai* generally means to worship, but more specifically it refers to the Congratulation of the Monarch (Chōhai or Chōga), a ceremony performed on the first day of the New Year at the Hour of the Dragon [7:00 A.M.-9:00 A.M.], when the entire court gathered at the Great Hall of State in ceremonial dress to pay homage to the monarch. By the early Heian period, it began to be replaced by the more private ceremony, Lesser Obeisance to the Monarch (Kojōhai), performed in the eastern courtyard of the Seiryōden, in which only holders of the highest six court ranks participated. By 990, the Lesser Obeisance to the Monarch had completely replaced the more elaborate T'ang style Congratulation of the Monarch in which the entire court assembled with banners, incense, and drums. Although the term *chōhai* is used in this entry, Tamai thinks that the Kojōhai ceremony is the one actually intended (McCullough and McCullough 1980, 1:381). The Great Hall of State, the most splendid building in the Greater Royal Palace located to the southwest of the Royal Residential Palace in the central portion of the complex, housed the monarch's throne. After fires in 876, 1056, and 1177, the enthronement ceremonies, which had been conducted at the Great Hall of State, were transferred to the Shishinden. For details, see McCullough and McCullough 1980, 2:836–37. In the Kamakura period, when residence within town palaces was prevalent, abdication ceremonies were conducted in such places as the Tominokōji Palace (Section 1), and the enthronement ceremonies in the Council of State (Section 2).

[Section 33]

1. The Green Horse Banquet (Aouma no Sechie) was a therapeutic ritual to ward off illnesses throughout the year by viewing "green" horses in early spring. According to the Yin-yang cosmology, the horse was a *yang* animal and green was the color of spring. The horses were probably light grays or roans, colors that fell within the definition of *ao* (green) but were written with the characters for "white" and " horse."

2. The function of interior controller (*naiben,* responsible for everything inside the Shōmei Gate) was usually performed by the minister of the left and that of exterior controller (*gaiben,* in charge of areas outside the Shōmei Gate) by the minister of the right. Here, a marginal note in the text indicates that the interior controller was the minister of the right, Fujiwara Tadaie (1228–75), aged nineteen at the time.

3. Presumably the sun is the major captain. The ceremony of the Green Horse Banquet revolved around an elaborate parade, viewed by the monarch and a host of other spectators, in which twenty-one horses from the Royal Stables were led through the Burakuin courtyard (later through the South Court of the Shishinden). Later the monarch and the court banqueted while dances were presented.

4. This is an allusion to the Lao Tzu passage that compares the rapid passage of time to the action of green horses parading by swiftly.

[Section 34]

1. Although innocent of any wrongdoing, the incumbent regent, Fujiwara (Ichijō) Sanetsune (1223–84), was forced to retire because his younger brother, the incumbent shogun Kujō Yoritsune (1218–44; shogun 1226–44), allegedly had plotted to take the life of the Hōjō regent Tokiyori (1227–23; shogunal regent 1246–56). The entire Kujō branch of the Fujiwara family was ousted from positions of power: Sanetsune from the post of regent, Yoritsune from the post of Shogun, and Sanetsune's father, the former regent Kujō Michiie, from influence in court society. The Konoe branch of the Fujiwara family replaced the Kujō branch at court, with Kanetsune selected as regent. Thus "regent" in Sections 1–34 refers to Ichijō Sanetsune, but in Sections 35–175, to Konoe Kanetsune.

2. Ben no Naishi sympathizes with the fate of the recently dismissed Sanetsune. She often uses the image of the moon clouded by haze or clouds to symbolize a sad occasion.

3. Upper Hot Water Room (Oyudono no Ue), a term not found in records during the Heian period when the Royal Residential Palace still existed. Apparently the term was coined during the Kamakura period when town palaces came into frequent use. A map of the Seiryōden in Ōta Seiroku's *A Study of the Sleeping-Hall Architectural Style* (*Shindenzukuri no Kenkyū*, 1987) situates the room in the northwestern corner of the Seiryōden at the Kan'in Palace. Iwasa Miyoko describes the room as another office where women of the upper ranks performed scribal duties. Uses of the term "Oyudono no Ue" in the Muromachi period place the room within the Seiryōden, where it was utilized by high-ranking female courtiers as an office for keeping records concerning annual events, drawing up royal documents, and the like. Another source places the Upper Hot Water Room in the northwestern corner of the Seiryōden, north of the Hand-Washing Room and the Dining Room (Yasuraoka 1967, 1:502–3). "Upper" suggests that the room may have been higher in elevation than others.

4. The attendance register (*chakutō*), made of paper that had been recycled and bound into book form, contained the names of officials on duty and visitors to the monarch, recorded by female courtiers on duty. There were separate attendance registers for female courtiers kept in the Upper Hot Water Room and for male courtiers in the Courtiers' Hall.

5. Kasuga Shrine, the tutelary shrine of the Fujiwara family in Nara, signified the importance of the regental family in the political and social life of the nation. Shōshō no Naishi intimates that vicissitudes, thought virtually to be unknown to the prosperous Fujiwara, have now ravaged the former regent Sanetsune and his family. Ben no Naishi and Shōshō no Naishi use the image of the evergreen as a symbol for stability to highlight the upheaval caused by the removal of the Kujō branch from power. The poem may also allude to *Shinkokinshū* 36 by Go-Toba in which he questions Sei Shōnagon's idea that evenings were best in autumn.

[Section 35]

1. There are two possible explanations for this term: it could refer to the Ōdairi or Daidairi (Greater Royal Palace), destroyed by fire in 1219 and not rebuilt

thereafter (Ōta 1987, 789–90), or it may be a sobriquet for Retired Sovereign Go-Saga.

2. Although Tamai is uncertain of the nature of the memoir, he thinks it was a record of royal activities written by Lady Chūnagon no Suke while she was in service to a former monarch, possibly Go-Saga. Lady Chūnagon no Suke was in her fifties at this time.

3. There are puns on *katami* (keepsake); *kata* (lagoon), and *urami* (regret); *ura* (bay, inlet), all of which are *engo* for *chidori* (plover). *Nami no ue* (on the waves) here means "circulating in unofficial quarters." *Hamachidori no ato* (plover tracks) refers to the handwriting. Ben no Naishi's poem is similar to an overdue notice from the library: the memoir must be returned.

[Section 36]

1. Attendants for the royal prayers (*gyohai no ontomo*) were female courtiers dispatched by the Office of Female Courtiers to assist the monarch in the Lime Altar Room to conduct daily royal prayers. For the Lime Altar Room, see Section 27, note 2.

2. The veranda (*sunoko*) of the Two-Bay Room, located to the east of the Two-Bay Room and the outer eaves (*magobisashi*), faced the eastern courtyard between the Seiryōden and the Jijūden where stood the two famous clusters of bamboo, the Black Bamboo (Kuretake) and the River Bamboo (Kawatake). The Black Bamboo was located on the eastern side of the courtyard, closest to the Jijūden.

3. Lady Chūnagon no Suke's remarks allude to a poem by Fun'ya no Yasuhide, a ninth-century poet, one of the Six Poetic Geniuses (Rokkasen), who has four poems in the *Kokinshū* (*Collection of Ancient and Modern Japanese Poetry*, ca. 905) and one poem in the *Gosenshū* (*Later Collection of Japanese Poetry*, ca. 950):

> *Kokinshū* 8. Fun'ya no Yasuhide. On the third of a certain first month, the Nijō Empress, who was then known as the Mother of the Crown Prince, summoned Yasuhide to receive some instructions. As he bowed below her veranda, she observed that snow was falling on his head while the sun was shining. She commanded him to compose a poem:

haru no hi no	Rare is the fortune
hikari ni ataru	of one who basks in the sun
ware naredo	on this springtime day,
kashira no yuki to	yet how can I not lament
naru zo wabishiki	that snow should whiten my head?

> (McCullough 1985a, 200)

Lady Chūnagon no Suke, who was in her fifties, comments that although Fun'ya no Yasuhide laments the white hairs upon his head (*kashira no yuki*), he was not as old as she.

4. Ben no Naishi's poem alludes to Fun'ya no Yasuhide's poem but commiserates with the sentiments of Lady Chūnagon no Suke because everyone dislikes the visible and physical effects of aging.

[Section 37]
  1. On the twenty-eighth day of the second month of the fifth year of Kangen (1247), the era name changed and became the first year of Hōji (1247). The Hōji era name was used until 1249. The change in era name was prompted by the need to remove any negative associations for the reign after power shifted from the Kujō to the Konoe branch of the Fujiwara family.
  2. Shining middle captain (Teru Chūjō) Minamoto Narinobu (b. 979) and Radiant lesser captain (Hikaru Shōshō) Fujiwara Shigeie (fl. 10th c.) decided to renounce the world in 1001 after the two felt they could not possibly eclipse the superior attainments of the "illustrious Four Counselors" (Shi Nagon: Fujiwara Tadanobu, Fujiwara Kintō, Minamoto Toshikata, and Fujiwara Yukinari) of Ichijō's court (980–1011; r. 986–1011).

[Section 38]
  1. The Light Offering (Gotō no Goshinji) was the offering of lighted torches to the North Star, worshipped as a protective deity, on the third day of the third month. For the first three days of the third month, the sovereign restricted his diet and avoided monks, nuns, people in mourning, and others who were ritually unclean. Buddhist monks and nuns were considered ritually unclean by Shintō standards because Buddhism dealt with death (funeral services) and illness (curative rites). Ritual defilements had to be avoided during the performance of Shintō ceremonies.
  2. During Ben no Naishi's period of light mourning (prescribed for the death of distant relatives), she was obliged to give up her regular duties and remain in seclusion.
  3. East Sanjō (Higashi Sanjō or Tō Sanjō), an area in the capital south of Nijō and east of Nishinotō'in. There also was a mansion of that name used as a town palace.
  4. Palace guards (*takiguchi*), military officers who handled duties similar to police with headquarters near a waterfall on the stream called Mikawamizu, which flowed through the palace grounds to the northeast of the Seiryōden.

[Section 39]
  1. "Goematsu Pine on Mt. Ryōzen" ("Ryōzen no Goematsu"), a line from a song sung at the Gosechi festivals.

[Section 41]
  1. The prayers were the Golden Wheel Ritual and the Buddha's Eye Ritual (Butsugenhō). For Golden Wheel Ritual, see Section 12, note 4. The Buddha's Eye Ritual was a rite addressed to the Goddess of Buddha's Eye (Buddhalocanā, J. Butsugenson) to prevent calamities. Apparently there were a series of strange occurrences, such as shooting stars, earthquakes, and a red tide near Kamakura, that necessitated the performance of various calamity-averting rituals of which these were a part.
  2. The manager, Fujiwara Munemasa, was also in charge of the Calamity-Averting Rite in Section 12.

3. Possibly the former chancellor, Fujiwara (Saionji) Saneuji (1194–1269), father of Ōmiya'in, Kinmoto, and Kinsuke. The incumbent chancellor was Minamoto Michimitsu.

4. Archbishop (Sōjō) Jigen. He resigned on the twenty-eighth day of the first month of 1247.

5. Calling the Roll (*Monjaku*), between 9-11 P.M., verified the presence of the palace guards on night duty.

6. During the official proceedings (*jin no kuji*), palace guards had to stay in attendance upon senior nobles during the meeting, causing a delay in "calling the roll."

[Section 42]

1. Seasonal Reading of the Sutra (Ki no Midokyō), refers to the reading of the Great Wisdom Sutra (Daihannya[haramitta]kyō, Skt. Mahāprajñā-pāramitā-sūtra), a fundamental philosophical work of the Mahāyāna school, recited as a protection against many kinds of evil. There were two seasons, spring and fall, during which the readings took place. Here, it is the spring (third month) reading.

2. When the Great Wisdom Sutra was being read in the Shishinden, the counselors, consultants, and other high-ranking nobles attended while others went before the sovereign's presence.

3. The little balls (*temari*) had nothing to do with the ceremony but were probably given to the child monarch to provide some amusement during the long reading.

4. There is a pun on *tomari* (stop; harbor) and *tō mari* (ten balls). The linked verses together produce a poem of longing for the former regent Sanetsune, under house arrest after his dismissal.

5. *Kakari* (anchor) is an *engo* for *fune* (boat), also a *kemari* (kickball) term indicating the four trees planted at the corners of the playing field. For details on *kemari*, see Section 87, note 1.

6. The poem's essence is: Why did rough waves (the Kamakura shogunate) confine the floating boat (the former regent Sanetsune) to harbor (his quarters)?

[Section 43]

1. Fujiwara Morotsugu's mother was the daughter of Fujiwara Muneyuki (d. 1221), who was a former provisional middle counselor of senior third rank.

2. Saionji was built in the Kitayama area by the former chancellor Fujiwara (Saionji) Saneuji. The Fujiwara branch descended from the former chancellor Saneuji was called "Saionji" to distinguish them from numerous other branch families of the northern or regental branch of the Fujiwara. Place name designations for branch families came into frequent use during the Kamakura period.

3. Ben no Naishi and Shōshō no Naishi's poems allude to a composition by Ariwara no Narihira in the *Tales of Ise:*

Once there was a man of rather low rank whose mother was a royal princess. The mother lived at Nagaoka and since the son was in royal service at the capital, he found it hard to visit her as often as she would have liked. He was her only child, and she loved him dearly. In the twelfth month of a certain year a letter came from her; it was, according to the messenger, a matter of the utmost urgency. In great alarm the man opened it and read this poem:

Oinureba	More than ever
Saranu wakare no	I yearn to see you,
Ari to ieba	For old age is said to bring
Iyoiyo mimaku	A parting
Hoshiki kimi kana	None can evade.

Weeping bitterly, the son wrote,

Yo no naka ni	For the sake of sons
Saranu wakare no	Who pray that their parents
Naku mo gana	May live a thousand years,
Chiyo mo to inoru	Would that in this world
Hito no ko no tame	There were no final partings.

(McCullough 1968, 128)

[Section 44]

1. Sen'ninmon'in (Fujiwara Genshi, 1232–62), consort of Shijō (1231–42; r. 1232–42), lost her father in early childhood, then her sovereign just a few years later. The act of women of the upper ranks cutting their hair (*migushi orosu*) signified taking Buddhist vows and renouncing the world. Aristocratic women sometimes had hair as long, if not longer, than their height. Therefore, when taking Buddhist vows, their hair was cut "short," to a length that reached the mid-back.

2. The Tō'in regent, Fujiwara Norizane (1209–35), father of Sen'ninmon'in, was a son of Fujiwara (Kujō) Michiie.

3. There are several puns: *ama* (fisherwoman; nun); *ura* (bay; lining [of robes]). *Koromo no ura* is a phrase taken from the Lotus Sutra, "the Jewel in the Lining," but here it is merely a pun on "bay." *Tatsu* (set out), *nare* (worn), and *ura* (lining) are *engo* for *koromo* (robe). *Tatsu* also means to sew cut cloth into robes, thus *tachinarenu* (not worn before) implies a recent change to a nun's habit. Ben no Naishi empathizes with the nun's sorrow.

4. More puns: *tsu* ([land of] Tsu; port); *naniwa* (proper name; what); *ama* (fisherwoman; nun). *Tsu no kuni* is a *jo* (decorative preface) for Naniwa. There is a play on Naniwa, the ancient name for Ōsaka in Settsu Province (Settsu no Kuni), for *nani wa* (why, or what).

[Section 45]

1. Lady Dainagon alludes to a poem by Ki no Tsurayuki (ca. 872–945):
Kokinshū 124. Tsurayuki. On kerria blossoming near the Yoshino River.

Yoshinogawa	Even their reflections
kishi no yamabuki	in the stream depths are scattered
fuku kaze ni	by the blowing wind:
soko no kage sae	kerria flowers on the bank
utsuroinikeri	of the Yoshino River.

(McCullough 1985b, 37)

2. Because the stream on the palace grounds also boasts kerria blooming nearby, the poem puns on *utsu* (reflect; transfer to) and alludes to Tsurayuki's poem.

[Section 46]

1. The former chancellor, Fujiwara (Saionji) Saneuji, is meant here. In office until the eleventh month of 1246, he was the father of Ōmiya'in and the maternal grandfather of Go-Fukakusa. The incumbent chancellor was Minamoto (Koga) Michimitsu, who came into office on the twenty-fourth day of the twelfth month of 1246.

2. There are puns on *matsu* (pine [tree]; pine [to long for]) and *kai* (ravine; efficacy). *Kai*, which can also mean "egg," is an *engo* for *yama* (mountain) and *hototogisu* (cuckoo).

3. The poem echoes the *kai* (ravine; efficacy) pun of the Chancellor's poem.

4. Ben no Naishi did not accompany the women who journeyed to Kitayama to hear the cuckoo. A headnote to her *kumoi yori* poem in the *Shokugosenshū* (*Later Collection of Gleanings of Japanese Poetry, Continued*, ca. 1251) states that she composed the poem after hearing about the exchange between the chancellor and her sister.

5. There is the same pun on *kai*. *Kumoi* (abode of clouds; Royal Palace) is an *engo* for *hototogisu* (cuckoo).

[Section 47]

1. The Records Office (Kirokudokoro), created in the reign of Sanjō (976–1017; r. 1011–16) to administer royal estates. Tamai thinks that it was located in the Tominokōji Palace, the residence of the Retired Sovereign Go-Saga. The purpose of the monarch's visit was to avoid a directional taboo.

2. Mock banquet festivities were staged presumably as an amusement for the child monarch by his father, Go-Saga.

3. *Ikan*, semi-formal attire worn by officials of fourth and fifth rank (such as the Takayuki mentioned here) and, less often, by more senior figures like the major counselor. For details, see Section 78, note 2.

4. One of the various songs sung on auspicious occasions. "Ah, the Clear Moon" is a line in a song sung at the Gosechi festivities. "Ten Thousand Years" was a dance with Chinese antecedents (said to have been set to music inspired by the parrot of Empress Wu [623–705]). The final song is unidentified.

[Section 48]

1. Golden Light Sutra (Konkōmyō Saishōkyō) annual lectures, held at the royal palace in the fifth month for five consecutive days, were conducted at the Seiryōden to ensure a peaceful reign.

2. The Demon Room (Oni no Ma), in the southwestern corner of the Seiryōden, was so called because the wall separating it from the Courtiers' Hall depicted an unidentified Chinese hero killing a demon. The precise function of the room is unknown, but it seems to have been a retiring room for those in need of privacy.

3. There is a pun on *hatsuka* (barely; twentieth).

[Section 49]

1. This implores Morotsugu not to forget Hyōe no Kami, even though in the midst of sorrow. Like the reply that follows, it alludes to a poem in the *Kokinshū*. *Kokinshū* 139. Anonymous. [Topic unknown].

satsuki matsu	Scenting the fragrance
hanatachibana no	of orange blossoms that await
ka o kageba	the fifth month's coming,
mukashi no hito no	I recall a perfumed sleeve
sode no ka zo suru	worn by someone long ago.

(McCullough 1985b, 41)

2. *Yatsuru* implies a change in one's appearance due to mourning, therefore, the poem suggests that the flower's fragrance will fade were it to touch his sleeves dyed by the colors of mourning.

[Section 50]

1. The Five Altars (Godan no Mishiho) were erected in front of the *myōō* (five divinities): Taisei Fudō (center), Gozanze Yasha (east), Gundari Yasha (south), Daiitoku Yasha (west), and Kongo Yasha (north). The ritual consisted of the simultaneous performance of prayers before the altars.

2. Lattice room dividers (*tatejitomi*), thin wooden slats placed together horizontally and vertically and backed by boards, used in a courtyard or inside a room to lend some privacy.

[Section 51]

1. Tamai suggests that the Table Room was the setting for the conversation because half-blinds were traditionally hung along the western side of that room.

2. Duty board (*nikkyū no onfuda*), a piece of paper placed on a board standing in the Courtiers' Hall upon which the names of those on duty were written.

3. Attendance register (*chakutō*), required the signatures of those in attendance at the Seiryōden. For details, see Section 34, note 4.

4. The Facilities Office (Tonomozukasa, also Tonomori no Tsukasa), one of the Twelve Offices of the Back Palace, was responsible for items related to lighting such as providing oil for torches and firewood for heating water for baths, and the like. Here the reference is to a female representative from that office.

5. Sounding boards (*nariita*, also *naruita*; *kenzan no ita*), located in the southern corner of the outer eaves corridor of the Seiryōden. Loose floor boards announced the arrival and departure of visitors to the royal residence.

6. Ryōzen, site of the Shōbō Temple on a mountain in the Higashiyama area.

[Section 52]

1. The date was the eighth day of the sixth month of 1247.

2. Apparently Akichika began an ascetic journey to Kumano soon after he renounced the world at Shōbō Temple. Kumano is located in the Muro-gun region in parts of Wakayama and Mie prefectures.

3. Repast in the Presence of a *Kami* (Jingonjiki) held on the eleventh day of the sixth and eleventh months. The monarch took freshly cooked rice, for which he

had lit the cooking fire, to the Shinkaden (part of the Chūwain) to worship the sun goddess Amaterasu Ōmikami and to invoke the spirits of the *kami*. After praying, he ate some of the rice. This ceremony resembled the First Fruits Service (Niinamesai), but used old rice rather than new. In this section, the ceremony was held in the Table Room of the Kan'in Palace.

4. *Mi no ke mo tatsu* (my hair stands on end) can also mean "my feathers are ruffled."

[Section 53]

1. Both Tamai and Iwasa think that "he" refers to the regent Konoe Kanetsune.

2. Fujiwara Tameuji (1222–86), eldest son of Fujiwara Tameie (1197–1275) and a grandson of Fujiwara Teika (1162–1241), inherited leadership of the Nijō school of poetry from Tameie but faced challenges from his brother Tamenori (1226–79), who founded the Kyōgoku school of poetry, and from his half-brother Tamesuke (1260–1328), who established the Reizei school under the direction of his mother the nun Abutsu. Later Tamenori's Kyōgoku school and Tamesuke's Reizei school joined forces, creating an innovative style of poetry known as the Kyōgoku-Reizei school of poetry. Tameuji appears a number of times in the memoir performing duties alongside Ben no Naishi. Although Tameuji and Ben no Naishi are distant relatives, their relationship is never mentioned in this account.

[Section 54]

1. For appointment ceremonies, see Section 12, note 1.

2. One of the secular duties of *naishi* was to announce the names of those who had received appointments to the monarch.

3. The more usual "kind of waiting" was that of a woman who longed for her lover's early arrival or who has stayed awake all night waiting for her lover as in the following by Akazome Emon in *Goshūishū* (*Later Collection of Gleanings of Japanese Poetry*, 1086):

Goshūishū 680 (also *Hyakunin Isshu* 59).

yasurawade	Would that I had slept
nenamashi mono o	without hesitating.
sayofukete	As night deepens,
katabuku made no	I watch the moon
tsuki o mishi kana	until it sets.

[Section 55]

1. Hidden censer (*soradakimono*), incense burned in a hidden place within a room or in an entirely different room, to provide fragrance for visitors. The character for *sora* suggests *atenonaranu* (unreliable), an antonym of *tanome* (to rely). A related word *soradanomi*, a combination of *soradaki* and *tanomi*, also means unreliable.

2. *Tanome* (rely) puns on *ta no mi* (fruits of rice fields) identified by Iwasa as a day to celebrate rice production. It refers directly to Ōmiya'in, the consort who provided the incense.

[Section 56]

1. The retired sovereign's Ben no Naishi refers to another female courtier with the same pseudonym as the author of *Ben no Naishi Nikki*. Apparently, the retired sovereign's Ben no Naishi had become familiar with the bush-clover (*hagi*) when Go-Saga lived at the Kan'in Palace while he was the titular monarch.

[Section 57]

1. The ceremony, first performed at the University (Daigakuryō) and later moved to the Council of State, consisted of reading and discussing Chinese Classics such as *The Book of Filial Piety* (*Hsiao Ching*), *The Book of Rites* (*Li Chi*), *The Book of Poetry* (*Mo Shih*), *The Book of History of the Lord of Shang* (*Shang Shu*), and *The Analects of Confucius* (*Lun Yü*). After this, the literati composed Chinese poems and scholars led their students in debates on the Chinese Classics, the Laws and Rituals, and the like.

2. On the day following the ceremony, the monarch usually ate *himorogi* (food originally offered to *kami*) in the Table Room. Iwasa and *Kōjien* agree with Tamai's explanation of *himorogi*. However, Holtom defines *himorogi* as a branch of the sacred evergreen tree called *sakaki* (*Cleyera japonica*) adorned with streamers of hemp and paper enclosed by a small fence similarly decorated. He states that it is the most primitive form of a Shintō shrine (75). Ellwood also defines *himorogi* as *sakaki* branches with strips of white cloth (43). Evidently there are two sets of compounds with different meanings. The first one applies here.

3. "Shikishima no michi" refers metaphorically to *waka*, contrasting native (Yamato) to Chinese (Kara) verse.

[Section 58]

1. Tokiwai Palace, the residence of Fujiwara (Saionji) Saneuji, was located between Ōimikado and Higashi Kyōgoku, on the border of Reizeinokōji and north of Tominokōji.

2. Fujiwara Tameie and two of his sons, Tameuji and Tamenori, appear together in this entry as participants in a linked-verse session sponsored by Go-Saga, who was an avid fan of linked-verse composition. For details on Tameie and his sons, see Section 53, note 2.

3. I have omitted an unintelligible phrase, "kore koso to ori ni mieshi."

4. Mikushigedono, the daughter of the former chancellor Fujiwara Kinfusa (d. 1249), died on the fifteenth day of the eighth month of 1247, less than a month after having given birth to Go-Saga's son Prince Seijo.

5. An allusion to a line from *Shinchokusenshū* (*New Royal Collection of Japanese Poetry*, ca. 1232):

Shinchokusenshū 1239. Fujiwara Kintsune.

aware nado	Indeed it is sad!
mata miru kage no	Why may I never see her again?
nakaruran	Even after the moon
kumogakurete mo	is obscured by clouds,
tsuki wa idekeri	it reappears.

6. There is a pun on *kage* (moonlight; form). *Kage* signifies a form or its projection, such as light.

[Section 59]

1. The Horse-Leading Ceremony (Komahiki), consisting of the presentation of horses sent from various provinces as tribute, was performed annually in the eighth month from the sixteenth to the twenty-eighth. On the sixteenth, sixteen horses from Shinano (Nagano prefecture) were presented. (Traditionally this took place on the fifteenth but because it would have affected the national mourning day for Suzaku, it was delayed until the sixteenth.) On the seventeenth, horses from Hosaka in Kai (Yamanashi prefecture) were presented. On the twentieth, horses from Ono in Musashi (Tokyo and Saitama prefectures), horses from Chichibu (in Saitama prefecture), and elsewhere were presented to the monarch. On the twenty-third, twenty horses from Mochizuki in Shinano were presented. On the twenty-eighth, fifty horses from Kōzuke (Gunma prefecture) were presented. Officials called *koma mukae* met the horses at Ōsaka Barrier outside the capital. After a preliminary statement by the presiding official at the guards' headquarters, senior nobles and others received horses, led them before the monarch, performed obeisance, and then withdrew. The remaining horses were distributed to retired sovereigns, the crown prince, or anyone else who was deemed appropriate. The messenger in charge of distributing the remaining horses was called the *hikiwake no tsukai*.

2. This sentence appears as a marginal note in the *Kangenki* text but in no other text. Sukesue did not become a provisional middle counselor until two years after this episode. An error of this type might have occurred during the course of revising the text at a later date.

3. I have followed Tamai in emending what appears to be a corrupt passage.

4. Tamai thinks that Akitomo had been in charge of the proceedings on the fifteenth.

5. Mikushigedono was Kinyasu's aunt.

6. An interlinear note names middle captain Kintada as Kinyasu's replacement.

7. There are references to *kirihara no koma* (horses of the misty field) in many old poems, beginning with *Shūishū* (*Collection of Gleanings of Japanese Poetry*, ca. 1005–11):

Shūishū 169. Takato.

ausaka no	Horses of the misty field
seki no iwa kado	emerge from the mountains,
fuminarashi	stamping underfoot
yama tachiizuru	the stone gate
kirihara no koma	at Ausaka Barrier.

Kirihara has been tentatively located at Kiri-mura, Chikuma-gun in Nagano prefecture. *Kumoi* (abode of clouds; Royal Palace) is an *engo* for *kiri* (mist).

[Section 60]

1. As the following poems make clear, "Takachika," added by a later hand, is an error for Kinchika. Fujiwara Kinchika had assumed the office of the master of the consort's household after Takachika resigned on the sixteenth day of the seventh month in 1247.

2. Kinchika's poem indirectly praises his ancestral home, Kan'in Palace, Go-Fukakusa's town palace. There is a pun on *sumu* (live; be clear).

3. The poem can be taken to mean, "Members of your family will always serve the monarch here."

[Section 61]

1. Saneo, the provisional major counselor, puns on [*okite*]*i* (stay [awake]; [Hour of] the Boar [9:00 P.M.-11:00 P.M.]).

2. Ben no Naishi puns on *ne* (sleep; [Hour of] the Rat [11:00 P.M.-1:00 A.M.]).

[Section 62]

1. The Consort's Apartment at the Kan'in Palace. Its exact location is not known, but Iwasa thinks it may have been located in the vicinity of the North Wing Chamber of the Jijūden. Ōmiya'in was not living at the Kan'in Palace, since she was in confinement at Fujiwara (Saionji) Saneuji's Imadegawa Mansion awaiting the birth of her second child by Go-Saga. The Imadegawa Mansion, the residence of Saneuji, was located north of Ichijō and west of Imadegawa Avenue in the northeastern part of Kyoto. Saneuji was the father of Ōmiya'in and the maternal grandfather of Go-Fukakusa.

2. *Wataru* (cross; span) acts as a pivot word (*kakekotoba*) for the phrases *kiri tachiwatari kari mo nakunari* (crossing the rising mist, wild geese cry) and *yoyo ni sakiwataru* (blooming for generations). *Kakekotoba* are words in which one sound (of one or more syllables) is to be read with two or more different meanings.

[Section 63]

1. Edge Apartment or Long Bridge Corner Apartment (Tsuma no Tsubone or Nagahashi no Sumi no Tsubone), one of the rooms located along a side of the corridor called the Long Bridge that connected the Seiryōden to the Shishinden.

2. Half-moon (*nakaba no tsuki*) is another name for the *biwa*, derived from the crescent moon-shaped holes on the body of the instrument. The poem can also mean, "Perhaps Kōtō no Naishi is weeping because she is growing old." Both Kōtō no Naishi and Azechi no Sanmi had borne children by Go-Saga.

[Section 64]

1. Resignation Request Ceremony (Jōhyō), in which the regent three times asked permission to resign from office. The request was usually ceremoniously refused by the monarch. This entry records what was probably the third time.

2. The sixty-second monarch, Murakami (926–67; r. 946–67), and the sixty-sixth monarch, Ichijō (980-1011; r. 986-1011).

3. Popular songs (*imayō*) were tunes considered modern in the Heian period.

4. *Kumoi* (abode of clouds; Royal Palace).

[Section 65]

1. There is a pun on *sumu* (live; be clear). *Wataru* (span; cross [a river]) is an *engo* for *kawa* (river).

[Section 66]

1. "Waka no Ura" (Waka Bay) and "matsu no arashi" (storm wind in the pines) are metaphors for poetry and *koto* music. Selden (personal communication) states that this clearly echoes Go-Toba's poem preserved in a chapter of *The Clear Mirror* (Niijimamori) after he was exiled to Oki:

*Masukagami, "*Niijimamori."

ware koso wa	Indeed I am
niijimamori ya	the new island guard.
oki no umi no	Stormy wave-wind
araki namikaze	in the seas of Oki,
kokoro shite fuke	blow with a sympathetic heart!

[Section 67]

1. For Takatsunji, see Section 50, note 3.

2. There are puns on *somuru* (begin [falling in love]; dye, steep) and *kokoro no iro* (color of the heart; sexual passion).

[Section 68]

1. Literally, "unkempt hair." Another name for *inutsuge* (*Ilex crenata* Thunb.), Japanese holly.

2. There is a pun on *tsuge* (boxwood; [*inu*]*tsuge*). Boxwood was used to make combs.

[Section 69]

1. The courtyard outside Go-Fukakusa's apartment, mentioned in Section 68.

2. "His Lordship" refers to the regent, Kanetsune.

[Section 70]

1. The Gosechi festival began on the sixteenth and continued for five consecutive days.

2. Thick-hemmed willow (*atsuzuma yanagi*) and the two color combinations that follow were assembled for special occasions and were named for their dominant color theme rather than by the usual seasonal floral phenomena (Dalby 1987, 15). Of the willow combination, Dalby states that there were two variations. In the first, all the robes were white with pale blue-green linings. In the second, all the robes were again white, but the blue-green linings deepened in hue from the outer to innermost layers. In either case, the chemise was scarlet-pink (Dalby 1987, 18).

3. Red-plum combination (*kōbai* [*no nioi*]) consisted of five robes in shades of plum-pink, deepening toward the innermost layer, with the chemise in blue-green or deep red (Dalby 1987, 17).

4. Pine combination (*matsugasane*), with shades of blue-green for the outer layers and maroon or purple for the innermost layers, had a chemise of scarlet-pink (Dalby 1987, 16).

5. For Gosechidokoro, see Section 9, note 1.

6. After the Gosechi Royal Rehearsal had taken place in the illuminated eastern garden, the dancers left combs, wrapped in colored paper, before the monarch, who watched the performance from behind bamboo blinds. The sovereign selected one of the combs as a sign of special favor (McCullough and McCullough 1980, 1:377). It also seems to have been customary for others to make presents of combs. The meaning of the minister's actions is not clear; Tamai suggests that dropping a gift comb may have been another custom.

7. Royal Viewing of the Girl Attendants (Warawa Goran) was held on the Day of the Hare during the Gosechi Festival.

[Section 71]

1. The banquet, which took place on the eighteenth (Day of the Hare), refers to the First Fruits Service (*Niinamesai*).

2. Iwasa states that at the commencement of the banquet a *naishi* went to the stairway on the eastern side of the Shishinden to summon all the courtiers to the banquet. Ben no Naishi was the female courtier chosen to summon the male courtiers.

3. Red plum under snow (*yuki no shita kōbai*) or plum under snow (*yuki no shita ume*) combination, worn from the height of winter through the end of spring, consisted of two top layers of white followed by three shades of plum-pink, with the darkest on top, and completed by a scarlet-pink chemise (Dalby 1987, 23). Although Tamai and Iwasa state that the color of the chemise was blue-green, Dalby states that blue-green too closely approximated the colors found in nature and was therefore artless. Iwasa states that some texts attribute the "omoiyare" poem to Shōshō no Naishi, but I followed Tamai's interpretation that the poetry exchange occurred between Ben no Naishi and middle counselor Saneo. Ben no Naishi and he exchanged numerous poems, such as those described in Section 78.

4. The Gosechi dancers were presented by senior nobles or other court officials

5. "Major counselor" is probably a mistake for provisional middle counselor Saneo.

[Section 72]

1. The exact nature of the *kujū kumo* or "ninety clouds" design is unknown. A hidden topic (*kakushidai*) poem concealed a specified word or phrase. In this case it was, "Naniwa uku shūku moeji," which means, "The topic is too hard; I can't think of anything witty."

2. In a broken stanza (*oriku*), the five initial syllables spell out the topic word, italicized in the transliteration. *Nigori*, indicating voiced syllables, were not used in medieval orthography.

[Section 73]

1. Promotion (*joi*) ceremonies were held regularly each year on the fifth or sixth day of the New Year and irregularly at various other times during the year. This appears to have been a special ceremony held at the end of the year 1247.

2. A line from an unidentified song.

3. "Ureshi ya mizu," a line taken from a song sung on happy occasions:

ureshi ya mizu	How splendid the waters!
naru wa taki no mizu	The sound is the roar
	of the cascade's waters.
hi wa teru tomo	Let the sun shine as it will,
taezu tōtari toutae	The flow never ceases.

(McCullough 1988, 40)

4. Ichirō, the title of the highest-ranking, most senior of the twenty royal guardsmen.

[Section 74]

1. For the Records Office, see Section 47, note 1. The date was the twenty-fourth day of the eleventh month of 1247.

2. *Kashiwagi* (oak [tree]), a sobriquet for members of the *Emon* (gate guards) and *Hyōe* (military guards). Here, it refers to Sanefuji.

3. Iwasa states that Ben no Naishi is expressing her preference for Arisuke's singing over Sanefuji's *koto*.

4. The provisional major counselor Saneo repeats lines from a *Kokinshū* poem:

Kokinshū 490. Anonymous. [Topic unknown].

yūzukuyo	Like the foliage,
sasu ya okabe no	indifferent to season,
matsu no ha no	of pines on a hill
itsu to mo wakanu	where the moon glimmers at dusk—
koi mo suru kana	so changeless is my yearning.

(McCullough 1985b, 115)

5. Goya, the Hour of the Tiger [3:00 A.M.-5:00 A.M.].

6. At the Kan'in Palace, the left gate guards' headquarters was located in the gate east of the Shunkyōden, south of the Giyōden.

[Section 75]

1. The Iwashimizu Special Festival (Iwashimizu no Rinji no Sai), was held annually on the second Day of the Horse in the third month. Although the Iwashimizu was called a "Special Festival" (*rinji no sai*), it was part of the regular Shintō observances. It featured a type of dancing known as Eastern Music (*Azuma-asobi*) or Eastern Dancing (*Azuma-mai*), as well as a royal messenger and horse racing. The Eastern Music ensemble usually included one or more singers, four or six dancers, and a small orchestra consisting of a Japanese zither (*wagon*, a six-stringed *koto*), a flute (*komabue*), an oboe (*hichiriki*), and a pair of clappers (*shakubyōshi*). The performers were usually members of the bodyguards who came from musical families. A day or two before the festival, an elaborate formal

banquet took place on the eastern side of the Seiryōden attended by the monarch and his entire court. Immediately thereafter, the trial performance (*shigaku*) took place in the courtyard. Later in the day, the sovereign inspected the horses to be raced by the guardsmen. On the day of the festival there was a royal purification ceremony in the Seiryōden, after which the monarch worshipped the offerings on display in the courtyard. After changing his costume, the sovereign returned to see the departure ceremony (*niwa no za*). The royal messenger and his party were called in before the assembled senior nobles and lesser figures by the head chamberlain in charge. Then ceremonial cups were drunk as the senior nobles and others inserted artificial flowers into the caps of the performers (wisteria for the messenger, usually a middle or lesser captain, and cherry blossoms for the dancers). The Messenger's Procession set out for Iwashimizu along streets filled with spectators. At one time there had been a Return Ceremony (*kaeridachi*) with dancing, but by the early eleventh century, it had been eliminated (McCullough and McCullough 1980, 1:404–5).

2. Spring decorations (*haru no kazashi*), the artificial flowers worn by the performers on the day of the festival.

3. In the lunar calendar, summer began in the fourth month. Female courtiers were given summer robes at this time, and Ben no Naishi received hers while she was at home in mourning.

4. There are puns not captured in the translation: *koro*[*mode*] (sleeves; around this time) and *tatsu* (begin; cut out [robes]).

[Section 76]

1. Tamai and Iwasa state that this event occurred on the nineteenth day of the intercalary twelfth month of 1249. Iwasa notes that the fact that there was bright moon confirms the validity of the nineteenth, for the full moon always occurred on the fifteenth in the lunar reckoning. For the Buddha's Names Ceremony, see Section 31, note 3.

2. On the second of the three successive nights of the Buddha's Names Ceremony, the chamberlains met to decide on the allotment of duties for the next year's services.

3. Tamai states that the remainder of the sentence, "sechi kakarishitai ni shirusu," is unintelligible. Iwasa emends the phrase in the base text "sechiyokuri' by consulting the Shōkōkan text to "sechi kakari. Gerō yori . . ." [The names of those whose roles were determined] were recorded in order from the lower grade."

4. For the Spirit-Pacifying Festival, see Section 22, note 2.

5. Probably a contest to determine which of the two sides could produce the most attractive *kosode* (small-sleeved robes).

[Section 77]

1. Obeisance to the Four Directions (Shihōhai), held on the first day of the New Year (which was also the first day of spring) during the Hour of the Tiger [3:00 A.M.-5:00 A.M.], was a ceremony performed by the monarch in the eastern courtyard of the Seiryōden. He made obeisance to the tombs of his royal ancestors, to the particular star thought to govern the destinies of sovereigns, and to the

"heavenly and earthly deities of the four directions." It was an important calamity-averting ceremony that also included prayers for prosperity and abundant harvests.

[Section 78]

1. The Gekka (Moon-flower) Gate was one of two gates leading to the Shishinden courtyard. The Gekka Gate stood to the west on the same side as the Orange Tree (*Tachibana*). The Nikka (Sun-flower) Gate stood to the east on the same side as the Cherry Tree (*Sakura*).

2. *Nōshi* was one of several styles of clothing worn by male aristocrats during the Heian and Kamakura periods: *sokutai* (formal attire), *ikan* (semiformal attire), *nōshi* (informal attire), and *kariginu* (casual attire). *Nōshi* consisted of a *hō* (full-length outer garment worn with *sokutai* attire) tied at the waist with a *hakoe* (sash), beneath which a *sashinuki* (gathered-hem full trousers) was worn. Unlike *sokutai*, there were no color prohibitions according to rank for *nōshi*, and because of this *nōshi* were sometimes called *zappō* (miscellaneous outer garments). During the Heian period, senior nobles of the third rank and higher were allowed to visit the palace wearing *nōshi* (Kinda'ichi 1972, 451 and 774). *Sokutai*, the most formal attire for monarchs and officials of the hundred governmental offices, was almost always worn for court ceremonies and for visits to the royal court. The *sokutai* were divided into two forms: civilian (*bunkan*) and military (*bukan*). Divided trousers called *ue no hakama* (straight-hem full trousers), *kanmuri* (formal court hats), *hōeki no hō* (outer garments), *shitagasane* (under robes), and *asagutsu* ("shallow" shoes elevated in front) were worn in this style (68). *Ikan*, a semiformal version of the *sokutai*, was not divided into civilian and military styles. In the *ikan* style, the divided trousers known as *ue no hakama* were replaced by the *sashinuki* (gathered-hem full trousers), but otherwise most items used in the *ikan* and *sokutai* styles are similar. During ceremonial occasions, when a *hitoe* (robe worn next to the body) and a *kinu* (robe) are added to the ensemble, it is called a *hitoe ikan* (64). *Kariginu*, the most casual style of clothing, consisted of an outer garment of three-quarter length with deep slits in the sides under the sleeves. The body and the sleeves were separate, with a slender sash sewn into the outside border of the sleeves' hemline. The outer garment was belted and bloused over, with the garment hanging down farther in the back than in the front. Originally *kariginu* were made of fabric woven from hemp and arrowroot, but later coarser fabrics were replaced by *aya* (damask or brocade). In the Heian period, the *kariginu* was the casual costume for aristocrats, and in the Kamakura period and later, it was used by both the nobility and members of the military class (271).

3. Aburanokōji Street, a north-south thoroughfare, formed the western border of the Kan'in Palace.

4. Fujiwara Takachika. He was appointed to the post of master of the dowager's household on the eighth day of the eighth month of 1248.

5. The day for hitting people (*hito utsu hi*) occurred in conjunction with preparations for the full moon gruel (*mochigayu*) eaten on the fifteenth day of the first month. Sticks that had been used to stir the full moon gruel were later used to hit the buttocks of others in sport. The practice seems to have evolved from ancient fertility customs.

6. Mashimizu and Sumutsuru may be transcription errors for the names of *nyōju*. I followed Iwasa in reading the names of female servants and Tamai in omitting an unintelligible phrase, *itsuruhiru*, which follows the name Mashimizu.

7. Kunming Lake Partition (Konmeichi no Shōji), a single-leaf partition that stood between the Two-Bay Room and the Kokiden Royal Apartment in the outer eaves chamber of the Seiryōden. On the side facing north, there was a picture of falconry in Sagano; on the side facing south, there was a scene depicting Kunming Lake in China.

8. For Upper Hot Water Room, see Section 34, note 3. The translation follows Tamai, who thinks that the phrase used here, "nageshi no shimo no ikken" [bay below the lintel], refers to a room which was on a level lower than the Upper Hot Water Room. Tamai leaves *Minotono* unidentified, but Iwasa thinks that "Minodono" may have been the name of a *nyōbō*, Lady Mino, who took up her post near the half-blinds (*kirimisu*) hanging along the western side of the Table Room. Here I followed Iwasa's interpretation of the scene.

9. Tamai states that Hyōe no Kami and the provisional major counselor were lovers.

10. Partition of the Annual Ceremonies (Nenjū Gyōji no Shōji), a free-standing single-leaf screen on the east side of the Courtiers' Hall. It depicted the annual ceremonies of the first through the sixth months on the eastern side and the ceremonies of the seventh through the twelfth months on the western side.

11. Tamai indicates the setting as His Majesty's Daytime Chamber (Hi no Omashi), located in the southeastern corner of the Seiryōden with the curtain-dais (*chōdai*) in the center of the room, cabinets for storage of musical instruments and valued documents, and a few furnishings (McCullough and McCullough 1980, 2:841). The curtain-dais, a four-sided raised *tatami* platform covered on all sides with curtains and a translucent *shōji* canopy, served as both a sitting room and sleeping area for the monarch.

12. A pun on *tsuki mide* (not seeing the moon; not hitting [you]) suggests that the women have been too preoccupied trying to hit him to enjoy the moon.

13. There is an implied word association, *tsuki izu* (the moon emerges) in the phrase *idenikeru ka na*; the phrase *ariake no* is partially included in the preceding phrase, *kokoro mo shirade ari*[*ake*].

14. Hand-Washing Room, where the monarch performed his ablutions, was located south of the Upper Hot Water Room on the northwestern side of the Seiryōden.

15. Saneo alludes to a poem in the *Tales of Ise*, Section 39:

Once a sovereign known as the Emperor of the Western Palace had a daughter, Princess Shūshi, who died. On the night of the funeral a man who lived nearby drove out with a lady in her carriage to watch the procession. A long time passed with no sign of the coffin, and the man, feeling that his tears had shown sympathy, decided to give up and go home. Just then the famous gallant Minamoto Itaru, who was also there to view the procession, came up to the carriage and began to flirt with the lady he imagined to be alone inside. Presently he caught a firefly and thrust it into the carriage. The lady started to extinguish it lest she be seen by its light—whereupon the man who was with her recited,

Idete inaba	When the princess emerges
Kagiri narubemi	It will be for the last time.
Tomoshi kechi	You would do well to heed
Toshi henuru ka to	The voices that lament
Naku koe o kike	This light's untimely extinction.

(McCullough 1968, 97)

16. Ben no Naishi's third poem directly challenges Saneo's assertion that he did not know the women were lying in wait to hit him. She states that she saw him standing with his back to the wall in the courtyard to avoid being beaten by gruel sticks and accuses him of only pretending to gaze at the moon.

[Section 79]

1. Probably the regent Kanetsune.

2. Jakusai, the Buddhist name of Ben no Naishi's father, Fujiwara Nobuzane (ca. 1177–1270). Nobuzane renounced the world in 1248, the year before the events recorded in this entry.

3. *Kazashi* were flowering branches attached to court caps or directly to the hair as ornaments on auspicious occasions.

4. *Haru no hikari* (spring sunlight; royal favor).

[Section 80]

1. Tamai and Iwasa state that Dainagon no Niidono was the daughter of either former chancellor Minamoto (Koga) Michimitsu or Fujiwara (Saionji) Kintsune, also a former chancellor. Tamai thinks that Dainagon no Niidono may have been Go-Fukakusa's wet nurse.

2. There are two *engo* for *na o nagasu*—make one's name flow, i.e., become known, (here, for loving)—*mizukuki [no ato]* (brush[tracks], translated here as "poems") and *nurasu* (drench).

3. There is a pun on *mizukuki no ato* (brush tracks; born after the writing [of those who wrote the love poems]).

[Section 81]

1. Go-Fukakusa was six years old at this time. Kunaikyō no Sukedono may have been the person referred to as Kunaikyōdono in Section 9.

2. In the Kan'in Palace, the Royal Dowager's Apartment refers to the residence of Senkamon'in, Royal Princess Gishi (see note 9 of this section). Her apartment, located in a building in the north part of the Kan'in Palace bordering on Nijō Avenue, was apparently where the fire was first detected.

3. Willow combination (*yanagi no usuginu*), worn from winter until spring, with outer robes of white and inner robes of blue. *Usuginu* (thin silk) may refer to robes worn on informal, leisure occasions. A Chinese jacket (*karaginu*) and train (*mo*) were required for female courtiers on formal occasions. Iwasa describes the lined Chinese jacket of golden yellow (*ura yamabuki no karaginu*) that Ben no Naishi had been wearing as yellow on the outside with a lining of red or spring

green. Ben no Naishi felt compelled to change from informal wear to a formal set of robes when she realized the fire would subject her to public scrutiny.

4. Maroon-plum combination robes (*suo naru umegasane no kinu*) consisted of a top robe of white with a very pale plum-pink tinge; a second robe of light plum-pink; a third of plum-pink; a fourth of scarlet-pink; and a fifth of maroon. The chemise was deep purple or blue-green (Dalby 1987, 22).

5. Royal Bedchamber (Yoru [Yon] no Otodo), a bed located in the north part of His Majesty's Apartment in the Seiryōden. Kōtō no Naishi was assigned the task of safeguarding the sacred sword, one of the most important duties of a female courtier. *Kenji* refer to the sacred sword and sacred jewels, two of the three regalia. Ben no Naishi, the junior female courtier on duty, was assigned the task of safeguarding the sacred jewels.

6. It is not clear whether Niidono is the Dainagon no Niidono who appears in Section 80. I followed Tamai in adding "no suke nite, onajiku Aburanokōji no kado no hō e irasetamau" after "Chūnagon."

7. Guardian Sword (*Ontachi*), kept near the sovereign for personal protection, not to be confused with the sacred sword, one of the regalia. In the daytime, it was kept near the southern edge of the His Majesty's Daytime Chamber; at night, it was kept south of the monarch's pillow in the Royal Bedchamber.

8. For double doors, see Section 14, note 9.

9. Royal Dowager (Kōgōgū no Onkata) refers to Royal Princess Gishi, a daughter (b. 1223) of Tsuchimikado, and a younger sister of Go-Saga. Known as Senkamon'in, she was given the title royal dowager, usually reserved for mothers of sovereigns, because she was Go-Fukakusa's aunt and godmother. She was the Ise Virgin in 1243, was in Nonomiya in 1244, and left the post in 1246, when Go-Fukakusa ascended the throne. She was twenty-six years old at the time of the fire.

10. Genjō was the name of a prized *biwa* housed in the Seiryōden shrine and was not to be handled by unclean hands. A variant text states that it was the daughter of Fujiwara Noritoki who brought the *biwa* to safety, rather than Noritoki himself. Noritoki appears in Section 141 playing the *biwa* (Tamai 1958a, 250–51; Iwasa 1994a, 244–45).

11. "The reigns of Engi and Tenryaku" were those of Daigo (885–930; r. 897–930) and Murakami. The Seiryōden burned down in Daigo's reign, and the entire palace went up in flames during the reign of Murakami; however, Ben no Naishi's use of the word *amatatabi* (repeated [fires]) is not accurate.

[Section 82]

1. The new town palace, Tominokōji, formerly housed Go-Fukakusa's parents, Go-Saga'in and Ōmiya'in.

2. For Spacious Hall, see Section 14, note 4.

3. In the next section, we learn that the unidentified person was none other than Go-Saga himself.

4. The line *iro mo ka mo* is also found in Ki no Tsurayuki and Ki no Tomomori's poems:

Kokinshū 851. Ki no Tsurayuki. On seeing plum blossoms at a house where the owner had died:

iro mo ka mo
mukashi no kosa ni
nioedomo
uekemu hito no
kage zo koishiki
(McCullough 1985, 185)

The hue is as rich
and the perfume as fragrant
as in days gone by,
but how I long for a glimpse
of the one who planted the tree.

Kokinshū 57. Ki no Tomomori. Lamenting his age under the cherry blossoms.

iro mo ka mo
onaji mukashi ni
sakuramedo
toshi furu hito zo
aratamarikeru
(McCullough 1985, 25)

In color and scent
they are probably the same
as blossoms of old,
but human beings must change
with the passing of the years.

[Section 83]

1. Refers to the apartment assigned to Kōtō no Naishi in the Tominokōji Palace. After the Kan'in Palace was destroyed (Section 81), Go-Saga and Ōmiya'in moved to the Reizei-Madenokōji Palace, located nearby in the northeastern quadrant of Kyōto, bordered on the north by Reizeinokōji, on the west by Madenokōji, on the east by Takakuranokōji, and on the south by Ōimikado. The Tominokōji Palace served as the town palace for Go-Fukakusa until 1251, when reconstruction of the Kan'in Palace was completed. Go-Fukakusa's court moved back to the Kan'in Palace, located southwest of the Tominokōji Palace. This event is recorded in Section 138 (Tamai 1958a, 243–45; Iwasa 1994a, 240–45).

2. Ōmiya'in, Go-Fukakusa's mother.

3. Fujiwara (Saionji) Saneo.

4. The former chancellor, Fujiwara (Saionji) Saneuji.

5. Refers to the poem in Section 82 by Go-Saga which begins with the line "iro mo ka mo." The chancellor criticizes Ben no Naishi and Saneo for composing allusive variations of lines from Go-Saga's poem in Section 82.

[Section 84]

1. It is not known which shrines Ben no Naishi is referring to here. In 1104 (Chōji gannen), the seven shrines were Ise, Iwashimizu, Kamo, Gion, Hiyoshi, Kitano, and Hirano. The *Journal of the Okamoto Regent (Okamoto Kanpaku Ki)* lists the following as "The Eight Shrines": Ise, Yahata, Kamo, Hirano, Kasuga, Gion, Hiyoshi, and Kitano. Apparently the practice of designating shrines in groups began in the mid-tenth century with those that received offerings of white cloth bestowed by the monarch (*heihaku*). These were the Sixteen Shrines (Jūroku-sha). Thereafter, several more were added, resulting in a new designation, the Twenty-six Shrines (Nijūrokusha). The list of designated shrines varies with the reference source consulted; however, the following shrines are included in most lists: Ise, Iwashimizu, Kamo, Matsunoo, Hirano, Inari, Kasuga, Ōharano, (Ō)miwa, Isonokami, Ōyamato, Hirose, Tatsuta, Sumiyoshi, Kibune, Yoshida, Hirota, Kitano and Gion (Ponsonby-Fane 1953, 118–19). In other sources Hie, Nibu, and Umenomiya appear as designated shrines.

2. The Seven Rivers Purification (Nanase no Onharae, also Nanase no Misogi) was performed on banks of rivers flowing into the sea. Yin-yang masters (*on'myōshi*) gave dolls to female courtiers, who made various robes to dress the them, after which they were placed in lidded boxes and conveyed to the monarch. The sovereign breathed on the dolls, then rubbed them over his body to transfer ritual pollutants onto them. Thereafter seven courtiers from the fourth or fifth ranks were selected as messengers to convey the dolls to the seven designated rivers for disposal, accompanied by Yin-yang masters who conducted the ceremony.

3. Dolls played an important part in purification rituals. Those used in the Seven Rivers Purification were probably similar to stuffed dolls known as "heaven's children" (*amagatsu*, protective charms representing babies at the crawling stage kept by children at their beds) which were sent downstream on their behalf at purification ceremonies (*Onharae*) (McCullough and McCullough 1980, 2:539). Small human figurines known as *katashiro*, similar to those used in purification rituals, were placed into coffins by relatives along with the personal belongings of the deceased (McCullough and McCullough 1980, 2:679). In Shirane Haruo's discussion on the function of dolls in the *Bridge of Dreams: A Poetics of "The Tale of Genji*," several new terms emerge: "replica" (*hitogata*), "paper figures rubbed against the body to remove pollution, evil influences, and other sins, then washed down a river as part of a purification (*misogi*) ceremony" (155); "doll, substitute" (*katashiro*) and "a thing to be rubbed" (*nademono*), all of which refer to a "replica" or "substitute" for a deceased loved one. A poetic exchange between Kaoru and Nakanokimi incorporating the two words are quoted in the analysis and allude to Ukifune's eventual fate: to be cast aside and washed downstream like a doll in a purification rite.

4. A reference to *kemari* (kickball), an aristocratic pastime. See Section 87.

5. The Karahashi major counselor, Minamoto Masachika, who was seventy years old at the time, is mentioned only in this entry.

6. A reference to Fun'ya no Yasuhide's poem, quoted in Section 36, note 3. "Flowers" imply royal favor.

[Section 85]

1. Cockfights (*toriawase*), popular in premodern times in India, Persia, Southeast Asia, and China, were introduced to Japan from China early in the eighth century. In the Nara (710–94) and Heian (794–1185) periods, cockfights were an amusement for the aristocracy, as had been the custom in China. During the Kamakura period (1185–1333), cockfighting matches were held annually on the third day of the third month in imitation of T'ang dynasty (618–905) practice; however, by the Edo period (1600–1867), cockfights became an occasion for gambling and, as a consequence, were held more frequently until they were banned in 1873 during the Meiji period (1868–1912). For details see *Nihon Rekishi Daijiten*, 13:213 and the *Kōdansha Encyclopedia of Japan* 1983, 1:333–34. I believe the *Ben no Naishi Nikki* is the only memoir written by a woman that mentions this activity. For further details on references to Chinese cockfights in prose and poetry, see Cutter 1989. Cutter also discusses the opposition voiced against cockfighting, simi-

lar to the sentiment expressed by Ben no Naishi in the poem lamenting the fate of the injured gamecock. I am indebted to Cynthia Chennault for this source.

2. For Spacious Hall see Section 14, note 4.

3. The names of a few roosters vary: Tamai reads "Harima" and "Naruaka," but Iwasa prefers "Hakama," and both Iwasa and Imazeki Toshiko read the latter "Nakaaka."

4. Inverted baskets (*fusego*) were usually used to perfume robes by burning incense beneath them. Here it refers to baskets under which the roosters were kept as pets in an empty apartment.

5. The Reizei major counselor composes the first seventeen syllables of a linked verse, expecting Kintada to add the final fourteen syllables to complete the linked verse; however, Kintada ignores the prompt, answering only with a curt three-syllable reply, "sa koso," noting his assent to the sentiment expressed by Kinsuke's link. Ben no Naishi notices Kintada's failure to complete the verse and composes a witty poem incorporating Kinsuke's imagery at Kintada's expense.

6. The poem plays on *engo, kumoi* (abode of clouds) and *sora* (sky), for the pillow word (*makurakobota*) *hisakata no* (celestial).

[Section 86]

1. This event took place on the twentieth day of the third month of 1249. Customarily, the Iwashimizu Special Festival was held on the second Day of the Horse of the third month, which on this particular year fell on the twenty-second day, but there was already another ceremony scheduled for that day. For further details, see Section 75, note 1.

2. *Mebu*, a low-ranking official of the royal stables of the left and right (Sayū Meryō).

3. *Kezuke*, an official assigned the task of recording the colors of the horses offered to the shrine at the ceremony. Fujiwara Suezane, son of Chikasue, is believed to be the official in charge of recording the color of the steeds. He was a senior fourth rank, lower grade, middle captain of the left at the time.

4. The *engo* here are *tsuki* (moon), *kumo* (clouds), and *kage* (moonlight or shadows). *Tsukige* (moon-hide) refers to horses with colors similar to the under feathers of a Japanese crested ibis (*toki*), perhaps a dapple-gray or a fawn-colored gray in which warm tones are evident. *Kage* (shadows) can refer to black horses, in which case Ben no Naishi seems to be suggesting the contrastive quality of *tsukige* (moonlight) and *kage* (shadows) to allude to light- and dark-colored horses.

[Section 87]

1. Managers (*bugyō*) were appointed to receive and carry out orders. Here, the manager was responsible for setting up the staging of the "kickball" (*kemari*) game. Unlike modern sports, managers were able to participate in the kickball games staged. For Tameuji's family connections, see Section 58, note 2.

2. *Kemari* (also *mari*, kickball) was an aristocratic sport played on a square field, called a *marigakari*, in an area enclosed by a fence. The ball itself was made of deer hide and was seven to eight inches in diameter. Trees were planted at each corner of the playing field: a cherry (*sakura*), a willow (*yanagi*), a pine (*matsu*),

and a maple (*kaede*). There were variations in the size of the playing field and the number of trees planted in the playing field, but the field was usually about fourteen meters square. Sometimes bamboo poles were staked into the ground to mark the outline of a makeshift playing field. The object of the *kemari* game was to keep the ball in play without letting it hit the ground. Success of the game was gauged by the number of kicks accumulated before the ball hit the ground. There were eight players, all of whom wore leather shoes and began seated in ranked order beneath a tree designated as the "first tree." The players stood up in ranked order with the player designated the "first player" standing first, followed by seven players standing in order of their rank. The game began when the eighth player moved from the corner of the "first tree" to a spot within three steps of the center of the playing field and placed the ball in the center of the field. Then the seventh player kicked the ball to the first player. The first player kicked the ball to the second player and so on until the ball reached the eighth player, who kicked it to the first player. The order was repeated until the ball hit the ground. The number of consecutive kicks was recorded, but when the ball hit the ground, counting began anew. Apparently each player kicked the ball three times: to receive the ball, to set up the pass, and to pass it to the next player. I chose to translate *kemari* literally as "kickball." Edward Seidensticker's translation of *kemari* as "football" suffers from a distracting association, in my mind, with the modern sport. The opening phrase *hana sakari* refers to the cherry tree in blossom on the *kemari* playing field during the third month of the lunar calendar.

3. "Sukehira" and "Takayuki" are probably references to Minamoto Sukehira, about whom little is known, and Fujiwara Takayuki, son of Takatsugu, who is otherwise unidentified.

4. Shōshō no Naishi's poem contains a pun, *amari* (too much, in excess), which contains sounds similar to *kemari* (kickball). Ben no Naishi's poem had stated that the ball falls and flowers scatter; Shōshō no Naishi's poem suggests the ball hangs on the mind much as the flowers stay in one's thoughts on such a special occasion.

5. Another pun on the homophonous *amari* and *kemari* in Ben no Naishi's poem. Unlike Ben no Naishi's poem, which supposes hearts to be calm in the spring, the following *Kokinshū* poem expresses the opposite:

Kokinshū 84. Ki no Tomomori. On cherry blossoms scattering.

hisakata no	On this springtime day
hikari nodokeki	when the celestial orb
haru no hi ni	diffuses mild light,
shizugokoro naku	why should the cherry blossom
hana no chiruran	scatter with unquiet hearts?

(McCullough 1985b, 30)

[Section 89]

1. Ben no Naishi's pun turns on *amari* (too much, in excess) indicating that the sound of the water flowing by the fishing weirs (*yana*) is too loud or that the water running through the weirs is overflowing its boundaries.

[Section 90]

1. For directional taboos, see Section 29, note 1.

2. For the Imadegawa Mansion, see Section 62, note 1.

3. The retired consort (*nyōin*) was Go-Fukakusa's mother, Ōmiya'in, who was about to go into confinement at the Imadegawa Mansion awaiting the birth of the future Kameyama. Kameyama, the younger brother of Go-Fukakusa, was born on the twenty-fifth day of the fifth month in 1249 at the Imadegawa Mansion, about a month after the date of this entry.

4. Fujiwara (Saionji) Sanefuji, the younger brother of Saneuji, was Ōmiya'in's uncle even though he was a year younger than she.

5. The royal sword (*gyoken*) was the sword worn by the monarch when he journeyed out of the royal residence.

6. The two head chamberlains are identified as Minamoto Mototomo, a head chamberlain of the left-middle captain, and Fujiwara Kinyasu, a head chamberlain of the right-middle captain.

7. *Nusa* (also *yūshide*), a strip of white cloth attached to a branch of a sacred *sakaki* tree as an offering to the *kami*. Iwasa thinks it may have been used in ceremonies.

8. *Tsure nakaraji* suggests that the cuckoo will keep the moon company. Conventional usage combined the images of *ariake* (dawn moon) and *hototogisu* (cuckoo) with *tsurenashi* (sadness). One such example follows:

Kokinshū 625. Mibu no Tadamine. [Topic unknown].

ariake no	The hours before dawn
tsurenaku mieshi	seem saddest of all to me
wakare yori	since that leave-taking
akatsuki bakari	when I saw in the heavens
uki mono wa nashi	the pale moon's indifferent face.

(McCullough 1985, 140)

[Section 91]

1. The Kamo Festival was celebrated annually on the middle Day of the Cock in the fourth month; therefore, the ceremony, known as the Summoning of the Guards, took place on the Day of the Sheep (two days before the Day of the Cock) or the Day of the Monkey (one day before the Day of the Cock). I followed Edward Seidensticker's translation of *aoi* as "heartvine" (*Futaba-aoi, Asarum caulescens* Maxim.), "the ivy-like plant with attractive pairs of heart-shaped leaves growing directly from rooted horizontal stems" (McCullough and McCullough 1980, 1:409). "Heartvine" leaves were used to decorate houses, carriages, and viewing stands for the Kamo Festival.

2. The guards, usually middle captains in the bodyguards, were summoned from the Six Guards' headquarters (Rokuefu).

3. For *nōshi*, see Section 78, note 2.

4. Guards dressed in the military style (*bukan*) formal attire (*sokutai*). Military style attire modified formal court hats with fan-shaped feather attachments (*oikake*) placed near the ears on both sides. Guards wore a quiver diagonally across their back with arrows (*ya*) arranged in a fan-shape, and carried a bow (*yumi*). The

outer garment (*hō*) was shorter than the civilian style and was adjusted to accommodate the quiver. Although military-style attire used the same divided trousers hemmed at the ankle (*ue no hakama*), guards wore boots rather than the "shallow" shoes with upturned toes (*asakutsu*).

5. Narrow swords (*hosodachi*), worn with formal attire, were for ceremonial use only. Narrow swords could be worn by bodyguards only by royal dispensation. Iwasa states that bodyguards usually wore swords known as "meadow swords" (*nodachi*).

[Section 92]

1. Kanetsune, who was forty years old at the time.

2. The original Japanese is *kagen no tsuki*, a waning half-moon in the fourth quarter. A moon in this phase was supposed to rise before eleven o'clock at night.

3. Ben no Naishi's poem alludes to the following in the *Shinkokinshū*:

Shinkokinshū 382 (Autumn 1). Retired Sovereign Sanjō.

ashihiki no	Might those who dwell
yama no anata ni	on the other side
sumu hito wa	of the foot-wearying mountains
matade ya aki no	see the autumn moon
tsuki o miruran	without having to wait.

[Section 93]

1. For the Golden Light Sutra, see Section 48, note 1.

2. In the replica Kan'in Palace and the original Royal Residential Palace, the Demon Room was located south of the Table Room and the Hand-Washing Room. The Tominokōji Palace was not designed as a replica of the original Royal Residential Palace as was the Kan'in, and therefore required authorial comment on its layout. See also Section 48, note 2.

3. Tomomi, son of the poet major counselor Minamoto Michitomo (1171–1227), rose to senior second rank as a major counselor. He was forty-seven years old at the time and was appointed to the post of palace minister in the second year of Kenchō (1250). Tamai Kōsuke notes a discrepancy in the first and second years of Kenchō for the reading of the Golden Light Sutra. He states that the readings were performed in the first year of Kenchō from the twenty-second to the twenty-sixth and in the second year of Kenchō from the twenty-third to the twenty-seventh [of the fifth month]. The dates recorded in *Ben no Naishi Nikki* correspond to the first year of Kenchō, but this does not explain why Tomomi is recorded as occupying a position he would not receive for two years, unless the error occurred when the text was revised.

4. There are two likely candidates to fit the sobriquet of the "new" major counselor: Fujiwara Michinaga (1234–59), the eldest son of the regent Yoshizane (regent, 1242–46), who was sixteen at the time and newly appointed to the post in the first year of Hōji (1247), and Fujiwara Yoshinori (1224–87), son of the poet provisional major counselor Motoyoshi, who was twenty-six at the time.

5. Sadahira, son of Minamoto Kanesada, rose to senior fourth rank lower grade, as a middle captain of the right.

6. The participants in the Buddhist rites "emerged" the next day, the twenty-third day of the fifth month. Shōgō'in, located in the Ukyō ward of Kyōto, was originally a Tendai temple whose priests were of royal lineage. Esoteric Buddhist rites (*shōkan onhō*) were performed by the archbishop (*sōjō*) to promote safety, tranquillity, and good health. The archbishop may have been Kiyotada, son of Konoe Motomichi (1160–1233), who was a regent (*sesshō-kanpaku*) and a palace minister (*naidaijin*) in the late Heian and early Kamakura periods.

7. Small handbells with clappers (*rei*, also *suzu*) arranged around a wooden handle forming a cluster with an inverted V-shape.

8. Ben no Naishi's poem contains a pun on *reiji* (the usual time; handbell).

[Section 94]

1. The regent is probably Kanetsune. Royal chairs (*goishi*), with four legs, armrests, and a backrest shaped like a Shintō gate (*torii*), were placed in the Shishinden, the Courtiers' Hall, and the Table Room for use by monarchs during ceremonies. They resembled chaise longues more than chairs since they supported an occupant's outstretched legs. The Table Room chairs were destroyed during the fire at the Kan'in Palace (Section 81), so the regent ordered new ones to be made for use at the Tominokōji Palace to which Go-Fukakusa's court had moved after the fire. The Table Room in the Seiryōden had three bays on a north-south axis. The royal chair was placed in the north bay, closest to the Dining Room.

2. Chairs for Sechie banquets were made of wood from the black persimmon; chairs for the Table Room were made of rosewood or red sandalwood.

3. Priestly Kanpyō Sovereign refers to Uda (r. 887–97) by the only era name used during his reign. The Priestly Sovereign (Hōō) title indicates that Uda had abdicated and taken Buddhist vows. Narihira no Ason refers to the poet Ariwara no Narihira, who served at Uda's court.

[Section 95]

1. Special Royal Prayers (Kotonaru Inori) to ward off calamities, prolong life, and the like were perhaps in reaction to the fire recorded in Section 81 that destroyed the Kan'in Palace.

2. Tamai notes that there were two Daytime Chambers at the Tominokōji Palace, one for the royal dowager Senkamon'in, Go-Saga's sister and aunt of the monarch, and the other for Go-Fukakusa

3. Jikken, the head priest (*zasu*) of Daigoji, the son of Fujiwara Motosuke, was seventy-four years old at the time.

4. Daigoji, a Shingon temple, was located in the Fushimi ward of Kyōto. The Golden Hall was built in 874 with the Yakushi Nyōrai as central image; the five-storied pagoda was erected nearby in 951.

5. Fugen Enmei Hō (Samantabhadra rite for longevity), a ritual performed for the Twenty-armed Bodhisattva Samantabhadra (Fugen) to pray for a long life, was one of the four great rituals (Sanmon Shika Daihō) of the Tendai school. Fugen represented the intrinsic principle of reason (*ri*), meditation (*jō*), and practice (*gyō*) of all Buddhas. He functioned as the right-hand attendant of Shakyamuni Buddha and is often depicted riding on a white elephant (Inagaki 1985, 52). The Seven-

Buddhas Healing Buddha (Shichibutsu Yakushi) consists of the Healing Buddha (Yakushi) and six other Buddhas who are his transfoprmed bodies. The six other Buddhas are Zenshōmyō Kichijōō, Hōgatsu Chigon Kōōn Jizaiō, Konjiki Hōkō Myōgyō Jōju, Muu Saishō Kichijō, Hōkai Raion, and Hōkai Shōe Yuge Jinzū. The Seven-Buddhas Healing Buddha prayers conducted [here before the image of the Yakushi in the Spacious Hall] to avert calamities, pray for an easy birth, and the like, was another of the four great rituals of the Tendai school.

6. Because there was no incumbent chancellor at the time, this must be a reference to the former chancellor Saneuji, father of Ōmiya'in, Kinsuke, and Kinmoto and grandfather of Go-Fukakusa.

[Section 96]

1. "One Who Plucks a Bowstring" (*tsruuchi*, also *meigen*), is a reference to the sixth-rank chamberlain summoned to twang a bowstring in the belief that the sound warded off ghosts, apparitions, and evil spirits. In this case, it was to allay the child monarch's fear of thunder.

2. The Ichikotsu tone is one of the keys in which *gagaku* (ancient court music) is played.

3. *Mono no ne* refers to the sound of music or musical instruments; *hiku* (to pull; or pluck strings) and *oshite* (to press down on a string with a finger, to finger a string; fingering [strings with the left hand]) are *engo* for *yumi* (bow); and *oshite* is a pillow word for *yumi* (bow). A related word is *shirabe* (song).

[Section 97]

1. The poetry gathering was held at the Reizei-Madenokōji Palace, to which Go-Saga and Ōmiya'in had moved after fire had destroyed the Kan'in Palace. For details, see Section 83, note 1. The retired sovereign is Go-Saga, father of Go-Fukakusa.

2. Ben no Naishi's poem alludes to the following in the *Kokinshū*:
Kokinshū 452. Prince Kagenori. Kawatake [thought to mean either a kind of bamboo or mushroom].

sayo fukete	The night has deepened,
nakaba takeyuku	and the celestial moon rides
hisakata no	halfway through the sky.
tsuki fukikaese	Blow her back again, I pray,
aki no yamakaze	autumn wind from the mountains.

(McCullough 1985, 107)

[Section 98]

1. For the significance of chrysanthemums during the Double Yang Banquet, see Section 11, note 1.

2. There is a pun on the antonyms *oku* (modern Japanese *okiru*, to be awake) and *nu* (modern Japanese *neru*, to sleep) in Shōshō no Naishi's poem. She implies that the major counselor ought to stay awake in anticipation of the Double Yang Banquet in which chrysanthemums play a major role. In her poem she alludes to a poem in the *Gosenshū*:

Gosenshū 396 (Autumn 2). Ise. On the death of a crane on the ninth day of the ninth month.

kiku no ue ni	The thousand-year crane
okiirubeku mo	has vanished like the dew,
aranaku ni	which should have gathered
chitose no mi o mo	on the chrysanthemums,
tsuyu ni nasu kana	though none is there.

3. The meaning of Madenokōji major counselor's phrase "kumo no uebushi" is a combination of *kumo no ue* (above the clouds, a metaphor for the Royal Palace) and *uebushi* (*fusu*, to lie down; to sleep), that is, to spend the night at the palace on night duty. *Fusu* is voiced in the compound *uebushi*.

4. The line "tsuyu o katashiku" that turns on *koromo katashiku*, implying a lover's rendezvous when one sleeve of each lover's robe overlaps as they are draped on the floor for use as a bed, in Ben no Naishi's poem insinuates that the Madenokōji major counselor had been lying down or sleeping during night duty.

[Section 99]

1. Shōshō no Naishi alludes to the following in *Goshūishū* (*Later Collection of Gleanings*, 1086):

Goshūishū 339 (Autumn 1). Sai'in no Nakatsukasa. It was a little past the tenth day of the ninth month when we heard that Princess Senshi was selected for the post of Kamo Virgin. We gazed at the moon until it was close to dawn and thought that such a significant night was not likely to be experienced again.

tsuki wa yoshi	The moon is beautiful.
hageshiki kaze no	Even the sound
oto sae zo	of the violent wind
mi ni shimu bakari	now pierces my body
aki wa kanashiki	with the sadness of autumn.

Shōshō no Naishi changes the original meaning of the poem in which the autumn wind pierces the body with sadness to one of being pieced by happiness at a promotion.

2. Ben no Naishi's poem borrows a line from *Shūishū* (*Collection of Gleanings of Japanese Poetry*):

Shūishū 281 (Congratulatory Poems). Yoshinobu. Having made a bamboo staff for the same person on his seventieth birthday celebration.

kuraiyama	Though the staff
mine made tsukeru	accompanied you to the peak
tsue naredo	of Rank Mountain,
ima yorozuyo no	now it is for the sake of climbing
saka no tame nari	a hill of myriad years.

Ben no Naishi's poem contains several puns: *mitsu* (three, third; to keep looking); *kai* (result, reward; ravine, gorge; also an *engo* for *yama* [mountain]); and *mayou* (to lose one's way or to lose heart [concerning advancement in rank]). *Mayou* is also an *engo* for *yama*, making parallels between climbing the bureaucratic ladder

Kyoko Selden (personal communication) states that Ben no Naishi's poem also commends her for not losing her way as did the Tsuchimikado palace minister as recounted in the following poem from the *Shinkokinshū*:

Shinkokinshū 1814 (Miscellaneous 2). Minamoto Morofusa.

kuraiyama	I ascended Rank Mountain
ato o tazunete	on paths sought after,
noboredomo	but I worry about
ko o omou michi ni	my child's road
nao madoinuru	all the more.

3. In her poem, Dainagon no Sanmi (major counselor of the third rank) alludes to a line in a *Shinkokinshū* poem:

Shinkokinshū 1314 (Love 4). Fujiwara Ariie.

mono omowade	Though without bitterness,
tada ōkata no	even when ordinary dew
tsuyu ni dani	wets autumn sleeves,
nurureba nururu	they are further wet
aki no tamoto o	by the tears of sorrow.

[Section 100]

1. For the Tokiwai Palace, see Section 58, note 1.

2. "This palace" refers to the Tominokōji Palace. For details, see Section 1, note 1.

3. The "water" in which the moon is reflected is the "spring pavilion" or "well pavilion" (*izumidono*) at the Tokiwai Palace. In "sleeping-hall" style architecture, the spring pavilion and the fishing pavilion (*tsuridono*) were located on the southernmost ends of covered corridors (*watadono*) that connected subsidiary buildings with the main south-facing residential hall.

[Section 101]

1. This entry refers to the moon-viewing excursion to the Tokiwai Palace to which Ben no Naishi and Go-Fukakusa's other female courtiers had been invited in Section 100. Therefore Sections 100 and 101 occurred almost at the same time, but Ben no Naishi and her colleagues did not learn of the visit of Ōmiya'in's female courtiers until they had returned from the Tokiwai Palace.

2. Hizendono could also be read Bizendono since classical texts do not distinguish between voiced and unvoiced syllables. If her name was Hizendono, it refers to Nagasaki prefecture; if her name was Bizendono, it refers to Okayama prefecture.

3. Shōshō no Naishi's poem borrows a line from *Goshūishū*:

Goshūishū 87 (Spring 1). Minamoto Akifusa. During the honorable reign of the monarch Shirakawa (r. 1072–86) as male courtiers were en route to view cherry blossoms, they were asked to stand in as messengers.

akugaruru	Enticed by the mountain
kokoro bakari wa	cherry blossoms,
yamazakura	I alone would gladly

tazunuru hito ni   go along with those
taguete zo yaru   who would request it.

4. *Chikaki kumoi* refers to the Tominokōji Palace, since it was located close to the Reizei-Madenokōji Palace where Go-Saga and Ōmiya'in lived. Hizendono's poem asks Shōshō no Naishi to be at the Tominokōji Palace next time Ōmiya'in's female courtiers chose to visit.

5. *Kuma* (corner, nook; shade, shadows) is an *engo* for the moon. Ben no Naishi states that there are no shadows or distance separating the hearts of the women at both palaces concerning their desire to view the moon together.

[Section 102]

1. "This palace" refers to the Tominokōji Palace.

2. The celebration began on the sixteenth day of the eleventh month. There is some discrepancy in the dates recorded in Ben no Naishi's memoir. Usually scheduled to begin on the Middle Day of the Ox in the eleventh month, the date in the year 1249 would have corresponded to the twenty-second day, rather than the sixteenth. Variant texts of *Ben no Naishi Nikki* and *Hyakurenshō* record that the Gosechi occurred on the twenty-second day of the eleventh month.

3. The Reizei Palace is usually referred to as the Reizei-Madenokōji Palace by Tamai Kōsuke because the palace borders these streets. For details, see Section 83, note 1.

4. *Kanzu* are head chamberlains.

5. Kisaimachi Boisterous Dancing (Kisaimachi no Ranbu) occurred on the Day of the Ox, when a banquet was held in conjunction with the Curtain-Dais Rehearsal. After the rehearsal, senior nobles and courtiers participated in boisterous dancing and singing outside the Jōneiden. For details, see Section 19, note 4.

6. The Retired Consort's Drinking Party (Nyōin no Onkata no Enzui) was held at the Reizei-Madenokōji Palace to which Ōmiya'in had just returned after giving birth to Kameyama at the Imadegawa Mansion. For details, see Section 90, note 2.

7. The Kan'in major counselors were Kinsuke, Kinmoto, Saneo, and Sanefuji, all of whom were descended from Fujiwara Kinsue (956–1029), founder of the Kan'in branch of the Fujiwara family (Kan'inryū), also called the Kinsue branch of the Fujiwara family (Kinsueryū). The Saionji, Sanjō, and Tokudaiji were further divisions of descendants from the Kinsue line.

8. The palace minister was Tokudaiji Sanemoto (1200–73), a son of Fujiwara Kintsugu and a member of one of the branch families descended from Kinsue. He is usually called the Tokudaiji major counselor in *Ben no Naishi Nikki*.

9. "Shirasagi koso shirahae nozokunare," a line from one of the songs performed at the Gosechi festival.

10. The white crane poem contains many metaphors: *tameshi* (former examples), *kage* (substitute for *sugata*, figure), and *iro* (color, which is an *engo* for *shirasagi* [white crane]). The fluttering sleeves of the young girl attendants during the dance are likened to the fluttering wings of the white crane, hence the substitution of *sode* (sleeves) for *hane* (wings).

11. Royal Viewing of the Girl Attendants (Warawa Goran) was another event in which the Gosechi dancers played a major role. The custom began during the reign of Murakami and was similar to the Gosechi Royal Rehearsal in that the ceremony occurred in the eastern Eaves-Chamber and Veranda of the Seiryōden. The ceremony served as an occasion for drinking and dancing by courtiers, with the selection of a comb as a mark of royal favor (McCullough and McCullough 1980, 1:377).

[Section 103]

1. The curative hot springs at Kinosaki (Kinosaki-machi, Kinosaki-gun, in Hyōgo prefecture) were said to have been discovered by the priest Dōchi. These hot springs were known for treating the ailments of old age.

2. Saneo's poem contains associated words (*engo*): *kokonoe* (Nine-fold Palace) and *fukaki* (deep).

3. Shōshō no Naishi's poem contains a play on *fumi* (to step on; letter), referring to Saneo's difficulty in walking through deep drifts of snow and to the letter he sent back to the palace by messenger.

4. Ben no Naishi's poem works along the same play on *fumi*, but rather than lending a sympathetic ear, she challenges Saneo's contention that the snow is deeper in mountains than in the Nine-fold Palace since Saneo's messenger was able to make his way back to deliver the letter.

[Section 104]

1. Sukeyasu's poem contains a play on *yumi toru kata* (side that takes the bow), referring to the left hand. The left hand is a metaphorical reference to Mototomo, who was the head chamberlain-middle captain of the left. This elicits praise from Azechi no Sanmi for a clever poetic answer to a command.

2. Ben no Naishi's poem is full of double entendres: *ya* (voice command for archers to draw back their bows; arrow), *hiku* (to draw [the bow]) referring to *ya*, and *iru* (to shoot; to enter) which is an *engo* for *yumi* ("bow") and a pillow word for *azusayumi* (birchwood bow). Ben no Naishi wondered whether or not she should have stopped Mototomo from leaving since he did not seem to know where he should be. Ben no Naishi thought that he should have joined them in the Demon Room for night duty.

[Section 105]

1. For the Buddha's Names Ceremony, see Section 31, note 3.

2. For details on Senkamon'in, see Section 81, note 9

3. Courtiers of ceremony (*idei no tenjōbito*) were those who performed specific functions after arriving at designated seats during ceremonies.

4. "This palace" refers to the Tominokōji Palace.

5. For covered corridors, see Section 100, note 3.

6. For Sadahira, Koreyori, Korenaga, and Motomasa, see Appendix C.

7. Ben no Naishi's poem alludes to the following in *Goshūishū*:
Goshūishū 390 (Winter). Izumi Shikibu. [Topic unknown].

sabishisa ni	It is said that even smoke
keburi o dani mo	cannot rise
tataji tote	due to loneliness,
shiba orikuburu	though kindling wood stokes the fire
fuyu no yamazato	at a mountain village in winter.

[Section 106]

1. For *kanzu*, see Section 102, note 4.

2. "His Majesty" refers to Go-Fukakusa who was eight years old at the time

3. "Small window" (*kojitomi*) refers to the window-like opening between the His Majesty's Daytime Chamber and the Courtiers' Hall in the Seiryōden. *Shitomi* were latticework windows, doors, or other openings, hinged at the top and opened by pushing the window out from the bottom, and propped in place by a stick. In the original Royal Residential Palace and at the detached Kan'in Palace, there was a comb-shaped window between the Daytime Chamber and the Courtiers' Hall through which the monarch could view male courtiers. The Tominokōji, an aristocratic mansion converted for use as a town palace, was not designed as a replica of the Royal Residential Palace and therefore lacked exact equivalents in rooms and other necessities.

4. For Sanetaka, Tsunetada, and Koremoto, see Appendix C.

5. An allusion to the following poem in *Goshūishū*:
Goshūishū 433 (Felicitations). Murasaki Shikibu. After the birth of the Retired Sovereign Go-Ichijō (b. 1008), people gathered to view the full moon in celebration of the seventh night after his birth.

mezurashiki	Rare light of the full moon
hikari sashisou	shines in the cup passed
sakazuki wa	from hand to hand—
mochinagara koso	indeed a full moon coursing
chiyo mo megurame	through a thousand-year reign.

There are several puns in Murasaki Shikibu's poem: *sakazuki* (full moon; cup), *mochinagara* (holding; full [moon]); and *meguru* (for the [cup] to have made the round to all participants; for the [moon] to course across the sky on its trajectory).

6. An allusion to the following in the *Shūishū*:
Shūishū 427 (Names of Things). Fujiwara Sukemi. Topic: "Kanoe saru" (*kanoe*, one of the ten stems [*jikkan*] and *saru*, one of the twelve branches [*jūnishi*], belonged to the premodern sexagesimal cycle used to calculate years.) *Kanoe saru* corresponds to the number 56 in the sixty-year cycle.

kanoe saru	Ship leaving the bay,
funa mate shibashi	please wait a moment—
koto towan	there is something I would ask
oki no shiranami	before the white waves
mada tatanu ma ni	rise in the offing.

[Section 107]

1. Kasuga Shrine, the tutelary shrine of the Fujiwara clan, located in Nara at the foot of Mount Mikasa. The Kasuga Festival, held twice annually on the first

Day of the Monkey in the second and eleventh months, featured a royal messenger (usually a Fujiwara middle captain), emissaries from the royal family, senior nobles, and *naishi*. The main events were the presentation of offerings, including horses conveyed by the messengers, recitation of *norito*, performances of sacred dances (*kagura*), and horse racing (McCullough and McCullough 1980, 1:400–1).

2. Nashihara, located in Nashihara-chō in Nara, was the designated resting place for royal messengers en route to the Kasuga Festival. Although the characters for the premodern Nashihara is "pear field," the characters used for the modern Nashihara-chō is that for "female courtiers" and "field," perhaps reflecting the historical usage of the site as a resting place for female royal messengers.

3. Iwasa Miyoko notes allusions made to the following from the *Kokinshū* and the *Shinkokinshū*:

    Kokinshū 1099 (Azuma-uta and Ise uta). Anonymous.

ou no ura ni	Let us sleep on it
katae sashiōi	and then discuss it—whether
naru nashi no	our love will ripen
nari mo narazu mo	like pears on laden branches
nete katarawan	stretching out toward Ou beach.
(McCullough 1985, 245)	

    Shinkokinshū 281 (Summer). Kunaikyō. At a poetry contest of 1,500 rounds.

katae sasu	Branches stretching out
ou no ura nashi	toward Ou beach—
hatsu aki ni	whether the pears ripen or not,
nari mo narazu mo	the early autumn wind
kaze zo mi ni shimu	pierces my body.

Tamai Kōsuke states that the "nashi" of the place name Nashihara may refer to a pear that bears fruit in the autumn on an unpredictable schedule. The same unpredictability is extended to the midnight moon, which requires one to stay awake all night if one wants to get a glimpse of it.

4. Sakuya, a *zōshi[me]* (maid), was one of the women employed by the Office of Female Courtiers to perform a variety of duties. Sakuya belonged to a class of female servants called *nyokan*, the lowest hierarchy of women in court service. It seems that their supervisors, *nyōkan* such as Takatsunji, were also called by their given names, but *naishi* and other *nyōbō* were known only by sobriquets that incorporated the names of a part of their official posts at court.

5. The line of the song they are singing contains the female servant's name in the line "ima wa harube to *saku ya* kono hana" from the following poem found in the preface of the *Kokinshū*:

    Kokinshū preface. Poem 1.

Naniwazu ni	Flowers on the trees
saku ya ko no hana	in bloom at Naniwazu
fuyu komori	say, "Now the winter
ima wa harube to	yields its place to the springtime!"
saku ya ko no hana	Flowers blooming on the trees.
(McCullough 1985, 4)	

6. *Waga mi hitotsu no* calls to mind Ariwara no Narihira's famous poem *Tsuki ya aranu*, preserved in both the *Kokinshū* (747) and *Ise Monogatari* (Section 4), in which the line *waga mi hitotsu wa* occurs.

[Section 108]

1. *Buppōsō*, a broad-billed roller or *Eurystomus orientalis*, with a cry that is homophonous with the *Sanbōe*, the Three Treasures of Buddhism: the Buddha (*butsu*), the Law (*hō*), and the Priest[hood] (*sō*).
2. Former chancellor Saneuji, father of Ōmiya'in.
3. The bird's name, *Buppōsō*, was based on the sound of its cry.
4. *Hiedori*, now known as *hiyodori*, a bird with ash-colored, bluish green body feathers and willow-colored head feathers, about the size of a *tsugumi* (a dusky thrush, *Merula eunomus*).

[Section 109]

1. "Edge" (*tsuma*) is used to indicate an exterior apartment, rather than one of the interior rooms in a building. A room at the edge of the building offered a view of the moon that an interior room could not. Perhaps related to the Edge Apartment of Section 63, note 1.
2. The Second Wing Chamber (Ni no Tai), a term used for subsidiary buildings within town palaces, was a building in the Tominokōji Palace where Ben no Naishi and Shōshō no Naishi were assigned living quarters.
3. Kyōgoku Avenue, bordering the east side of the Tominokōji Palace, was one of the north-south thoroughfares on the easternmost border of Heian-kyō. Located near the famous large willow on the palace grounds facing Kyōgoku Avenue was a building known as the Great Willow Hall (Sumi no Gosho, also Ōyanagiden).
4. Shōshō no Naishi's poem contains several puns: *yoru* (twist [thread], come close, approach; night). Her poem challenges the traditional concept that willows should be viewed in close proximity, as in a poem from the *Shūishū*. This poem also uses *yoru* (twist [thread] and approach) as an *engo* for *ito* (thread).

Shūishū 33 (Spring). Ōnakatomi Yoshinobu.

chikakute zo	Indeed the colors increase
iro mo masareru	the closer one gets—
aoyagi no	green strands of the willow
ito wa yorite zo	should be viewed
miru bekarikeru	close at hand.

5. Ben no Naishi's poem opposes the idea that willow strands are usually blown into disorder by the wind. Iwasa Miyoko cites the following traditional example from the *Shūishū*:

Shūishū 32 (Spring). Anonymous.

tomosureba	When the wind comes
kaze no yoru ni zo	with the night,
aoyagi no	green strands of the willow
ito wa nakanaka	are dyed
midare somekeru	into considerable disorder.

[Section 110]

1. For Seven Rivers Purification, see Section 84, notes 1 and 2.
2. For Eaves Corridor (Konrō), see Section 5, note 2.
3. Shōshō no Naishi's poem compares the Tominokōji Palace to the former Kan'in Palace after the topic was introduced during a conversation among female courtiers. Iwasa Miyoko notes that her poem refers to the following poem from the *Shikashū* (*Collection of Verbal Flowers*, ca. 1151-54):

Shikashū 29 (Spring). Ise no Tayū.

inishie no	Eight-fold cherry blossoms
nara no miyako no	of the Nara capital
yaezakura	of the distant past,
kyō kokonoe ni	today their fragrance
nioinuru kana	covers the Nine-fold Palace.

4. Ben no Naishi uses "shinobu mukashi no kumoi" to refer to the Kan'in Palace, destroyed by fire in 1249 (Section 81), as the superior palace, but politely commends the Tominokōji Palace for its fragrant flowers.

[Section 111]

1. For details on kickball (*kemari*), see Section 87, note 2.
2. Tokitsune, son of Minamoto Nobuyasu, was the nephew of Arisuke.
3. A reference to cherry blossoms.
4. The royal cavalryman (*mizuijin*) Yorimine is otherwise unidentified
5. *Goematsu*, a tree known as a *himematsu* (*Pinus pentaphylla*), a Japanese white pine. Iwasa states that here the beautifully decorated kickball may have been attached to a branch made of gold or silver into the likeness of a *goematsu* pine. This kickball may have been used to start the game, in which case it would have been called an *agemari*.
6. Thin white paper (*ganpishi*) made from the bark of the shrub *jinchōge* (*Daphne odora*), a sweet-smelling daphne that grows wild in the western mountains of Japan with small yellow flowers that bloom in summer.
7. Retired Sovereign Go-Saga's composition puns on the meaning of *osamari* (end, conclude; quell, subdue). There are three *engo* related to kickball: *mari* (ball), *keru* (kick), and *kazu(f)uru* (count). For details on kickball, see Section 87, note 2. Iwasa Miyoko states that Go-Saga'in's poem alludes to one in the *Shoku-kokinshū* by his grandfather, Go-Toba'in:

Shokukokinshū 105 (Spring). Go-Toba'in.

fuku kaze mo	Joyful that at night
osamareru yo no	even the blowing wind
ureshiki wa	has settled down—
hana miru toki zo	we recalled our joy
mazu oboekeru	when we first saw the flowers.

Cherry blossoms, an *engo* for *kemari*, refers to the corner at which play begins in kickball. The absence of wind augured good playing conditions.

8. Ben no Naishi's poem puns on the similarities of *ari* (*kakegoe* [a voice prompt] in kickball) and *amari* (in excess; ball), and *kazu* (count) and *kazu(f)u* (to

count). All subsequent poems echo her use of puns and *engo*. Ben no Naishi follows Go-Saga's lead with auspicious number and counting words. Counting the number of consecutive kicks is the main object of kickball.

9. Iwasa quotes the following poem from the *Shinkokinshū* as being related to Shōshō no Naishi's:

Shinkokinshū 1490 (Miscellaneous 1). Fujiwara Shunzei.

samidare wa	In the rains of the fifth month,
amaya no nokiba no	raindrops from the eaves
amasosogi	of the thatch-roof hut
amari naru made	are so abundant
nururu sode kana	my sleeves are drenched.

Shunzei's poem plays on the similarity of *amasosogi* (raindrops, eavesdrop) and *amari* (the roofs' eaves). *Nokiba* (edge of the eaves) and *maya* (thatched-roof hut) are *engo* for *amari*.

10. Iwasa states Ben no Naishi may be alluding to a poem from the *Shinkokinshū*:

Shinkokinshū 732 (Felicitations). Fujiwara Norikane.

kimi ga yo ni	In His Majesty's reign,
aeru wa tare mo	anyone able to meet him
ureshiki o	is happy—
hana wa iro ni mo	the color of the cherry blossom
idenikeru kana	also emerges!

11. The word *harukaze* (spring breeze; spring cold) in Shōshō no Naishi's poem is echoed in the next poem in this section by Kinmoto. Shōshō no Naishi was ordered by the monarch to chastise Kinmoto for refusing to manage the kickball game.

12. Kinmoto's poem claims he was genuinely down with a spring cold (*harukaze*).

13. Ben no Naishi, who was not ordered to attack Kinmoto, defends him on the basis of his good looks, stating that anyone who looks as elegant as a flower ought to be trustworthy as well. Her poem puns on *kaze* (wind; a cold).

[Section 112]

1. The Buddha's Anointment Ceremony (Kanbutsue) was performed by pouring hydrangea tea (*amacha*) over an image of the infant Buddha to celebrate his birthday on the eighth day of the fourth month. This ceremony has its origins in the legend that Buddha's body was drenched with perfumed water by dragons. At the Japanese court, the ceremony was conducted in the Seiryōden. After priests (*dōshi*) concluded their meeting, first they and next the senior nobles anointed the image of the Buddha with water of five colors that had been poured into five bowls. Afterwards, the priests received alms and then withdrew.

2. Sanefuji was actually a provisional middle counselor at the time; he was appointed provisional major counselor in the following year. Although scholars do not think that *Ben no Naishi Nikki* was written in retrospect, errors of this type may have occurred during revision at a later time.

3. A "crimson glossed silk robe" (*kurenai uchi no iro*) is given sheen and luster by having been beaten over a fulling block (*kinuta*). In *The Tale of Genji*, when Genji was staying at Yūgao's house, he heard the sounds of someone plying a wooden mallet over a fulling block, indicating that her house in the capital was a poor one located among the dwellings of laborers.

4. "Grapevine," an approximate translation for *tsuta* (*Parthenocissus tricuspidata*), belonging to the grape (*budō*) family, is a vine-like plant whose leaves are used in designs of family crests (*mon*).

5. *Kaede*, a sweet maple (*Aceraceae*). The *tsuta* and *kaede* refer to Section 9 of *The Tales of Ise*, which follows the section in which the *kakitsubata* poem is composed and precedes the *miyakodori* poem: "Continuing their journey, they arrived in the province of Suruga. When they arrived at Mt. Utsu, the path they were entering was very dark and hemmed in by abundant growths of *tsuta* and *kaede*. They were disheartened." Utsu no yama, now called Utsunoya Tōge, is located between Okabe-chō and Shizuoka-shi in Shizuoka prefecture.

6. Female courtiers thought that a poem ought to be written formally introducing Sanefuji as the one who brought the late offering. Mitsukuni, a chamberlain, was chosen to be the manager (*bugyō*) to handle Sanefuji's offering.

[Section 113]

1. Although not specified in the text, this is the Kamo Festival, which took place on the fourteenth day of the fourth month.

2. Female messengers (*onnazukai*) of *suke* rank (middle level of *naishi* ranking) were dispatched from the Naishidokoro to the Kamo Festival as their representative.

3. Wild pinks combination (*nadeshiko no kinu*) was a summer color combination with the outer layers either in shades of crimson (*kōbai*) or burgundy (*suo*) with a greenish-blue lining (*ao*). Another explanation for this combination has it with crimson outer layers and a light purple lining (*usu murasaki*). There are a variety of wild pinks (*nadeshiko*): *Dianthus superbus* (wild pinks), the light-colored Yamato wild pinks (*Caryophyllaceous corolla*), and the darker Chinese wild pinks.

[Section 114]

1. For Repast in the Presence of a *Kami* (Jingonjiki), see Section 52, note 3.

2. Michiyuki, son of Minamoto Michichika, held senior third rank at the age of forty-nine.

3. Akimasa, son of Fujiwara Chikafusa, was forty-four years old at the time, holding the post of controller.

4. Iwasa states that the unspecified *naishi* must refer to Ben no Naishi, who had already gone to the Shinkaden, the main building within the Chūwain located just west of the Royal Residential Palace in the Greater Royal Palace, where the ceremony was to take place.

[Section 115]

1. The Black Door (Kurodo) was a long narrow bay north of the Bush-Clover

Room in the Seiryōden and southwest of the palace guards' headquarters (Takiguchi no Jin). Stars Meeting (Hoshiai), another way of referring to the Tanabata Festival, celebrates the meeting of the stars, the Weaver Maid and the Herdsman, as their trajectories cross once a year near the Heavenly Stream. Shōshō no Naishi's poem suggests that it is as rare for Saneo to report for duty as the Black Door guard as it is for the yearly rendezvous of the ill-fated lovers.

2. Iwasa states that Shōshō no Naishi's poem alludes to the following poem from *Gosenshū*:

Gosenshū 239 (Autumn 1). Anonymous.

ama no gawa	Though it is not far
tōki watari wa	from the crossing
nakeredomo	of the Heavenly Stream,
kimi ga funade wa	I wait the year long
toshi no koso mate	for your ship to embark.

[Section 116]

1. In Section 81, a fire destroys the Kan'in Palace; in Section 138, Go-Fukakusa and his court move back to the newly rebuilt Kan'in Palace, the setting for the remainder of the memoir (Tamai 1958a, 243-45; Iwasa 1994a, 240-41). The Tominokōji Palace is the setting for Sections 83 through 137.

[Section 117]

1. Go-Saga, age thirty-one, invited them to a moon-viewing (*kangetsu*) poetry gathering. "The usual" implies that Ben no Naishi and her sister were accustomed to being invited to poetry parties sponsored by Go-Saga to compose linked verse. The party was held at Go-Saga's residence, the Reizei-Madenokōji Palace.

2. For double doors, see Section 14, note 9.

3. "He" refers to Go-Saga.

4. *Amida Butsu Renga* is linked verse in which a syllable from the name Amida Buddha, *na mo Ami ta (fu) tsu (fu* is not pronounced), becomes in that order the initial sound for each linked sequence. "Namu Amida Butsu" is the modern Japanese pronunciation of this phrase.

5. Iwasa states that Go-Saga's poem alludes to the following in *Shūishū*:

Shūishū 758 (Love 2). Fujiwara Koretada.

kakurenu no	How am I to respond
soko no kokoro zo	to your indifference?
urameshiki	I seek what is in the depths
ika ni se yo tote	of your heart
tsurenakaruran	as in a hidden marsh.

Kakerenu (hidden marsh) alludes to the *kundoku* reading of *komori nu* found in the *Collection of Ten Thousand Leaves* (*Man'yōshū*, ca. 759). There is a pivot word, *soko* (bottom; over there), playing on the figurative pillow word for *nu* (marsh). Kyoko Selden (personal communication) states that *ika ni seyo tote kaeruran* is a set phrase from a famous *Shinkokinshū* poem:

Shinkokinshū 210 (Spring 1). Fujiwara Shunzei.

waga kokoro	What are you telling
ika ni seyo tote	my heart to do?
hototogisu	The cuckoo cries
kumoma no tsuki no	in the moonlight
kage ni kakuran	from between the clouds.

6. Go-Saga's poem alludes to the following in the *Kokinshū* (also *Tales of Ise*, Section 82):

Kokinshū 884 (Miscellaneous 1). Ariwara no Narihira.

akanaku ni	Not content,
madaki mo tsuki no	the moon hides
kakaruru ka	quickly,
yamanoha nigete	would that the mountains' rim
irezu mo aranan	prevent its escape.

Iwasa also cites the following poem from *Shūishū* as a reference:

Shūishū 470 (Miscellaneous 1). Tachibana Tadamoto.

wasuruna ya	Do not forget me,
hodo wa kumoi ni	until we meet again.
narinu tomo	Though in the meantime,
sora yuku tsuki mo	we are as distant as the abode of clouds
meguriau made	where the moon courses the sky.

7. Ben no Naishi introduces the topic of a lover's parting, suggestive of the word *kinuginu* (robe on robe) written with the character for *koromo* or "morning after" as in morning-after poems exchanged by lovers who have spent the night together. Her link also contains *engo* of *meguriau* (go round) and *oguruma* (little carriage [with wheels turning]).

8. Go-Saga's poem alludes to the following example in *Man'yōshū*:

Man'yōshū 694 (Book IV). Hirokawa no Ōkimi.

koikusa o	Love grasses
chikaraguruma ni	piled onto seven
nanaguruma	hand-drawn carriages;
tsumite kouraku	loving thoughts of you
waga kokoro kara	from my heart.

Selden (personal communication) states that in Man'yō times *koikusa* indicated just plain grass, but that by Ben no Naishi's time *koigusa* (love/passion grass) probably came to be associated with *hanaguruma* (flower carriages), often a *makie* theme. *Makie* are designs or pictures on lacquerware, embellished with mother-of-pearl inlays.

9. Shōshō no Naishi's poem alludes to the following in *Kokinshū*:

Kokinshū 556 (Love 2). Abe no Kiyoyuki (sent to Ono no Komachi).

tsutsumedomo	Though I wrap them,
sode ni tamaranu	the sleeves cannot contain them;
shiratama wa	the white jewels are
hito o minu me no	tears from eyes
namida narikeri	that cannot see my beloved.

10. Formerly called Dainagon no Suke. She was promoted to the third rank in Section 99, prompting the use of a new sobriquet.

11. This passage suggests that it was common knowledge that Ben no Naishi kept records of the poetry she composed at court. One of the variant titles for the text, *Ben no Naishi Ie no Shū* or *Ben no Naishi Kashū*, seems to verify the existence of at least a personal poetry collection by Ben no Naishi. Perhaps Ben no Naishi used the poetry collection as a basis for revising and compiling the present text, thus accounting for the inconsistencies in dates and offices of characters who appear in the work. Mistakes of this nature are often found in works revised at a later date.

12. There are *engo* in Ben no Naishi's poem: *ha* (leaves [of pages]; [from trees]) and *tsumu* (to pluck; pick).

[Section 118]

1. For the Horse-Leading Ceremony, see Section 59, note 1.

2. Iwasa states that Kinmoto is sending his respects to the female courtiers to mark the first time he served as the presiding official of this ceremony. Full-moon steeds (*mochizuki no uma*), found in all three poems from this entry, are horses sent from Mochizuki in Shinano province (now Nagano prefecture).

3. Shōshō no Naishi's poem puns on *hiku* (lead, pull; quote, cite), to cite a precedent for the poem and to lead the horses.

[Section 119]

1. For the Imadegawa Mansion, see Section 62, note 1.

2. Seven people, one after another, took turns holding various cords that held the crossed portion of the tripod on the bottom part of the torches. It was a ritual performed when clear weather was desired. After the last person had his or her turn, that person had the task of chanting "tere tere hi no ko" (Shining, shining Sun-child) while dancing. This ritual seems to be similar to the modern Japanese children's song "Teru-teru Bōzu," sung to ward off rain and bring clear skies.

3. Torch stakes (*tōdai no kui*) were made of three thin stakes of which about one-fifth of the upper part was bound and twisted together with the bottom part extending into a tripod foot. A dish of oil placed on the crossed portion provided fuel for the torchlight.

4. Ben no Naishi's poem seeks to justify her refusal to sing and dance to "tere tere hi no ko." The boatman is a metaphor that refers to Shōshō no Naishi who usually performs this function. She suggests that she, a mere amateur, could not possibly succeed in praying for good weather in the absence of the customary boatman, Shōshō no Naishi.

[Section 120]

1. *Kami* Observances (Goshinji), ceremonies performed in worship of *kami*. Courtiers went to the site of the rites for purification and abstinence, so there were only a few people left to serve at court. The monarch was also to abstain from entertainment as penitence during this time. Boredom caused the child monarch to command Ben no Naishi to amuse him.

2. The Large Room (Daidokoro), the office for the lowest-ranking *nyōbō* (*gerō no nyōbō*), is not to be confused with the Table Room (Daibandokoro), the headquarters for higher-ranking *nyōbō* such as *naishi*. Iwasa states that the location of the Daidokoro is not known, but suggests that the use of this word in the *Memoirs of Nakatsukasa no Naishi*, *The Confessions of Lady Nijō*, and *The Clear Mirror* indicates that it is a distinct and separate room from the similar-sounding Daibandokoro. Judging by this entry, it seems that the Large Room was located by the exterior corridors near the gardens, although it does not state which building served as the setting for this entry. (Daidokoro has nothing to do with the homophonous modern Japanese word for "kitchen.")

3. *Ōban* guards, warriors sent from various provinces to perform martial duties at court, performed duties similar to palace guards.

4. Abstinence charms or cards (*monoimi no fuda*) let others know that persons wearing them were not allowed to communicate with people, even though they sometimes had to wear charms while they performed necessary errands in the city.

5. Ben no Naishi is referring to her father, Nobuzane, known as Jakusai after he had taken Buddhist vows. Iwasa proposes that word of her antics had reached home and that Nobuzane wanted her to return home to undergo penance for having acted foolishly and for having fallen into the courtyard stream (*yarimizu*) during a time of solemn preparations for Shintō rites. Undergoing penance might provide a chance for her recent actions to be reconsidered by the *kami* (Iwasa 1994a, 225).

[Section 121]

1. This section refers to the staging of mock state banquets, special festivals and *shidai* (catalogs containing the correct procedural order in which rites were to be executed), to teach the young eight-year-old monarch how to play his part in these ceremonies and festivals when they occurred. Although they were called "special" festivals, the Iwashimizu Special Festival celebrated on the middle Day of the Ox in the third month and the Kamo Special Festival celebrated on the last Day of the Cock in the eleventh month, were performed annually in addition to scheduled, regular festivals. This was part of the informal education courtiers, both male and female, were required to provide the young monarch.

2. Actually the former chancellor Saionji Saneuji.

3. Batons (*shaku*) made of long narrow pieces of wood were held in the right hand when men wore formal costumes. The "Palace Snow" (Uchino no Yuki) chapter in *The Clear Mirror* states that the chancellor had the female courtiers make the batons "intentionally small."

4. "Chancellor-Lay Priest" refers to Saionji Kintsune.

5. The Lay Priest, Takatoki, was a famous virtuoso of the Seiryū Biwa. It is no wonder that Kōtō no Naishi also became a virtuoso of the *biwa* with such a teacher.

6. Iyo no Naishi, the unidentified Iyo of Section 119 who danced "tere tere hi no ko" instead of Ben no Naishi.

7. Socks (*shitauzu*) worn with formal *sokutai* costumes. Unlike *tabi*, *shitauzu* had no divided section for the big toe. Chūnagon no Suke invents an excuse to get out of playing the palace controller (naiben) role.

8. Ben no Naishi's poem puns on *ashi* (feet; reeds) and *shitauzu* (socks) and *shitane* (roots) with related meaning and sounds. Iwasa quotes Chūnagon no Suke's reply as recorded in *The Clear Mirror*:

tsu no kuni no	My wretched heart
ashi no shitane no	floats and quakes
midare wabi	like the roots of the reeds
kokoro mo nami ni	disordered by waves
ukite furu kana	in Tsu Province.

Tsu no Kuni (Settsu province) is now part of Hyōgo prefecture.

9. The "person himself" refers to Kinchika, the Sanjō middle counselor.

10. "Director" (*ninjō*) refers to the lead dancer in charge of the all the other *kagura* dancers.

11. Hoop, wheel, or ring (*rin*), a sacred object (*torimono*) held by *kagura* dancers to attract *kami*, sometimes attached to a branch of the sacred *sakaki*.

12. Whistling (*uso o fuku*), an activity of uncertain ceremonial function, was assigned to Ben no Naishi during an outing.

13. Only among female courtiers who knew each other well.

14. Round singing, taking turns singing songs from the Gosechi festival repertoire, was an activity known as *idashiuta*.

15. Boisterous dancing (*ranbu*). In Section 27, note 1, courtiers performed on a platform (*rodai no ranbu*), singing and dancing in a boisterous manner.

16. The room below the lintel (*nageshi no shimo no hitoma*) was apparently the room from which Kinmoto was showing the women how to dance by sticking only his arms through the bamboo blinds to their room. Kinmoto's room seems to have been on a lower level than the main room inhabited by female courtiers, hence the name.

17. Sanefuji, who was an expert musician, dampened the spirit of the concert conducted by female courtiers who were all amateur musicians. When Sanefuji came in they could perform no longer because a true musician had invaded a gathering of friends.

18. Wrapped brush (*makiage no fude*), a line from the song "White Tissue Paper" (*Shirousuyō*). Also mentioned in Section 19, note 4. *Iu* (tie together) is an *engo* for *fude* (brush). *Makiage* can also mean "to pinch, pilfer, take away," hence, the "pilfered brush."

[Section 122]

1. The Toba Mansion, a town palace located in Shimo Toba in the Fushimi ward of Kyoto. It was the palace of Retired Sovereign Shirakawa, but after Retired Sovereign Go-Toba lived there, it went to ruin. Go-Saga rebuilt it. The Morning Audience was set up for Go-Fukakusa to see his parents, Go-Saga and Ōmiya'in.

2. Morning Audience (Chōkin), a ceremony during which monarchs visited their parents. This event is also recorded in the "Palace Snow" (Uchino no Yuki) chapter of *The Clear Mirror*.

3. Dragon-Head-Bird-Neck (*Ryūtōgekisu*), pleasure boats with prows carved into heads of dragons and imaginary waterfowl. Used to entertain the nobility with

musicians playing their instruments while floating on lakes located on the mansion grounds.

4. For the "formal style" (*kamiage no naishi*), see Section 21, note 2.

5. The telling and transmitting of tales (*katariiden*), introduced as a topic of conversation, is taken up as a topic by Shōshō no Naishi and Ben no Naishi in their poems. The events of that day were so memorable that the participants will narrate the topic of conversation to their offspring and grandchildren in their old age

6. From this section on, words enclosed in brackets indicate lacunae (*ketsuji*) in the text. Here, Iwasa suggests *niwa* or *niwa no* as the three missing syllables in Ben no Naishi's poem. I followed the former even though it is missing a syllable because the latter did not make sense to me. This is the first of many lacunae.

7. *Some shitagasane*, robes dyed with colors suitable to rank and season. During the Ceremony for Clear Weather (Hare no Gishiki) everyone was allowed to dye robes any color they wanted rather than wear white outer robes with dark burgundy inner robes. See Section 70, note 4, for the pine combination.

8. White-on-white combination robes could only be worn by people of advanced age who had received special permission to wear them. No one besides the chancellor was allowed to wear exclusively white robes.

9. Ben no Naishi's poem plays on the white-on-white so-called *some shitagasane* (dyed combination robes) because white is not a color produced by dyeing.

APPENDICES

Appendix A
Ben no Naishi's Literary Heritage and Family Tree

Ben no Naishi's family traced their lineage back to the Heian-period scholar-statesman Fuyutsugu (775–826). There were several generations of poets and writers in her family. The following highlights the literary and artistic accomplishments of her immediate ancestors, beginning with Ben no Naishi's great-great-grandfather Tametada and ending with her father Nobuzane.

Tametada (d. 1136)

Ben no Naishi's great-great-grandfather, Tametada, was known as the Tokiwa governor of Tango province (part of Kyōto prefecture) after his detached villa, Tokiwa. His father was Fujiwara Tomonobu of junior fifth rank, lower grade, and his mother was the daughter of Fujiwara Arisuke, the governor of Ōmi province (Shiga prefecture). Tametada is credited with compiling the *Poetry Contest of the Tametada Family* (*Tametada Ke no Uta'awase*) and a personal poetry collection, the *Collection of Fujiwara Tametada* (*Fujiwara Tametada Ason no Shū*) with 267 compositions.[1] He had nine poems included in several royal poetry anthologies beginning with the *Collection of Golden Leaves* (*Kin'yōshū*, 1124–27).

Tametada followed his parents into court service relatively young. Like his father, he attended closely upon Retired Sovereign Shirakawa (1053–1129; r. 1072–86). His mother was a wet nurse to Shirakawa's daughter, Ikuhōmon'in, which further strengthened the ties between the royal family and his own. The royal couple was fond of Tametada and his parents.

His favored position gave him access to choice posts and promotions. He was appointed the governor of Tango province, placed in charge of rebuilding the palace, and became one of Shirakawa's close retainers. In 1135, the *Mirror of the Present* (*Imakagami*) states that Tametada built the palace at Sanjō and Karasumaru avenues (Sanjō Karasumaru Gosho) for the use of Retired Sovereign Toba, after which he was promoted to senior fourth rank, lower grade, and made the provisional head of the Woodworking Bureau (Mokkō Gon no Kami).

His favored position at the court of Retired Sovereign Shirakawa also made him a valued guest at poetry contests sponsored by one of the leading members of the Rokujō school of poetry, Fujiwara Akisuke (1090–1155), with whom he developed a close friendship. During 1131 and 1132, Tametada sponsored poetry contests to which he invited budding poets, among them his three sons (known at the time as the "Three Jaku of Tokiwa"), Minamoto Yorimasa, and Fujiwara Shunzei.

Of Tametada's several sons, the three later known as the "Three Jaku of Ōhara" renounced the world at an early age to devote themselves to the composition of poetry. The poems of Ben no Naishi's great-grandfather, Tametsune (ca. 1114–80; also Tametaka; Jakuchō), and those of his brothers, Tamenari (ca. 1113–81; Jakunen) and Yorinari (ca. 1119–73; Jakuzen), are represented in the *Collection of a Thousand Years* (*Senzaishū*, ca. 1188) and later royal anthologies.

Tametada's favored status is reflected in the posts he received, such as the governorship of Tango province, which kept him near the capital and his royal patron Shirakawa, who exercised power as *in* during the reigns of Horikawa, Toba, and Sutoku (1119–64; r. 1123–41). Tametada was probably in his forties when he died in 1136 during Sutoku's reign.

Tametsune (1113–ca.1181)

Ben no Naishi's great-grandfather Tametsune (Jakuchō) served as a chamberlain (*kurōdō*) and as governor of Bingo (Okayama prefecture) and Nagato provinces (Yamaguchi prefecture) and rose to the junior fifth rank, upper grade, before taking Buddhist vows at the age of thirty in 1143. Because Tametsune took the tonsure so young, he did not compile a lengthy record of court service.

Before taking vows, Tametsune compiled a twenty-scroll anthology, *Later Collection of Leaves* (*Goyōwakashū*),[2] that was to rival the sixth royal anthology, *Collection of Verbal Flowers* (*Shikashū*, ca. 1151–54), compiled by Fujiwara Akisuke of the Rokujō school. Imitating the form and content of a royal anthology, Tametsune began his collection with a *kana* preface and included poems from the reign of Murakami (926–67; r. 946–67) to that of Konoe (1139–55; r. 1141–55). His anthology echoed topics found in royal anthologies, such as the four seasons, felicitations, parting, travel, names of things, love, and the like. Tametsune also wrote the historical tale, *The Mirror of the Present* (*Imakagami*, 1170), one of the three later historical "mirrors" that followed *The Great Mirror* (*Ōkagami*, late 11th or early 12th c.).

Takanobu (1142–1205)

Ben no Naishi's grandfather, Takanobu, was a respected court poet with compositions included in the final fifteen royal anthologies and the author of two works that no longer survive: a fictional tale known as *Floating Waves* (*Ukinami*) and a historical tale, *Still More Generations* (*Iya Yotsugi*).[3] After Tametsune renounced the world to join his brothers at Ōhara, his wife Bifukumon'in no Kaga decided to send Takanobu, then only two years old, to the home of her father, Fujiwara Chikatada (d. 1186), so that she could marry the influential poet Fujiwara Shunzei, who had been married earlier to one of Tametada's daughters. Bifukumon'in no Kaga's second marriage produced several children, among them the outstanding thirteenth-century poet Fujiwara Teika and his elder full sister, Kenzu Omae. Although Takanobu was the elder half-brother of Teika, the twenty-year age difference seems to have inhibited the growth of brotherly affection between them. In fact, Teika has often been criticized for sending a surrogate to visit Takanobu on his deathbed, another indication of a rather distant relationship.[4]

Takanobu's poetry collection, *The Poetry Collection of Fujiwara Takanobu* (*Fujiwara Takanobu no Ason Shū*),[5] contains the expected poetic exchanges with members of his stepfather's Mikosa (also Mikohidari, and later Nijō) school of poetry, but it also includes a surprising number of affectionate poetic exchanges with members of the rival Rokujō school. It seems that Takanobu and the Rokujō school leader, Akisuke's son Kiyosuke (1104–77), the compiler of the *Secrets of Waka* (*Okugishō*), *Pocket Book of Waka* (*Fukurō Sōshi*), *First Book of Waka* (*Waka Shogakushō*), *A Collection of Verbal Flowers Continued* (*Shoku Shikashū*), and *A Shepherd's Flute Chronicle* (*Bokuteki Ki*), were very close friends.[6] But because Shunzei and Teika were leaders of the Mikosa school, they probably resented Takanobu's friendship with the leader of the rival school.

Takanobu benefited from his grandfather Chikatada's position as a court favorite of Toba (1103–56; r. 1107–23). As the foster father of Toba's consort, Bifukumon'in (1117–60), Chikatada was able to procure for his grandson appointments as chamberlain, governor of the provinces of Kōzuke, Echizen, and Wakasa, and provisional head of the royal stables of the right of fifth rank, all before he had reached the age of fourteen.[7]

After the deaths of Toba in 1156 and Bifukumon'in in 1160, Takanobu's career languished for some time. He entered the service of Hachijō'in, a daughter of Toba and Bifukumon'in, but was expelled from court in 1160 by Go-Shirakawa ostensibly for neglecting his duties in the Courtiers' Hall, and was not recalled for five years. He was not promoted to the fourth rank until 1179, when he was already in his late thirties.

Around 1173, Takanobu married the young daughter of a close friend, Fujiwara Nagashige (fl. late 12th c.), a Rokujō poet who was one of three other men also expelled from the Courtiers' Hall by the royal decree of 1160.[8] It is believed that Takanobu waited for Nagashige's daughter to attain a marriageable age much as Genji waited for Murasaki in *The Tale of Genji*; however, Takanobu's wife died after only five years of marriage.[9] Takanobu's liaison with Ukyō no Daibu (fl. mid-12th c.), which is described in her account, *The Poetic Memoirs of Lady Daibu*, probably began around the autumn of 1178, shortly after the death of his young wife. Although Ukyō no Daibu was quite a bit younger than Takanobu, she was still involved with him when she fell passionately in love with Taira no Sukemori. Thereafter, it seems that her affections fluctuated between the two until she ended her relationship with Takanobu after Sukemori's death in 1185.[10]

Takanobu was thus a literary figure of some importance, but he is best known for his *yamato-e* portrait paintings (*nise-e*). In 1173, he was commissioned to paint the courtiers taking part in the processions to the Shintō shrines of Hie and Hirano and the Buddhist monastery of Mt. Kōya. Apparently the portraits by Takanobu were so realistic that the courtiers were shocked by them; Fujiwara Kanezane, the minister of the right at the time, expressed relief in his diary that he had been absent during those occasions (*Gyokuyō* [entry for the ninth day of the ninth month of 1173]). Takanobu is also traditionally given credit for the famous portraits of Minamoto Yoritomo, Taira no Shigemori (1138–79), and Fujiwara Mitsuyoshi at Jingoji, although this theory is now much debated. Under the influence of Hōnen Shōnin, whose portrait Retired Sovereign Go-Shirakawa is said to have commissioned, Takanobu renounced the world in 1201 and died four years later. A number of his poems were included in the *New Collection of Ancient and Modern Japanese Poetry* (*Shinkokinshū*, 1205) compiled by his younger half-brother, Teika, and others.

Nobuzane (ca. 1177–1270)[11]

Little is known about Nobuzane's childhood. An entry dated the fourth day of the eighth month of 1199 in Teika's diary, *Bright Moon Chronicle*

(*Meigetsuki*), refers to him as Takazane and states that he occupied no post while holding the fifth rank at the age of twenty-three. He is known to have been a participant in a poetry contest held in 1200, the *Second Hundred-Sequence Poetry Contest of 1200* (*Dainido Hyakushu Uta'awase*).[12] Soon afterward, in either 1200 or 1201, he adopted the name Nobuzane.

As a courtier, Nobuzane may have been in the service of Hachijō'in or Shunkamon'in, since he wrote poems lamenting their loss when they died not five months apart in 1211. Hachijō'in was the aforementioned daughter of Toba and Bifukumon'in; Shunkamon'in was a daughter of Go-Toba by a daughter of Fujiwara (Kujō) Kanezane (1149–1207).[13]

Despite Nobuzane's kinship relationship with Teika, who was emerging as the most influential critic of the day, Nobuzane's name is conspicuously absent from the major poetry competitions and anthologies of the first decade of the century. His budding career as a poet was dealt a severe setback when his poems were excluded from the prestigious *New Collection of Ancient and Modern Japanese Poetry*. Of the eleven people who were invited to the *Second Hundred-Sequence Poetry Contest of 1200*, Nobuzane was the only participant whose poems were not selected for inclusion in the *New Collection of Ancient and Modern Japanese Poetry*. In fact, Nobuzane does not emerge on the public poetry scene until 1216 when he was invited to be the head judge of the *Hundred-Poem Sequence of the Palace Minister Michiie* (*Naidaijin Michiie Hyakushu*), sponsored by the powerful court figure Kujō Michiie. Shortly thereafter, he was invited to poetry-composition parties sponsored by Retired Sovereign Juntoku (1197–1242; r. 1210–21), Michiie, and others.[14] Perhaps as revenge for having been excluded from the *New Collection of Ancient and Modern Japanese Poetry*. Nobuzane refused to invite Teika's son Tameie to participate in the *Priestly Prince Michisuke's Fifty-Poem Sequence* (*Michisuke Hōshinnō Gojūshu Waka*, ca. 1215), on the grounds that he was too inexperienced.

Nobuzane was promoted to senior fifth rank, lower grade, in the spring of 1216 by Juntoku. In the following year, he was appointed provisional master of central affairs. Around 1219 or earlier, he was appointed governor of the province of Bingo, and in 1226 he was promoted to the fourth rank. Then in 1231, Teika recorded in his diary that Nobuzane, the provisional master of the right capital, had visited him in order to thank him for assisting him in some official capacity. This promotion was probably due to Teika's intercession on Nobuzane's behalf; however, Nobuzane did not progress beyond senior fourth rank, lower grade, after 1231; neither did he receive any further appointments.

In the interval between the compilation of the *New Collection of Ancient and Modern Japanese Poetry* in 1205 and that of the *New Royal*

Collection (*Shinchokusenshū*, 1232), of which Teika was the sole compiler, Nobuzane's relationship with Teika must have improved dramatically, for a number of his poems appear in the later collection. It is apparent that Nobuzane maintained a delicate balance between the two rival schools of poetry: the Mikohidari (later Nijō) school of his relatives, Teika and Tameie, and the Rokujō school of his close friends.[15]

Nobuzane seems to have begun to make a name for himself as a painter midway in his forties. Early mentions of him in the *Bright Moon Chronicle* and elsewhere do not contain any particular references to his skill as an artist; however, medieval texts such as the *Mirror of the East* (*Azumakagami*, ca. 1289), *The Clear Mirror,* and the *Jōkyū Era Chronicle* (*Jōkyūki,* late Kamakura-early Nanbokuchō period) make frequent reference to paintings by Nobuzane. Most notable of these is the portrait of Retired Sovereign Go-Toba commissioned for presentation to his mother, Shichijō'in, thought to be preserved today at Minase Shrine.[16] Unfortunately, none of the other titles found in the Kamakura histories can be related to extant paintings. There are, however, two scrolls of portraits commonly attributed to Nobuzane: the *Royal Cavalryman Scroll* (*Zuijin Teiki Emaki,* ca. 1247) and the *Thirty-Six Immortal Poet Portraits* (*Sanjūrokkasen-e,* 1240s).[17]

Nobuzane's literary corpus can be more reliably identified. He left a personal anthology, *The Poetry Collection of Fujiwara Nobuzane* (*Fujiwara Nobuzane Ason no Shū*), which he is thought to have completed a year before he renounced the world in 1248.[18] Furthermore, 122 of his compositions appear in royal anthologies from the *New Royal Collection* on. According to one theory, he also compiled the *Tales of the Present* (*Ima Monogatari,* ca. 1239), a medieval collection of brief stories about poems, polite accomplishments, ethical behavior, the gods, and the like.[19] Here he seems to have been perpetuating the family tradition of writing historical works that began with his grandfather's *Mirror of the Present* and his father's *Still More Generations.* Although Nobuzane achieved neither high rank nor lucrative appointments within the court bureaucracy, his poetic and artistic gifts afforded him ample opportunity to cultivate patronage relationships with influential members of society on behalf of his offspring.

Of Nobuzane's five sons, Tametsugu (d. 1265) is the best known. Although not prominent as a poet, Tametsugu followed in the footsteps of his father and grandfather as a portrait painter. He also became the first male member of his family to rise as high as junior third rank, a promotion granted him by Go-Fukakusa in 1258. He was probably the artist who painted a portrait of Konoe Kanetsune in 1247 to commemorate

Kanetsune's appointment as regent.[20] His descendants were able to remain prominent in artistic circles until the fifteenth century.[21]

In addition, Nobuzane had at least five daughters. He placed one of his elder daughters, Sōhekimon'in Shōshō no Naishi (d. ca. 1270), in the service of Kujō Michiie's daughter Sōhekimon'in (consort to Go-Horikawa and mother of Shijō [1231–42; r. 1232–42]). Sōhekimon'in Shōshō no Naishi probably retired from service when Sōhekimon'in died at the early age of twenty-five and never returned to court service.[22]

The epithet by which another of Nobuzane's daughters is known, Shijō'in Shōshō no Naishi (fl. early 13th c.), indicates that she was in the service of Retired Sovereign Shijō. Since she is listed in the *Genealogy of the Exalted and the Base* before Sōhekimon'in Shōshō no Naishi, she might have been the older of the two, but nothing is known of her life.

Nobuzane was able to secure for his two younger daughters, Ben no Naishi and Shōshō no Naishi (d. 1265), similar positions at the court of Go-Fukakusa. Since Go-Fukakusa was a child of only three when he ascended the throne, Nobuzane's relationships with Kujō Michiie and Go-Fukakusa's father, Retired Sovereign Go-Saga, probably had much to do with his daughters' placement at court.

As he approached the age of sixty, Nobuzane began compiling his personal poetry collection. He may have begun collecting suitable poems around the year 1246; from internal evidence, it seems the compilation was completed sometime in 1247. While selecting the poems and reviewing the events of his life, he apparently reached the decision to renounce the world, for he took Buddhist vows in 1248.

When Nobuzane died between the years 1266 and 1270, he had outlived most of his children. He was survived by two daughters, Sōhekimon'in Shōshō no Naishi and Ben no Naishi, the former of whom wrote the following lament in the *Collection of Gleanings Continued* (*Shokushūishū*, 1278):[23]

Shokushūishū 1285, (Miscellaneous 2). In the spring after Nobuzane Ason died, Sōhekimon'in Shōshō no Naishi composed this poem upon seeing the verdant grasses growing over the place where he was buried.

toshitoshi no	Although I keep longing
haru no kusa ni mo	for traces of the withered one,
nagusa made	it is consoling
karenishi hito no	to see that spring grasses
ato o koitsutsu	are renewed year after year.

Notes

1. *Gunsho Ruijū* (*GR*), 15:80–93.
2. *GR*, 10:31–60.
3. Miyajima, 8.
4. Ibid.
5. *Shinkō Gunsho Ruijū* 12:12–74.
6. Miyajima, 8.
7. Ibid., 5.
8. Ibid., 6.
9. Inoue, 379.
10. Miyajima, 6.
11. Inoue Muneo bases his calculation of the date of Nobuzane's death on the fact that Nobuzane's name appears in the *Index to the Ancient and Modern Japanese Poetry Continued* (*Shokukokin Wakashū Mokuroku*) as one of the living authors who submitted texts to the monarch on the eighth day of the fourth month of 1266. *The Poetry Collection of Hitoie* (*Hitoie Wakashū*), compiled in 1271 (Bun'ei 8) states that Nobuzane's recent death required the compiler to go into mourning. Therefore, Inoue concludes that Nobuzane must have died no later than 1270.
12. Yonekura, 22.
13. Ibid.
14. Ibid., 23.
15. Ibid., 24.
16. Ibid., 23; Graybill, 148–50.
17. Graybill, 143–56. Several sets of paintings of the *Thirty-Six Immortal Poets* following the selections of Fujiwara Kintō (966-1041) survive. The oldest of these, known as the *Satake-bon*, was formerly housed in the Lower Kamo Shrine (Shimogamo Jinja) in Kyoto. Stylistic analysis suggests that the *Satake-bon* is the product of a collaboration among members of Nobuzane's family, including Nobuzane himself (M. Graybill personal communication). Fujiwara Teika's *Bright Moon Chronicle* (*Meigetsuki*) refers to a different set of thirty-six poets selected by Kujō Motoie; apparently Nobuzane was commissioned to paint them as a present for Retired Sovereign Go-Toba after the former monarch had been banished to the island of Oki.
18. *Shikashū Taisei*, 4:266–73.
19. *Shinkō Gunsho Ruijū*, 21:230–44.
20. Yonekura, 54.
21. Ibid., 51.
22. *Gunsho Kaidai*, 11:75–76.
23. Yonekura, 26.

Ben no Naishi's Family Tree

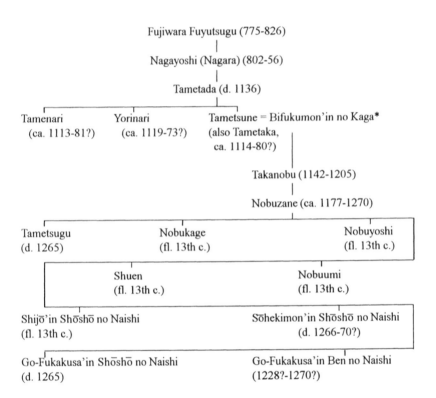

Fujiwara Fuyutsugu (775-826)
|
Nagayoshi (Nagara) (802-56)
|
Tametada (d. 1136)

Tamenari
(ca. 1113-81?)

Yorinari
(ca. 1119-73?)

Tametsune = Bifukumon'in no Kaga*
(also Tametaka,
ca. 1114-80?)

Takanobu (1142-1205)
|
Nobuzane (ca. 1177-1270)

Tametsugu
(d. 1265)

Nobukage
(fl. 13th c.)

Nobuyoshi
(fl. 13th c.)

Shuen
(fl. 13th c.)

Nobuumi
(fl. 13th c.)

Shijō'in Shōshō no Naishi
(fl. 13th c.)

Sōhekimon'in Shōshō no Naishi
(d. 1266-70?)

Go-Fukakusa'in Shōshō no Naishi
(d. 1265)

Go-Fukakusa'in Ben no Naishi
(1228?-1270?)

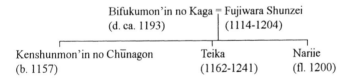

*Bifukumon'in no Kaga's Second Marriage:

Bifukumon'in no Kaga = Fujiwara Shunzei
(d. ca. 1193)   (1114-1204)

Kenshunmon'in no Chūnagon
(b. 1157)

Teika
(1162-1241)

Nariie
(fl. 1200)

Source: *Genealogy of the Exalted and the Base*, 2:157-58.

Appendix B
The Succession

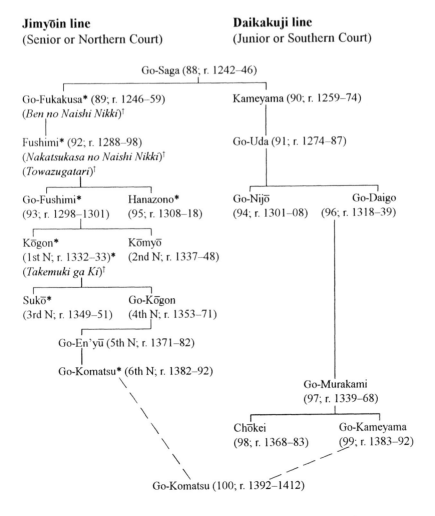

Jimyōin line
(Senior or Northern Court)

Daikakuji line
(Junior or Southern Court)

Go-Saga (88; r. 1242–46)

Go-Fukakusa* (89; r. 1246–59)
(*Ben no Naishi Nikki*)[†]

Kameyama (90; r. 1259–74)

Fushimi* (92; r. 1288–98)
(*Nakatsukasa no Naishi Nikki*)[†]
(*Towazugatari*)[†]

Go-Uda (91; r. 1274–87)

Go-Fushimi*
(93; r. 1298–1301)

Hanazono*
(95; r. 1308–18)

Go-Nijō
(94; r. 1301–08)

Go-Daigo
(96; r. 1318–39)

Kōgon*
(1st N; r. 1332–33)*
(*Takemuki ga Ki*)[†]

Kōmyō
(2nd N; r. 1337–48)

Sukō*
(3rd N; r. 1349–51)

Go-Kōgon
(4th N; r. 1353–71)

Go-En'yū (5th N; r. 1371–82)

Go-Komatsu* (6th N; r. 1382–92)

Go-Murakami
(97; r. 1339–68)

Chōkei
(98; r. 1368–83)

Go-Kameyama
(99; r. 1383–92)

Go-Komatsu (100; r. 1392–1412)

Note: The first number in the parentheses following a monarch's name indicates that monarch's position in the order of succession. The Arabic numerals 88 through 99 indicate the uneven alteration of sovereigns from the Jimyōin and Daikakuji lines. The designations 1st N through 6th N indicate the Jimyōin line during the Nanbokuchō period when monarchs from each line occupied the throne simultaneously. The two lines of succession were reunified in the person of Go-Komatsu, the 100th sovereign of Japan in the traditional reckoning.

*Indicates extant "royal diaries" (*Go-Fukakusa'in Shinki, Fushimi'in Gyoki, Go-Fushimi'in Shinki, Hanazono Tennō Shinki, Kōgon'in Shinki,* and *Go-Komatsu'in Shinki*).

†Indicates extant "literary diaries" written by women who served at court during a titular monarch's reign.

Appendix C
Biographic List

(Section of first appearance in parentheses. Listed by personal names to facilitate identification of individuals as given in the translation.)

Akichika, Minamoto (1219–?). "Tsuchimikado middle counselor." Son of Sadamichi, grandson of Michichika, and brother of Akisada. A provisional middle counselor of junior second rank when he took Buddhist vows in 1247. (Section 51)

Akimasa, Fujiwara (ca. 1206–?). "Controller." Son of Fujiwara Chikafusa. (Section 114)

Akisada, Minamoto (d.1283). "Tsuchimikado major counselor." Son of Sadamichi, grandson of Michichika, and brother of Akichika. A provisional major counselor of senior second rank when he took Buddhist vows in 1255. (Section 3)

Akitomo, Fujiwara (1211–66). "Head chamberlain–controller," also in Section 105, "major controller of the left–consultant." Became a provisional major counselor of senior second rank. (Section 9)

Arisuke, Minamoto (1203–72). "Commander of the [right] military guards." Died as former provisional middle counselor of senior second rank. (Section 22)

Aritsugu, Sugawara (d. 1303). Royal tutor to Fushimi (r. 1288–98), Go-Fushimi (r. 1298–1301), and Go-Nijō (r. 1301–8). (Section 57)

Azechi no Sanmi (fl. mid-13th c.). Older sister of Azechi no Suke; daughter of Fujiwara Takahira (d. 1254). Bore Go-Saga's son Prince Saijohō. (Section 63)

Azechi no Suke (fl. mid-13th c.). Daughter of Fujiwara Takahira; younger sister of Azechi no Sanmi; served Go-Fukakusa. (Section 28)

Ben no Naishi 1. (1228?–1270?). Author of the poetic account that bears her name; daughter of Fujiwara Nobuzane and sister of Shōshō no

247

Naishi. 2. An unidentified female courtier who served at the retired sovereign's residence. (Section 56)

Chamberlain. *See* Mitsukuni.

Chamberlain. *See* Munemasa.

Chamberlain. *See* Tsunetoshi.

Chamberlain–assistant master. *See* Tsunetoshi.

Chamberlain–gentleman-in-waiting. *See* Munemasa.

Chancellor. *See* Michimitsu.

Chancellor. *See* Saneuji.

Chikayori, Fujiwara (1223–?). A provisional middle counselor of senior second rank when he took Buddhist vows. (Section 4)

Chūnagon no Suke (fl. mid-13th c.). Fujiwara Shinshi; either a daughter of major counselor Fujiwara Sanemune (1145–1207?) or major counselor Fujiwara Saneie (1145–94); over fifty years old in 1246. (Section 9)

Commander of the left gate guards. *See* Sanefuji.

Commander of the military guards. *See* Arisuke.

Commander of the right gate guards. *See* Michinari.

Commander of the right military guards. *See* Arisuke.

Consort. *See* Ōmiya'in.

Controller. *See* Chikayori.

Dainagon (fl. mid-13th c.). "Lady Dainagon no Sanmi" after Section 99; daughter of the chancellor Fujiwara (Saionji) Kintsune (although *The Clear Mirror* states that she was the daughter of Fujiwara Takachika). Bore Go-Saga two children. (Section 8)

Dainagon no Niidono (fl. ca. mid-13th c.). Either the daughter of the Koga chancellor, Minamoto Michimitsu or Fujiwara (Saionji) Kintsune, another former chancellor. Probably Go-Fukakusa's wet nurse. (Section 80)

Dainagon no Suke (fl. mid-13th c.). Daughter of Minamoto Takachika, known as Sukedai. She was the mother of Lady Nijō, the author of *The Confession of Lady Nijō*. (Section 121)

Former Tendai Abbot. *See* Jigen.

Fujiwara major counselor. *See* Tameie.

Fun'ya no Yasuhide. A ninth-century poet with four poems in *Kokinshū* and one in *Gosenshū*. (Section 36)

Fuyutada, Fujiwara (1216–68). "Provisional middle counselor," also known as Ōimikado Fuyutada. Son of palace minister Ietsugu; died as former palace minister of senior second rank. (Section 91)

Go-Fukakusa (1243–1304; r. 1246–59). "His Majesty." Eighty-ninth sovereign; son of Go-Saga and Ōmiya'in; older brother of Kameyama (r. 1259–74); the reigning monarch during Ben no Naishi's court service. (Section 6)

Go-Saga (1220–72; r. 1242–46). "Retired sovereign." Eighty-eighth monarch; father of Go-Fukakusa and ninetieth monarch, Kameyama, and husband of Ōmiya'in. (Section 1)

Hachijō major counselor Michitada. *See* Michitada.

Head chamberlain–controller. *See* Akitomo.

Head chamberlain–middle captain. *See* Masaie.

Head chamberlain–middle captain of the left. *See* Mototomo.

Head chamberlain–middle captain of the right. *See* Kinyasu.

His Lordship (The Regent). *See* Sanetsune (up through Section 34) and Kanetsune (after Section 34).

His Majesty. *See* Go-Fukakusa.

Hizen, Lady. Unidentified female courtier who served the retired consort Ōmiya'in. (Section 101)

Hōjō Tokiyori (1227–63). Regent who was the target of an assassination plot by his uncle Mitsutoki and the fourth shogun of the Kamakura period, Kujō Yoritsune. (Section 34, n. 1)

Horikawa minister of the center. *See* Tomomi.

Hyōe no Kami (fl. mid-13th c.). Probably the granddaughter of provisional middle counselor, Fujiwara Iemichi (1142–87). (Section 49)

Interior controller, the Kujō major captain of the right. *See* Tadaie.

Iyo no Naishi. Unidentified female courtier. (Section 119)

Jakusai. *See* Nobuzane.

Jigen (b. 1218). "Former Tendai abbot." Son of chancellor Kujō Michiie; resigned from the position of archbishop in 1247. (Section 41)

Jikken (b. 1175). "Head priest" (*zasu*) of Daigoji, the son of Fujiwara Motosuke. (Section 95)

Junshi (809–71). Aunt of the Nijō consort, Fujiwara Kōshi. (Section 9, n. 3)

Kanehira, Fujiwara (1227–?). "Takatsukasa minister of the left." Served as both regent and chancellor on and off from 1252 to 1287; took Buddhist vows in 1290 as the former regent. Also appears in *Confessions of Lady Nijō. (Section 48)*

Kanemine. Unidentified royal cavalryman. (Section 86)

Kanetomo. Unidentified carriage officer. (Section 4)

Kanetsune, Konoe Fujiwara (1210–59). "Lord Okanoya." Third son of Konoe Iezane; served as regent from 1237–42; chancellor in 1242; regent from 1247–52. (Section 34)

Kazan'in consultant–middle captain. *See* Morotsugu.

Kazan'in major counselor. *See* Sadamasa.

Kinchika, Fujiwara (1221–?). "Sanjō middle counselor" and "master of the consort's household." Promoted to provisional major counselor in 1250 (Kenchō 2). In Section 121, he is referred to as the Sanjō major counselor. A former palace minister of senior second rank when he took Buddhist vows in 1286. (Section 50)

Kinmasa, Fujiwara (fl. mid-13th c.). Consultant of the right-middle captain, of senior third rank. (Section 105)

Kinmoto, Fujiwara (Saionji) (1219–74). "Madenokōji major counselor." Eldest son of chancellor Fujiwara (Saionji) Saneuji (1194–1269); older brother of Ōmiya'in (Fujiwara Kitsushi), uncle of Go-Fukakusa and Kameyama, and the older brother of Kinsuke; died as former minister of the right of senior second rank. (Section 9)

Kinsuke, Fujiwara (1222–67). "Ōmiya and Reizei major counselor." Second son of Fujiwara (Saionji) Saneuji; older brother of Ōmiya'in and younger brother of Kinmoto; died as the former chancellor of junior first rank. (Section 12)

Kintada, Fujiwara (fl. mid-13th c.). "Middle captain Kintada." A senior noble (*hisangi*) of junior second rank when he took Buddhist vows in 1278. (Section 14)

Kinyasu, Fujiwara (1230–?). "Middle captain of the left," also "head chamberlain of the right." A former provisional middle counselor of senior second rank when he took Buddhist vows in 1291. (Section 39)

Koga Chancellor. *See* Michimitsu.

Koremoto, Fujiwara (fl. mid-13th c.). A middle captain of junior fourth rank, upper grade. Son of Korenari. (Section 106)

Korenaga, Fujiwara (fl. mid-13th c.). A middle captain of senior fourth rank, lower grade. Son of Koretoki. (Section 105)

Koreyori, Takatsukasa (1240–83). A middle captain of the right. Son of Korehira. Advanced to provisional major counselor of senior second rank before his death. (Section 105)

Kōshi, Fujiwara (842-910). Nijō consort famous for her liaison with Ariwara no Narihira. (Section 9)

Kōtō no Naishi (fl. mid-13th c.). Daughter of punishments minister and later lay priest Fujiwara Takatoki known as a virtuoso of the Seiryū biwa. Served Go-Saga, bore him three children; she was also a famous *biwa* virtuoso. (Section 7)

(Kujō) Fujiwara Michiie. *See* Michiie.

(Kujō) Fujiwara Yoritsune. *See* Yoritsune.

Kunaikyō, or Kunaikyō no Suke (fl. mid-13th c.). May be the same person or two people with similar pseudonyms. Kunaikyō was a daughter of senior noble (*hisangi*) Fujiwara Akiuji (1206–74). (Section 9)

Lesser captain. *See* Michiyo.

Lesser captain. *See* Sukeyasu.

Lord Okanoya Kanetsune (Okanoya). *See* Kanetsune.

Lord Ōkura (Ōkurakyō). *See* Sadatsugu.

Madenokōji major counselor. *See* Kinmoto.

Major controller of the left–consultant. *See* Akitomo.

Masachika, Minamoto (1179–1249). "Karahashi major counselor." A senior noble who died on the fifth day of the Twelfth Month of 1249 as a major counselor with senior second rank. Makes only one appearance in the account as an infirm seventy-year-old man. (Section 84)

Masaie, Minamoto (1213–?). "Tsuchimikado consultant–middle captain" of senior third rank in final appearances in the poetic account. A former provisional major counselor of senior second rank when he took Buddhist vows in 1268. (Section 8)

Masamitsu, Minamoto (1225–67). "Nakanoin third rank middle captain." Son of chancellor Michimitsu; brother of Masatada. Died as the former provisional middle counselor of senior second rank. (Section 22)

Masatada, Minamoto (Koga) (1224–72). "Middle captain of the right Masatada." Son of chancellor Michimitsu; brother of Masamitsu, father of Lady Nijō. (Section 28)

Mashimizu. Unidentified female assistant (*nyōju*). (Section 78)

Master of the consort's household. *See* Takachika.

Master of the consort's household. *See* Kinchika.

Michiie, (Kujō) Fujiwara (1193–1252). Regent in 1221; chancellor from 1228 to 1231; and regent from 1235 to 1237. Father of regent Sanetsune and fourth shogun Yoritsune. (Section 6, n. 3)

Michimitsu, Minamoto (1187–1248). "Koga chancellor." Son of Tsuchimikado Michichika (1145–1202); father of Masamitsu and Masatada. Died as former chancellor of junior first rank. (Section 30)

Michinari, Minamoto (1221–?). "Provisional master of the consort's household," also "commander of the right gate guards." Son of Minamoto Michikata (d. 1238). A former palace minister of senior second rank when he took Buddhist vows in 1270. (Section 19)

Michitada, Minamoto (d. 1250). "Hachijō major counselor." Died as a major counselor of senior second rank. (Section 37)

Michiyo, Minamoto. "Lesser captain Michiyo." Fifth son of Michikata (d. 1238). A former consultant of junior second rank when he took Buddhist vows in 1270. (Section 19)

Michiyuki, Minamoto (ca. 1201–?). "Tsuchimikado middle counselor." Son of Michichika. Senior third rank in 1250. (Section 114)

Middle captain. *See* Korenaga.

Middle captain. *See* Sukeyasu.

Middle captain of the left. *See* Kinyasu.

Middle counselor of junior second rank. *See* Yoshinori.

Middle captain of the right. *See* Koreyori.

Middle captain of the right. *See* Masatada.

Mikushigedono (d. 1247). Daughter of former chancellor Fujiwara Kinfusa (d. 1249). Died giving birth to Go-Saga's son, Prince Seijo. (Section 58)

Minodono. "Lady Mino." Unidentified female courtier. (Section 78)

Mitsukuni, Fujiwara (Hino) (1205–70). Died as senior noble (*hisangi*) of junior third rank. (Section 12)

Morotsugu, Fujiwara (1222–81). "Kazan'in consultant–middle captain," also "provisional master of the dowager's household." Son of lay priest–minister of the right, Tadatsune; descended from Yorimichi (990–1072). Died while holding the post of palace minister. (Section 14)

Motomasa, Fujiwara (Saitō) (d. ca. 1264). An officer in the military guards of the left. Son of Mototaka. Took Buddhist vows in 1264. (Section 105)

Mototomo, Minamoto (1231–?). A head chamberlain of the left-middle captain. (Section 76)

Munemasa, Fujiwara (1216–69). "Chamberlain–gentleman-in-waiting." Died as a consultant. (Section 12)

Nakanoin third rank middle captain. *See* Masamitsu.

Nakayasu. Unidentified. Highest-ranking palace guard (*takiguchi no ichirō*). (Section 73)

Narihira, Ariwara (825–80). Famous lover and poet alluded to in Section 9 for his liaison with the Nijō consort. Served during Uda's reign and mentioned as having played *sumō* with the monarch. (Section 9, n. 3, Section 94)

Narinobu, Minamoto (979–?). "Shining middle captain." Son of Munehira (951–1041); adopted son of Michinaga (966–1027). Took Buddhist vows in 1001 with his friend Fujiwara Shigeie. (Section 37)

Nijō Consort. *See* Kōshi, Fujiwara.

Nijō middle counselor Sukesue. *See* Sukesue.

Nobuzane, Fujiwara (ca. 1177–1270). "Jakusai" after taking Buddhist vows in 1248. Father of Ben no Naishi and Shōshō no Naishi. Famous as a portrait artist and court poet. (Section 79)

Norizane, Fujiwara (1209–35). "Tō'in regent." Eldest son of Michiie; father of Sen'ninmon'in; chancellor 1231–32 and regent 1232–35. (Section 44)

Ōmiya major counselor. *See* Kinsuke.

Ōmiya'in (1225–92). "Consort," also "retired consort." Fujiwara Kitsushi; daughter of Saionji Saneuji and younger sister of Kinmoto and Kinsuke. Consort of Go-Saga and mother of Go-Fukakusa and Kameyama. (Section 11)

Palace minister. *See* Sanemoto.

Priestly Kanpyō Sovereign. Nickname for Uda (r. 887–97) based on an era name. (Section 94)

Provisional master of the consort's household. *See* Michinari

Provisional middle counselor. *See* Fuyutada.

Provisional major counselor. *See* Saneo.

Radiant lesser captain. *See* Shigeie.

Reizei major counselor. *See* Kinsuke.

Retired Consort. *See* Ōmiya'in.

Retired Sovereign. *See* Go-Saga.

Royal Dowager. *See* Senkamon'in.

Sadahira, Minamoto. Middle captain of the right. Son of Kanesada. Achieved senior fourth rank, junior grade as middle captain of the right. (Section 93)

Sadamasa, Fujiwara (1217–94). "Kazan'in major counselor." Died while holding the post of the minister of the right. (Section 24)

Sadamura. Unidentified general assistant. (Section 107)

Sadatsugu, Fujiwara (d. 1272). "Lord Ōkura." Son of Mitsuchika. Took Buddhist vows in 1250. (Section 37)

Sakuya. A maid (*zōshi/me*). (Section 107)

Sanefuji, Fujiwara (1226–98). "Commander of the left gate guards." Younger brother of Fujiwara (Saionji) Saneuji (1194–1269). Took Buddhist vows and died in 1298 as a provisional major counselor of senior second rank. (Section 9)

Sanekata, Fujiwara (d. 908). A former governor of Mutsu province alluded to as the source of the *katsumi* legend. (Section 6. n. 1)

Sanemoto, Fujiwara (1200–73). "Tokudaiji major counselor" with the concurrent post of major captain of the right; also "palace minister." Son of Kintsugu, a major counselor of senior second rank. A former chancellor of junior first rank when he took Buddhist vows in 1265. (Section 20)

Saneo, Fujiwara (Saionji) (1216–73). "Provisional major counselor." Third son of Fujiwara (Saionji) Kintsune (1171–1244), younger brother of Saneuji. Died after taking Buddhist vows as the former minister of the left of junior first rank. (Section 45)

Sanetaka, Fujiwara (1208–ca. 1288). A *hisangi* of junior third rank who was later described as a senior noble of second rank in the *Memoirs of Nakatsukasa no Naishi* dated 1288. Son of Fujiwara Kintaka. (Section 106)

Sanetsune, Fujiwara (Ichijō) (1223–84). "Regent, also "His Lordship." Chancellor in 1246, regent from 1246 to 1247, and chancellor from

1265 to 1267. Son of former regent Fujiwara (Kujō) Michiie (1193–1252); mother was daughter of the chancellor Fujiwara Kintsune (1171–1244); brother of the shogun Yoritsune. Replaced by Konoe Kanetsune as regent when Yoritsune was implicated in a plot to assassinate the Hōjō regent Tokiyori. Died after taking Buddhist vows as a minister of the left and the former regent of junior first rank. (Section 6)

Saneuji, Fujiwara (Saionji) (1194–1269). "Former chancellor." Father of Ōmiya'in, Kinmoto and Kinsuke. A former chancellor of junior first rank when he took Buddhist vows in 1260. (Section 46)

Sanjō middle counselor. See Kinchika.

Senkamon'in, Royal Dowager (b. 1223). Royal princess Gishi, daughter of Tsuchimikado and sister of Go-Saga. Served as Ise Virgin from 1243 to 1246 until Go-Fukakusa became monarch. Given the title of royal dowager for her position as godmother and aunt of Go-Fukakusa. (Section 81)

Sen'ninmon'in (1232–62). Fujiwara Genshi, daughter of Fujiwara Norizane and consort to Shijō (r. 1232–42). (Section 44)

Shigeie, Fujiwara (fl. early 11th c.). "Radiant lesser captain." Son of the minister of the left Akimitsu. Took Buddhist vows at the age of twenty-five in the year 1001 with his friend Minamoto Narinobu. (Section 37)

Shijō major counselor. See Takachika.

Shining middle captain. See Narinobu.

Shōnagon no Naishi. Unidentified female courtier. (Section 27)

Shōshō no Naishi (d. 1265). Younger sister of Ben no Naishi. Also served Go-Fukakusa. (Section 4)

Sixth-rank chamberlain. See Sukeyoshi.

Suezane. Unidentified middle captain. (Section 86)

Sukehira, Minamoto. Unidentified kemari player. (Section 87)

Sukesue, Fujiwara (fl. mid-13th c.). A former provisional major counselor of senior second rank when he took Buddhist vows in 1268. (Section 59)

Suketsugu. Unidentified. (Section 3)

Sukeyasu. Unidentified. First called lesser captain and later middle captain. (Section 45)

Sukeyoshi. Unidentified sixth-rank chamberlain. (Section 64)

Sumutsuru. Unidentified female assistant (nyōju). (Section 78)

Tadaie, Fujiwara (1228–75). "Interior controller," also "major captain of the right." Died as the former minister of the right and former regent of junior first rank. (Section 33)

Taie. Unidentified. May be an abbreviation for Tameie. (Section 7)

Takachika, Minamoto (b. 1202). "Master of the dowager's household," also "Shijō major counselor." Grandfather of Lady Nijō. (Section 78)

Takatoki, Fujiwara. (fl. early 13th c.). Father of Kōtō no Naishi. Known as the lay priest Takatoki. (Section 121)

Takatsukasa minister of the left. *See* Kanehira.

Takatsune, Fujiwara (1217–85). "Yoshida Takatsune." Died as a senior noble (*hisangi*) of senior third rank. (Section 39)

Takatsunji. Unidentified female assistant (*nyōju*). (Section 50)

Takayuki, Fujiwara. (fl. mid-13th c.). Son of Fujiwara Takatsugu. (Section 87)

Tameie, Fujiwara (1198–1275). "Fujiwara major counselor." Son of Teika (1162–1241) and husband of Abutsu-ni, author of *Utatane* and *Izayoi Nikki*. Succeeded Teika as head of the Nijō school of poetry. (Section 58)

Tamemochi. Unidentified. (Section 15)

Tamenawa. Unidentified. (Section 4)

Tamenori, Fujiwara (1226–79). Son of Tameie and younger brother of Tameuji. Founder of the Kyōgyoku school of poetry. (Section 58)

Tametsugu. May refer to the author's older brother, Fujiwara Tametsugu. (Section 7, n. 2)

Tametsune, Fujiwara (1209–56). "Yoshida middle counselor." Son of Suketsune; died as middle counselor of senior second rank. (Section 58)

Tameuji, Fujiwara (1222–86). Eldest son of Tameie; grandson of Teika. A middle captain of the left in 1247. Inherited leadership of the Nijō school of poetry from Tameie. (Section 53)

Tō'in Regent. *See* Norizane.

Tokitsugu, Taira (d. 1294). "Controller Tokitsugu." A former provisional major counselor of senior second rank when he took Buddhist vows in 1290. (Section 52)

Tokitsuna. General assistant. (Section 3)

Tokitsune, Minamoto (fl. mid-13th c.). Nephew of Minamoto Arisuke. (Section 111)

Tokudaiji major captain [of the right]. *See* Sanemoto.

Tokudaiji major counselor. *See* Sanemoto.

Tomomi, Minamoto (1202–?). "Horikawa palace minister." Son of Minamoto Michitomo (1171–1227), a poet who held the office of major counselor of second rank and who was one of the compilers of the *Shinkokinshū*. Highest position achieved was senior second rank as major counselor. (Section 93)

Tsuchimikado consultant–middle captain. *See* Masaie.

Tsuchimikado major counselor. *See* Akisada.

Tsuchimikado middle counselor. *See* Akichika.

Tsunemitsu, Fujiwara (1212–74). "Counselor Tsunemitsu." Died as the former middle counselor of senior second rank. (Section 38)

Tsunetada, Fujiwara (fl. mid-13th c.). Later changed his name to Chikatada. A middle captain of the left holding senior fourth rank, lower grade, in 1250. Son of Yōbai Michitsugu of the Northern branch of the Fujiwara family; listed under both Konoe and Nijō branch of the Fujiwara family in the *Genealogy of the Exalted and the Base*. (Section 106)

Tsunetoshi, Fujiwara (1213–77). "Controller Tsunetoshi," "chamberlain-assistant master," and "Yoshida Tsunetoshi." Died while holding the post of middle counselor of senior second rank. (Section 3)

Uda (r. 887–97). Also known as Priestly Kanpyō Sovereign, a nickname based on an era name. (Section 94)

Yoritsune, Fujiwara (Kujō) (1218–56). Fourth shogun; son of Michiie; and brother of regent Sanetsune. By being implicated in a plot to assassinate the Hōjō regent Tokiyori, Yoritsune caused his family members to be ousted from powerful positions at court. (Section 34, n. 1)

Yoshida middle counselor. *See* Tametsune.

Yoshinori, Fujiwara (1224–1287). "Middle counselor of junior second rank." Later became a major counselor of junior first rank. Poet who took Buddhist vows in 1287 and died at age 64. Son of the poet Motoyoshi, a provisional major counselor of senior second rank. (Section 4)

Appendix D
Bibliographic Essay

Previous Scholarship

Information in English on *Ben no Naishi Nikki* is limited to Karen Brazell's introduction in *The Confessions of Lady Nijō* (1971), Edward Putzar's *Japanese Literature* (1973), Hisamatsu Sen'ichi's *Biographical Dictionary of Japanese Literature* (1976), Donald Keene's *Travelers of a Hundred Ages* (1989), Robert N. Huey's *Kyōgoku Tamekane: Poetry and Politics in Late Kamakura Japan* (1989), Konishi Jin'ichi's *A History of Japanese Literature, Volume Three: The High Middle Ages* (1991), and Chieko Mulhern's *Japanese Women Writers: A Bio-Critical Sourcebook* (1994). Most merely mention *Ben no Naishi Nikki* in passing.

Japanese scholarship on *Ben no Naishi Nikki* dates back nearly eighty years, but is limited. In *Literary Diaries by Women at Court* (1927), Ikeda Kikan devoted three of the book's eight chapters to Kamakura works: one each to *Journal of the Sixteenth-Night Moon, Memoirs of Nakatsukasa no Naishi,* and *Ben no Naishi Nikki.* The chapter on *Ben no Naishi Nikki,* the shortest of the eight, nevertheless exerted great influence on several generations of scholars. Ikeda cites excerpts from *The Clear Mirror, The Collection of Jeweled Leaves,* and *Notes from a Frog at the Bottom of a Well* to prove that what remains of the text is only part of the original.

In this pioneer study, Ikeda also noted inaccuracies in the recording of dates and in the use of titles, and advanced the theory that these errors were the result of a faulty memory of an author writing in retrospect. He thought that the only source materials for the *nikki* were the poems Ben no Naishi had composed on various occasions.

Ikeda stated that Sōhekimon'in Shōshō no Naishi and Ben no Naishi were the oldest and youngest of Nobuzane's three daughters, and that Shōshō no Naishi, who does not appear in the *Genealogy of the Exalted and the Base,* was the middle sister. (I follow Tamai's theory advanced in *A New Annotation of Ben no Naishi Nikki* [*Ben no Naishi Nikki Shinchū,* 1958a] that Shōshō no Naishi was the youngest of the three sisters.)

Ikeda's concluding remarks, in which he stated that Ben no Naishi was an "eternal maiden" who recorded entries with a "cheerfulness" attributable to her youth, proved to have a great impact on later writers. There are still scholars today who perpetuate the image of Ben no Naishi as an innocent girl who recorded only pleasant aspects of court life without any literary intent. Ikeda stated that Ben no Naishi wrote the account after she had completed court service, but the account contains no hint of retrospection, suggesting instead extensive revision after the date of composition.

A short article by Nomura Hachirō (1930) and an entry in Fujimura Tsukuru's literary dictionary (1933) were the only other significant references to *Ben no Naishi Nikki* before the Second World War.

In 1951, Tamai Kōsuke announced that he was preparing a collated, annotated text, and in 1958 published *A New Annotation of Ben no Naishi Nikki,* the first comprehensive study of the work. Meanwhile, in 1954, Yoshihira Toshio had published "*Ben no Naishi Nikki*: The Eternal Maiden" ("*Ben no Naishi Nikki,* Eien no Otomegokoro"), a short article based entirely on Ikeda's earlier work.

The 1960s produced eleven works in which *Ben no Naishi Nikki* was discussed, the largest number to appear since research had begun on the topic in the 1920s, but only those of Ōuchi Mayako and Kidō Saizō made significant contributions to the study of *Ben no Naishi Nikki.* In 1964 Ōuchi Mayako, published "Treatise on *Ben no Naishi Nikki*" ("*Ben no Naishi Nikki* Kō"), which provided both new information and a new critical approach. Ōuchi began by proposing that Ben no Naishi might have already been in service at court prior to the birth of the future Go-Fukakusa.[1] She also provided internal evidence that it was common knowledge at court that Ben no Naishi had been keeping some sort of written record of her court service. Ōuchi was the first to state that Ben no Naishi's stance was formal and public and the first to consider *Ben no Naishi Nikki* as a forerunner of the *Journal of the Upper Hot Water Room,* an official court journal compiled by women from 1477 to 1826, in which daily events were recorded in a terse manner reminiscent of *kanbun* diaries kept by court nobles. She also discussed the relationships between the women with whom Ben no Naishi worked, drawing parallels with Murasaki Shikibu's critique of her fellow female courtiers, analyzed Ben no Naishi's use of imagery, and discussed Ben no Naishi's talent in the area of linked-verse composition. The new approach and information provided by Ōuchi was to profoundly affect the writing and views of Imazeki Toshiko and Iwasa Miyoko, two of the leading *Ben no Naishi Nikki* scholars of the 1980s and 1990s.

In 1969, Kidō Saizō included a section entitled "*Ben no Naishi Nikki*" in *A History of Japanese Literature by Women* (*Nihon Joryū Bungaku Shi*). Discussing linked-verse composition as a social game in the mid-Kamakura period, he ranked Ben no Naishi and her relatives high among linked-verse poets of that time. (See also Kidō's remarks on early linked-verse poets in "Linked Verse of the Mid-Kamakura Period" ["Kamakura Chūki Renga"], a section in his book *A Study of the History of Linked Verse* [*Rengashi Ronkō*, 1973]). Ōuchi Mayako's 1964 article had first introduced the idea of Ben no Naishi as a linked-verse poet, in which speed of composition was highly prized.

Only three publications in the 1970s dealt with *Ben no Naishi Nikki* in a substantive fashion. The first was "Ben no Naishi Notes: Concerning Buddhist Ceremonies" ("Ben no Naishi Nōto: Hōgo to no Kakawari"), a chapter in Kobayashi Chisō's *Continuation of Thoughts on Medieval Literature* (*Zoku Chūsei Bungaku no Shisō*, 1974), which discussed the memoir in terms of its significance to historians of religion. The second was an article in *Fūzoku* by Kiyota Tomoko, "The Nature of Tradition in *Ben no Naishi Nikki*: Court Customs and Literary Arts" ("*Ben no Naishi Nikki* no Denshosei: Kyūtei Fūzoku to Bungei," 1977), which dealt with costumes, color combinations, musical instruments, Buddhist ceremonies, court ceremonies, and other subjects of interest to cultural historians. The third, a short article by Matsumoto Yasushi, "Retired Sovereign Go-Fukakusa's Ben no Naishi: Wit and Humor" ("Go-Fukakusa'in Ben no Naishi: Kichi to Yūmoa," 1979), pointed out some examples of Ben no Naishi's wit and resourcefulness and discussed similarities between her personality and that of Sei Shōnagon.

The 1980s brought forth a new burst of interest in *Ben no Naishi Nikki*. Twelve articles appeared in print between 1981 and 1987, six of them by Imazeki Toshiko, who emerged as one of the leading authorities on *Ben no Naishi Nikki* since the death of Tamai Kōsuke, and who published a new annotated edition with modern Japanese translation in 1989.

In the 1980s, Imazeki published a series of articles devoted exclusively to *Ben no Naishi Nikki*, which were republished in 1987 as a chapter in *Views on Medieval Literary Diaries by Women* (*Chūsei Joryū Nikki Bungaku Ronkō*). In these articles, Imazeki, like Ōuchi, considered the work a public account of a woman who served in an official capacity at court. Imazeki stated that this public stance determined the way Ben no Naishi treated family members who appeared in the *nikki*. She also stated that the shared perspective between Ben no Naishi and her sister remained constant whether the topic was happy or sad, and further maintained that the shared point of view prevented any intensification of emotional value. She noted that there is a nostalgia for the distant past, which served as the model for courtly elegance and behavior. Imazeki interpreted this longing for the past as a sign of anxiety about the present. Imazeki suggested that Ben no Naishi emphasized the tone of cheerfulness in the *nikki* to counterbalance the feelings of insecurity about the present in which she lived and that the public stance that excluded everything of a private nature and the shared point of view with her sister were two other reasons for emphasizing the tone of cheerfulness in the account.

Iwasa Miyoko, another leading authority on *Ben no Naishi Nikki*, produced three short essays. Two of them, "Ben no Naishi Nikki" in a chapter of *A New History of Japanese Literature* (*Nihon Bungaku Shinshi*, 1985) and "*Ben no Naishi Nikki*" (1987) in the journal *Kokubungaku Kaishaku to Kyōzai no Kenkyū*, are short introductions. A third provides a bibliography and valuable notes on textual history as part of an introduction to the Shokōkan manuscript.

Two other articles in the 1980s bore the same title: Tsumoto Nobuhiro, "Memoirs of Ben no Naishi and Nakatsukasa no Naishi" ("*Ben no Naishi Nikki* to *Nakatsukasa no Naishi Nikki*," 1981) and Matsumoto Yasushi, "*Ben no Naishi Nikki* to *Nakatsukasa no Naishi Nikki*" (1983). These short articles reflect the tendency, which had begun early in the study of medieval *nikki* by women, to discuss *Ben no Naishi Nikki* and *Nakatsukasa no Naishi Nikki* as sister works. The Tsumoto article suggests that *Ben no Naishi Nikki* resembles a *rekishi monogatari* (historical tale) because it seeks to preserve for posterity the mode of life important to court society; the Matsumoto article merely distills information obtained from earlier studies.

In the 1980s, Donald Keene discussed *Ben no Naishi Nikki* briefly in his *Hakutai no Kakaku* (*Travelers of a Hundred Ages*). Keene compared *Ben no Naishi Nikki* with the *Memoirs of Nakatsukasa no Naishi* and used some of Ikeda's ideas, but his five-page essay offers some commentary on Ben no Naishi's wit and resourcefulness, her exacting nature, her extroversion, and the like, gleaned from internal information. Robert Huey mentions Ben no Naishi in passing in his book, *Kyōgoku Tamekane: Poetry and Politics in Late Kamakura Japan* (1989). In the English translation of Konishi Jin'ichi's *History of Japanese Literature, Volume Three: The High Middle Ages*, published in 1991, *Ben no Naishi Nikki* is mentioned as being derivative of eleventh-century Heian masterpieces.

In the 1990s, Imazeki and Iwasa continued to publish articles on *Ben no Naishi Nikki*. In 1990, Imazeki Toshiko published "A Reconsideration of *Ben no Naishi Nikki*—Sense of Crisis and Expression" ("*Ben no Naishi Nikki* Saikō—Kikikan to Hyōgen," 1990), which explored the function of the *nikki* to preserve a way of life on the verge of extinction. By 1996, she had turned her attention to the concept of sacred time and sacred space, as manifested in *Ben no Naishi Nikki*, considering sacred time to be cyclical in nature and citing studies in religion that stated that cyclical time allowed one to return to the origin of "time." She contrasted sacred time with profane (or secular) time, denoting the linear flow of time by which the past is measured as being behind the present, the present as a point between the momentary flow of the past and the future, and the future as a point somewhere before us.

Iwasa Miyoko published two articles on *Ben no Naishi Nikki* in the 1990s: "People in *Ben no Naishi Nikki*" ("*Ben no Naishi Nikki* no Hitobito," 1992) focusing on notable male and female personalities who appear frequently in the work; and "Ideas on Lacunae in *Ben no Naishi Nikki*" ("*Ben no Naishi Nikki* Ketsuji Kō," 1993), which reports on the reconstruction of missing portions from the extant text of *Ben no Naishi Nikki*. She also produced a new annotation and translation of *Ben no Naishi Nikki* in volume 48, *A Collection of Medieval Diaries and Travelogues* (*Chūsei Nikki Kikō Shū*), in *A New Collection of Classical Japanese Literature* (*Shinpen Nihon Koten Bungaku Zenshū*), published by Shōgakukan in 1994, firmly situating *Ben no Naishi Nikki* within the premodern literary canon.

During the years 1990–92, Morita Kaneyoshi published three articles on *Ben no Naishi Nikki* in the journal *Nihon Bungaku Kenkyū*: "Views on *Ben no Naishi Nikki*, One" ("*Ben no Naishi Nikki* Ron Ichi: Keitai no Kakunin," 1990); "Views on *Ben no Naishi Nikki*, Two: Ben no Naishi and Shōshō no Naishi" ("*Ben no Naishi Nikki* Ron Ni: Ben no Naishi to Shōshō no Naishi," 1991); and "Views on *Ben no Naishi Nikki*, Three: Its Literary Quality" ("*Ben no Naishi Nikki* Ron San: Sono Bungakusei," 1992), but no new lines of investigation emerged from these.

Texts

Relatively little work has been done on the extant texts of *Ben no Naishi Nikki*. The summary below is based on Tamai 1951 (6–10) and Tamai 1958a (301–6), both of which deal mainly with texts consulted during his preparation of *A New Annotation of Ben no Naishi Nikki* and on Iwasa 1986 (215–17), which restates Tamai's findings and provides slightly more extensive discussion of one manuscript.

According to Tamai, Iwasa, and standard references, there are seven printed editions, of which I have seen all but the first:

1. *Ben no Naishi Nikki*. In Tokugawa Mitsukuni, *Fusō Shūyōshū* (compiled 1689; published 1899).

2. *Ben no Naishi Nikki.* In volume 14 of *Gunsho Ruijū* (1820; reprinted in 1938–39).

3. *Ben no Naishi Nikki.* In volume 3 of *Nihon Bungaku Zensho* (1890–91).

4. Tamai Kōsuke, *Ben no Naishi Nikki Shinchū* (1958).

5. Iwasa Miyoko, ed., *Ben no Naishi Nikki* (1986).

6. Imazeki Toshiko, ed., *Kōchū Ben no Naishi Nikki* (1989).

7. Iwasa Miyoko, *Ben no Naishi Nikki,* in *Chūsei Nikki Kikō Shū,* in volume 48 of *Shinpen Nihon Koten Bungaku Zenshū* (1994).

Tamai does not mention either the *Fusō Shūyōshū* or the *Nihon Bungaku Zensho* edition; Iwasa mentions the former in passing but says nothing about the latter. Iwasa's 1986 work is a facsimile reproduction of the *Shōkōkan* manuscript described below, and Tamai's is an annotated edition based on the *Gunsho Ruijū* text, with emendations drawn primarily from the *Shōkōkan* manuscript and two others, *Kangen Ki* and *Wagaku Kōdansho.* Imazeki's 1989 brief annotated work is also based on the *Shōkōkan* manuscript. Iwasa's 1994 annotated translation, too, is based on the *Shōkōkan* manuscript with emendations provided from the *Matsudaira* manuscript, entitled *Go-Fukakusa'in Ben no Naishi Ie no Shū.*

As discussed earlier, *Ben no Naishi Nikki* is demonstrably incomplete in its present form. Tamai surmises that all extant copies stem from a damaged original. Earlier sources state that originally there were two scrolls, of which the second is lost and the end of the first badly damaged.

The *Gunsho Ruijū* text contains two colophons. The first, which is believed to derive from the manuscript selected for inclusion by the compiler, Hanawa Hoki'ichi, identifies Ben no Naishi and gives her antecedents; the second deals with editorial matters. Since neither provides information concerning the age or provenance of the manuscript, we can say only that it must have been one available to Hanawa around the end of the eighteenth century or the beginning of the nineteenth. In addition to the damage at the end, the Hanawa text is flawed by three conspicuous lacunae and one duplication, as shown below. (Section numbers were devised by Tamai and used in his *Shinchū;* the *Gunsho Ruijū* text contains no subdivisions. Iwasa and I also use Tamai's numbering.)

Section 46: 20 lines omitted

Section 61: 12 characters omitted

Section 120: 8 characters omitted

Section 139: 8 lines repeated

Tamai was able to identify and correct all four errors by referring to extant manuscripts, of which he and Iwasa list over a dozen.[2] The ones he singles out for discussion, five in all, can be described briefly as follows.

1. *Ben no Naishi Kangen Ki* (1 *satsu* [volume])
This manuscript, owned by the Cabinet Library, bears the title *Ben no Naishi Kangen Ki* (*Ben no Naishi's Kangen Chronicle*), presumably because a large number of the events described in the memoir, which covers the years 1246–52, took place during the Kangen era (1243–47). It contains the three passages missing from *Gunsho Ruijū* but has small lacunae of its own in Sections 74 and 171, as well as the duplication in Section 139. The lack of any colophon leads Tamai to think that it may be the oldest extant manuscript.

2. *Shōkōkan* text (1 *satsu*)
This manuscript, preserved originally by the Mito branch of the Tokugawa clan, contains a note identifying the copyist as the scholar Andō Tameakira (1659–1716). Tamai tentatively regards it as second in age to *Ben no Naishi Kangen Ki*. It contains a colophon essentially identical to the first one in *Gunsho Ruijū*, provides additional information about Ben no Naishi's antecedents and a note about Shōshō no Naishi, includes the three passages missing from *Gunsho Ruijū*, and lacks the duplication in Section 139. A four-line omission in Section 108 has been corrected by a later hand. Tamai calls it the most complete extant manuscript.

Iwasa and Imazeki hold that fire damaged the Shōkōkan manuscript. They describe the pattern of damage in this manuscript as being caused by burning and note that the extant scroll was rolled in reverse fashion, with the end of the scroll on the outside, thereby accounting for the worst damage to the end of the text. (Normally, scrolls are rolled with the beginning of the text on the outside.)

3. *Wagaku Kōdansho* text (2 *satsu*)
This manuscript bears the title *Ben no Naishi Nikki* on the outside cover and the title *Go-Fukakusa'in Ben no Naishi Ie no Shū* (*Personal Poetry Collection of Retired Sovereign Go-Fukakusa Ben no Naishi*) on the inside cover. Its colophon is essentially identical to the first one in *Gunsho Ruijū*.

It lacks the four major *Gunsho Ruijū* flaws but has an error in Section 120, probably introduced in the process of correcting the mistake in *Gunsho Ruijū*, which Tamai believes this copyist was using in conjunction with another text. Since the usual *satsu* contains ten lines per page, and since pages 27 and 28 of the first *satsu* here correspond exactly to the missing twenty lines in Section 46 of *Gunsho Ruijū*, Tamai argues persuasively that the error in *Gunsho Ruijū* arose when someone turned an extra page while copying a text similar to this one. (The passage is also present in the *Kangen Ki* and *Shōkōkan* manuscripts, but the pagination differs.)

4. *Komoro* text (2 *satsu*)

This manuscript, formerly owned by the Komoro clan, contains both a colophon essentially identical to the first one in *Gunsho Ruijū* and a fairly long note concerning Ben no Naishi's father and grandfather, Nobuzane and Takanobu. There are the three lacunae in Sections 46, 61, and 120, but they have been filled in by a later hand. The duplication in Section 139 is absent.

5. *Ban Naokata* text (2 *satsu*)

This manuscript, owned by the Cabinet Library, carries a colophon essentially identical to the first one in *Gunsho Ruijū* and another, dated 1838, identifying the copyist as the national scholar Ban Naokata (1790–1842). Tamai takes it to be a copy of the wood block edition of *Gunsho Ruijū*.

A review of the above information shows that there is apparently no manuscript known to date from before the seventeenth century, and that nothing seems to be deducible at present about the ancestry and history of any text. It is hoped that further research will yield additional information.

The translation in the present study comprises the first 122 of Tamai's 175 sections. It follows the text in *Ben no Naishi Nikki Shinchū*, with frequent reference to Iwasa Miyoko's annotation of *Ben no Naishi Nikki* in *Chūsei Nikki Kikō Shū*, volume 48 of *Shinpen Nihon Koten Bungaku Zenshū*.

Notes

1. Ōuchi parts company with Ikeda by suggesting that Ben no Naishi was not extremely young at the time of Go-Fukakusa's accession in 1246. She proposes that if Ben no Naishi had been about eighteen in 1246, she would have been nineteen when the change of regents occurred (Section 34), around twenty-one when the Kan'in Palace burned down (Section 81), and around twenty-two when she put

on the demon mask (Section 120). Ōuchi's speculations are based on the fact that Kameyama died in 1305 and, therefore, 1305 was the last year Kameyama could have commanded Ben no Naishi to write the Tanabata poem. If she was eighteen in 1246, she might have been seventy-two in 1300. Although we do not know if she even lived past the year 1270, this estimated calculation of her age does not seem unreasonable. If she began service three years prior to Go-Fukakusa's accession, then she would have been around fifteen when she first entered court. Serving throughout Go-Fukakusa's thirteen-year reign would have placed her age at around thirty-one when the monarch was forced to abdicate in 1259 (Ōuchi 1964, 246-47). That would place her birth date at around 1228 and her death date at around 1270.

2. There are manuscripts and parts of manuscripts in the possession of the Cabinet Library, the Imperial Household Agency, the Shimabara Municipal Cultural Center, Tokyo University, Tsukuba University, Kyushu University, Keiō University, the Sumiyoshi Shrine, the Matsudaira family, and other public and private owners.

Appendix E
Royal Poetry Anthology List

Man'yōshū (*Collection of Ten Thousand Leaves,* ca. 759) 175 (n.6.1), 226 (n.117.5), 227 (n.117.8)

Of the twenty-one royal poetry anthologies (*chokusenshū*), those mentioned in the text are listed below:

1. *Kokinshū* (*Collection of Ancient and Modern Japanese Poetry,* ca. 905) 190 (n.36.3), 193 (n.45.1), 195 (n.49.1), 202 (n.74.4), 207 (n.82.4), 211 (n.88.5), 212 (n.90.8), 215 (n.97.2), 221 (n.107.3, n.107.5), 227 (n.117.6, n.117.9)

2. *Gosenshū* (*Later Collection of Japanese Poetry,* ca. 950) 190 (n.36.3), 215-16 (n.98.2), 226 (n.115.2)

3. *Shūishū* (*Collection of Gleanings of Japanese Poetry,* ca. 1005-11) 198 (n.59.7), 216 (n.99.2), 220 (n.106.6), 222 (n.109.4, n.109.5), 226 (n.117.5, n.117.6)

4. *Goshūishū* (*Later Collection of Gleanings of Japanese Poetry,* 1086) 196 (n.54.3), 216 (n.99.1), 217 (n.101.3), 219-20 (n.105.7), 220 (n.106.5)

5. *Kin'yōshū* (*Collection of Golden Leaves,* 1124-27) 235

6. *Shikashū* (*Collection of Verbal Flowers,* ca. 1151-54) 223 (n.110.3), 236

7. *Senzaishū* (*Collection of a Thousand Years,* ca. 1188) 236

8. *Shinkokinshū* (*New Collection of Ancient and Modern Japanese Poetry*, ca. 1205) 189 (n.34.5), 213 (n.92.3), 217 (n. 99.2, n.99.3), 221 (n.107.3), 224 (n.111.9, n.111.10), 226-27 (n.117.5), 238, 239

9. *Shinchokusenshū* (*New Royal Collection of Japanese Poetry*, ca. 1232) 197 (n.58.5), 239-40

10. *Shokugosenshū* (*Later Collection of Gleanings of Japanese Poetry Continued*, ca. 1251) 12, 194 (n.46.4)

11. *Shokukokinshū* (*Collection of Ancient and Modern Japanese Poetry Continued*, ca. 1265) 12, 16-17, 223 (n.111.7)

12. *Shokushūishū* (*Collection of Gleanings Continued*, 1278) 241

13. *Shingosenshū* (*New Later Collection of Japanese Poetry*, 1303) 17-18

14. *Gyokuyōshū* (*Collection of Jeweled Leaves*, ca. 1313) 14-15, 18

19. *Shinshūishū* (*New Collection of Gleanings*, 1364) 7, 17

Appendix F
Kyoto and Environs, ca. 1250

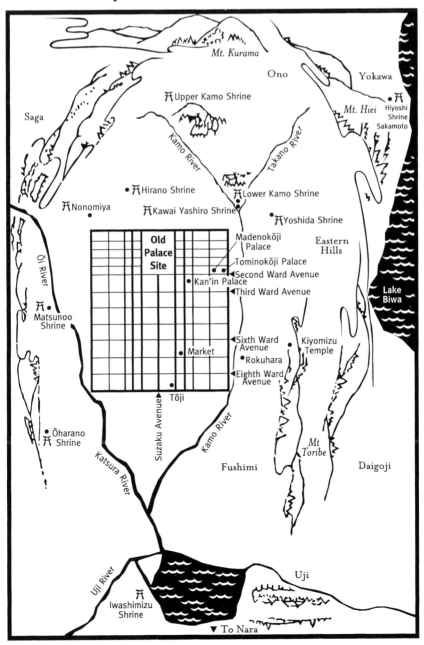

Appendix G
Kan'in Palace Reconstruction Layout

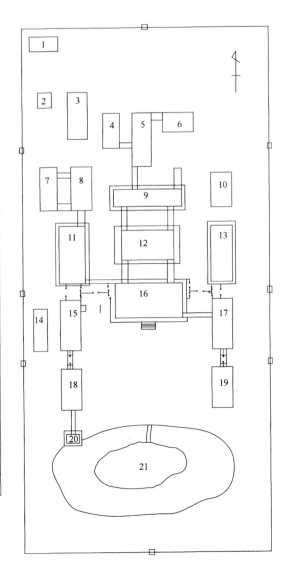

LEGEND

1. Naizenya (Tray Office)
2. Kamaya (Utensil Office)
3. Mizushidodokoro (Palace Kitchen Office)
4. Nishi no Ya (West Office)
5. Kita no Hirogosho (North Spacious Office)
6. Gosechidokoro (Five Banquets Office)
7. Nishi no Ni no Tai (Second Western Wing Chamber)
8. Nishi no Ichi no Tai (First Western Wing Chamber)
9. Kita no Tai (North Wing Chamber)
10. Kogosho (Lesser Palace)
11. Seiryōden (Sovereign's Royal Residence)
12. Jijūden (Benevolent Longevity Hall)
13. Higashi no Kita no Tai (North East Wing Chamber)
14. Kurōdodokoro (Chamberlain's Office)
15. Kyōshoden (Proofreading Hall)
16. Shishinden (Main Ceremonial Hall)
17. Giyōden (Proclamation Sun Hall)
18. Anpukuden (Tranquil Fortune Hall)
19. Shunkyōden (Spring Pleasure Hall)
20. Tsuridono (Fishing Pavilion)
21. Man-made lake and island

Appendix H
Kan'in Palace Seiryōden Layout

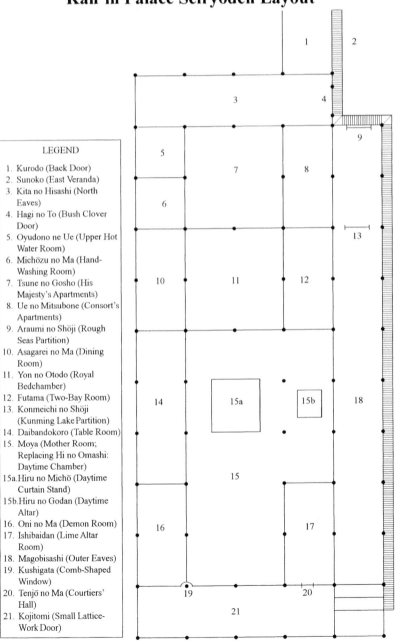

LEGEND

1. Kurodo (Back Door)
2. Sunoko (East Veranda)
3. Kita no Hisashi (North Eaves)
4. Hagi no To (Bush Clover Door)
5. Oyudono ne Ue (Upper Hot Water Room)
6. Michōzu no Ma (Hand-Washing Room)
7. Tsune no Gosho (His Majesty's Apartments)
8. Ue no Mitsubone (Consort's Apartments)
9. Araumi no Shōji (Rough Seas Partition)
10. Asagarei no Ma (Dining Room)
11. Yon no Otodo (Royal Bedchamber)
12. Futama (Two-Bay Room)
13. Konmeichi no Shōji (Kunming Lake Partition)
14. Daibandokoro (Table Room)
15. Moya (Mother Room; Replacing Hi no Omashi: Daytime Chamber)
15a. Hiru no Michō (Daytime Curtain Stand)
15b. Hiru no Godan (Daytime Altar)
16. Oni no Ma (Demon Room)
17. Ishibaidan (Lime Altar Room)
18. Magobisashi (Outer Eaves)
19. Kushigata (Comb-Shaped Window)
20. Tenjō no Ma (Courtiers' Hall)
21. Kojitomi (Small Lattice-Work Door)

273

Appendix I
Kanji List

Abutsuni   阿仏尼

Antoku   安徳

Ben no Naishi   弁内侍

Ben no Naishi Nikki   弁内侍日記

"*Ben no Naishi Nikki* Kō"   弁内侍日記考

Bifukumon'in   美福門院

Bifukumon'in no Kaga   美福門院加賀

Bingo province   備後

Bokuteki Ki   牧笛記

Chūden no Gyokaizu   中殿御会図

Daijōdaijin   太政大臣

Dainido Hyakushu Uta'awase   第二度百首歌合

Dan no Ura   壇の浦

Dōjo Hōshinnō Gojusshu Waka   道助法親王五十首 和歌

Echizen province   越前

Eigu Uta'awase   影供歌合

Fujiwara and branch families   藤原家

    Akisuke   顕輔

    Chikatada   親忠

    Fuyutsugu   冬嗣

    Ieyoshi   家良

    Kaneie   兼家

    (Takatsukasa) Kanehira   鷹司兼平

    (Konoe) Kanetsune   近衛兼経

275

(Kujō) Kanezane	九条兼実
Kinchika	公親
Kinmasa	公雅
(Saionji) Kinmoto	西園寺公基
(Saionji) Kinmune	西園寺公宗
(Saionji) Kinsuke	西園寺公相
Kintada	公忠
Kintsune	公経
Kinyasu	公泰; 公保
Kiyosuke	清輔
Koremoto	伊基
Korenaga	伊長
Koreyuki	伊行
(Hosshōji) Masahira	法性寺雅平
(Kujō) Michiie	九条道家
Michinaga	道長
Michitaka	道隆
Michitsuna no Haha	道綱の母
Mitsutoshi	光俊
Mitsuyoshi	光良
(Kujō) Motoie	基家
Motomasa	基政
Nagako (Chōshi)	長子
Nagashige	長重
Nagatsune	長経
Nagayoshi (or Nagara)	長良
Nariie	成家
Nobuyoshi	信義
Nobukage	信蔭
Nobutaka	信隆
Nobuumi	信海
Nobuzane, also Jakusai	信実, 寂西
Norizane	教実
(Saionji) Sanefuji	西園寺実藤
Sanekata	実方
(Tokudaiji) Sanemoto	徳大寺実基
(Saionji) Saneo	実雄
Sanetaka	実隆

(Ichijō) Sanetsune	一条実経
(Saionji) Saneuji	西園寺実氏
Shōshi	彰子
Shuen	守円
Shunzei (Toshinari)	俊成
Shunzei-kyō no Musume	俊成卿女
Tadahira	忠平
Tadaie	忠家
Takanobu	隆信
Tameie	為家
Tamenari, also Jakuzen or Jakunen	為業, 寂念
(Kyōgoku) Tamenori	京極為教
(Reizei) Tamesuke	冷泉為相
Tametada	為忠
Tametaka, see Tametsune	
Tametsugu	為継
Tametsune, also Tametaka and Jakuchō	為経, 為隆, 寂超
Tameuji	為氏
Teika (Sadaie)	定家
Teishi	定子
Yorinari, also Jakuzen	頼業, 寂然
(Kujō) Yoritsune	九条頼経
Yukiie	行家
Fujiwara Nobuzane Ason no Shū	藤原信実朝臣集
Fujiwara Takanobu Ason no Shū	藤原隆信朝臣集
Fujiwara Tametada Ason no Shū	藤原為忠朝臣集
Fukuro Sōshi or *Fukuro Zōshi*	袋草紙
Fumi no Tsukasa	書司
Genji	源氏
Genji Monogatari	源氏物語
Genpei	源平
Genson (or *Genzon*) *Waka Rokujō*	現存和歌六条
Gishi Naishinnō, Senkamon'in	曦子内親王、仙花門院
Go-Fukakusa	後深草
Go-Fukakusa'in Nijō	後深草院二条
Go-Horikawa	後堀川

Go-Ichijō	後一条
Go-Saga	後嵯峨
Go-Shirakawa	後白河
Go-Toba	後鳥羽
Go-Toba'in Zō	後鳥羽院像
Gosechi	五節
Goyōwakashū	後葉和歌集
Gyokuyō Wakashū	玉葉和歌集
Hachigatsu Izayoi Uta'awase	八月十六夜歌合
Hachijō'in	八条院
Hino Meishi	日野名子
Hitoie Wakashū	人家和歌集
Hōji Hyakushu	宝治百首
Hōji Ninen no Hyakushu	宝治二年百首
Hōji Onhyakushu	宝治御百首
Hōjō Mitsutoki	北条光時
Hōjō Tokiyori	北条時頼
Hōnen Shōnin	法然上人
Horikawa	堀河
ie no shū	家の集
Imakagami	今鏡
Ima Monogatari	今物語
In no Onhyakushu	院御百首
In no On'uta'awase	院御歌合
Insei	陰政
Iwashimizu Wakamiya Uta'awase	石清水若宮歌合
Iya Yotsugi	弥世継
Izayoi Nikki	十六夜日記
Izumi Shikibu Nikki	和泉式部日記
Jingoji	神護寺
jishin	侍臣
jokan	女官
Jōkyūki, also *Shōkyūki*	承久記
Juntoku	順徳
Kagerō Nikki	蜻蛉日記

Kameyama	亀山
Kameyamadono Goshu *On'uta'awase*	亀山殿五首御歌合
kanajo	仮名序
kana nikki	仮名日記
kanbun	漢文
Kanemotokō Ki	兼基公記
Kanimori no Tsukasa	掃司
Kan'in Palace	閑院殿
Kashiwade no Tsukasa	膳司
kashū	家集
Kawaisha Uta'awase	河合社歌合
Kengozen Nikki see *Kenshun-* *mon'in Chūnagon Nikki;* also *Tamakiharu*	建御前日記
Kenreimon'in	建礼門院
Kenreimon'in Ukyō no Daibu	建礼門院右京大夫
Kenreimon'in Ukyō no Daibu *Shū*	建礼門院右京大夫集
Kenshunmon'in	建春門院
Kenshunmon'in no Chūnagon	建春門院中納言
Kenshunmon'in no Chūnagon Nikki, also *Tamakiharu* and *Kengozen Nikki*	建春門院中納言日記; たまきはる、 建御前日記
Kin'yō Wakashū	金葉和歌集
kiroku kanbun	記録漢文
Kitsushi, Saneo's daughter	佶子
Kokin Wakashū	古今和歌集
Kokon Chomonjū	古今著聞集
Kōkyū	後宮
Kōmyōbuji Nyūdō Saki no Sesshōke no *Aki Sanjusshu Uta*	光明峯寺入道前摂政 家秋三十首歌
Konoe	近衛
kotobagaki	詞書
Kōzuke	上野
(Kugatsu jūsan'yo no) Kameyama- *dono Goshu On'uta'awase,* see *Kameyamadono Goshu* *On'uta'awase*	

kujū kumo	九十雲
Kura no Tsukasa	蔵司
Kusuri no Tsukasa	薬司
Madenokōji (also Reizei-Madenokoji)	
Palace	万里小路殿
Makura no Sōshi	枕草紙
Masukagami	増鏡
Meigetsuki	明月記
Mikado no Tsukasa	闈司
Mikawa	三河
Mikohidari (Mikosa)	御子左
Minamoto no Takachika	源隆親
Minasedono no Shiki no E Shikan	みなせ殿の四季の絵四巻
Miyuki On'aramashizu	御幸御あらまし図
mochigayu no hi	望粥の日
Moitori no Tsukasa	水司
mono no na	物の名
Murakami	村上
Murasaki	紫
Murasaki Shikibu Nikki	紫式部日記
myōbu	命婦
Naidaijin Michiie Hyakushu	内大臣道家百首
naishi	内侍
naishi no jō	内侍掌
naishi no kami	内侍尚
naishi no suke	内侍典
Naishidokoro	内侍所
Naishi no Tsukasa	内侍司
Nakatsukasa no Naishi Nikki	中務内侍日記
Nijō	二条
nikki	日記
nikki bungaku	日記文学
nise-e	似絵
nōshi	直衣
Nui no Tsukasa	縫司
nyōbō	女房
nyōju	女孺

nyōkan, nyokan	女官
Nyokudokoro, Nyokodokoro	女工所
nyokurōdo	女工人
Ōgi	仰木
Ōhara no San Jaku	大原三寂
Ōkagami	大鏡
okashi	をかし
Okugisho	奥儀書
Ōmiya'in	大宮院
"Oriiru kumo"	をり居る雲
oriku	折り句
otona otonashiki suke	おとなおとなしき典侍
Oyudono no Ue no Nikki	御湯殿上日記
rekishi monogatari	歴史物語
renga	連歌
renku	連句
Rokujō	六条
Sakamoto	坂本
Sake no Tsukasa	酒司
Sanjūrokkasen-e	三十六歌仙絵
sanshu no jingi	三種の神器
Sanuki no Suke Nikki	讃岐典侍日記
Sarashina Nikki	更級日記
satodairi	里内裏
Sei Shōnagon	清少納言
Senkamon'in	仙花門院
Sen'ninmon'in	宣仁門院
Senzai Wakashū	千載和歌集
Shijō	四条
Shijō'in Shōshō no Naishi	四条院少将内侍
Shika Wakashū	詞花和歌集
Shinchokusen Wakashū	新勅選和歌集
Shingosen Wakashū	新後選和歌集
Shin'in Ben no Naishi	新院弁内侍
Shinkokin Wakashū	新古今和歌集
Shinshūi Wakashū	新拾遺和歌集

Shin'yōmeimon'in	新陽明門院
Shin'yōmeimon'in nyōbō Chūnagon	新陽明門院女房中納言
Shokugosen Wakashū	続後選和歌集
Shokukokin Wakashū	続古今和歌集
Shokukokin Wakashū Mokuroku	続古今和歌集目録
Shokushika Wakashū	続詞花和歌集
Shokushūi Wakashū	続拾遺和歌集
Shoku Yotsugi	続世継
Shōshō no otōto	少将の弟
Shōshō no Naishi	少将内侍
Shūfūshō	秋風抄
Shunkamon'in	春華門院
Sōhekimon'in	藻壁門院
Sōhekimon'in Shōshō no Naishi	藻壁門院少将内侍
Sugawara Takasue's Daughter	菅原孝標女
Suia ganmoku, Suia shō	水蛙眼目, 水蛙抄
Sutoku	崇徳
Taira no Shigemori	平重盛
Taira no Sukemori	平資盛
Takano Nikki	高野日記
Takemuki ga Ki	竹むきが記
Taketori Monogatari	竹取物語
Tamakiharu, see *Kenshunmon'in Chūnagon Nikki*	
Tanba province	丹波
Toba	鳥羽
Tōgū no Ben	東宮弁
Tokiwai Palace	常磐井殿
Tominokōji Palace	富の小路殿
Tonomozukasa, or Tonomori no Tsukasa	殿司
Tosa Nikki	土佐日記
Towazugatari	問はずがたり
Tsukuba Mondō	筑波問答
Tsukubashū	筑波集
Tsuwamono no Tsukasa	兵司
"Uchino no yuki"	内野の雪

Ukinami	うきなみ
uneme	采女
uta'awase	歌合
uta'awase nikki	歌合日記
Utatane	うたたね
Wakasa province	若狭
Waka Shogakushō	和歌初学抄
yamato-e	大和絵
zōshime	雑仕女
Zuijin Teiki Emaki	随身庭騎絵巻

References

(Place of publication is Tokyo unless otherwise noted.)

Abutsu ni. *Izayoi Nikki* 十六夜日記. In *Chūsei Nikki Kikō Shū* 中世日記紀行集, vol. 51 of *Shin Nihon Koten Bungaku Taikei* 新日本古典文学大系, ed. Fukuda Hide'ichi 福田秀一 et. al. 1990- .

____. *Utatane* うたたね. In *Chūsei Nikki Kikō Shū* 中世日記紀行集, vol. 51 of *Shin Nihon Koten Bungaku Taikei* 新日本古典文学大系, ed. Fukuda Hide'ichi 福田秀一 et. al. 1990- .

Araki Yoshio 荒木良雄. *Chūsei Bungaku Jiten* 中世文学事典. 1966.

Arntzen, Sonja, trans. *The Kagerō Diary*. Ann Arbor, Mich. 1997.

Asai Torao 浅井虎夫. *Shintei Jokan Tsūkai* 新訂女官通解. 1985.

Aston, W. G., trans. *Nihongi: Chronicles of Japan from the Earliest Times to A.D. 697*. 1978.

Backus, Robert L., trans. *The Riverside Counselor's Stories: Vernacular Fiction of Late Heian Japan*. Stanford, Calif., 1985.

Ben no Naishi Nikki 弁内侍日記. In *Shinkō Gunsho Ruijū*, 新交群書類従 vol. 14, 1928.

Ben no Naishi Nikki 弁内侍日記. In *Nihon Bungaku Zensho* 日本文学全書, vol. 3, ed. Ochiai Naobumi 落合直文. 1912.

Bowring, Richard, trans. *Murasaki Shikibu, Her Diary and Poetic Memoirs: A Translation and Study*. Princeton, N.J., 1982.

Brazell, Karen, trans. *The Confessions of Lady Nijō*. Stanford, Calif., 1973.

____. "*Towazugatari*: Autobiography of a Kamakura Court Lady." *Harvard Journal of Asiatic Studies* 31 (1971): 220-33.

Brewster, Jennifer, trans. *The Emperor Horikawa Diary: Sanuki no Suke Nikki*. Honolulu, 1977.

Brower, Robert H., and Earl Miner. *Japanese Court Poetry*. Stanford, Calif., 1961.

Cranston, Edwin A., trans. *The Izumi Shikibu Diary: A Romance of the Heian Court*. Cambridge, Eng., 1969.

285

Cutter, Robert Joe. *The Brush and the Spur: Chinese Culture and the Cockfight*. Hong Kong, 1989.

Dalby, Liza. "The Cultured Nature of Heian Colors." Colloquium for Center for Japanese Studies, University of California, Berkeley, 1987.

Dōjo Hōshinnō Gojusshu Waka 道助法親王五十首和歌. In *Gunsho Ruijū*, vol. 11, 1938-39.

Eigu Uta'awase 影供歌合. In *Shinkō Gunsho Ruijū*, vol. 9, 1928.

Ellwood, Robert S. *The Feast of Kingship: Accession Ceremonies in Ancient Japan*, 1972.

Fujimura Tsukuru 藤村作. "Ben no Naishi Nikki." In *Nihon Bungaku Daijiten* 日本文学大辞典, vol. 6, 1933.

Fujiwara (Kujō) Kanezane 藤原九条兼実. *Gyokuyō* 玉葉. 1906-7.

Fujiwara Nobuzane Ason no Shū 藤原信実朝臣集. In *Shikashū Taisei*, vol. 4, 1975.

Fujiwara Takanobu Ason no Shū 藤原隆信朝臣集. In *Shinkō Gunsho Ruijū*, vol. 12, 1928.

Fujiwara Tametada Ason no Shū 藤原為忠朝臣集. In *Gunsho Ruijū*, vol. 15, 1938-39.

Fukuda Hide'ichi 福田秀一. *Chūsei Bungaku Ronkō* 中世文学論考, 1975.

Genealogy of the Exalted and the Base (*Sonpi Bunmyaku* 尊卑分脈). In *Kokushi Taikei* 国史大系, vols. 58-60, 1929-64.

Gensonwaka Rokujō 現存和歌六条. In *Gunsho Ruijū*, vol. 10, 1938-39.

Go-Fukakusa'in Nijō 後深草院二条. *Towazugatari Zenshaku Jo/Ge* 問はずがたり全釈、上下, compiled by Kuretake Dōbunkai 黒竹同文会, 1978.

Goyō Wakashū 後葉和歌集. In *Gunsho Ruijū*, vol. 10, 1938-39.

Graybill, Maribeth. *Kasen-e: An Investigation into the Origins of the Tradition of Poet Pictures in Japan*. Ph.D. diss., University of Michigan. Ann Arbor, 1983.

Gunsho Kaidai 群書解題. 31 vols. Compiled by Ōta Takeshi 太田節, 1960-67.

Gunsho Ruijū 群書類従. 30 vols. Reprint compiled by Hanawa Hoki'ichi 塙保己一, 1903.

Gyokuyō Wakashū 玉葉和歌集. In *Kokka Taikan*, vol. 1, 1968.

(Hachigatsu) Izayoi Uta'awase 八月十六夜歌合. In *Gunsho Ruijū*, vol. 15, 1938-39.

Hall, John W., and Jeffrey P. Mass. *Medieval Japan: Essays in Institutional History*. New Haven, Conn., 1976.

Harries, Phillip Tudor, trans. *The Poetic Memoirs of Lady Daibu*. Stanford, Calif., 1980.

Hino Meishi 日野名子. *Takemuki ga Ki* 竹むきが記. Ed. Iwasa Miyoko 岩佐美代子 et. al. In *Chūsei Nikki Kikō Shū* 中世日記紀行集, vol. 51 of *Shin Nihon Koten Bungaku Taikei* 新日本古典文大系, 1990- .

Hisamatsu Sen'ichi 久松潜一. "Ben no Naishi." In *Biographical Dictionary of Japanese Literature*, 1976.

Hisamatsu Sen'ichi et. al., eds. "*Ben no Naishi Nikki*" 弁内侍日記. In *Waka Bungaku Daijiten* 和歌文学大辞典, 1962.

____. "Nikki Bungaku" 日記文学. In *Nihon Bungaku Shi: Chūsei* 日本文学史：中世, 1977.

Hochstedler, Carol, trans. *The Tale of Nezame: Part Three of Yowa no Nezame Monogatari*. Cornell East Asia Papers, No. 22. Ithaca, N.Y., 1979.

Hōji Hyakushu 宝治百首, *Hōji Ninen no Hyakushu* 宝治二年百首, and *Hōji Onhyakushu* 宝治御百首 are variant titles of *In no Onhyakushu*.

Holtom, D. C. *The Japanese Enthronement Ceremonies with an Account of the Imperial Regalia*, 1972.

Huey, Robert N. *Kyōgoku Tamekane: Poetry and Politics in Late Kamakura Japan*. Stanford, Calif., 1989.

Hulvey, S. Yumiko. "Abutsu-ni." In *Japanese Women Writers: A Bio-Critical Sourcebook*. Ed. Chieko Irie Mulhern. Westport, Conn., 1994.

____. "Ben no Naishi." In *Japanese Women Writers: A Bio-Critical Sourcebook*. Ed. Chieko Irie Mulhern. Westport, Conn., 1994.

Hurst, G. Cameron, III. *Insei: Abdicated Sovereigns in the Politics of Late Heian Japan, 1086-1185*. New York, 1976.

Ichiko Teiji 市古貞次, ed. *Nihon Bungaku Zenshi: Chūsei* 日本文学全史ー中世. Vol. 3, 1978.

Ikeda Kikan 池田亀鑑. "*Ben no Naishi Nikki*" 弁内侍日記. In *Kyūtei Joryū Nikki Bungaku* 宮廷女流日記文学, 1927.

____. *Heian Jidai no Bungaku to Seikatsu* 平安時代の文学と生活, 1978.

Imakagami 今鏡. *Nihon Koten Zensho*, vol. 53. Ōsaka, 1957.

Ima Monogatari 今物語. In *Shinkō Gunsho Ruijū*, vol. 21, 1938-39.

Imazeki Toshiko 今関敏子. "*Ben no Naishi Nikki*" 弁内侍日記. In *Chūsei Joryū Nikki Bungaku Ronkō* 中世女流日記文学論考. Ōsaka, 1987.

____. "*Ben no Naishi Nikki* Chūshaku, sono Hitotsu: Kangen Yonen Haru-Aki" 弁内侍日記注釈その一つ寛元四年春秋. *Teikoku Gakuen Kiyō* 帝国学園紀要 13 (1987):1-8.

_____. "*Ben no Naishi Nikki* kō: Akarusa o Megutte" 弁内侍日記一明るさをめぐって. *Teikoku Gakuen Kiyō* 8 (1982):1-8.

_____. "*Ben no Naishi Nikki* ni Okeru 'Kyō (Ke[f]u)': Sei Naru Jikū e no Sanbi"弁内侍日記における「今日（けふ）」一聖なる時空への讃美. *Kokubun* 国文 85 (1996):43-52.

_____. "*Ben no Naishi Nikki* no Shipittsu Ito" 弁内侍日記の執筆意図. *Nihon Bungaku* 日本文学 519 (1996):20-28.

_____."*Ben no Naishi Nikki* Saikō Kikikan to Hyōgen"「弁侍日記」再考一危機感と表現. *Kokusai Kenkyū Ronsō* 2, no. 2 (1990):83-94.

_____. 弁内侍日記小論一荒涼さへの視点をめぐって. *Teikoku Gakuen Kiyō* 11 (1985):11-20.

_____. *Kōchū Ben no Naishi Nikki* 校注弁内侍日記. Ōsaka, 1989.

_____. "Nikki Bungaku ni Okeru 'Jiko'" 日記文学に於ける自己. *Teikoku Gakuen Kiyō* 10 (1984):13-21.

_____. "Tsuki Akari no Kyūtei: *Ben no Naishi Nikki* Shōkō" 月明りの宮廷：弁内侍日記小考. *Teikoku Gakuen Kiyō* 9 (1983: 1-8.

Inagaki Hisao. *A Dictionary of Japanese Buddhist Terms*. Kyōto, 1985.

In no Onhyakushu 院御百首. In *Kokka Taikan*, vol. 4, 1968.

In no On'uta'awase 院御歌合. In *Gunsho Ruijū*, vol. 12, 1938-39.

Inoue Muneo 井上宗雄. "Fujiwara Nobuzane Nenpu Kōshō: Jōkyū made" 藤原信実年譜考証一承久まで. *Waka Bungaku Shinron* 和歌文学新論, ed. Morimoto Motoko 森本元子, 1982.

Ishida Yoshisada 石田吉貞. "Chūsei Nikki-Kikō Bungaku" 中世日記紀行文学. In *Shinkokin Sekai to Chūsei Bungaku* 新古今世界と中世文学, 1972.

Ishii, Susumu. "The Decline of the Kamakura Bakufu." Trans. Jeffrey P. Mass and Hitomi Tonomura. In *The Cambridge History of Japan: Medieval Japan*, vol. 3, ed. Kōzō Yamamura. Cambridge, Eng., 1990.

Iwasa Miyoko 岩佐美代子. "*Ben no Naishi Nikki*" 弁内侍日記. In *Nihon Bungaku Shinshi* 日本文学新史, ed. Koyama Hiroshi, 1985.

_____. *Ben no Naishi Nikki* 弁内侍日記. Ōsaka, 1986.

_____. "*Ben no Naishi Nikki*" 弁内侍日記. *Kokubungaku Kaishaku to Kyōzai no Kenkyū* 国文学解釈と教材の研究 32, no. 4 (1987): 140-41.

_____. "*Ben no Naishi Nikki* Ketsuji Kō" 弁内侍日記欠字考. *Nikki Bungaku Kenkyū* 日記文学研究 1, no. 5 (1993):308-22.

____. "*Ben no Naishi Nikki* no Hitobito" 弁内侍日記の人々. *Kokubun Tsurumi* 国文鶴見 37 (1992):14-23.

____. "Chūsei no Joryū Nikki Bungaku" 中世の女流日記文学. *Chūsei Bungaku* 中世文学 22, no. 10 (1977):4-6.

____. "Nyōbō no Nikki" 女房の日記. In "Shinpojiumu, Nikki to Bungaku—'Shinjitsu' no Hyōgen o Meggute" シンポジウム、日記と文学：真実の表現をめぐって. *Kobun* 古文 85 (1993): 6-17.

____. "Tennō no Isshō to Nyōbō Nikki Bungaku" 天皇の一生と女房日記文学. *Kokubun Tsurumi* 国文鶴見 25 (1990):39-48.

Iwasa Miyoko 岩佐美代子 et. al., *Ben no Naishi Nikki* 弁内侍日記. In *Chūsei Nikki Kikō Bungaku* 中世日記紀行文学, vol. 48 of *Shinpen Nihon Koten Bungaku Zenshū* 新編日本古典文学全集, 1994.

____ et. al., *Izayoi Nikki* 十六夜日記. In *Chūsei Nikki Kikō Shū* 中世日記紀行集, vol. 48 of *Shinpen Nihon Koten Bungaku Zenshū* 新編日本古典文学全集, 1994.

____ et. al., *Nakatsukasa no Naishi Nikki* 中務内侍日記. In *Chūsei Nikki Kikō Shū* 中世日記紀行集, vol. 51 of *Shin Nihon Koten Bungaku Taikei*. 新日本古典文学大系, 1990.

____ et. al., *Takemuki ga Ki* 竹むきが記. In *Chūsei Nikki Kikō Shū* 中世日記紀行集, vol. 51 of *Shin Nihon Koten Bungaku Taikei* 新日本古典文学大系, 1990.

Iwashimizu Wakamiya Uta'awase 石清水若宮歌合. In *Gunsho Ruijū,* vol. 12, 1938-39.

Izayoi Nikki 十六夜日記. In *Nihon Bungaku Zensho* 日本文学全書, vol. 3, ed. Ochiai Naobumi.

Izumi Shikibu Nikki 和泉武部日記. In *Nihon Koten Bungaku Taikei*, vol. 18, ed. Fujioka Tadaharu 藤岡忠美, 1956-68.

Kagerō Nikki 蜻蛉日記. In *Nihon Koten Bungaku Taikei*, vol. 9, ed. Kimura Masanori 木村正中 and Imuta Tsunehisa 伊牟田経久.

Kameyamadono Goshu On'uta'awase 亀山殿五首御歌合. In *Gunsho Ruijū*, vol. 9, 1938-39.

Kaneko Kinjirō 金子金治郎. *Rengashi to Kikō* 連歌師と紀行, 1990.

Kawaisha Uta'awase 河合社歌合. In *Gunsho Ruijū*, vol. 12, 1938-39.

Keene, Donald. *Hakutai no Kakaku* 百代の価格. Vol. l, 1984.

____. *Seeds in the Heart: Japanese Literature from Earliest Times to the Late Sixteenth Century.* New York, 1993.

_____. *Travelers of a Hundred Ages: The Japanese as Revealed Through 1,000 Years of Diaries*. New York, 1989.

Kenreimon'in Ukyō no Daibu Shū 建礼門院右京大夫集. In *Gunsho Ruijū*, vol. 15, 1938-39.

Kenshunmon'in Chūnagon Nikki 建春門院中納言日記, see *Tamakiharu Zenchūshaku*.

Kinda'ichi Haruhiko 金田一春彦. *Shinmeikai Kogo Jiten* 新明解古語典. 1972.

Kidō Saizō 木藤才蔵. "Ben no Naishi-Nakatsukasa no Naishi" 弁内侍中務内侍. In *Nihon Joryū Bungakushi* 日本女流文学史, ed. Hisamatsu Sen'ichi, vol. 1, 1969.

_____. "Kamakura Chūki no Renga" 鎌倉中期の連歌. In *Rengashi Ronkō* 連歌史論考, vol. 1, 1973.

Kiyota Tomoko 清田倫子. "*Ben no Naishi Nikki* no Denshōsei: Kyūtei Fūzoku to Bungei" 弁内侍日記の伝承性ー宮廷風俗と文芸. *Fūzoku* 風俗15, no. 4 (1977):1-20.

Kobayashi Chishō 小林知昭. "Ben no Naishi Nōto: Hōgo to no Kakawari" 弁内侍ノートー法語とのかかわり. In *Zoku Chūsei Bungaku no Shisō* 続中世文学の思想, vol. 2, 1974.

Kōdansha Encyclopedia of Japan. 9 vols. 1983.

Kokin Wakashū 古今和歌集. In *Nihon Koten Bungaku Taikei*, ed. Saeki Umetomo 佐伯梅友, vol. 8, 1956-68.

Kokka Taikan 国歌大観. Compiled by Matsushita Daisaburō 松下大三郎 and Watanabe Fumio 渡辺文男. 4 vols. 4th rev. ed., 1968.

Kokushi Taikei 国史大系. Compiled by Kuroita Katsumi. Rev. ed. 66 vols, 1929-64.

Kokusho Sōmokuroku 国書総目録. 9 vols., 1963-76.

Kōmyōbuji Nyūdō Saki no Sesshōke no Aki Sanjusshu Uta 光明峰寺入道前摂政家の秋三十首歌. In *Shinkō Gunsho Ruijū*, vol. 9, 1928.

Konishi Jin'ichi. *A History of Japanese Literature, Volume Three: The High Middle Ages*. Trans. Aileen Gatten and Mark Harbison. Ed. Earl Miner. Princeton, N.J., 1991.

_____. *A History of Japanese Literature, Volume Two: The Early Middle Ages*. Trans. Aileen Gatten. Ed. Earl Miner. Princeton, N.J., 1986.

Kugyō Bunin 公御補任. Vols. 53-57 of *Kokushi Taikei* 国史大系, 1929-64.

Marra, Michele. *The Aesthetics of Discontent: Politics and Reclusion in Medieval Japanese Literature*. Honolulu, 1991.

Masukagami 増鏡. In *Nihon Koten Bungaku Taikei*, vol. 87, ed. Kidō Saizō 木藤才蔵, 1956-68.

Matsumoto Yasushi 松本寧至. *"Ben no Naishi Nikki to Nakatsukasa Naishi Nikki*: Ben no Naishi Ron" 弁内侍日記と中務内侍日記 ―弁内侍論. In *Chūsei Joryū Nikki Bungaku no Kenkyū* 中世女流日記文学の研究, 1983.

_____. "Chūsei Joryū Nikki Bungaku: Shinpojiumu Yōshi" 中世女流日記 文学シンポジウム要旨. *Chūsei Bungaku* 中世文学 22-23, no. 10 (1977):1-3.

_____. "Go-Fukakusa-in Ben no Naishi: Kichi to Yūmoa Yōshi" 後深草院 弁内侍：機知とユーモア要旨. *Kokubungaku Kaishaku to Kyōzai no Kenkyū* 国文学解釈と教材の研究 24, no. 1-6 (1979):96-97.

McCullough, Helen Craig. "Aristocratic Culture," in *The Cambridge History of Japan: Vol. 2 Heian Japan,* ed. Donald H. Shively and William H. McCullough. Cambridge, Eng., 1999.

_____. *Brocade by Night: Kokin Wakashū and the Court Style in Japanese Classical Poetry.* Stanford, Calif., 1985.

_____, ed. *Classical Japanese Prose: An Anthology.* Stanford, Calif., 1990.

_____, trans. *Genji and Heike: Selections from The Tale of Genji and The Tale of the Heike.* Stanford, Calif., 1994.

_____, trans. *Kokin Wakashū: The First Imperial Anthology of Japanese Poetry.* Stanford, Calif., 1985.

_____, trans. *Ōkagami: The Great Mirror, Fujiwara Michinaga (966-1027) and His Times.* Princeton, N.J., 1980.

_____, trans. *The Taiheiki: A Chronicle of Medieval Japan.* Rutland, Vt., 1979.

_____, trans. *The Tale of the Heike.* Stanford, Calif., 1988.

_____, trans. *Tales of Ise: Lyrical Episodes from Tenth-Century Japan.* Stanford, Calif., 1968.

McCullough, William H. "Japanese Marriage Institutions in the Heian Period." *Harvard Journal of Asiatic Studies* 27 (1967):103-167.

_____. "The Heian Court" in *The Cambridge History of Japan: Vol. 2 Heian Japan,* ed. Donald H. Shively and William H. McCullough. Cambridge, Eng., 1999.

_____. "The Capital and its Society" in *The Cambridge History of Japan: Vol. 2 Heian Japan,* ed. Donald H. Shively and William H. McCullough. Cambridge, Eng., 1999.

McCullough, William H., and Helen Craig McCullough, trans. *A Tale of Flowering Fortunes: Annals of Japanese Aristocratic Life in the Heian Period.* 2 vols. Stanford, Calif., 1980.

Miner, Earl, Hiroko Odagiri, and Robert E. Morrell. *The Princeton Companion to Classical Japanese Literature.* Princeton, N.J., 1985.

Mintzer, Robert Alfred. "Jōjin Ajari no Haha Shū: Maternal Love in the Eleventh Century, An Enduring Testament." Ph.D. diss., Harvard University, 1978.

Miyajima Shin'ichi 宮島新一. "Fujiwara Takanobu no Shōgai to Saigei" 藤原隆信の生涯と才芸. *Museum: Tōkyō Kokuritsu Hakubutsukan Bijutsushi* 4 (1984):4-11.

Miyake, Lynne. "The Tosa Diary: In the Interstices of Gender and Criticism" in *The Woman's Hand: Gender and Theory in Japanese Women's Writing.* Stanford, Calif., 1996.

Morita Kaneyoshi 森田兼吉."*Ben no Naishi Nikki* Ron Ichi: Keitai no Kakunin" 弁内侍日記論一：形態の確認. *Nihon Bungaku Kenkyū* 日本文学研究 25 (1989):105-16.

_____. "*Ben no Naishi Nikki* Ron Ni: Ben no Naishi to Shōshō no Naishi" 弁内侍日記論二：弁内侍と小将内侍. *Nihon Bungaku Kenkyū* 26 (1990):59-69.

_____. "*Ben no Naishi Nikki* Ron San: sono Bungakusei" 弁内侍日記論 三：その文学性. *Nihon Bungaku Kenkyū* 27 (1991):49-61.

Morris, Ivan. trans. *As I Crossed a Bridge of Dreams: Recollections of a Woman of Eleventh-Century Japan.* New York, 1971.

_____, trans. *The Pillow Book of Sei Shōnagon.* 2 vols. New York, 1967.

_____. *The World of the Shining Prince: Court Life in Ancient Japan.* New York, 1964.

Mulhern, Chieko Irie, ed. *Japanese Women Writers: A Bio-Critical Sourcebook.* Westport, Conn., 1994.

Murasaki Shikibu 紫式部. *Genji Monogatari* 源氏物語. In *Nihon Koten Bungaku Zenshū,* vols. 12-17, ed. Abe Akio 阿部秋生, Akiyama Ken 秋山虔, and Imai Gen'e 今井源衛, 1970-76.

_____. *Murasaki Shikibu Nikki* 紫式部日記. In *Nihon Koten Bungaku Zenshū,* vol. 18, ed. Nakamura Kōichi 中村幸一.

Nagazumi Yasuaki 永積安明. *Chūsei Bungaku no Tenbō* 中世文学の展望, 1963.

Nakatsukasa no Naishi Nikki 中務内侍日記. In *Shinkō Gunsho Ruijū,* vol. 14, 1928.

Nakatsukasa no Naishi Nikki. In *Chūsei Nikki Kikō Shū,* vol. 51, of *Shin Nihon Koten Bungaku Taikei,* 1990- .

Nihon Bungaku Zensho 日本文学全書. Edited by Ochiai Naobumi 落合直文, 1912.

Nihon Koten Bungaku Daijiten Henshū Iinkai 日本古典文学大辞典編集 委員会. *Nihon Koten Bungaku Taikei* 日本古典文学大系. Ed. Takagi Ichinosuke 高木市之助 et. al. 102 vols., 1956-68.

Nihon Koten Bungaku Zenshū 日本古典文学全集. Ed. Akiyama Ken 秋山虔, et. al. 51 vols., 1970-76.

Nihon Rekishi Daijiten 日本歴史大辞典. 20 vols. 1964.

Niwa Tamako. *Nakatsukasa Naishi Nikki.*" Ph.D. diss., Radcliffe, 1955.

Nomura Hachirō 野村八郎. "*Ima Monogatari*" 今物語. In *Kamakura Jidai Bungaku Shinron* 鎌倉時代文学新論, 1930.

_____. "*Minamoto Ienaga Nikki, Ben no Naishi Nikki oyobi Nakatsukasa no Naishi Nikki*" 源家長日記弁内侍日記および中務内侍日記. In *Kamakura Jidai Bungaku Shinron* 鎌倉時代文学新論, 1930.

Ōta Seiroku 太田静六. *Shindenzukuri no Kenkyū* 寝殿造の研究, 1987.

Ōuchi Mayako 大内摩耶子. "*Ben no Naishi Nikki Kō*" 弁内侍日記考. *Ōsaka Furitsu Daigaku Kiyō* 大阪府立大学紀要 Vol. 12, Series C (1964): 239-57.

Oyudono no Ue no Nikki 御湯殿上日記. Vol. 16 of *Shinkō Gunsho Ruijū* 新交群書類従.

Perkins, George. *A Study and Partial Translation of Masukagami.* Ph.D. diss., Stanford University. 2 vols, 1977.

_____. *The Clear Mirror: A Chronicle of the Japanese Court During the Kamakura Period (1185-1333).* Stanford, Calif., 1998.

Philippi, Donald L., trans. *Kojiki,* 1969.

Piggott, Joan R. *The Emergence of Japanese Kingship.* Stanford, Calif., 1997.

Ponsonby-Fane, R. A. B. *Studies in Shintō and Shrines.* Kyōto, 1953.

Reischauer, Edwin O., and Joseph K. Yamagiwa. *Translations from Early Japanese Literature.* Cambridge, Mass., 1951.

Sansom, George B. *A History of Japan to 1334.* Vol. 1. Stanford, Calif., 1958.

_____. *A History of Japan, 1334-1615.* Vol. 2. Stanford, Calif., 1961.

Sanuki no Suke Nikki 讃岐典侍日記. In *Nihon Koten Bungaku Zenshū*, vol. 18, ed. Ishii Fumio 石井文夫.

Sarashina Nikki 更級日記. In *Nihon Koten Bungaku Taikei*, vol. 20, ed. Nishishita Kyōichi 西下経一, 1956-68.

Sarra, Edith. *Fictions of Femininity: Literary Inventions of Gender in Japanese Court Women's Memoirs.* Stanford, Calif., 1999.

Satō Kiyoe 佐藤清衛. "*Ayashi* yori *Ajikinashi* e" あやしよりあじきなしへ. In *Chūsei Nihon Bungaku* 中世日本文学, 1966.

Sei Shōnagon 清少納言. *Makura no Sōshi* 枕草紙. In *Nihon Koten Bungaku Taikei.*, vol. 19, ed. Ikeda Kikan 池田亀鑑, Kishigami Shinji 岸上慎二, and Akiyama Ken 秋山虔.

Seidensticker, Edward, trans. *The Gossamer Years: The Diary of a Noblewoman of Heian Japan.* Rutland, Vt., 1975.

_____, trans. *The Tale of Genji*. New York, 1978.

Shikashū Taisei: Chūsei II 私歌集大成：中世二. Ed. Wakashi Kenkyūkai, 1975.

Shingosen Wakashū 新後選和歌集. In *Kokka Taikan*, vol. 1, 1968.

Shinkō Gunsho Ruijū 新交群書類従. 24 vols. Compiled by Hanawa Hoki'ichi 塙保己一, 1938-39.

Shin Nihon Koten Bungaku Taikei 新日本古典文学大系. 1990–.

Shin Wakashū 新和歌集. In *Gunsho Ruijū*, vol. 10, 1938-39.

Shirane, Haruo. *The Bridge of Dreams: A Poetics of The Tale of Genji*. Stanford, Calif., 1987.

Shokukokin Wakashū 続古今和歌集. In *Kokka Taikan*, vol. 1, 1968.

Shokushūi Wakashū 続拾遺和歌集. In *Kokka Taikan*, vol. 1, 1968.

Shūfūshō 秋風抄. In *Gunsho Ruijū*, vol. 10, 1938-39.

Sonpi Bunmyaku 尊卑分脈. In *Kokushi Taikei* 国史大系, vols. 58-60, 1929-64.

Sugita Haruko 杉田春子. *Heian Jidai Kōkyū oyobi Joshi no Kenkyū* 平安時代後宮および女詞の研究, 1982.

Suia Shō 水蛙抄 (also *Suia ganmoku* 水蛙眼目). In *Shinkō Gunsho Ruijū*, vol. 13.

Suzuki Kazuo 鈴木一雄, ed. "Joryū Nikki Bungaku Kaidai" 女流日記文学解題. *Kokubungaku Kaishaku to Kanshō* 国文学解釈と鑑賞 31, no. 1-4 (1966):107-108.

Suzuki, Tomi. "Gender and Genre: Modern Literary Histories and Women's Diary Literature" in *Inventing the Classics: Modernity, National Identity, and Japanese Literature*. Stanford, Calif., 2000.

Taiheiki 太平記. In *Nihon Koten Bungaku Taikei*, vol. 35.II, ed. Gotō Tanji 後藤丹治 and Kamada Kisaburō 釜田喜三郎, 1971.

Taiheiki 太平記. In *Shinpen Nihon Koten Bungaku Zenshū*, vol. 55, ed. Hasegawa Tadashi 長谷川端, 1996.

Takahashi Bunji 高橋文二 and Asai Shin'ichi 浅井伸一. *Heian Kamakura Joryū Kajin Shū* 平安鎌倉女流歌人集, 1979.

Takehana Isao 竹鼻いさお. "*Ben no Naishi Nikki*" 弁内侍日記. *Kokubungaku Kaishaku to Kanshō* 41, no. 3 (1966):107-8.

Takamure Itsue 高群逸枝. *Dai Nihon Josei Jinmei Jisho* 大日本女性人名辞書, 1980.

Takemuku ga Ki. See Hino Meishi.

Taketori Monogatari 竹取物語. In *Nihon Koten Bungaku Taikei*, vol. 9, ed. Sakakura Atsuyoshi 坂倉篤義, 1956-68.

Tamai Kōsuke 玉井孝助. "*Ben no Naishi Nikki* no Honbun Kōsho" 弁内侍日記の本文考書 *Gakuen* 学園 9 (1951):6-10.

_____. *Ben no Naishi Nikki Shinchū* 弁内侍日記新注, 1958.

_____. *Nakatsukasa no Naishi Nikki Shinchū* 中務内侍日記新注, 1958.

_____. *Nikki Bungaku no Kenkyū* 日記文学の研究, 1965.

Tamakiharu Zenchūshaku たまきはる前注釈. Edited by Kobara Mikio 小原幹雄 et. al., 1983.

Tosa Nikki 土佐日記. In *Nihon Koten Bungaku Zenshū*, vol. 9, ed. Matsumura Sei'ichi 松村誠一, 1970-76.

Towazugatari. See Go-Fukakusa'in Nijō.

Tsukubashū 筑波集. In *Nihon Koten Zensho* 日本古典全書, vols. 73-74, ed. Fukui Kyūzō 福井久蔵.

Tsumoto Nobuhiro 津基信宏. "*Ben no Naishi Nikki to Nakatsukasa Naishi Nikki*" 弁内侍日記と中務内侍日記. *Kokubungaku Kaishaku to Kanshō* 国文学解釈と鑑賞 46, no. 1 (1981):115-19.

Tsunoda Bun'e 角田文衛. "Kōkyū no Rekishi" 後宮の歴史. In *Kōkyū no Subete* 後宮のすべて. *Kokubungaku Kaishaku to Kyōzai no Kenkyū* 国文学解釈と教材の研究 25, no. 13 (1980):35-78.

_____. *Nihon no Kōkyū* 日本の後宮, 1973.

Tsurezuregusa 徒然草. In *Nihon Koten Bungaku Taikei,* vol. 30, ed. Nishio Minoru 西尾実, 1971.

Wallace, John, trans. "Fitful Slumbers: Nun Abutsu's *Utatane.*" *Monumenta Nipponica* 43, no. 4 (1988):391-416.

Webb, Herschel, and Marleigh Ryan. *Research in Japanese Sources: A Guide.* New York, 1963.

Yasuraoka Kōsaku 安良岡幸作. *Tsurezuregusa Zenchūshaku* 徒然草全注釈. 2 vols., 1967.

Yonekura Michio 米倉道雄. "Fujiwara Nobuzane Kō" 藤原信実考. *The Bijutsu Kenkyū* 305 (1977):20-31.

_____. "Nobuzane no Shisontachi (jō)" 信実の子孫たち (上). *The Bijutsu Kenkyū* 342 (1988):51-59.

Yoshida Sei'ichi 吉田精一. "Nihon no Josei Shi," 日本女性史. *Kokubungaku Kaishaku to Kanshō* 国文学解釈と鑑賞 24, no. 3 (1979):6-224.

Yoshihara Toshio 吉原敏雄. "*Ben no Naishi Nikki:* Eien no Otomegokoro" 弁内侍日記：永遠の乙女心. *Kokubungaku Kaishaku to Kanshō* 国文学解釈と鑑賞 19, no. 1 (1954):57-61.

Index of First Lines

Index

CORNELL EAST ASIA SERIES

61 Emily Groszos Ooms, *Women and Millenarian Protest in Meiji Japan: Deguchi Nao and Ōmotokyō*

62 Carolyn Anne Morley, *Transformation, Miracles, and Mischief: The Mountain Priest Plays of Kyōgen*

63 David R. McCann & Hyunjae Yee Sallee, tr., *Selected Poems of Kim Namjo*, afterword by Kim Yunsik

64 HUA Qingzhao, *From Yalta to Panmunjom: Truman's Diplomacy and the Four Powers, 1945-1953*

65 Margaret Benton Fukasawa, *Kitahara Hakushū: His Life and Poetry*

66 Kam Louie, ed., *Strange Tales from Strange Lands: Stories by Zheng Wanlong*, with introduction

67 Wang Wen-hsing, *Backed Against the Sea*, tr. Edward Gunn

68 Brother Anthony of Taizé & Young-Moo Kim, trs., *The Sound of My Waves: Selected Poems by Ko Un*

69 Brian Myers, *Han Sŏrya and North Korean Literature: The Failure of Socialist Realism in the DPRK*

70 Thomas P. Lyons & Victor Nee, eds., *The Economic Transformation of South China: Reform and Development in the Post-Mao Era*

71 David G. Goodman, tr., *After Apocalypse: Four Japanese Plays of Hiroshima and Nagasaki*, with introduction

72 Thomas P. Lyons, *Poverty and Growth in a South China County: Anxi, Fujian, 1949-1992*

74 Martyn Atkins, *Informal Empire in Crisis: British Diplomacy and the Chinese Customs Succession, 1927-1929*

76 Chifumi Shimazaki, *Restless Spirits from Japanese Noh Plays of the Fourth Group: Parallel Translations with Running Commentary*

77 Brother Anthony of Taizé & Young-Moo Kim, trs., *Back to Heaven: Selected Poems of Ch'ŏn Sang Pyŏng*

78 Kevin O'Rourke, tr., *Singing Like a Cricket, Hooting Like an Owl: Selected Poems by Yi Kyu-bo*

79 Irit Averbuch, *The Gods Come Dancing: A Study of the Japanese Ritual Dance of Yamabushi Kagura*

80 Mark Peterson, *Korean Adoption and Inheritance: Case Studies in the Creation of a Classic Confucian Society*

81 Yenna Wu, tr., *The Lioness Roars: Shrew Stories from Late Imperial China*

82 Thomas Lyons, *The Economic Geography of Fujian: A Sourcebook*, Vol. 1

83 Pak Wan-so, *The Naked Tree*, tr. Yu Young-nan

84 C.T. Hsia, *The Classic Chinese Novel: A Critical Introduction*

85 Cho Chong-Rae, *Playing With Fire*, tr. Chun Kyung-Ja

86 Hayashi Fumiko, *I Saw a Pale Horse and Selections from Diary of a Vagabond*, tr. Janice Brown

87 Motoori Norinaga, *Kojiki-den, Book 1*, tr. Ann Wehmeyer

88 Chang Soo Ko, tr., *Sending the Ship Out to the Stars: Poems of Park Je-chun*

89 Thomas Lyons, *The Economic Geography of Fujian: A Sourcebook*, Vol. 2

Order online: www.einaudi.cornell.edu/eastasia/CEASbooks, or contact Cornell East Asia Series Distribution Center, 95 Brown Road, Box 1004, Ithaca, NY 14850, USA; toll-free: 1-877-865-2432, fax 607-255-7534, ceas@cornell.edu

2-05/.5M pb/.2M hc/SB